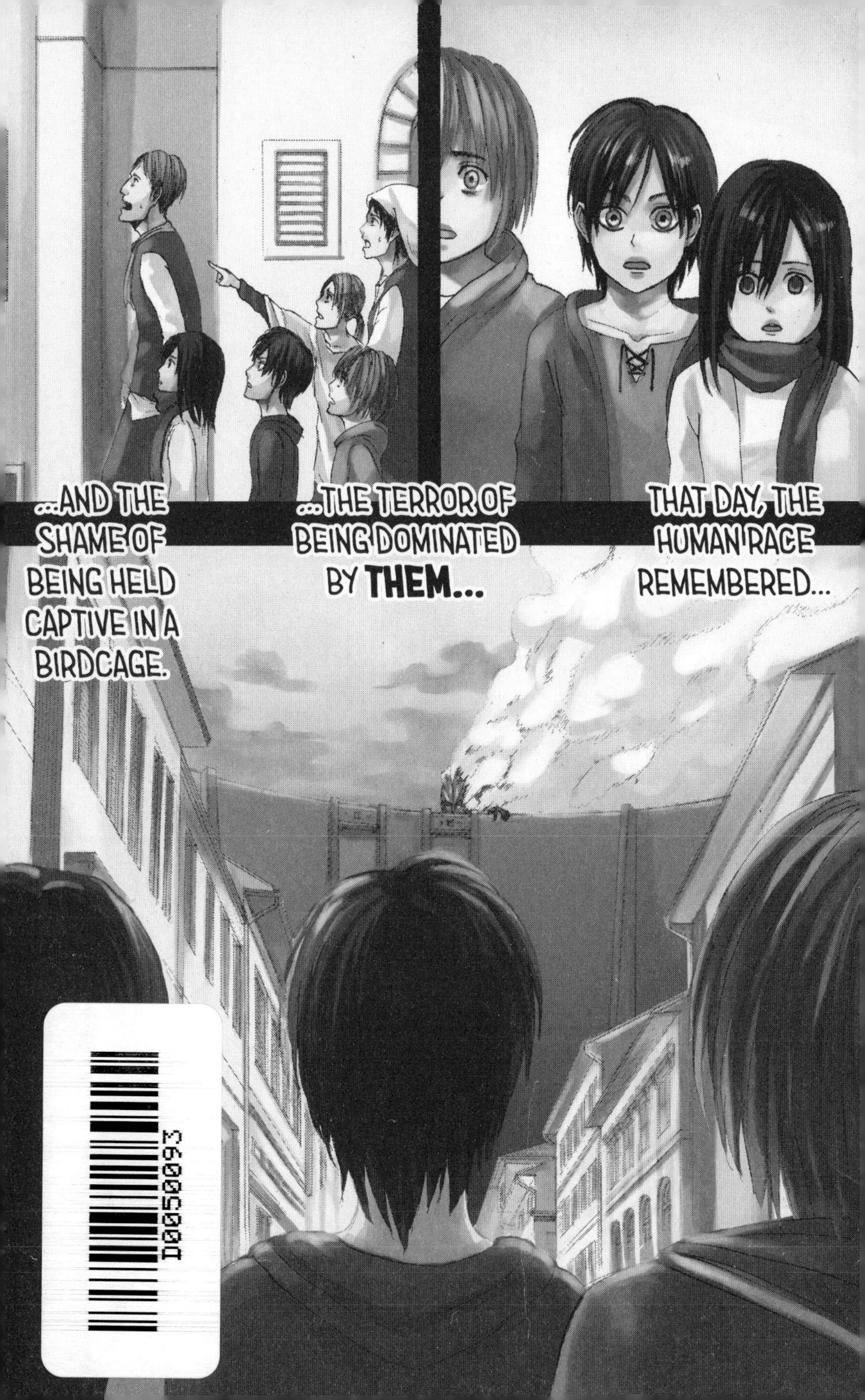
THAT DAY, THE HUMAN RACE REMEMBERED...
...THE TERROR OF BEING DOMINATED BY **THEM**...
...AND THE SHAME OF BEING HELD CAPTIVE IN A BIRDCAGE.

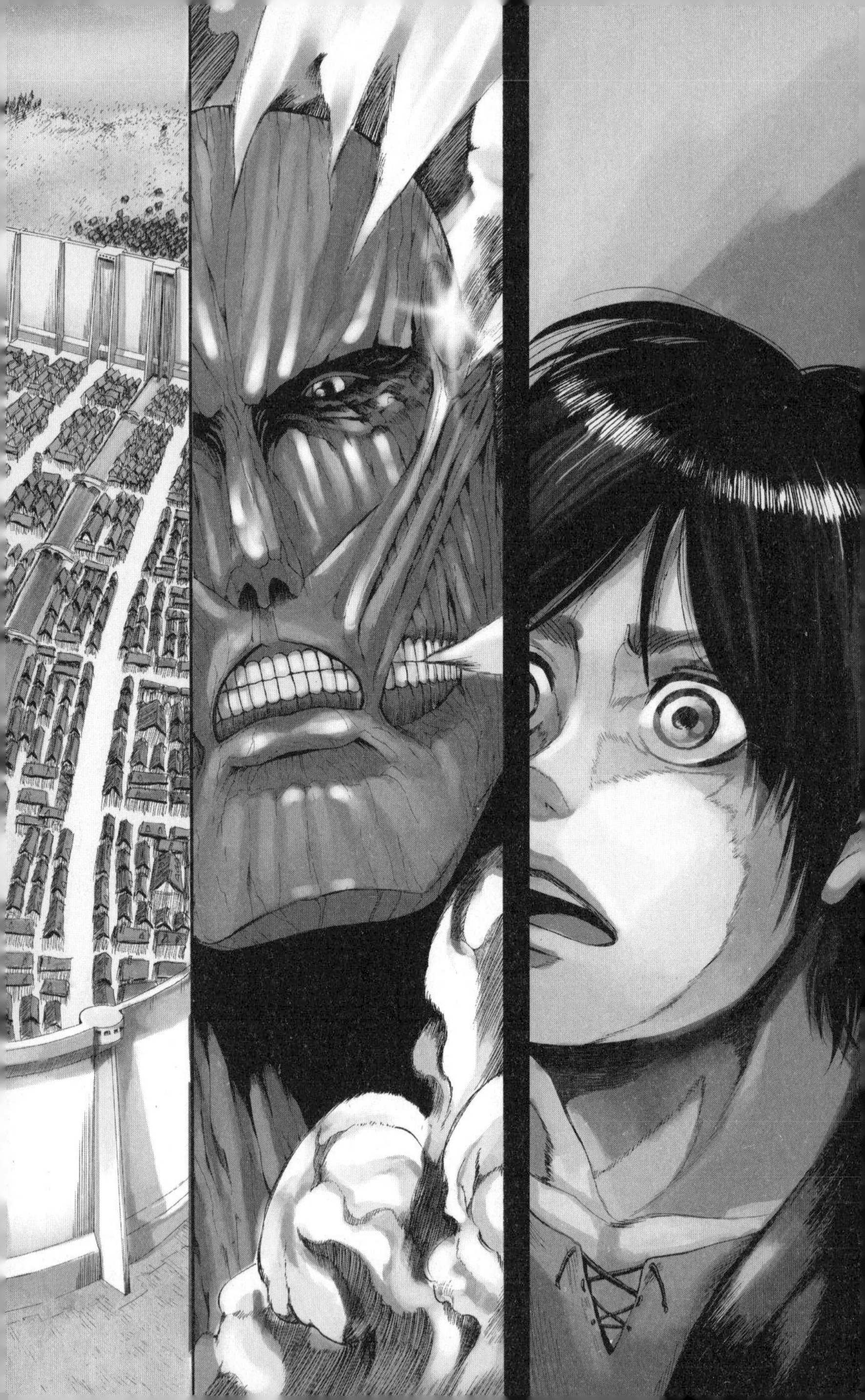

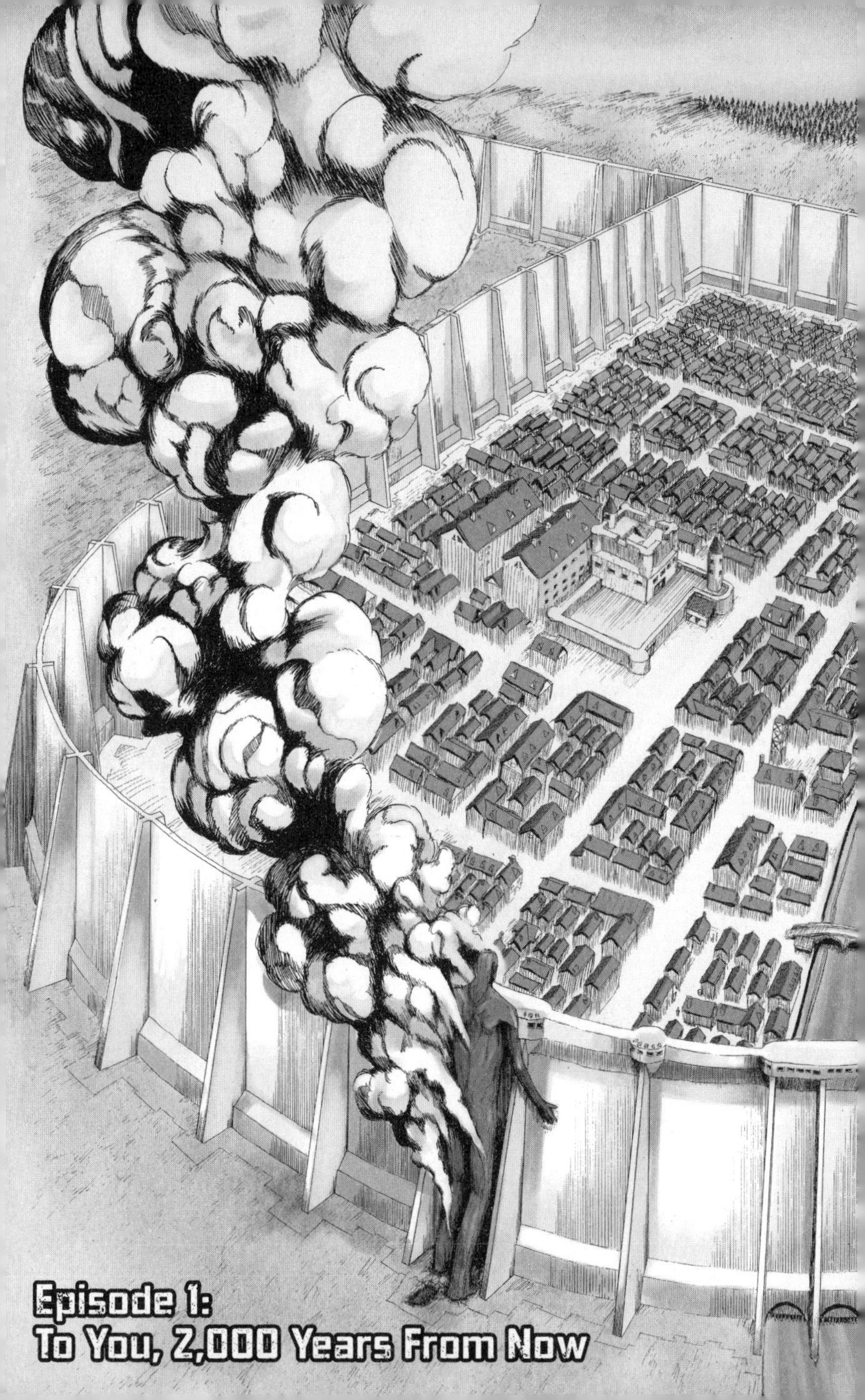
Episode 1:
To You, 2,000 Years From Now

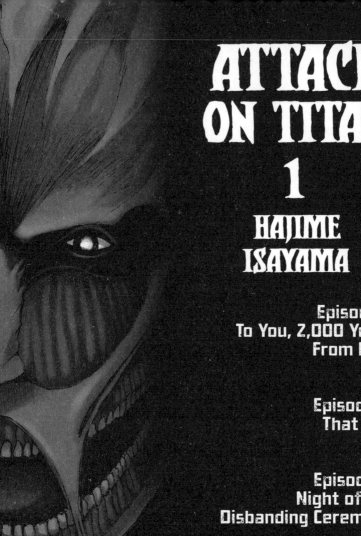

ATTACK ON TITAN

1

HAJIME ISAYAMA

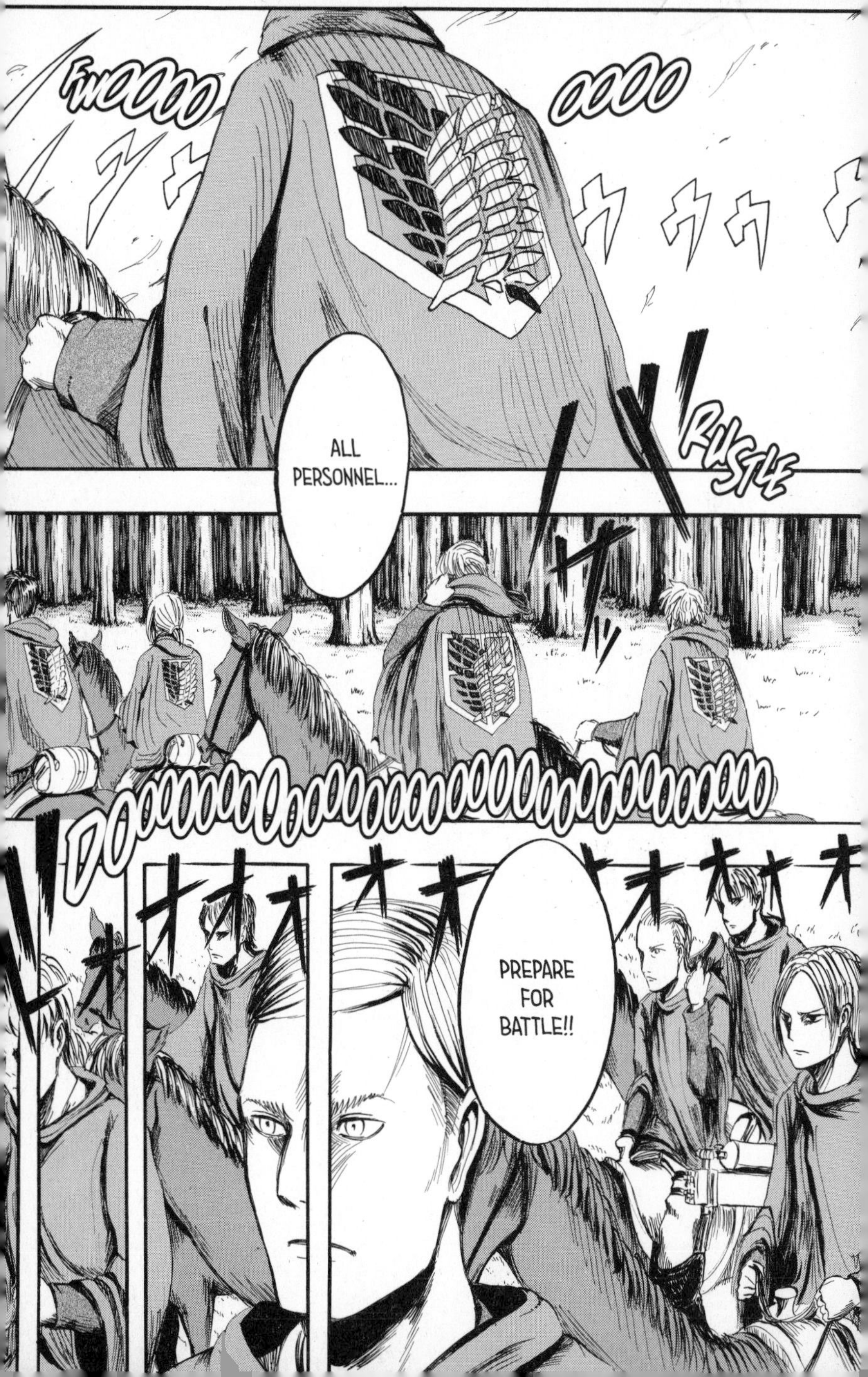
FWOOOO OOOO
ALL PERSONNEL...
RUSTLE
DOOOOOOOOOOOOOOOOOOOOOOOOOOOOOOO
PREPARE FOR BATTLE!!

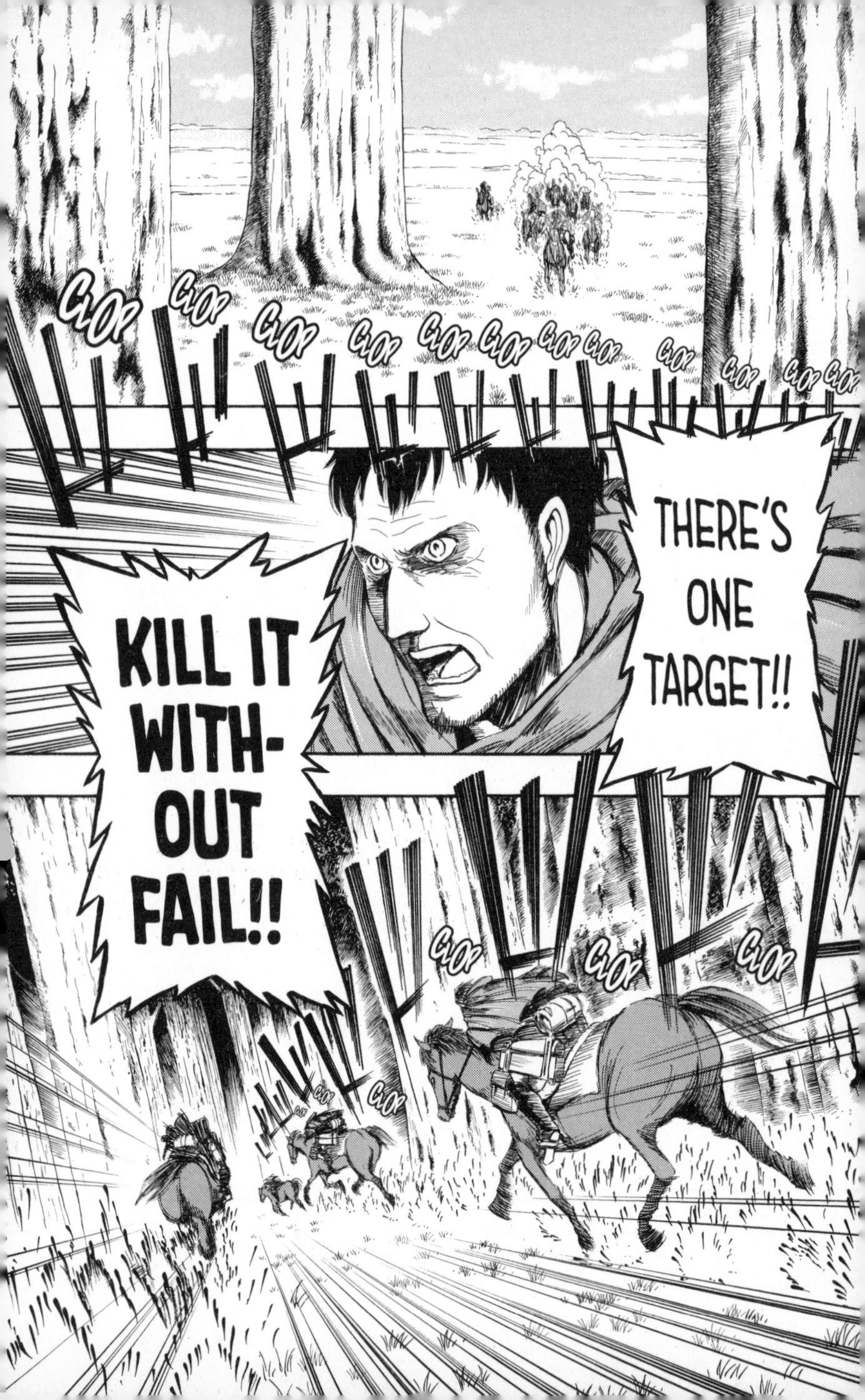
CLOP CLOP CLOP CLOP CLOP CLOP CLOP CLOP CLOP CLOP CLOP CLOP
THERE'S ONE TARGET!!
KILL IT WITH-OUT FAIL!!
CLOP CLOP CLOP
CLOP

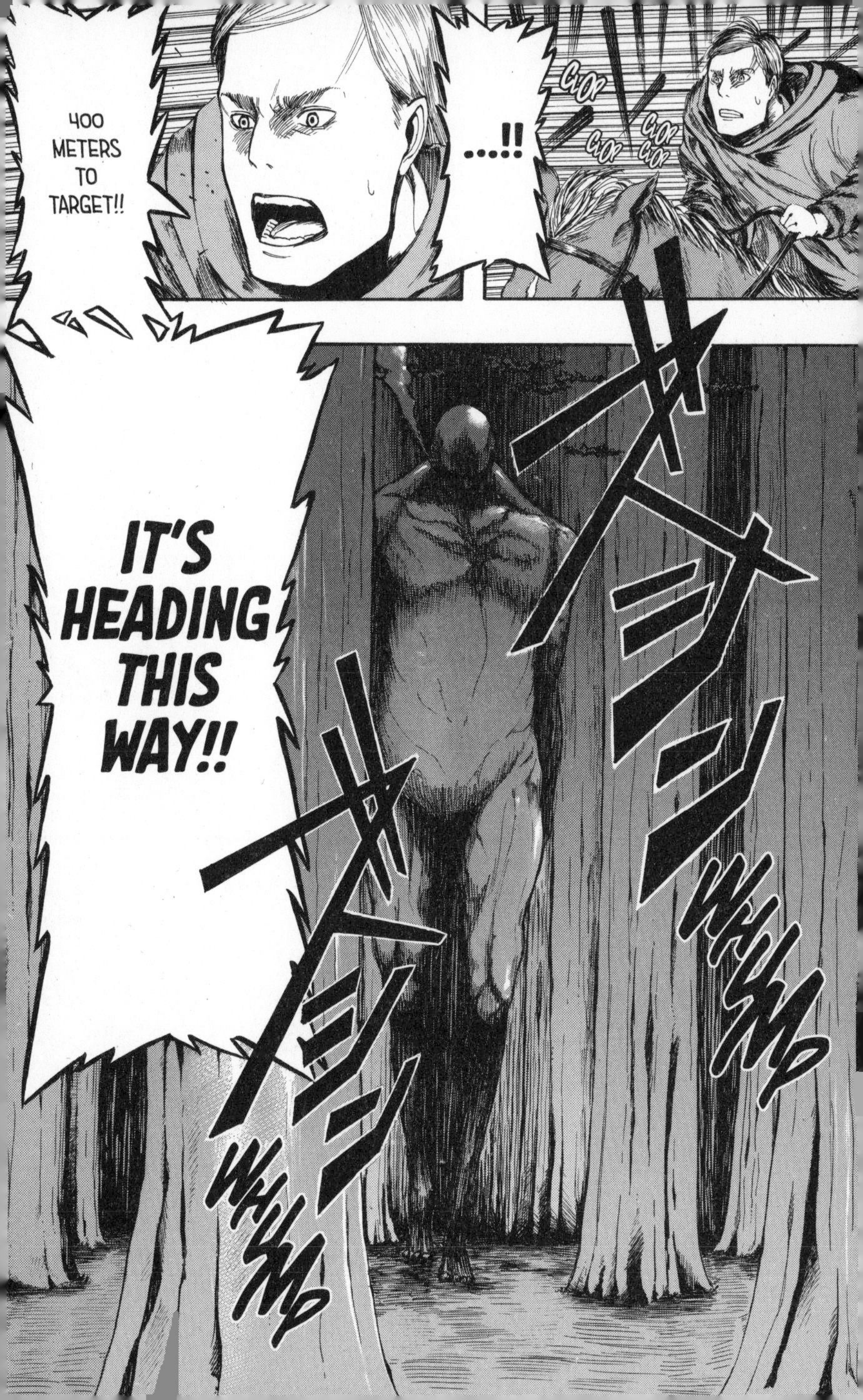
CLOP
CLOP
CLOP
CLOP CLOP
...!!
400 METERS TO TARGET!!
IT'S HEADING THIS WAY!!
WHUMP
WHUMP

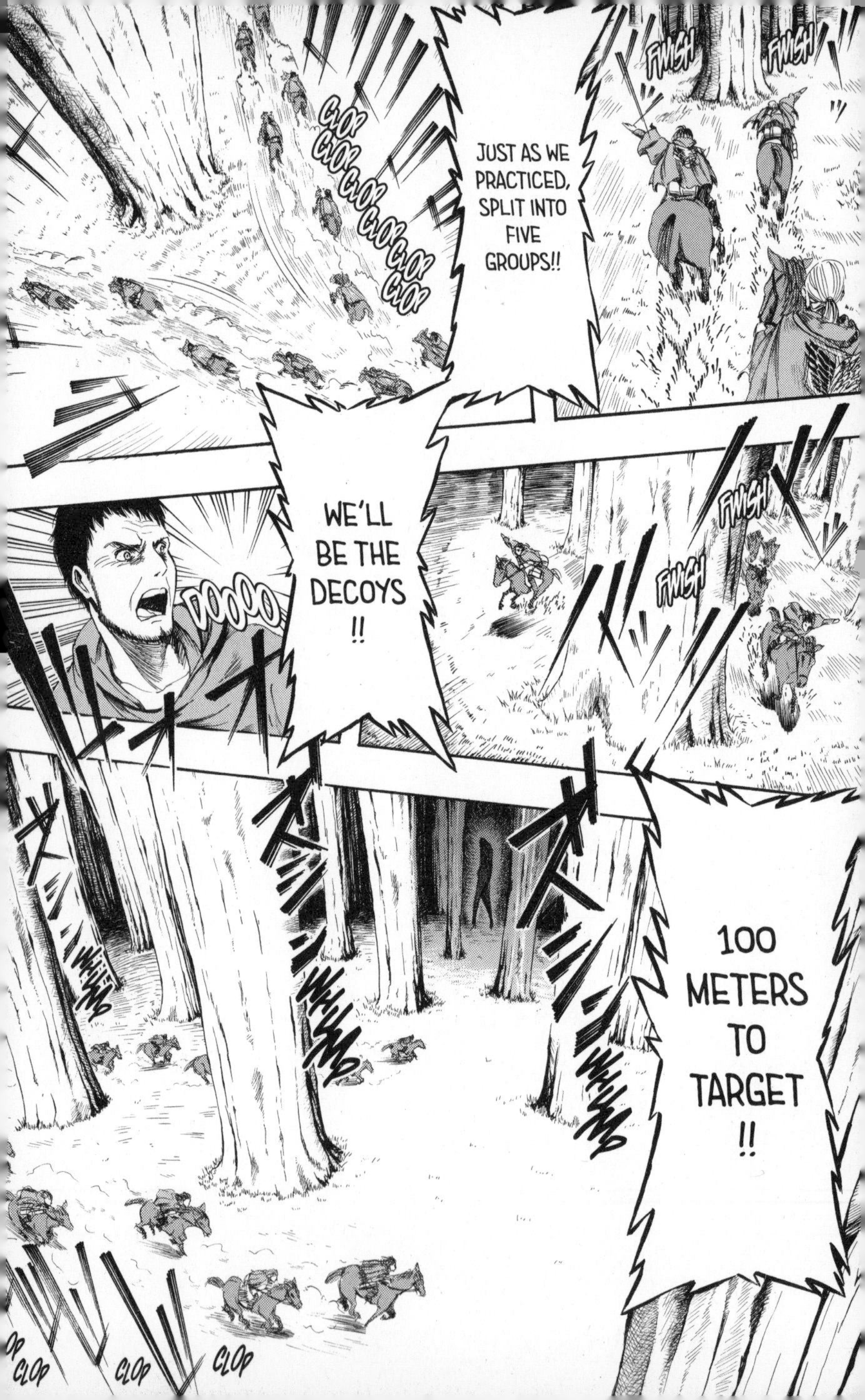
FWISH
FWISH
JUST AS WE PRACTICED, SPLIT INTO FIVE GROUPS!!
CLOP CLOP CLOP CLOP CLOP CLOP
FWISH
FWISH
WE'LL BE THE DECOYS !!
DOOOO
100 METERS TO TARGET !!
CLOP
CLOP
CLOP

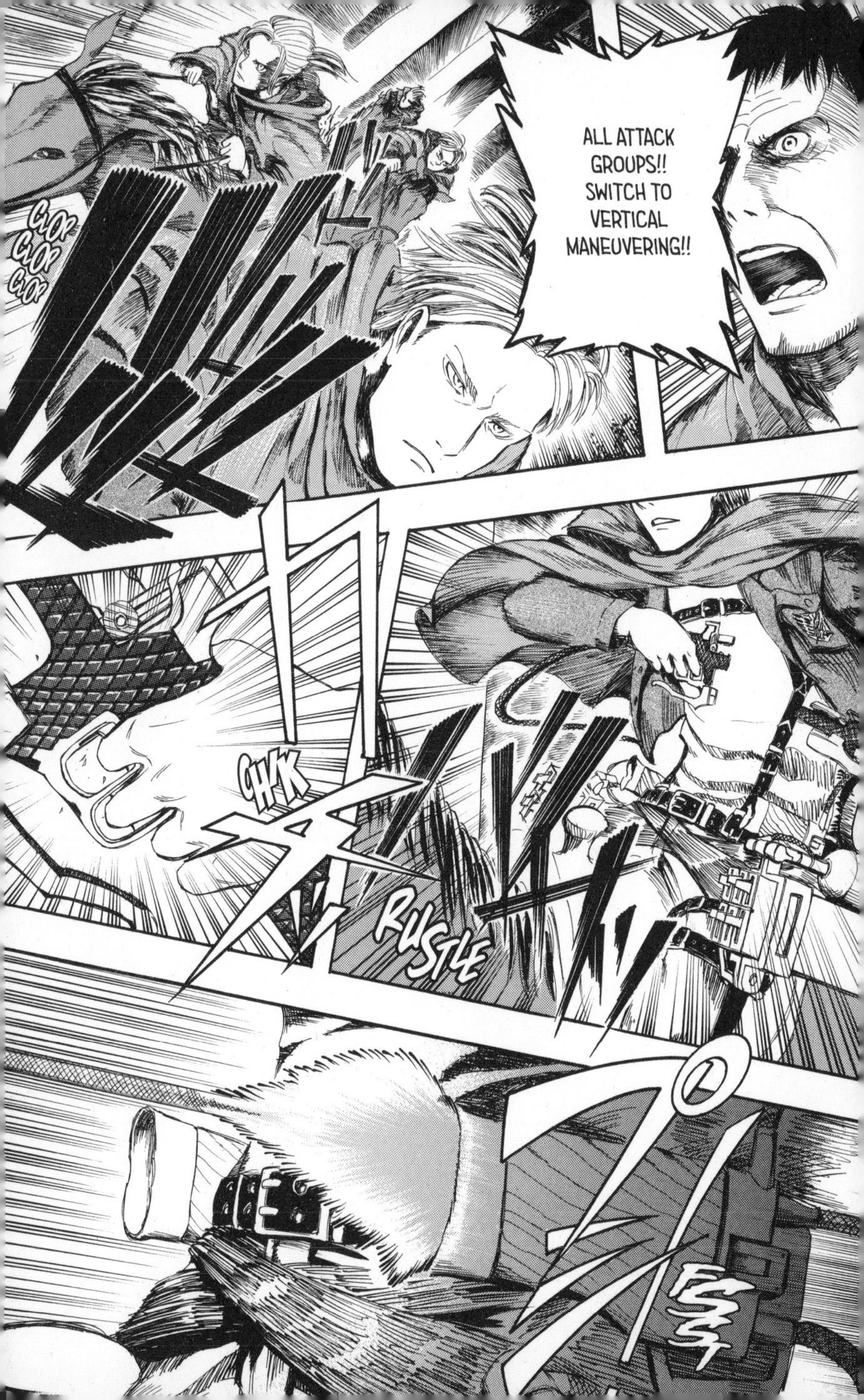
ALL ATTACK GROUPS!! SWITCH TO VERTICAL MANEUVERING!!
CLOP CLOP CLOP
CHAK
RUSTLE
FSST

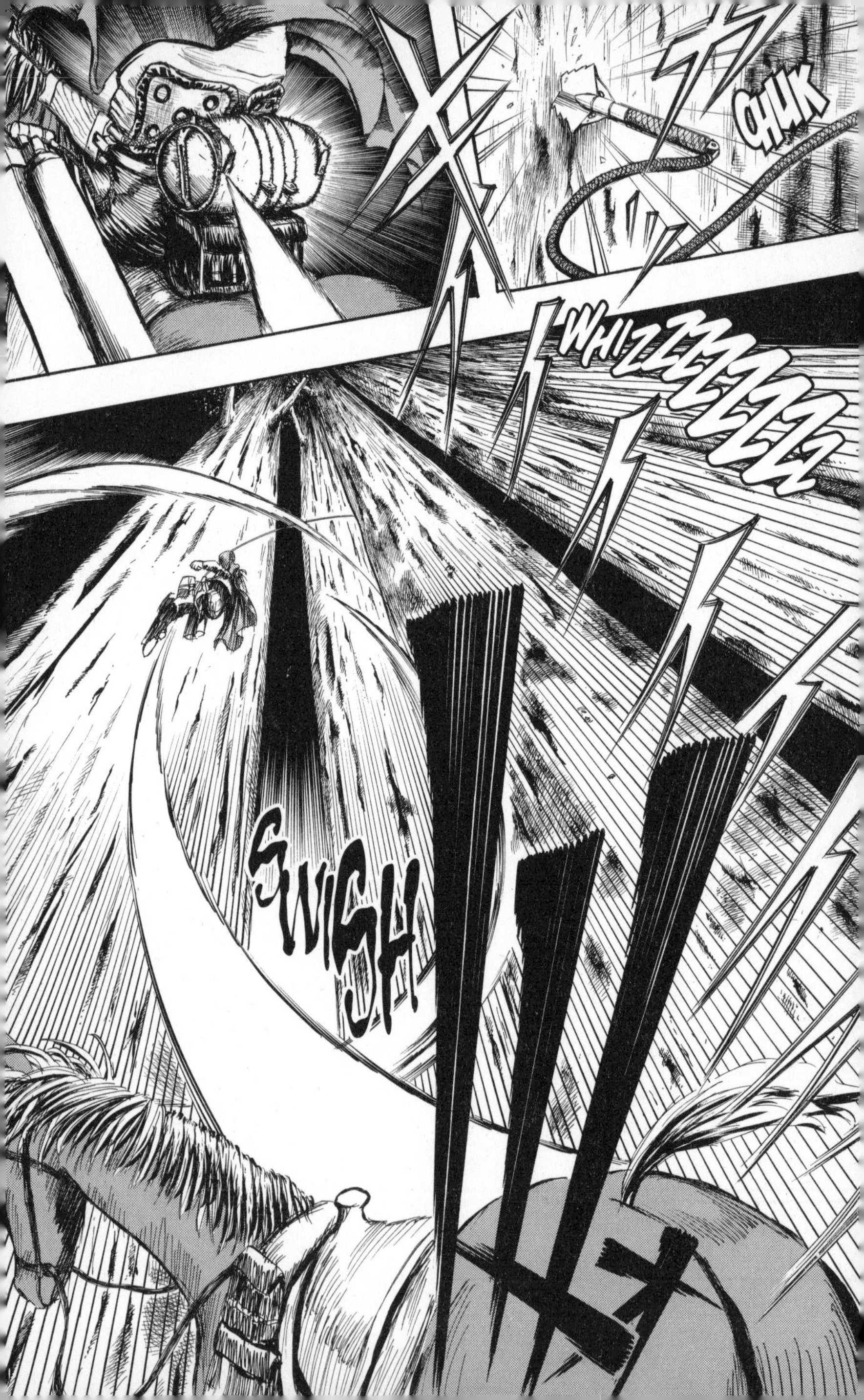
CHUK
WHIZZZZZZZ
SWISH

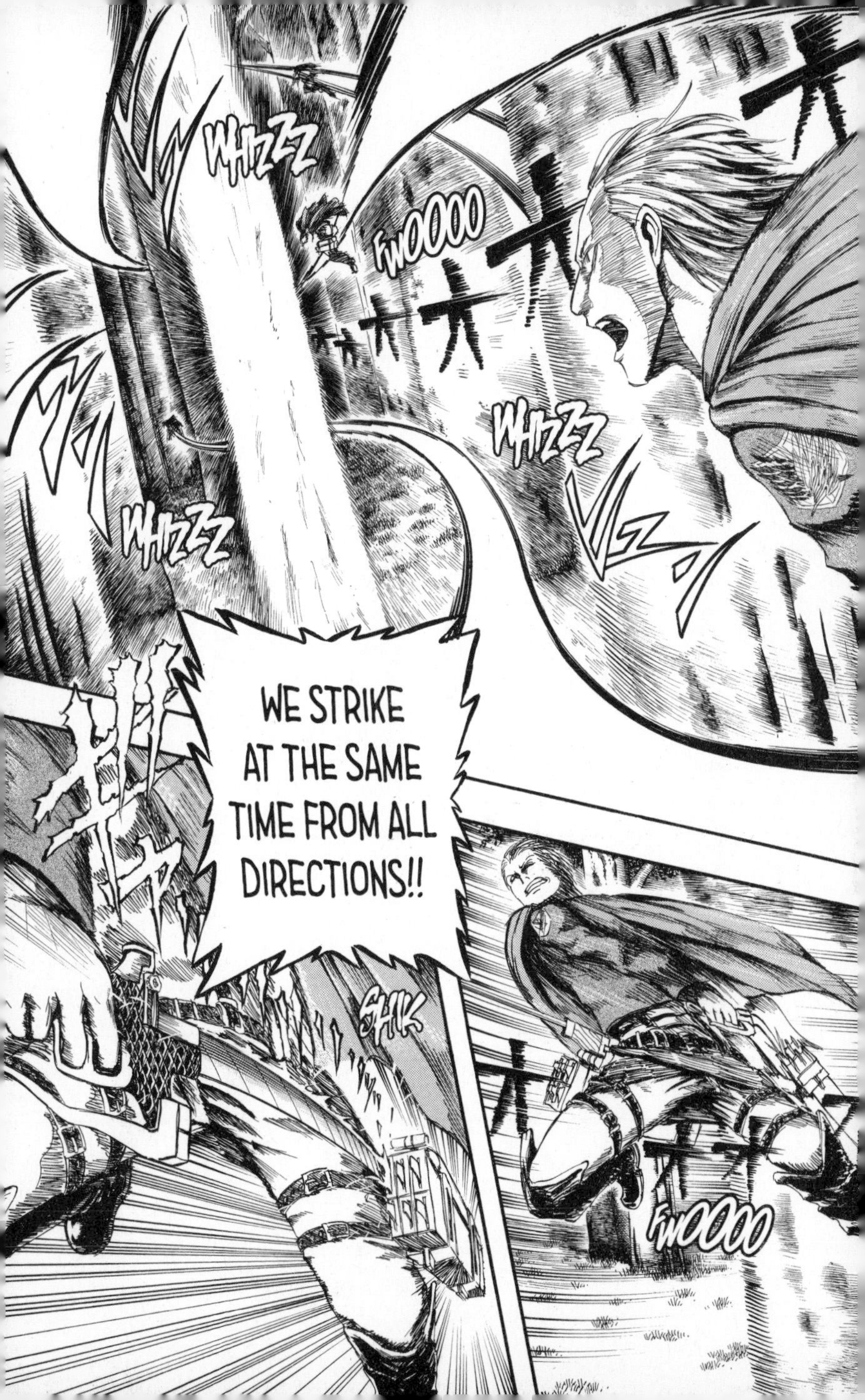
WHIZZZ
FWOOOO
WHIZZZ
WHIZZZ
WE STRIKE AT THE SAME TIME FROM ALL DIRECTIONS!!
FWOOOO
SHIK

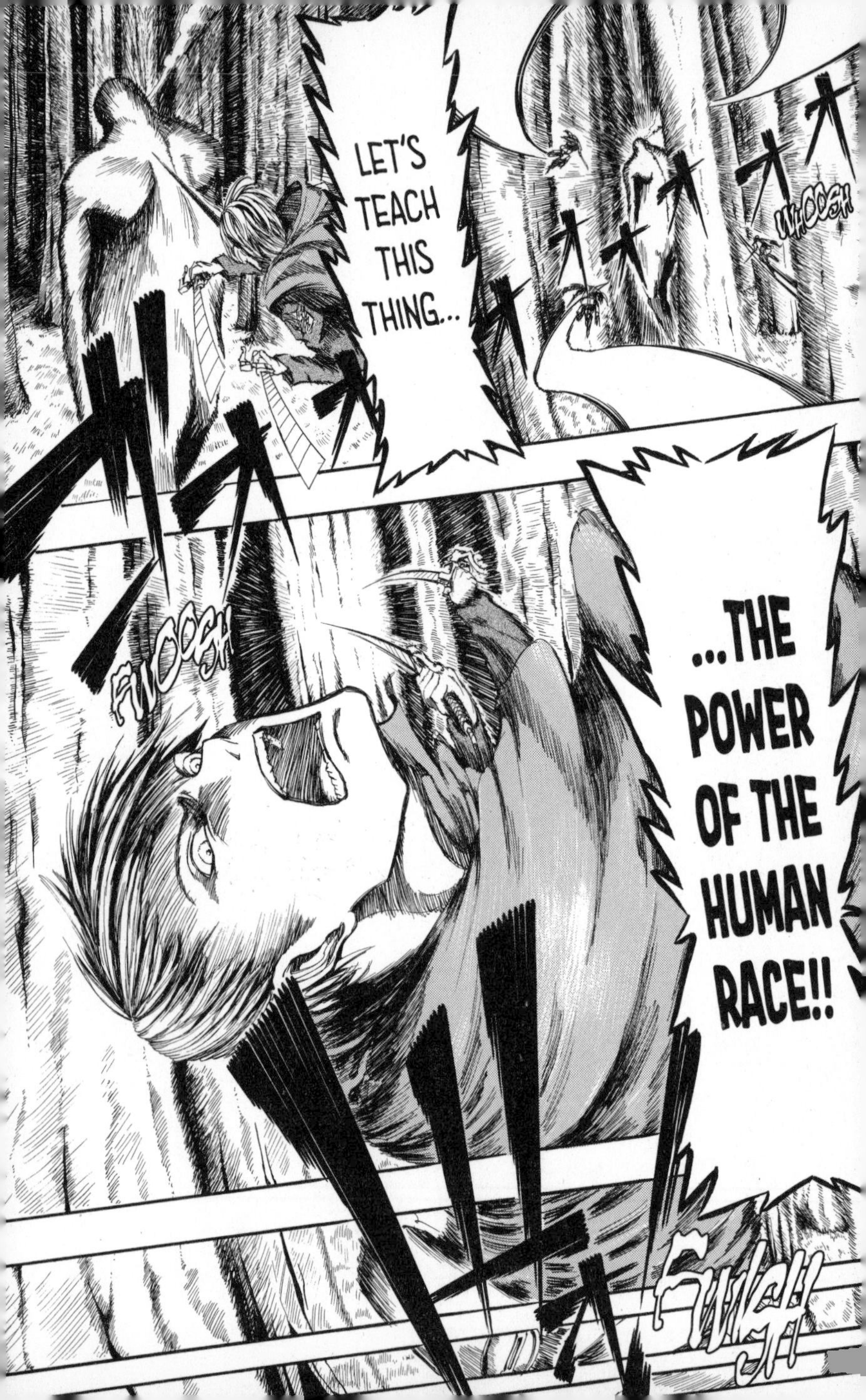
WHOOSH
LET'S TEACH THIS THING...
...THE POWER OF THE HUMAN RACE!!
FWOOSH
SWISH

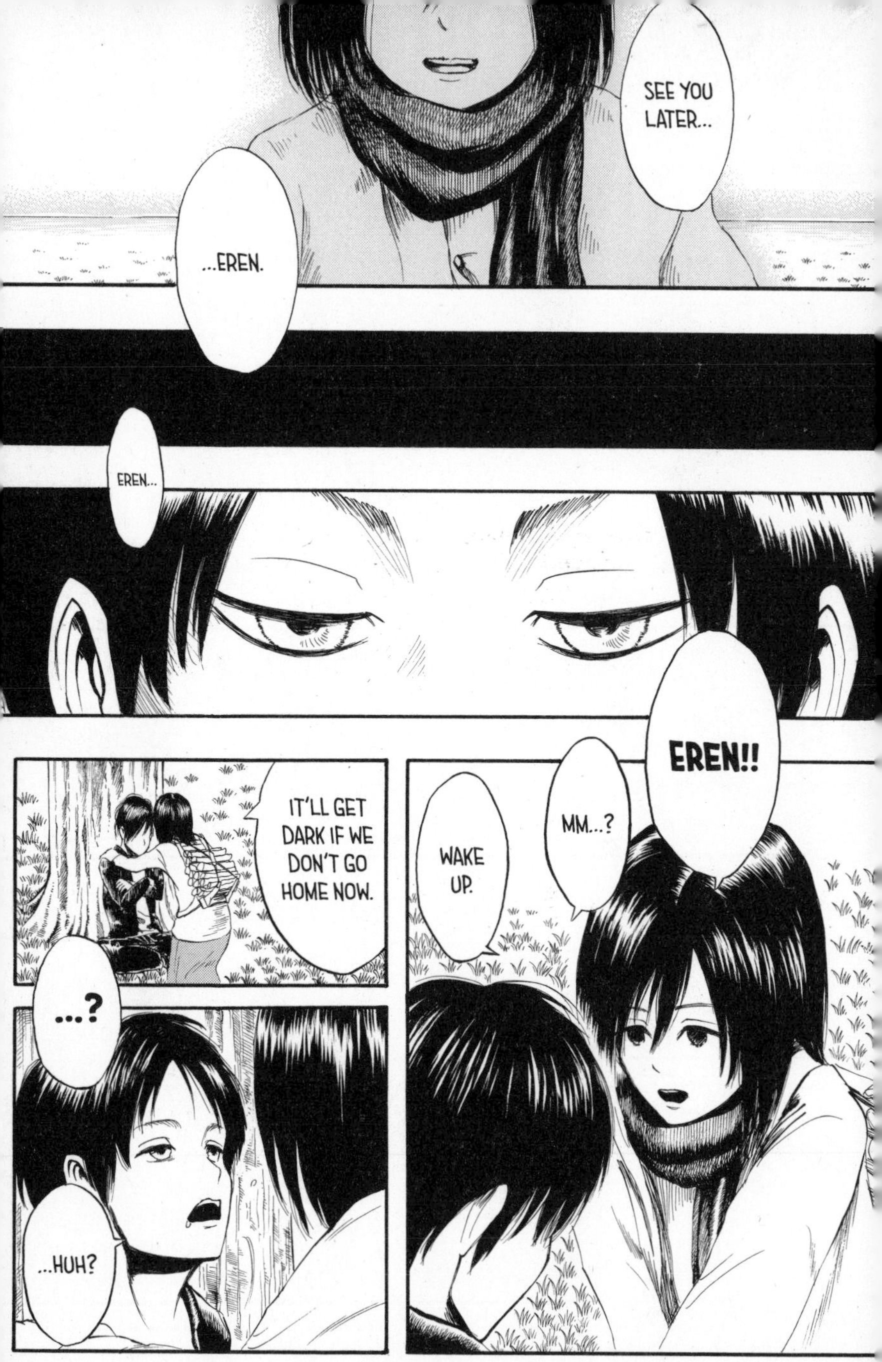
SEE YOU LATER...
...EREN.
EREN...
EREN!!
MM...?
WAKE UP.
IT'LL GET DARK IF WE DON'T GO HOME NOW.
...?
...HUH?

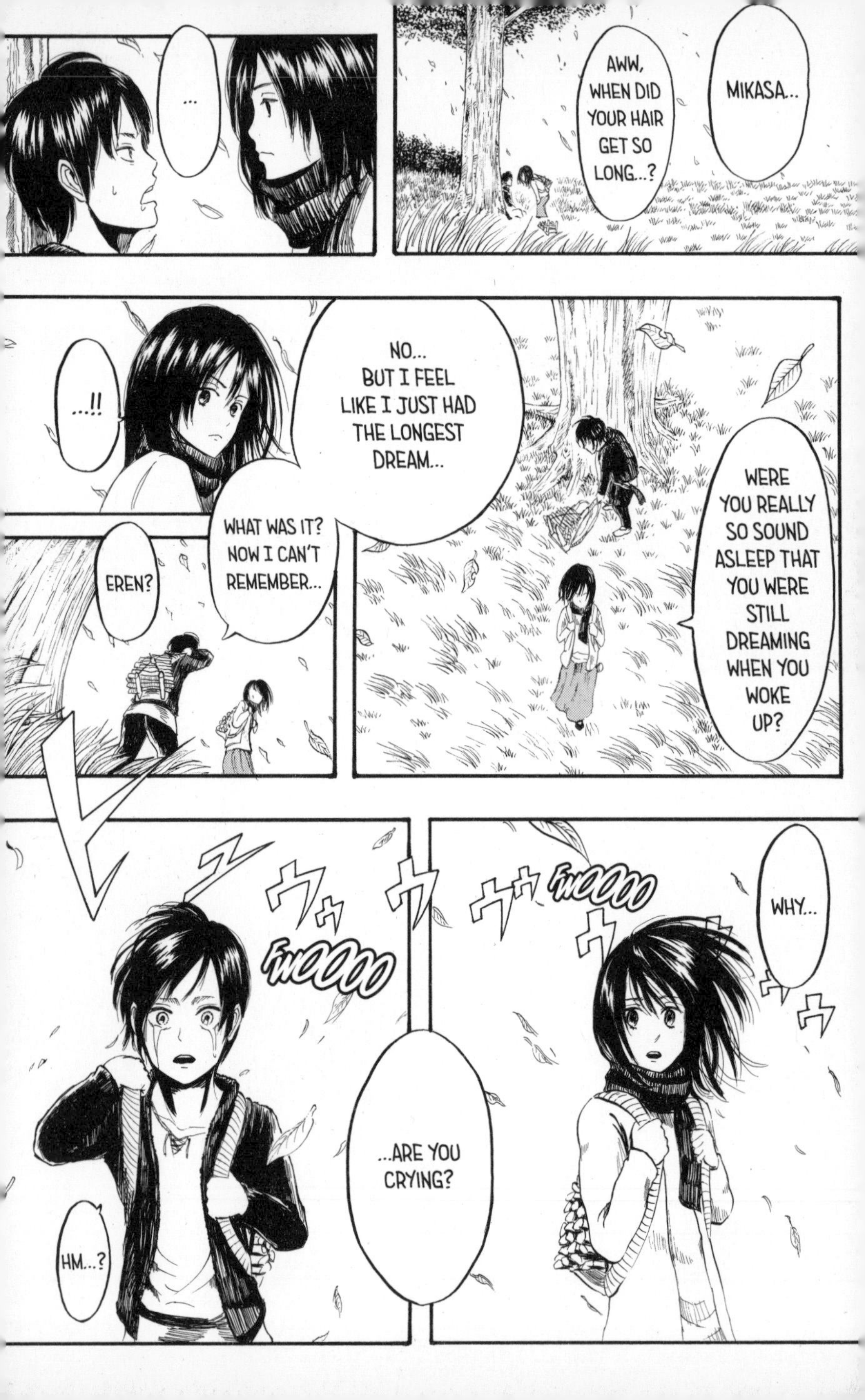
MIKASA...
AWW, WHEN DID YOUR HAIR GET SO LONG...?
...
WERE YOU REALLY SO SOUND ASLEEP THAT YOU WERE STILL DREAMING WHEN YOU WOKE UP?
NO... BUT I FEEL LIKE I JUST HAD THE LONGEST DREAM...
...!!
WHAT WAS IT? NOW I CAN'T REMEMBER...
EREN?
WHY...
FWOOOOO
...ARE YOU CRYING?
FWOOOOO
HM...?

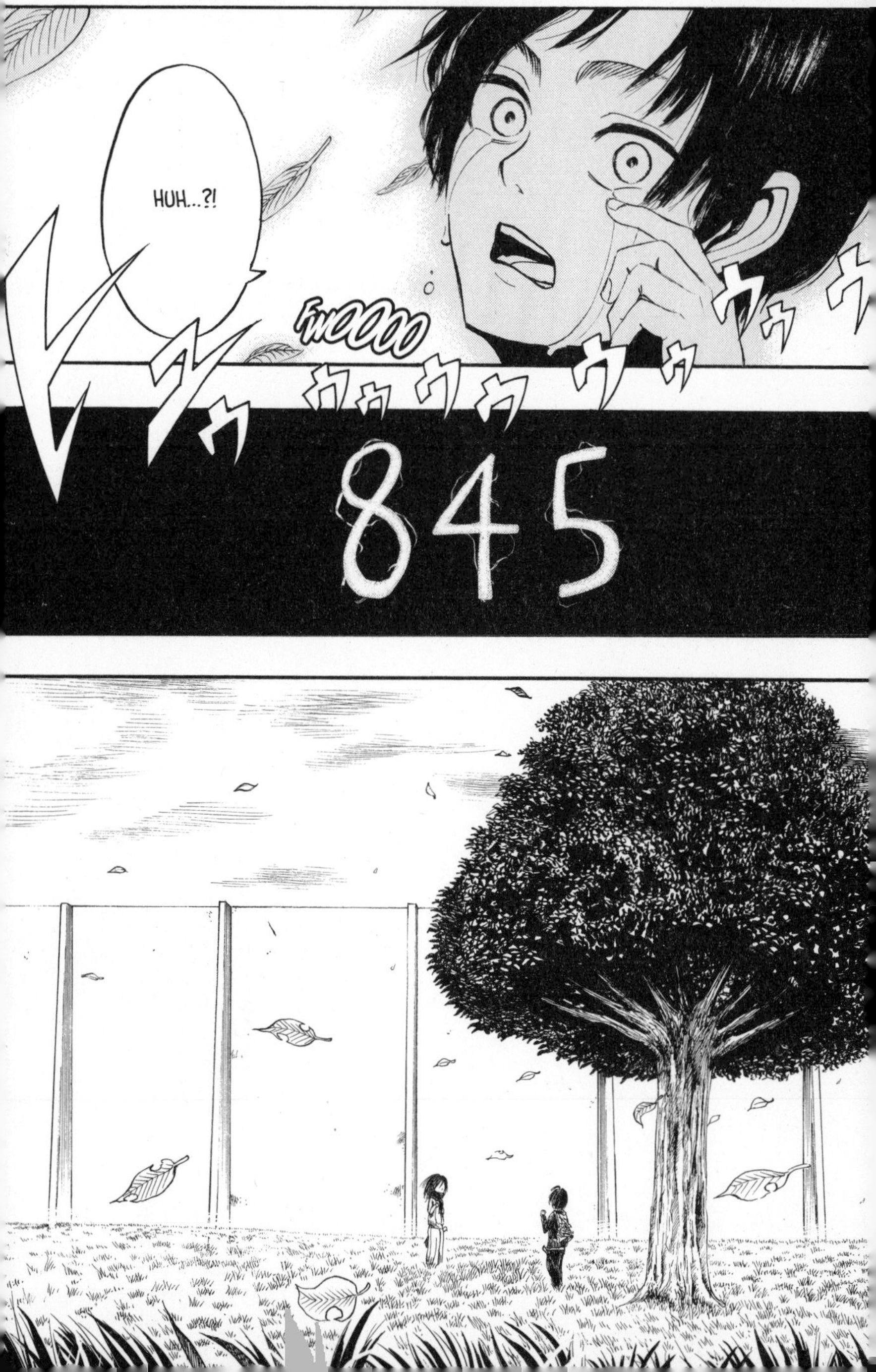
HUH...?!
FWOOOO
845

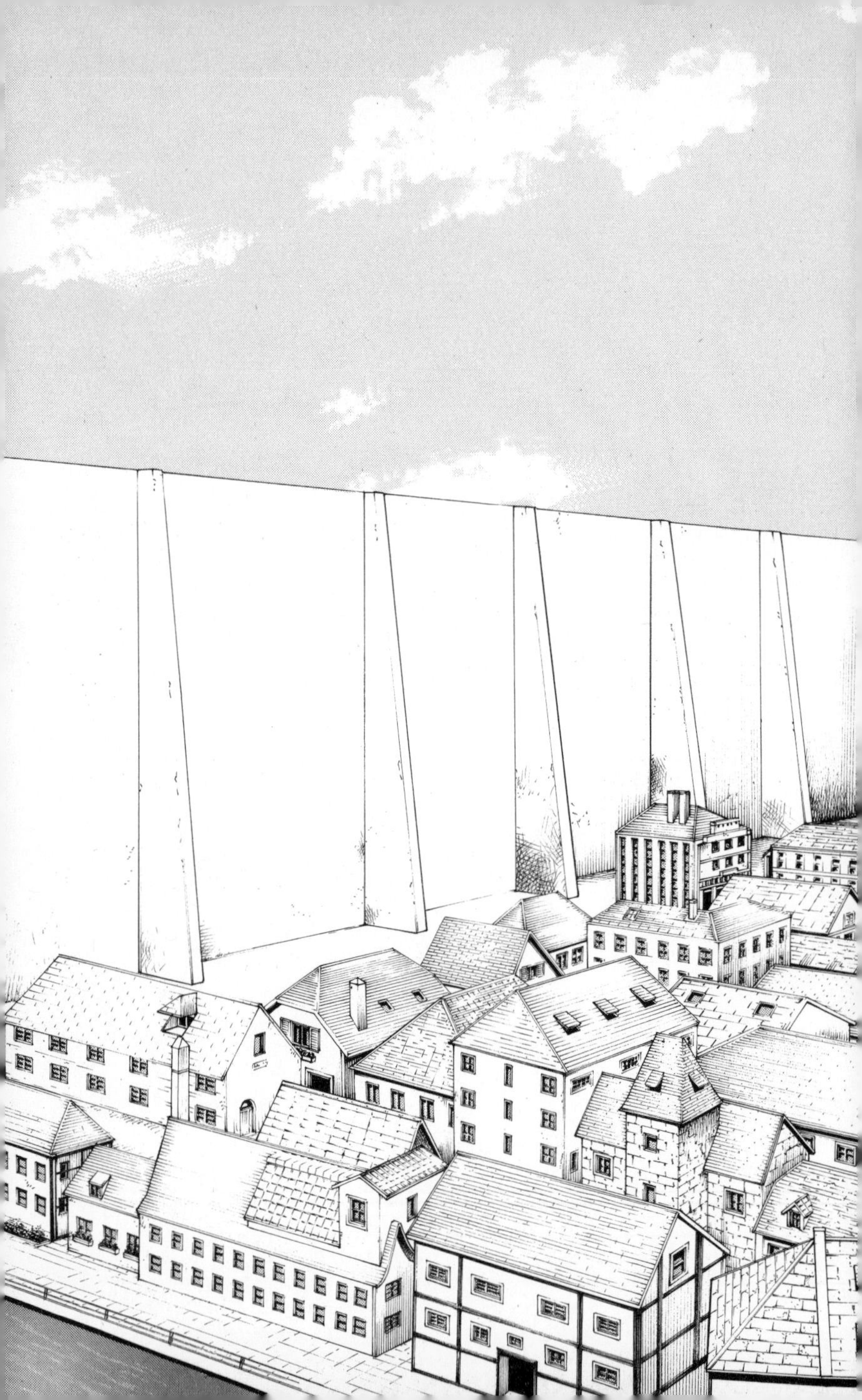

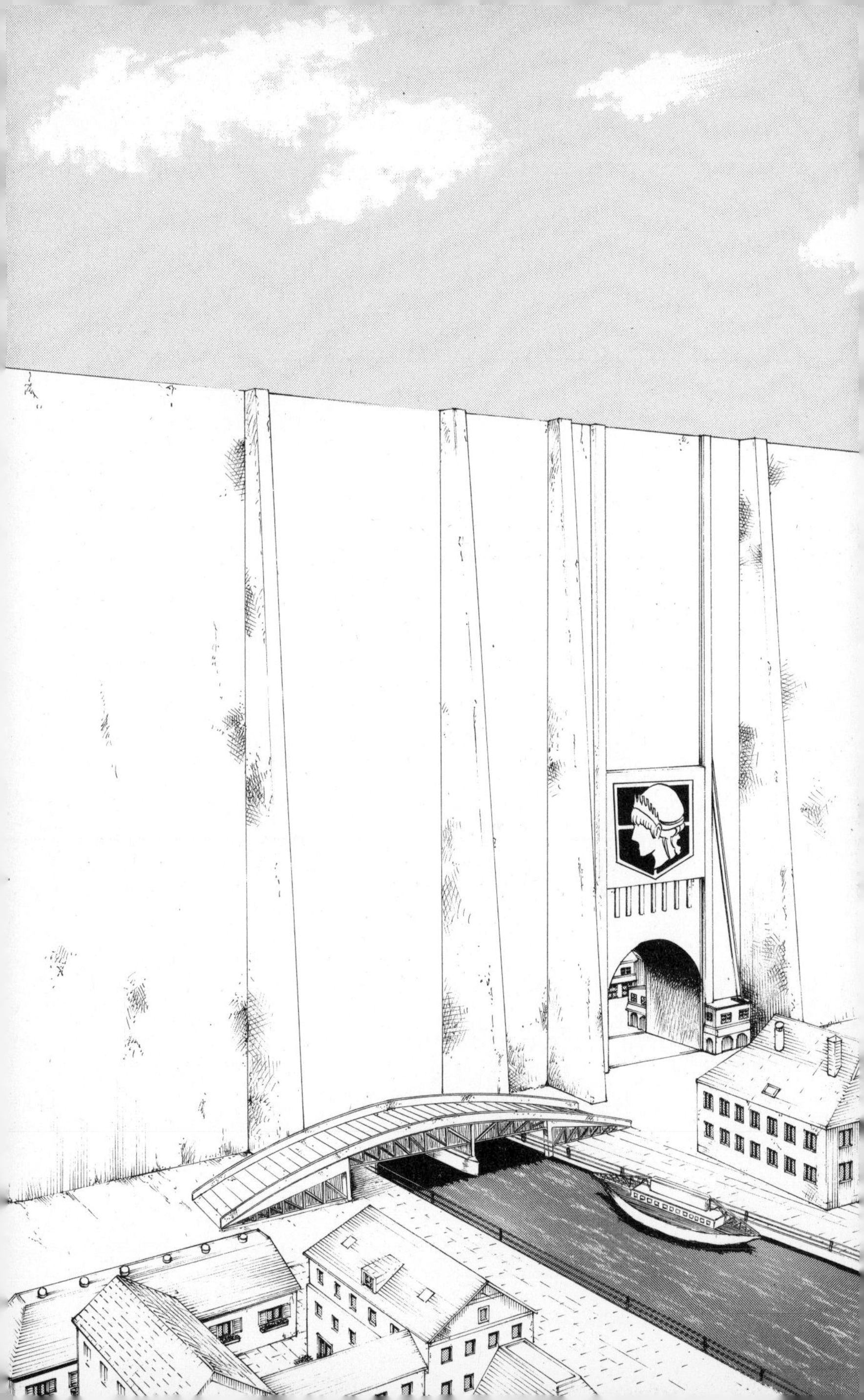

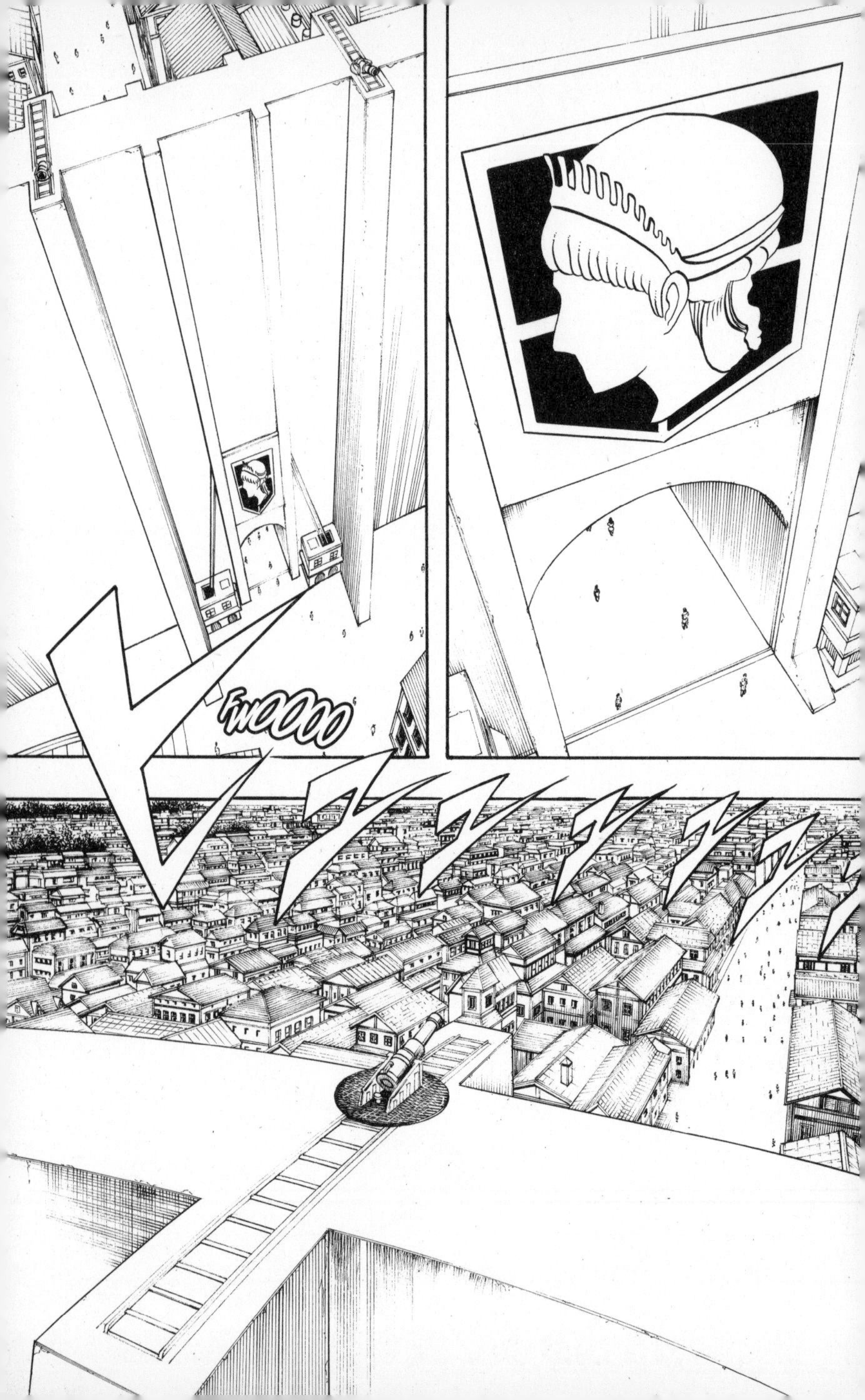
FWOOOO

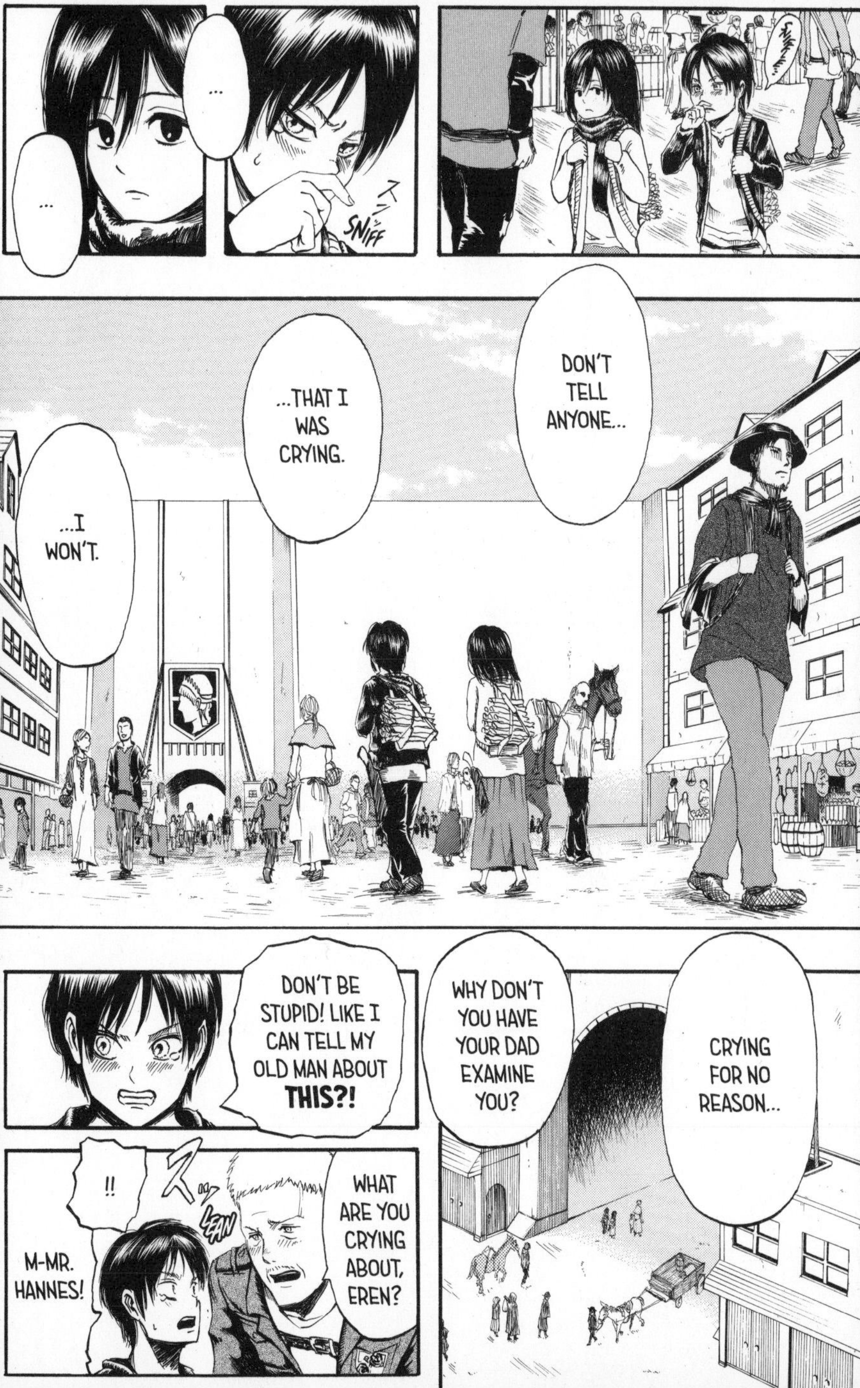
...
SNIFF
...
DON'T TELL ANYONE...
...THAT I WAS CRYING.
...I WON'T.
CRYING FOR NO REASON...
WHY DON'T YOU HAVE YOUR DAD EXAMINE YOU?
DON'T BE STUPID! LIKE I CAN TELL MY OLD MAN ABOUT **THIS?!**
WHAT ARE YOU CRYING ABOUT, EREN?
LEAN
!!
M-MR. HANNES!

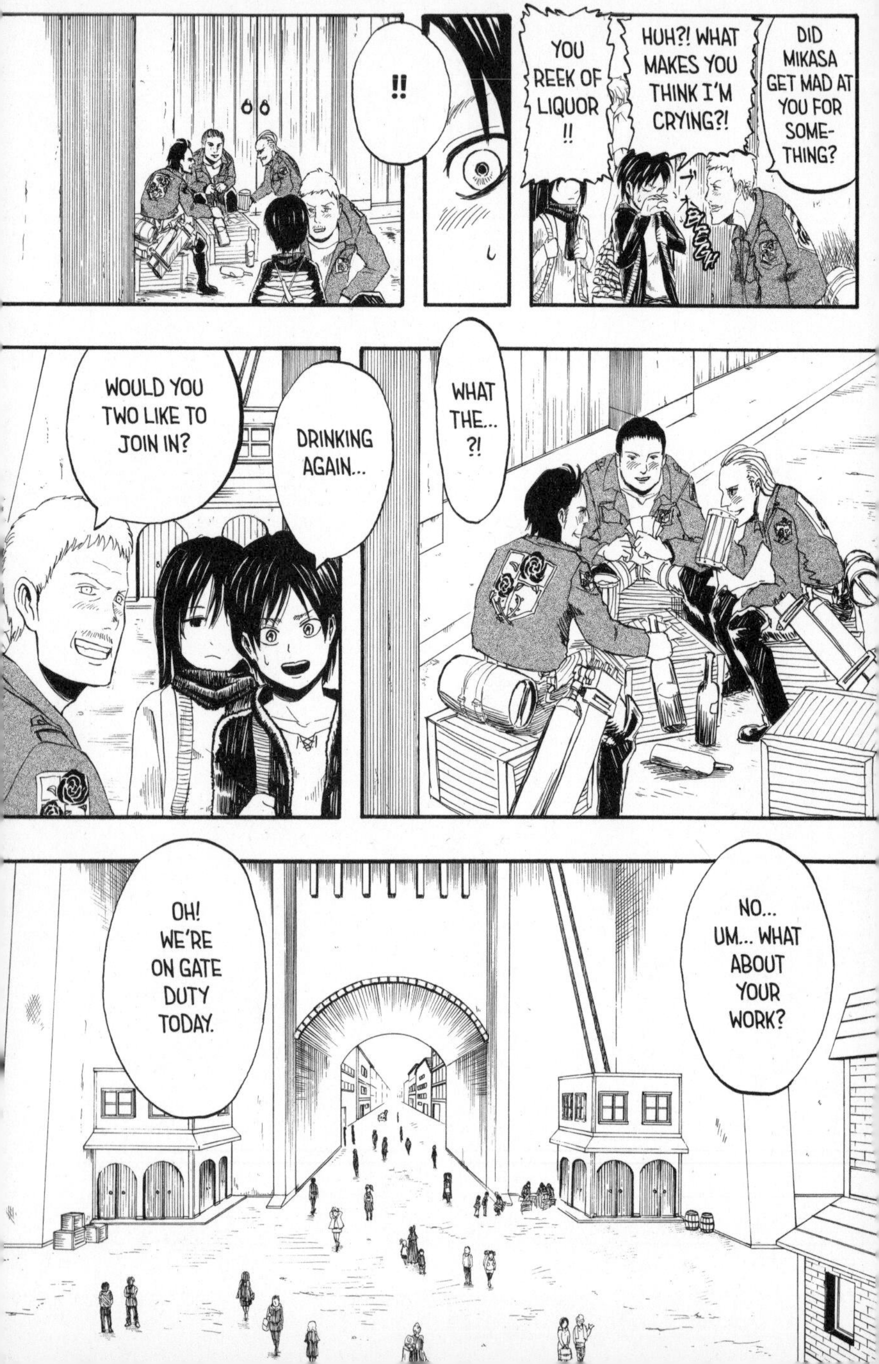
DID MIKASA GET MAD AT YOU FOR SOME-THING?
HUH?! WHAT MAKES YOU THINK I'M CRYING?!
BLECH
YOU REEK OF LIQUOR !!
!!
WHAT THE... ?!
DRINKING AGAIN...
WOULD YOU TWO LIKE TO JOIN IN?
NO... UM... WHAT ABOUT YOUR WORK?
OH! WE'RE ON GATE DUTY TODAY.

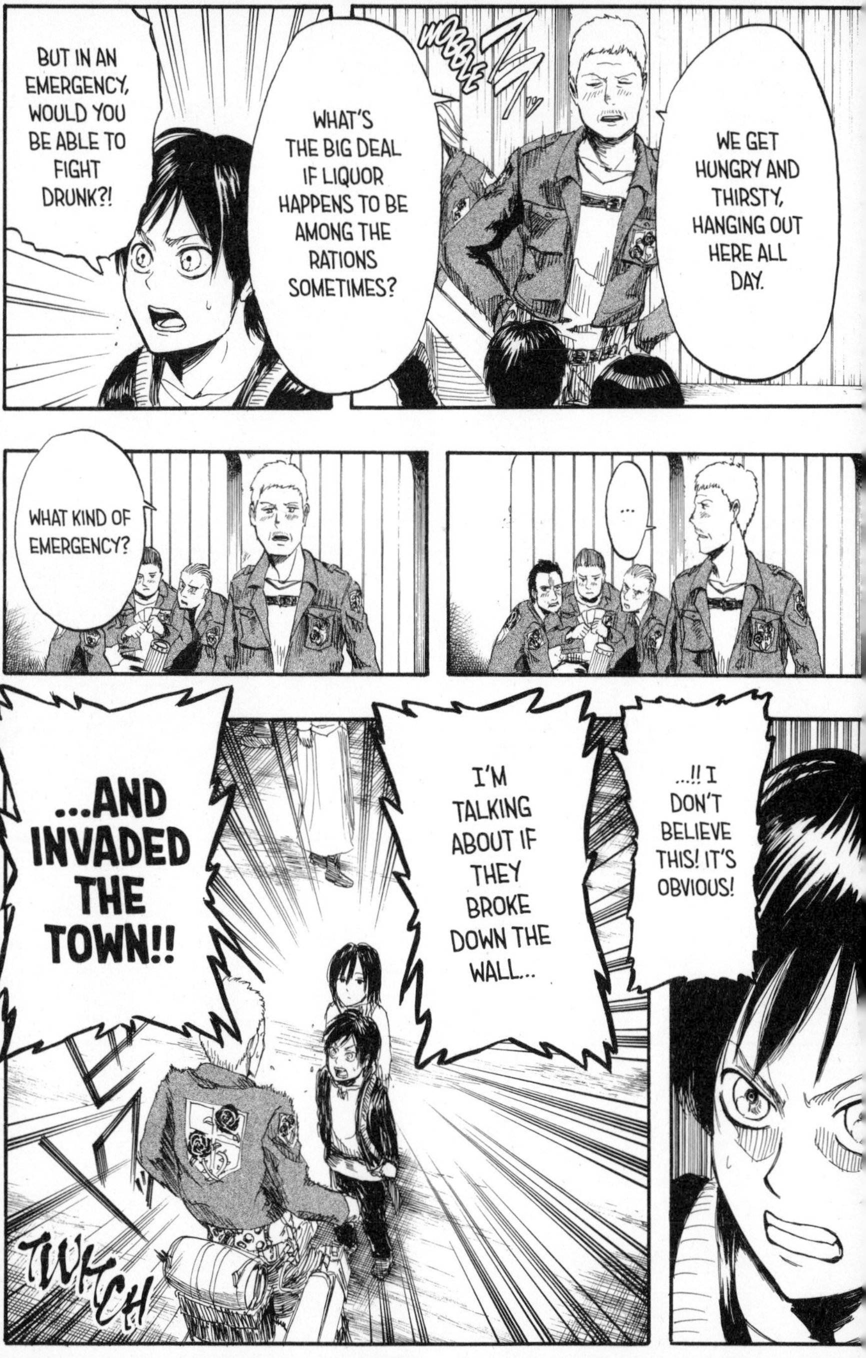
WOBBLE
WE GET HUNGRY AND THIRSTY, HANGING OUT HERE ALL DAY.
WHAT'S THE BIG DEAL IF LIQUOR HAPPENS TO BE AMONG THE RATIONS SOMETIMES?
BUT IN AN EMERGENCY, WOULD YOU BE ABLE TO FIGHT DRUNK?!
...
WHAT KIND OF EMERGENCY?
...!! I DON'T BELIEVE THIS! IT'S OBVIOUS!
I'M TALKING ABOUT IF THEY BROKE DOWN THE WALL...
...AND INVADED THE TOWN!!
TWITCH

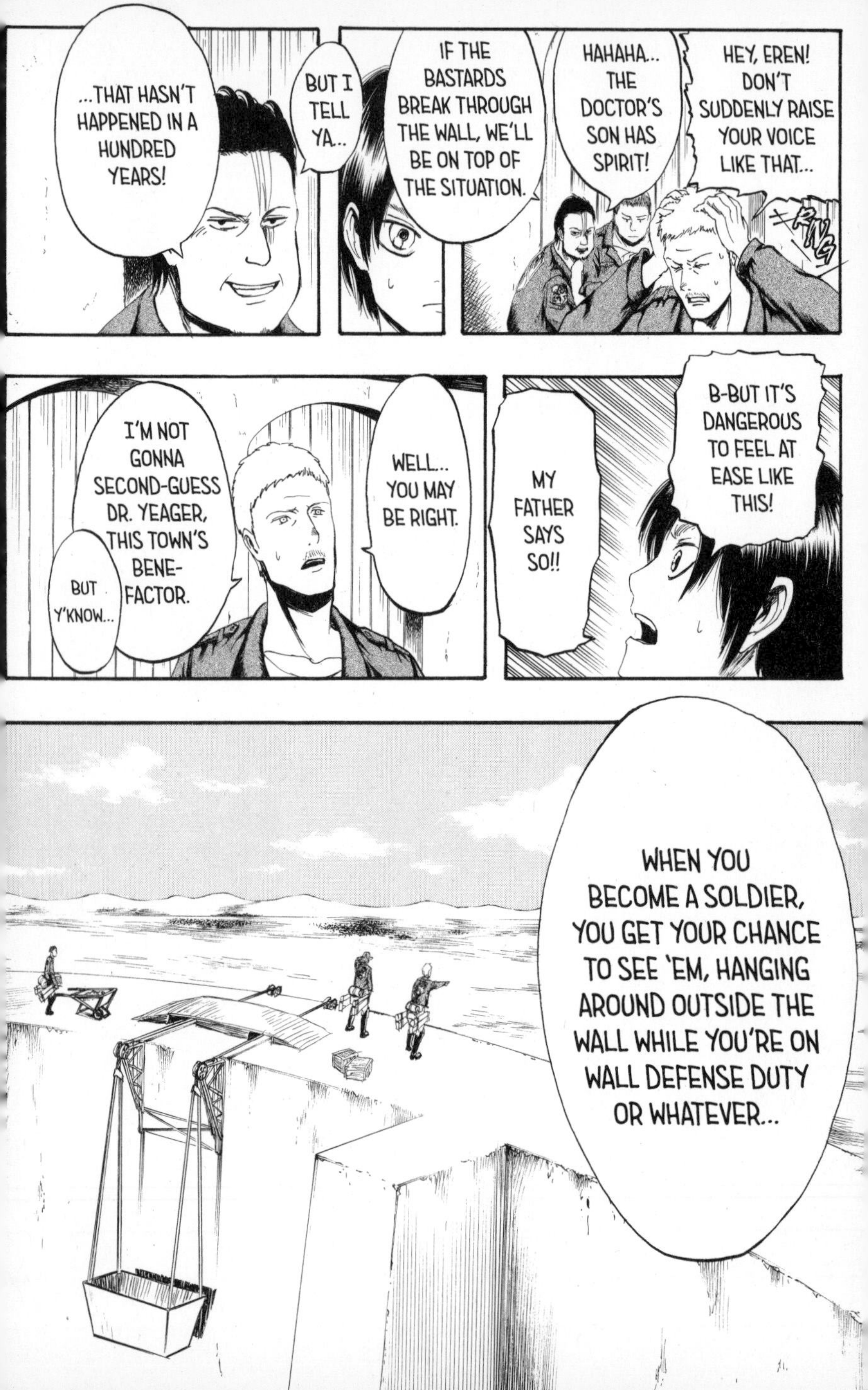
HEY, EREN! DON'T SUDDENLY RAISE YOUR VOICE LIKE THAT...
HAHAHA... THE DOCTOR'S SON HAS SPIRIT!
IF THE BASTARDS BREAK THROUGH THE WALL, WE'LL BE ON TOP OF THE SITUATION.
BUT I TELL YA...
...THAT HASN'T HAPPENED IN A HUNDRED YEARS!
B-BUT IT'S DANGEROUS TO FEEL AT EASE LIKE THIS!
MY FATHER SAYS SO!!
WELL... YOU MAY BE RIGHT.
I'M NOT GONNA SECOND-GUESS DR. YEAGER, THIS TOWN'S BENE-FACTOR.
BUT Y'KNOW...
WHEN YOU BECOME A SOLDIER, YOU GET YOUR CHANCE TO SEE 'EM, HANGING AROUND OUTSIDE THE WALL WHILE YOU'RE ON WALL DEFENSE DUTY OR WHATEVER...

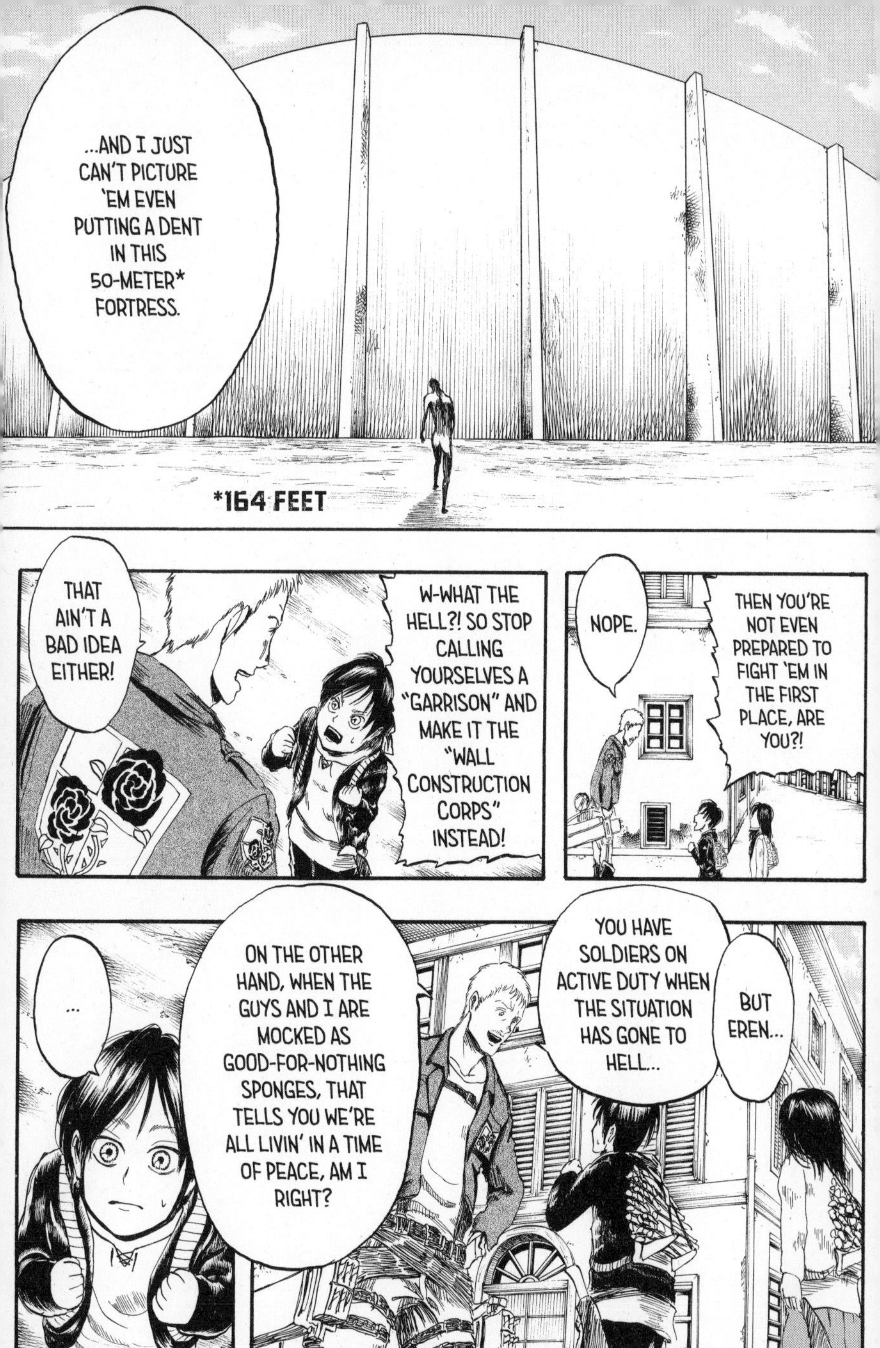
...AND I JUST CAN'T PICTURE 'EM EVEN PUTTING A DENT IN THIS 50-METER* FORTRESS.
*164 FEET
THEN YOU'RE NOT EVEN PREPARED TO FIGHT 'EM IN THE FIRST PLACE, ARE YOU?!
NOPE.
W-WHAT THE HELL?! SO STOP CALLING YOURSELVES A "GARRISON" AND MAKE IT THE "WALL CONSTRUCTION CORPS" INSTEAD!
THAT AIN'T A BAD IDEA EITHER!
BUT EREN...
YOU HAVE SOLDIERS ON ACTIVE DUTY WHEN THE SITUATION HAS GONE TO HELL...
ON THE OTHER HAND, WHEN THE GUYS AND I ARE MOCKED AS GOOD-FOR-NOTHING SPONGES, THAT TELLS YOU WE'RE ALL LIVIN' IN A TIME OF PEACE, AM I RIGHT?
...

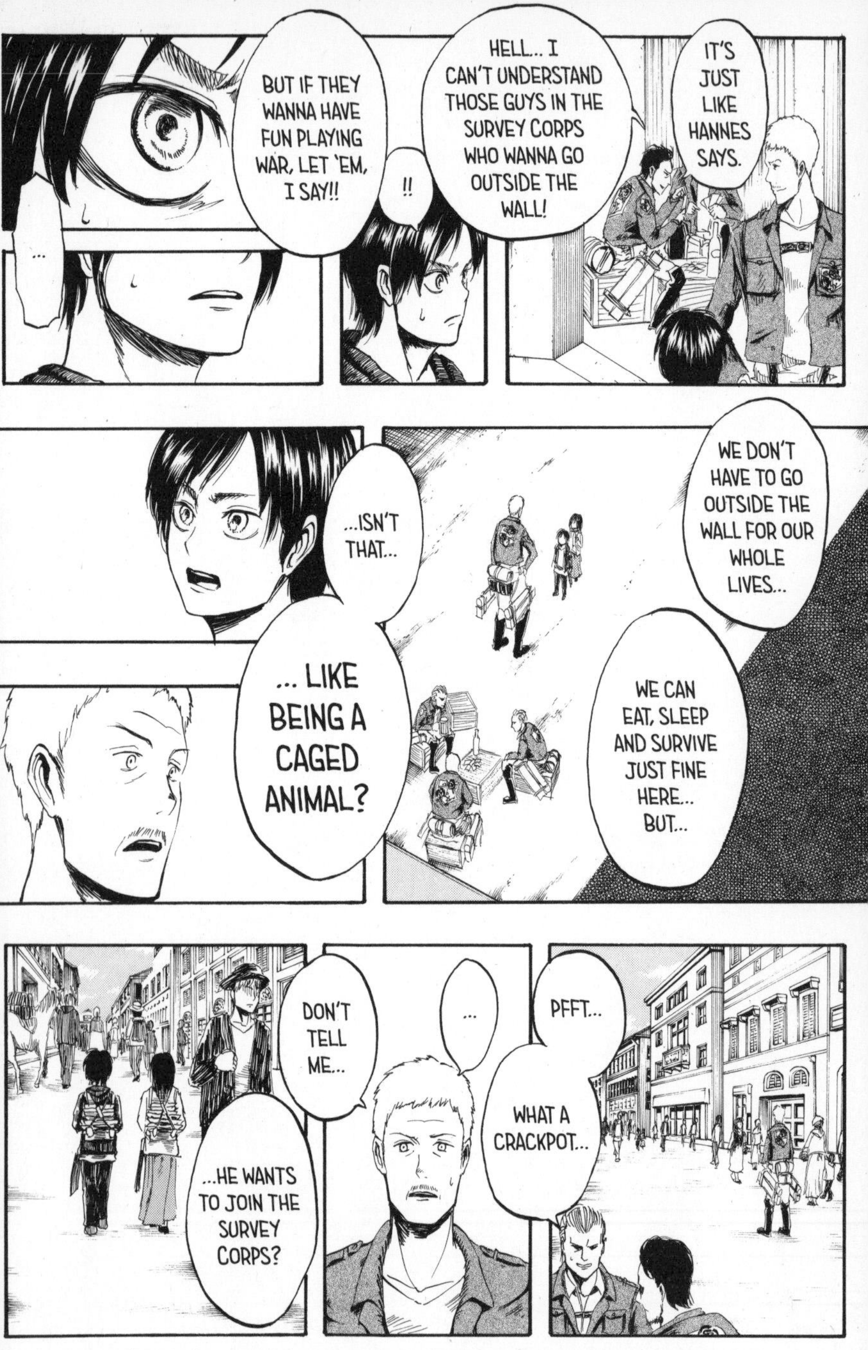
IT'S JUST LIKE HANNES SAYS.
HELL... I CAN'T UNDERSTAND THOSE GUYS IN THE SURVEY CORPS WHO WANNA GO OUTSIDE THE WALL!
BUT IF THEY WANNA HAVE FUN PLAYING WAR, LET 'EM, I SAY!!
!!
...
WE DON'T HAVE TO GO OUTSIDE THE WALL FOR OUR WHOLE LIVES...
WE CAN EAT, SLEEP AND SURVIVE JUST FINE HERE... BUT...
...ISN'T THAT...
... LIKE BEING A CAGED ANIMAL?
PFFT...
WHAT A CRACKPOT...
...
DON'T TELL ME...
...HE WANTS TO JOIN THE SURVEY CORPS?

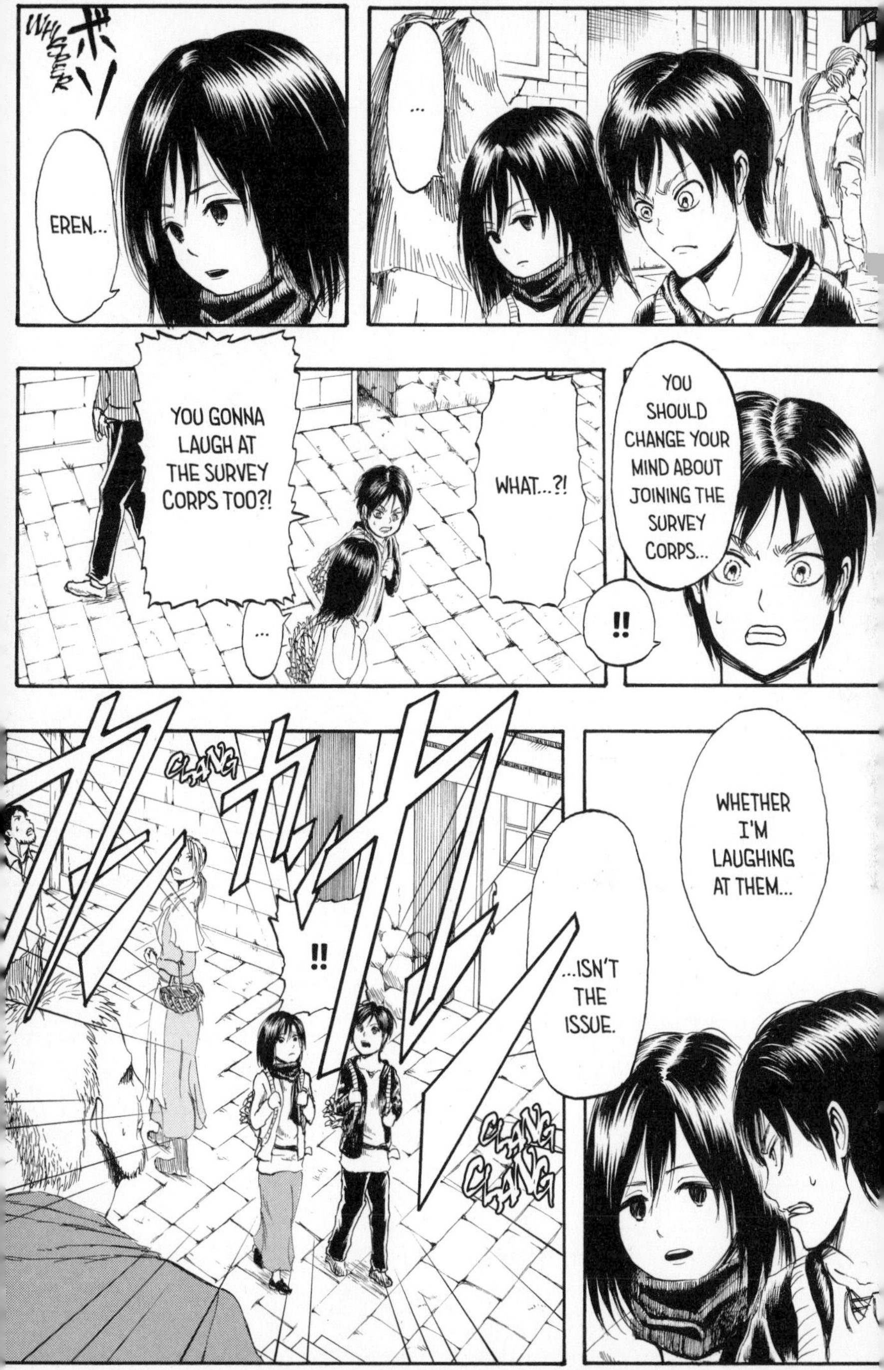
...
WHISPER
ボソ
EREN...
YOU SHOULD CHANGE YOUR MIND ABOUT JOINING THE SURVEY CORPS...
!!
WHAT...?!
YOU GONNA LAUGH AT THE SURVEY CORPS TOO?!
...
WHETHER I'M LAUGHING AT THEM...
...ISN'T THE ISSUE.
CLANG
!!
CLANG CLANG CLANG

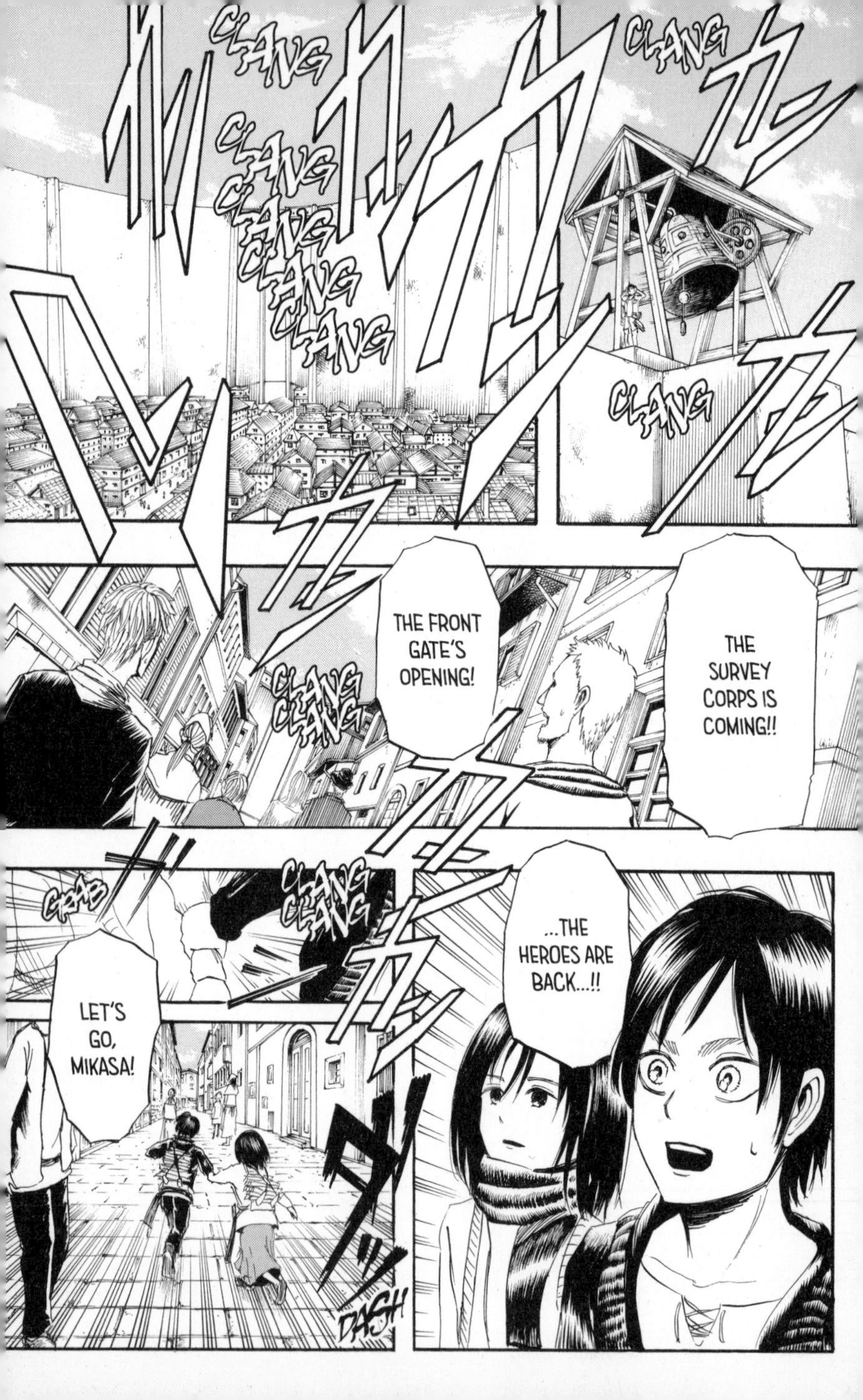
CLANG
CLANG
CLANG
CLANG
CLANG
CLANG
CLANG
THE SURVEY CORPS IS COMING!!
THE FRONT GATE'S OPENING!
CLANG CLANG
...THE HEROES ARE BACK...!!
CLANG CLANG
GRAB
LET'S GO, MIKASA!
DASH!

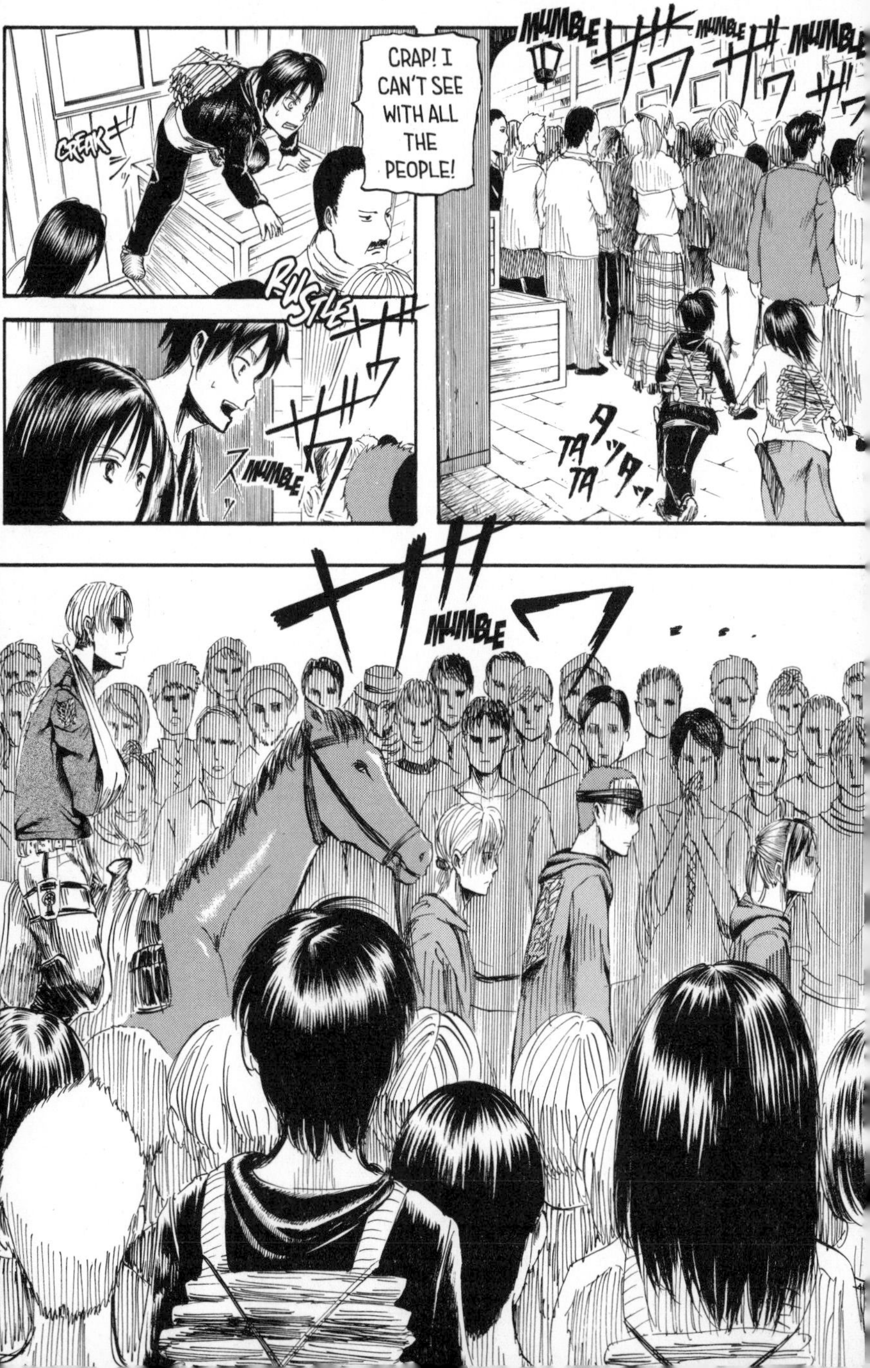
MUMBLE
MUMBLE
MUMBLE
ザワ ザワ ザワ
TA TA
タッタッ
CRAP! I CAN'T SEE WITH ALL THE PEOPLE!
CREAK
RUSTLE
ザワ
MUMBLE
MUMBLE
ザワ…

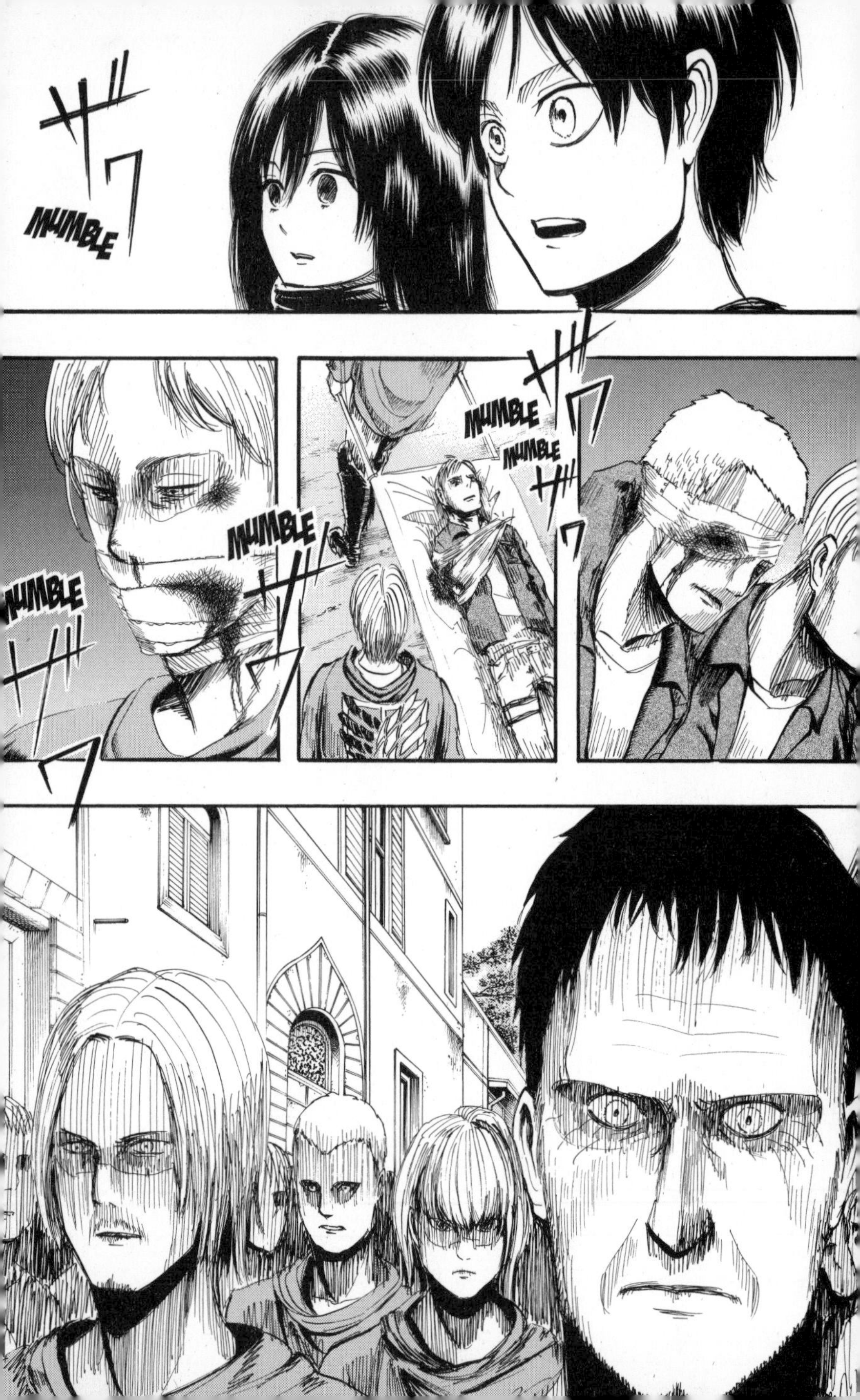
ザワ
MUMBLE
ザワ
MUMBLE
MUMBLE
ザワ
MUMBLE
ザワ
MUMBLE
ザワ

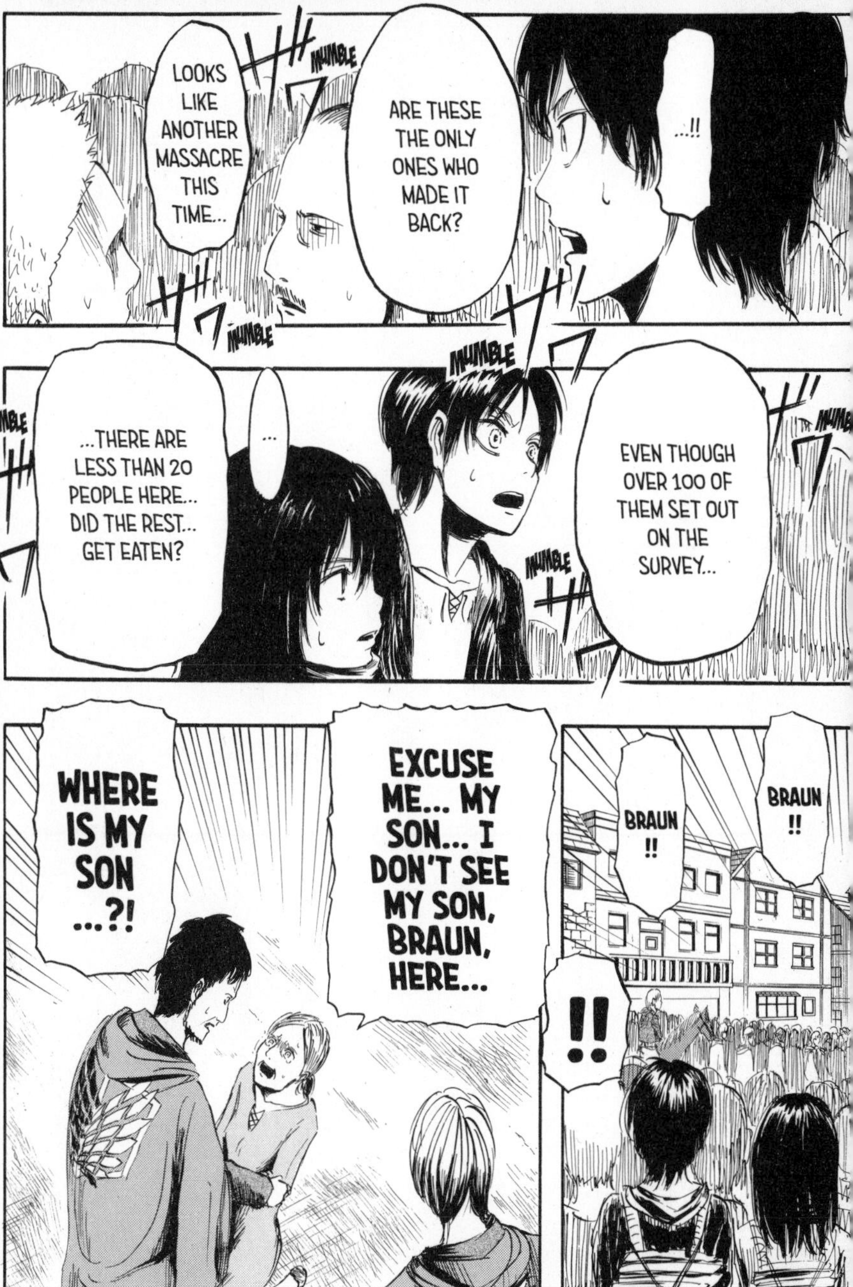
...!!
MUMBLE
ARE THESE THE ONLY ONES WHO MADE IT BACK?
MUMBLE
LOOKS LIKE ANOTHER MASSACRE THIS TIME...
MUMBLE
MUMBLE
MUMBLE
EVEN THOUGH OVER 100 OF THEM SET OUT ON THE SURVEY...
MUMBLE
...
...THERE ARE LESS THAN 20 PEOPLE HERE... DID THE REST... GET EATEN?
MUMBLE
BRAUN!!
BRAUN!!
!!
EXCUSE ME... MY SON... I DON'T SEE MY SON, BRAUN, HERE...
WHERE IS MY SON...?!

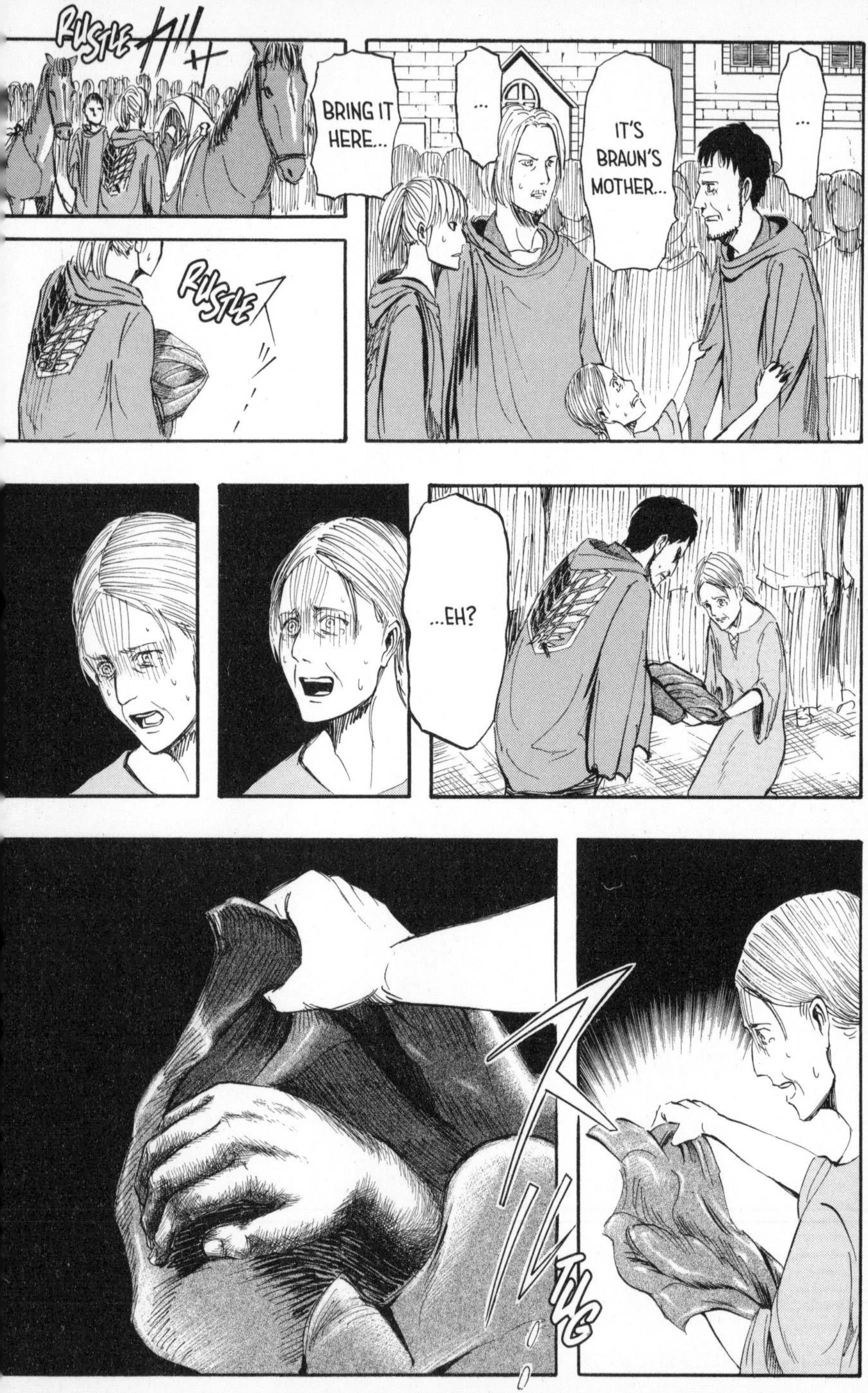
...
IT'S BRAUN'S MOTHER...
...
BRING IT HERE...
RUSTLE
RUSTLE
...EH?
TUG

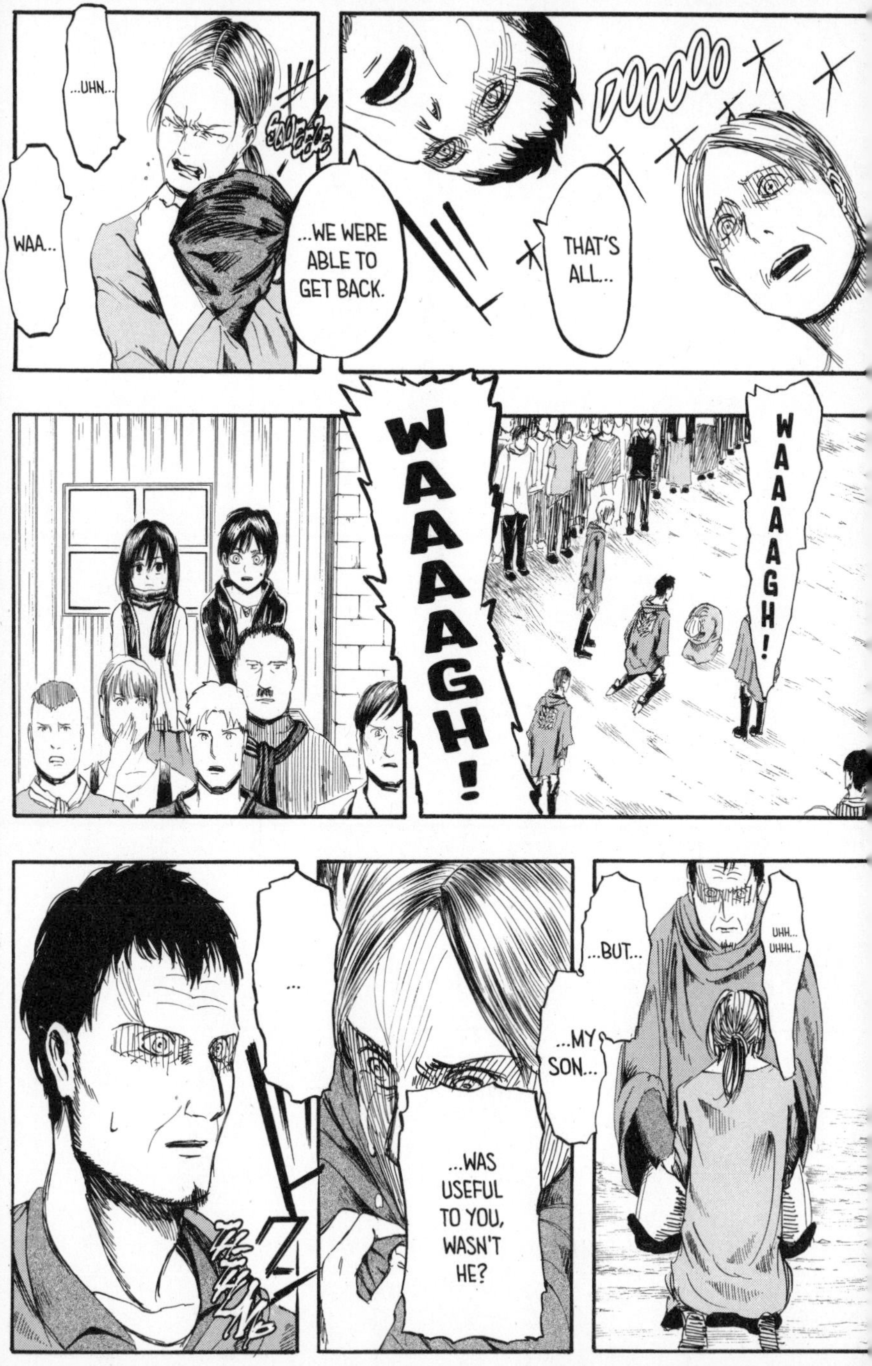
DOOOOO
THAT'S ALL...
...WE WERE ABLE TO GET BACK.
...UHN...
WAA...
WAAAAAGH!
WAAAAGH!
UHH... UHHH...
...BUT...
...MY SON...
...WAS USEFUL TO YOU, WASN'T HE?
...

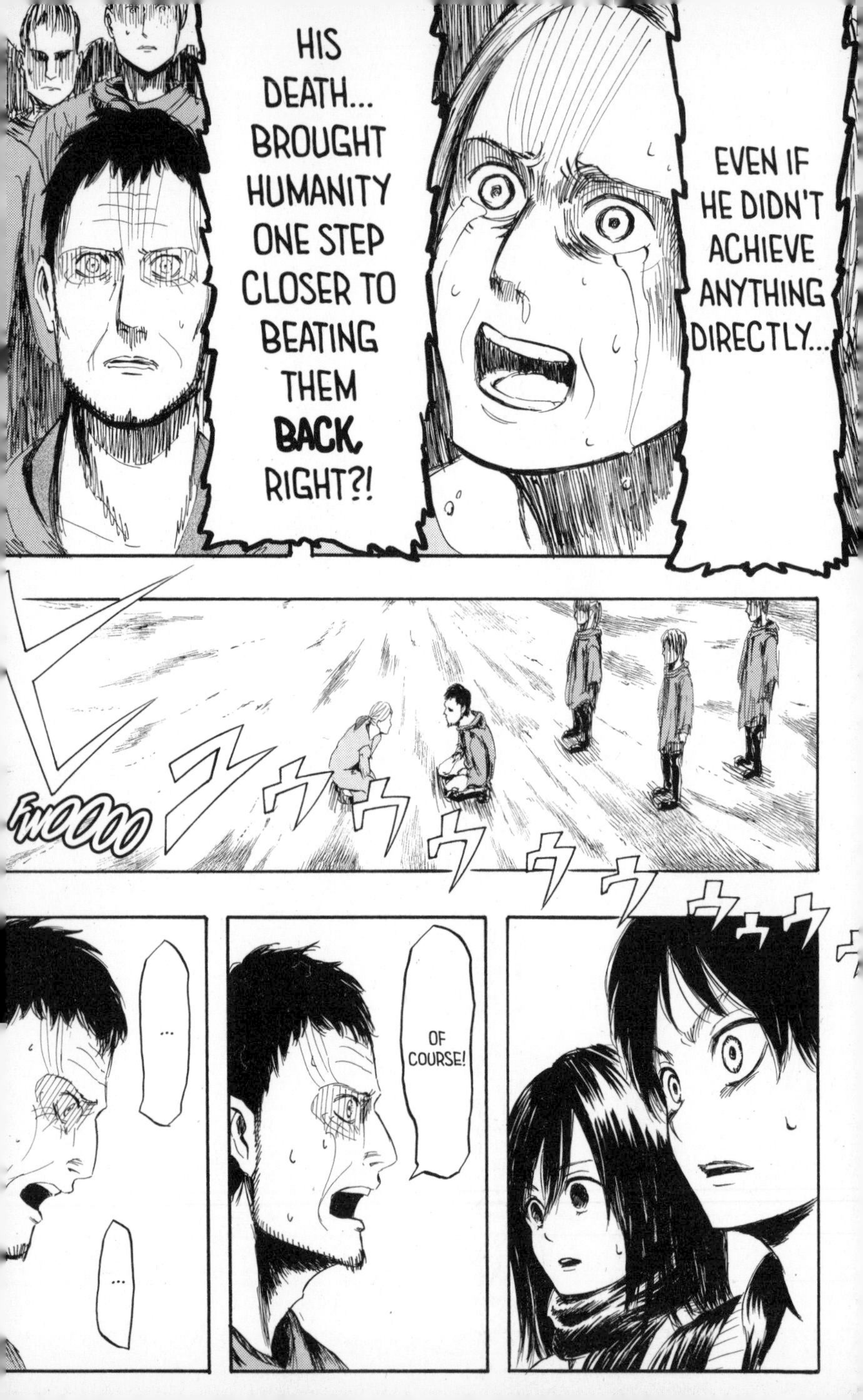
EVEN IF HE DIDN'T ACHIEVE ANYTHING DIRECTLY...
HIS DEATH... BROUGHT HUMANITY ONE STEP CLOSER TO BEATING THEM BACK, RIGHT?!
FWOOOO
OF COURSE!
...
...

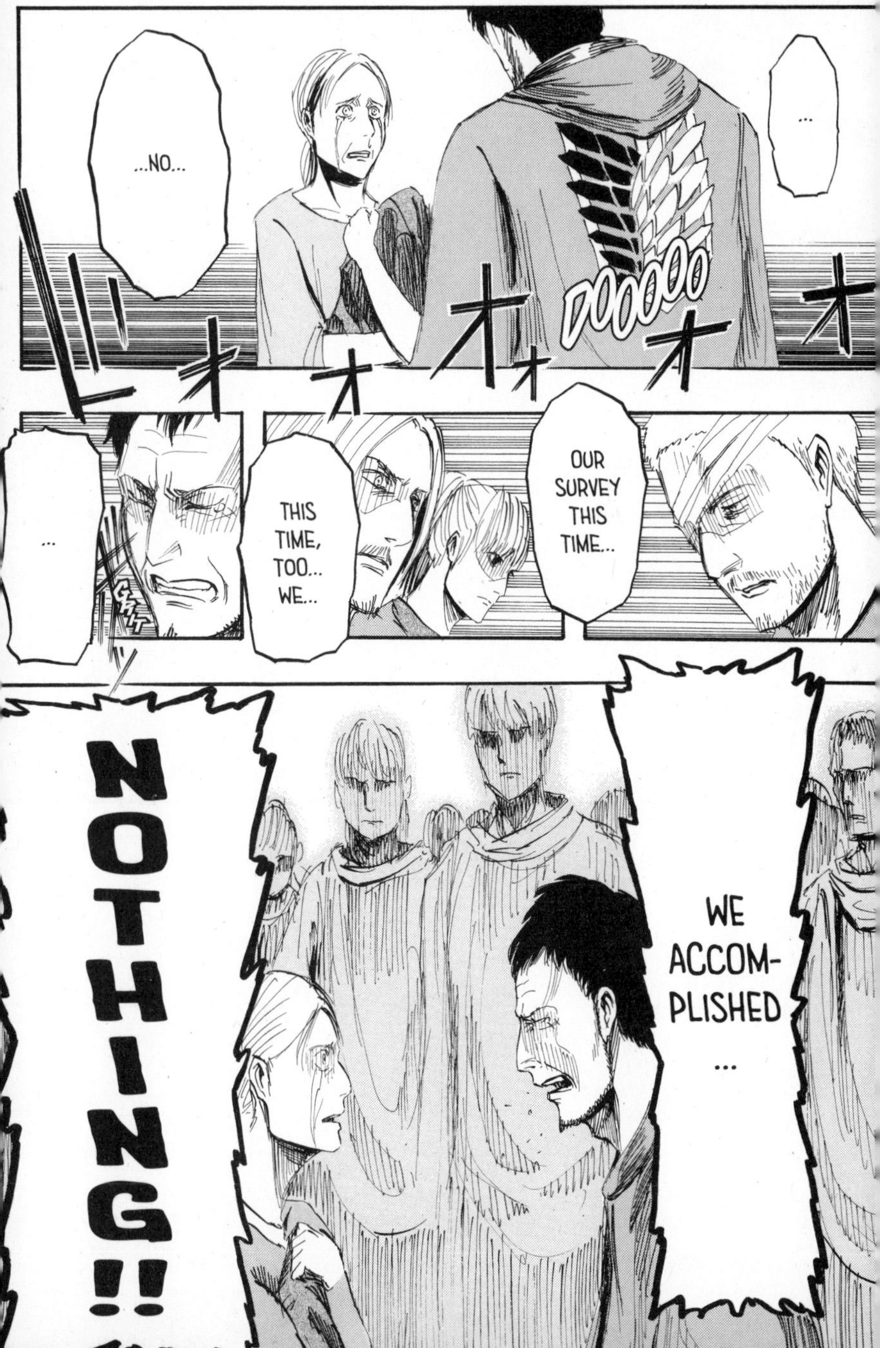
...
DOOOOOO
...NO...
OUR SURVEY THIS TIME...
THIS TIME, TOO... WE...
...
GRIT
WE ACCOM-PLISHED ...
NOTHING!!

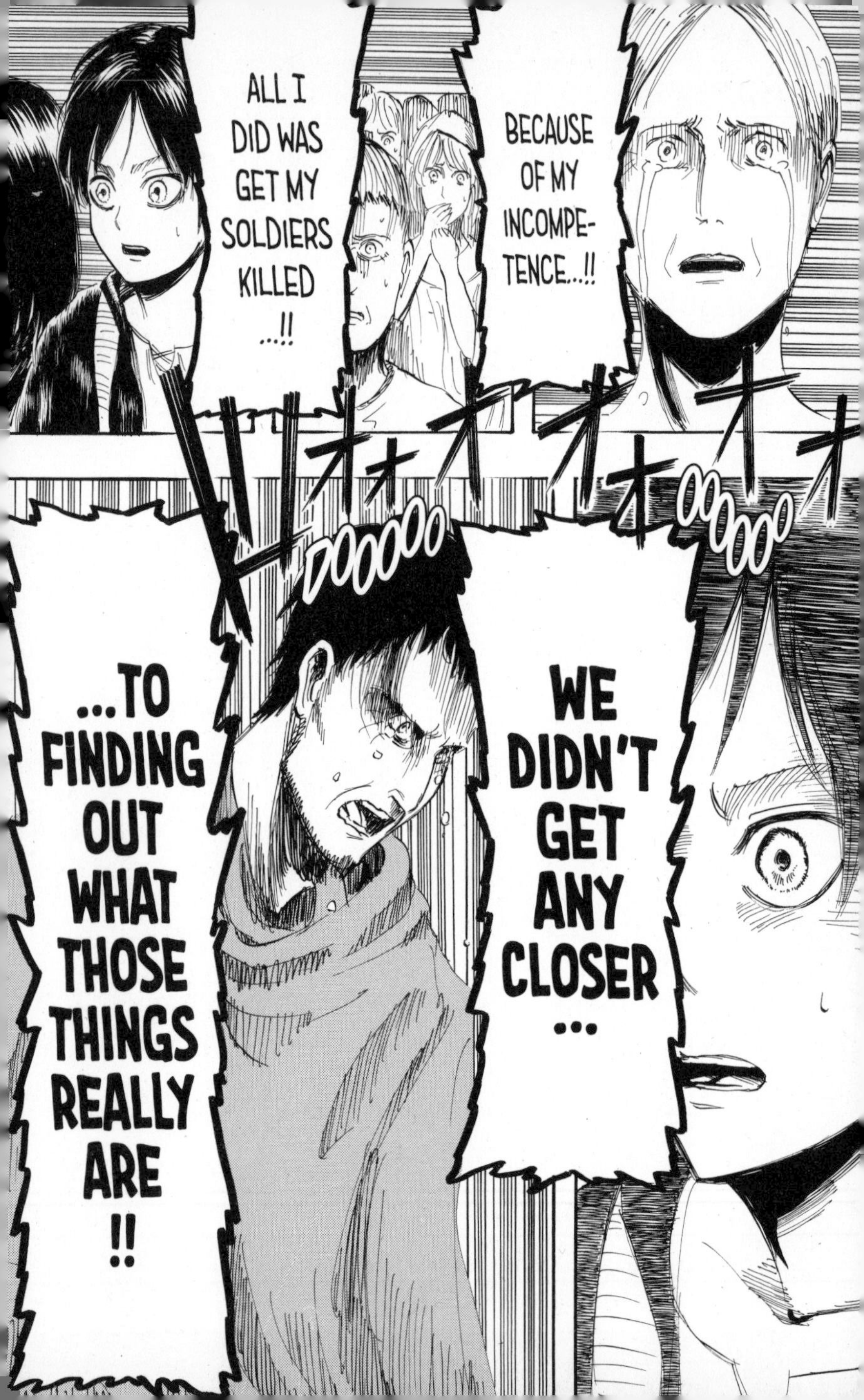
BECAUSE OF MY INCOMPETENCE...!!
ALL I DID WAS GET MY SOLDIERS KILLED ...!!
DOOOOO
OOOOOO
WE DIDN'T GET ANY CLOSER ...
...TO FINDING OUT WHAT THOSE THINGS REALLY ARE !!

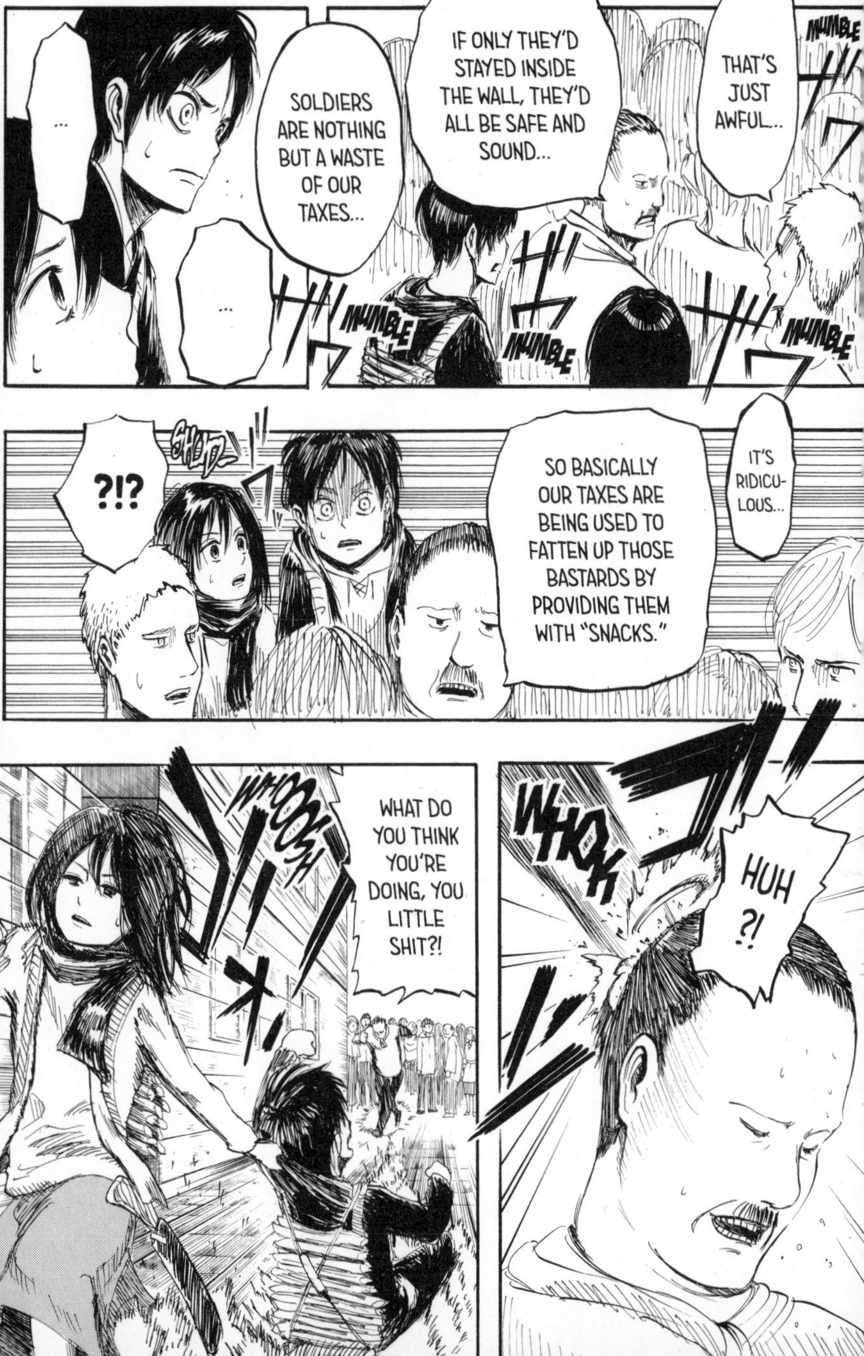
MUMBLE
THAT'S JUST AWFUL...
IF ONLY THEY'D STAYED INSIDE THE WALL, THEY'D ALL BE SAFE AND SOUND...
SOLDIERS ARE NOTHING BUT A WASTE OF OUR TAXES...
MUMBLE
MUMBLE
MUMBLE
...
...
IT'S RIDICULOUS...
SO BASICALLY OUR TAXES ARE BEING USED TO FATTEN UP THOSE BASTARDS BY PROVIDING THEM WITH "SNACKS."
SHOVE
?!?
WHOK
HUH ?!
WHOOOM
WHAT DO YOU THINK YOU'RE DOING, YOU LITTLE SHIT?!

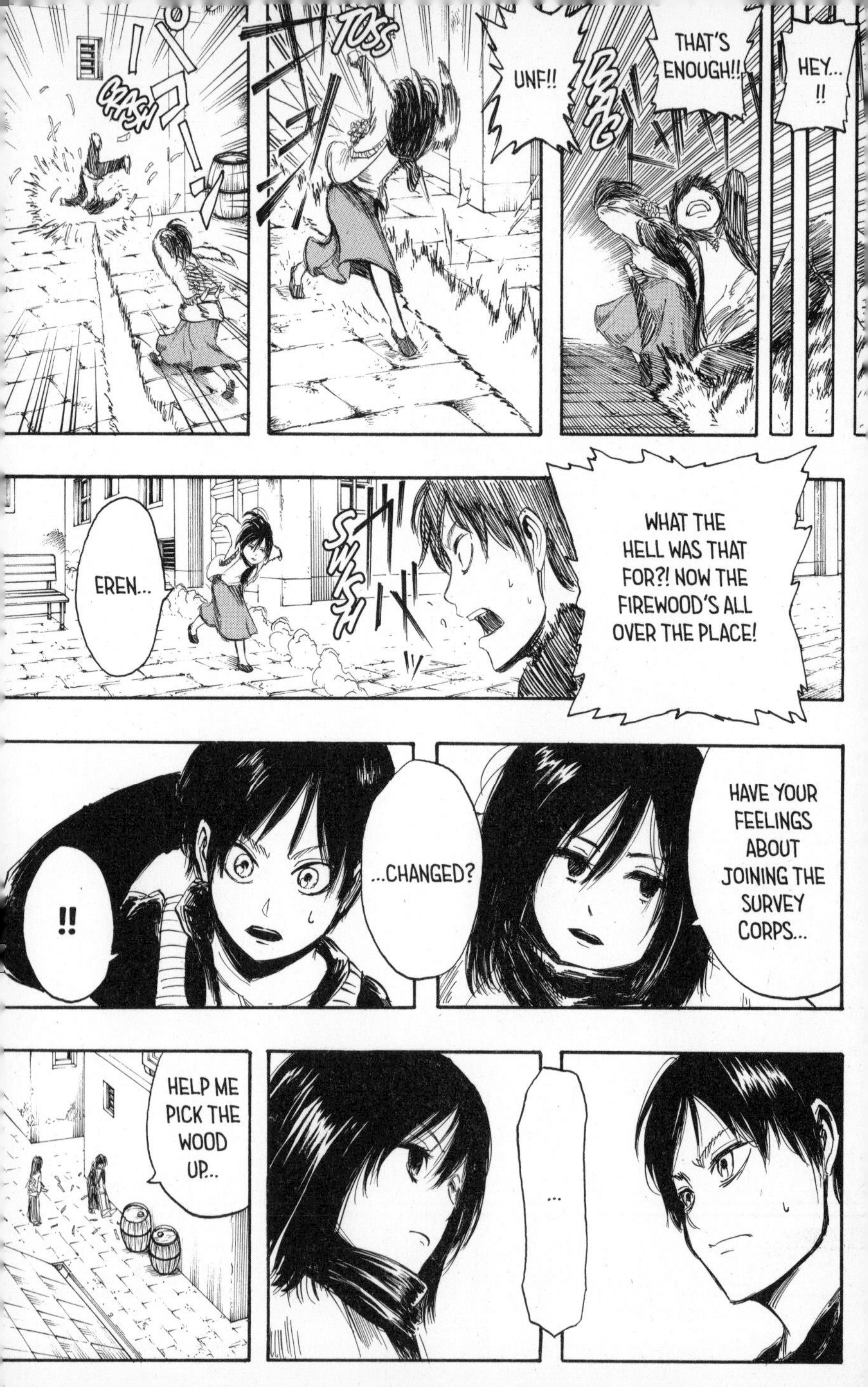
HEY... !!
THAT'S ENOUGH!!
DRAG
UNF!!
TOSS
CRASH
WHAT THE HELL WAS THAT FOR?! NOW THE FIREWOOD'S ALL OVER THE PLACE!
SWISH
EREN...
HAVE YOUR FEELINGS ABOUT JOINING THE SURVEY CORPS...
...CHANGED?
!!
...
HELP ME PICK THE WOOD UP...

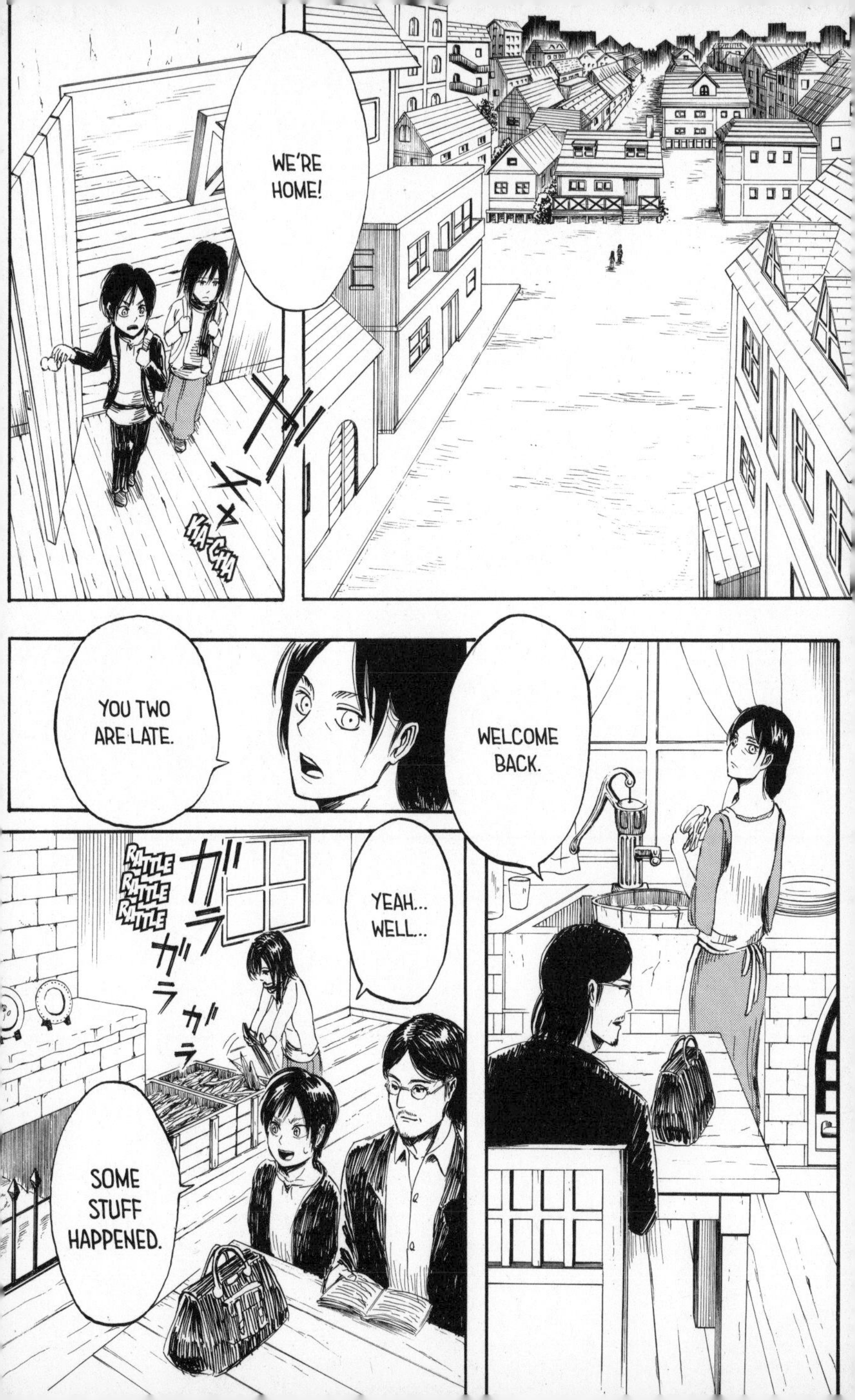
WE'RE HOME!
ガチャ
KA-CHA
WELCOME BACK.
YOU TWO ARE LATE.
YEAH... WELL...
ガラガラガラ
RATTLE RATTLE RATTLE
SOME STUFF HAPPENED.

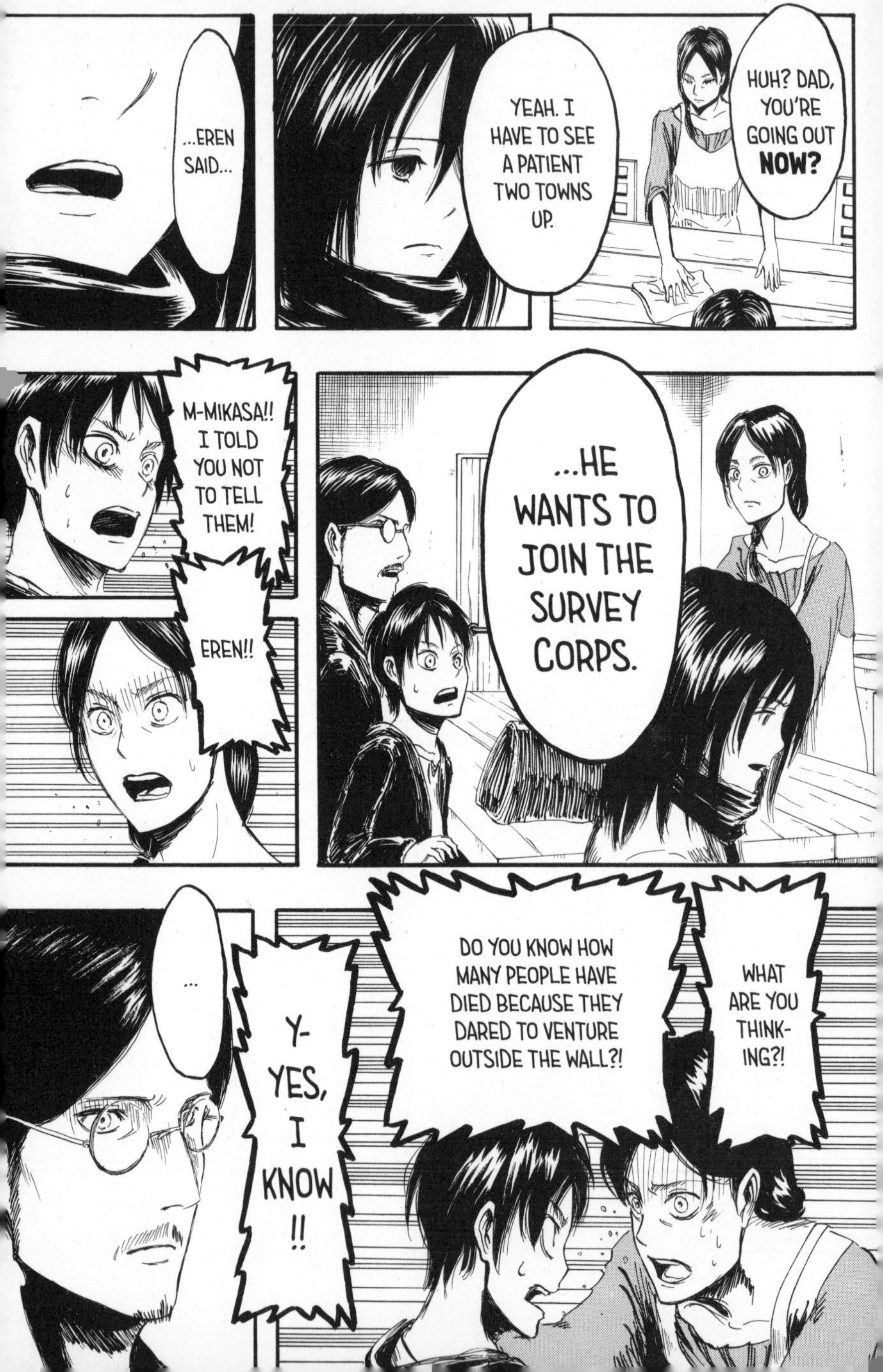
HUH? DAD, YOU'RE GOING OUT **NOW?**
YEAH. I HAVE TO SEE A PATIENT TWO TOWNS UP.
...EREN SAID...
...HE WANTS TO JOIN THE SURVEY CORPS.
M-MIKASA!! I TOLD YOU NOT TO TELL THEM!
EREN!!
WHAT ARE YOU THINK-ING?!
DO YOU KNOW HOW MANY PEOPLE HAVE DIED BECAUSE THEY DARED TO VENTURE OUTSIDE THE WALL?!
Y- YES, I KNOW!!
...

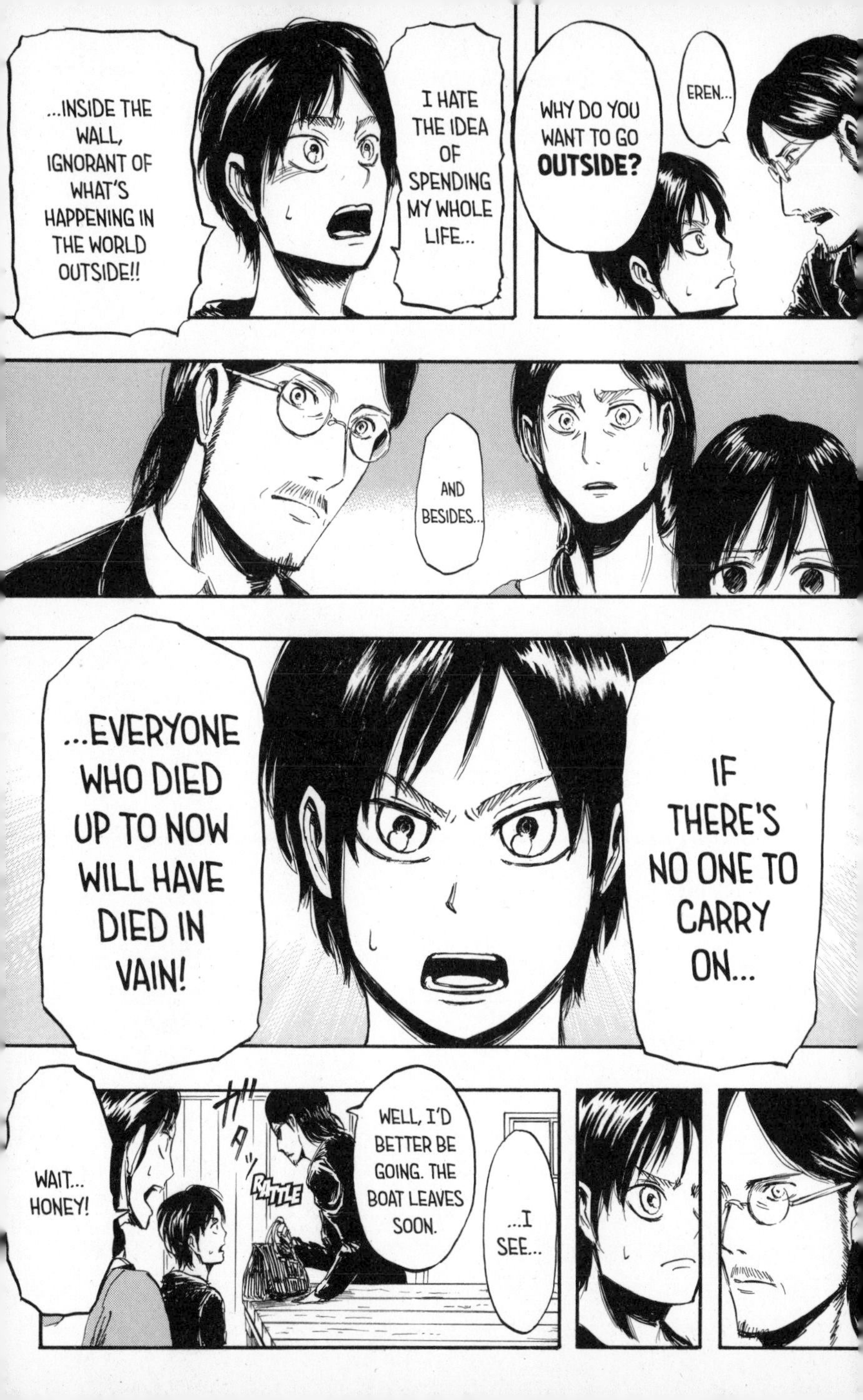
EREN...
WHY DO YOU WANT TO GO OUTSIDE?
I HATE THE IDEA OF SPENDING MY WHOLE LIFE...
...INSIDE THE WALL, IGNORANT OF WHAT'S HAPPENING IN THE WORLD OUTSIDE!!
AND BESIDES...
IF THERE'S NO ONE TO CARRY ON...
...EVERYONE WHO DIED UP TO NOW WILL HAVE DIED IN VAIN!
...I SEE...
WELL, I'D BETTER BE GOING. THE BOAT LEAVES SOON.
RATTLE
WAIT... HONEY!

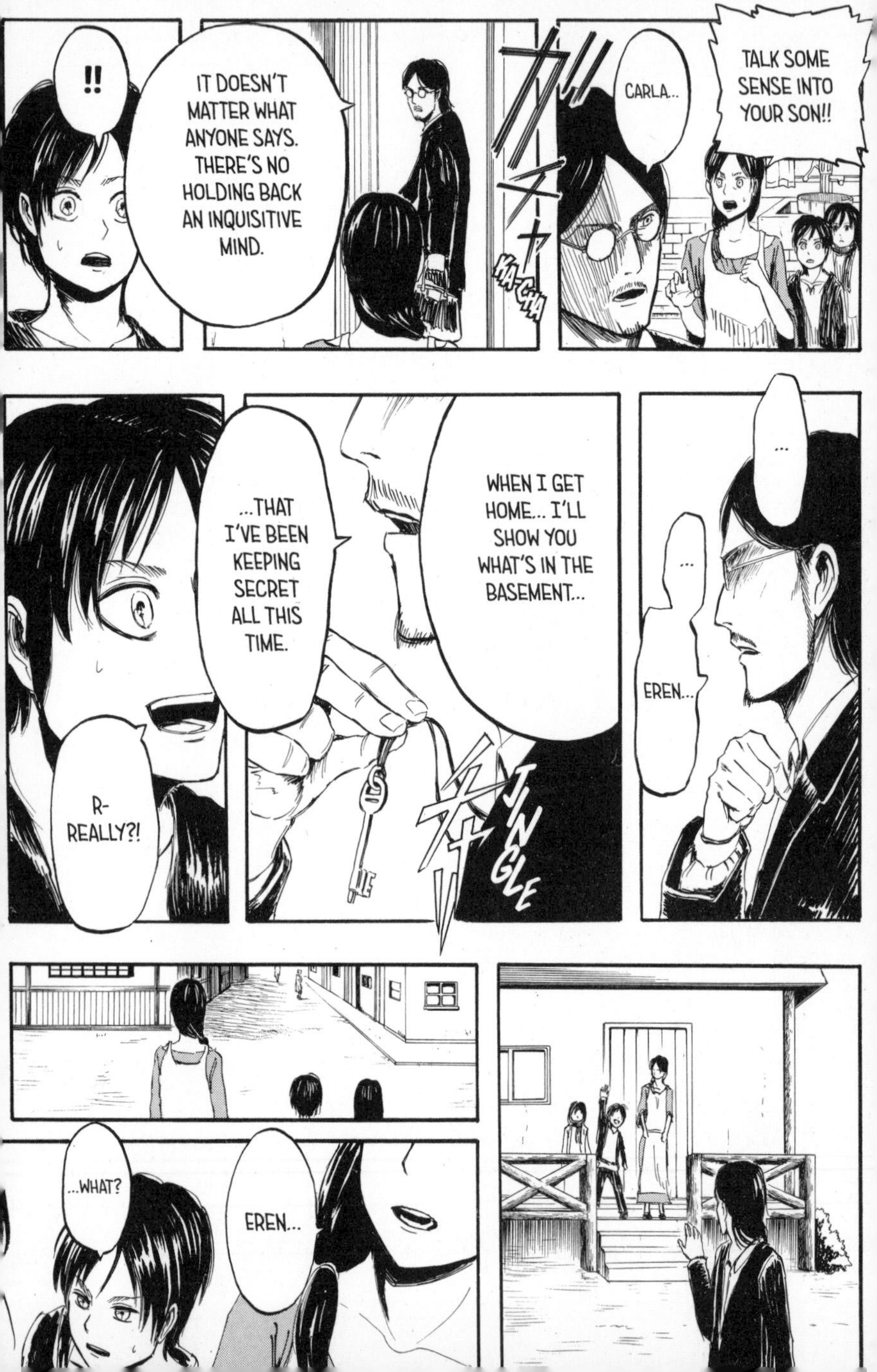
TALK SOME SENSE INTO YOUR SON!!
CARLA...
KA-CHA
IT DOESN'T MATTER WHAT ANYONE SAYS. THERE'S NO HOLDING BACK AN INQUISITIVE MIND.
!!
...
...
EREN...
WHEN I GET HOME... I'LL SHOW YOU WHAT'S IN THE BASEMENT...
JINGLE
...THAT I'VE BEEN KEEPING SECRET ALL THIS TIME.
R-REALLY?!
EREN...
...WHAT?

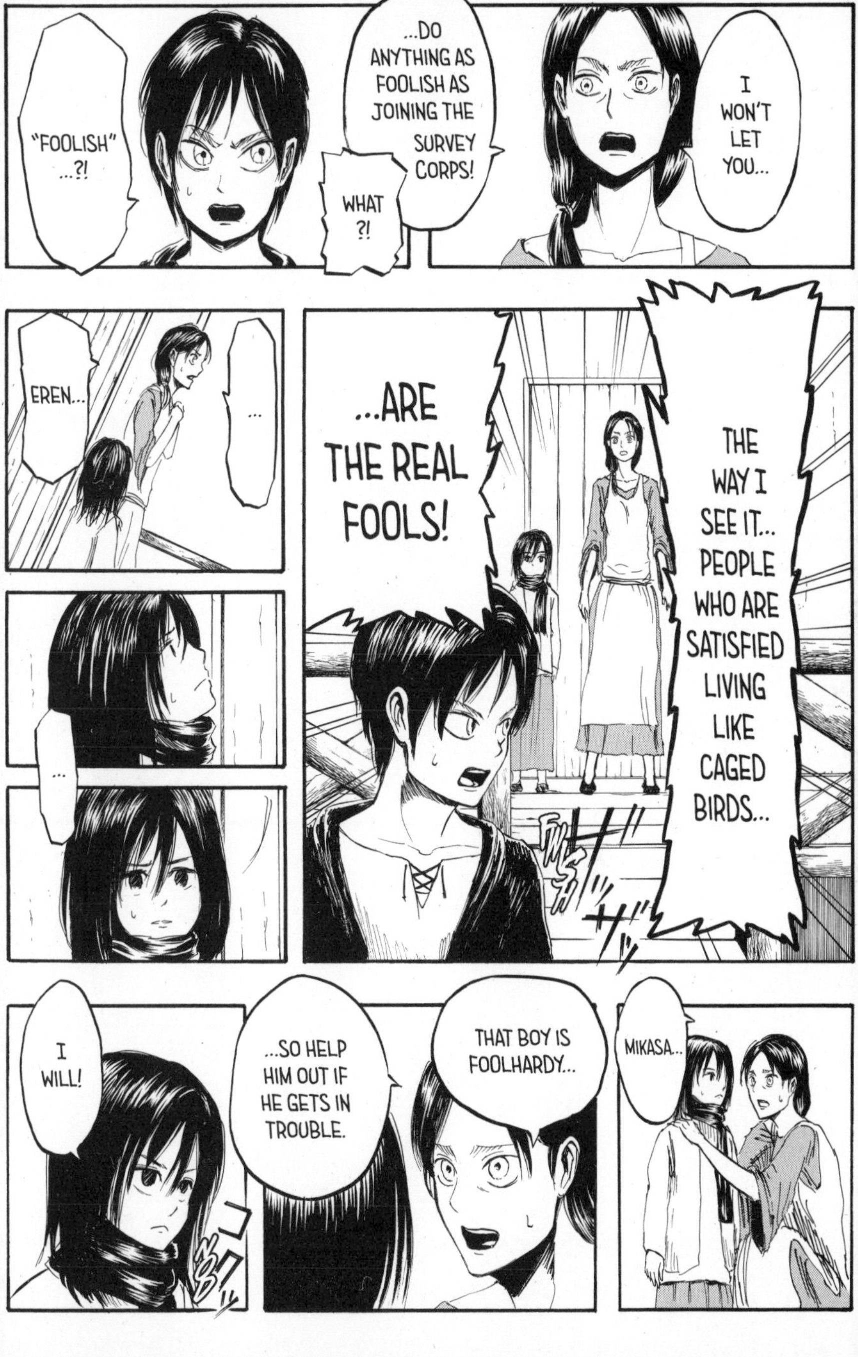
I WON'T LET YOU...
...DO ANYTHING AS FOOLISH AS JOINING THE SURVEY CORPS!
WHAT ?!
"FOOLISH" ...?!
THE WAY I SEE IT... PEOPLE WHO ARE SATISFIED LIVING LIKE CAGED BIRDS...
...ARE THE REAL FOOLS!
FWSH
...
EREN...
...
MIKASA...
THAT BOY IS FOOLHARDY...
...SO HELP HIM OUT IF HE GETS IN TROUBLE.
I WILL!

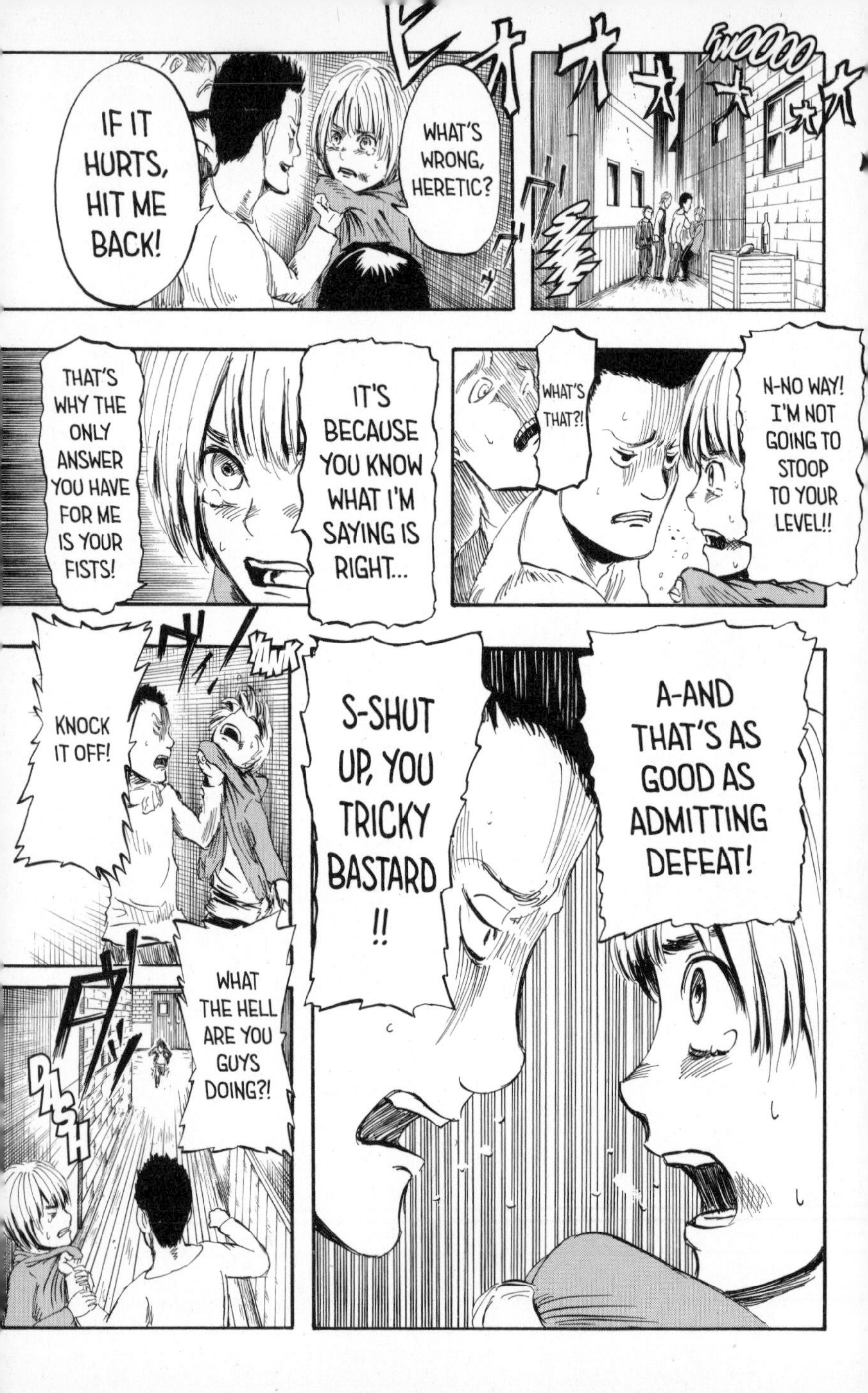
FWOOOO
WHAT'S WRONG, HERETIC?
IF IT HURTS, HIT ME BACK!
N-NO WAY! I'M NOT GOING TO STOOP TO YOUR LEVEL!!
WHAT'S THAT?!
IT'S BECAUSE YOU KNOW WHAT I'M SAYING IS RIGHT...
THAT'S WHY THE ONLY ANSWER YOU HAVE FOR ME IS YOUR FISTS!
A-AND THAT'S AS GOOD AS ADMITTING DEFEAT!
S-SHUT UP, YOU TRICKY BASTARD!!
YANK
KNOCK IT OFF!
WHAT THE HELL ARE YOU GUYS DOING?!
DASH

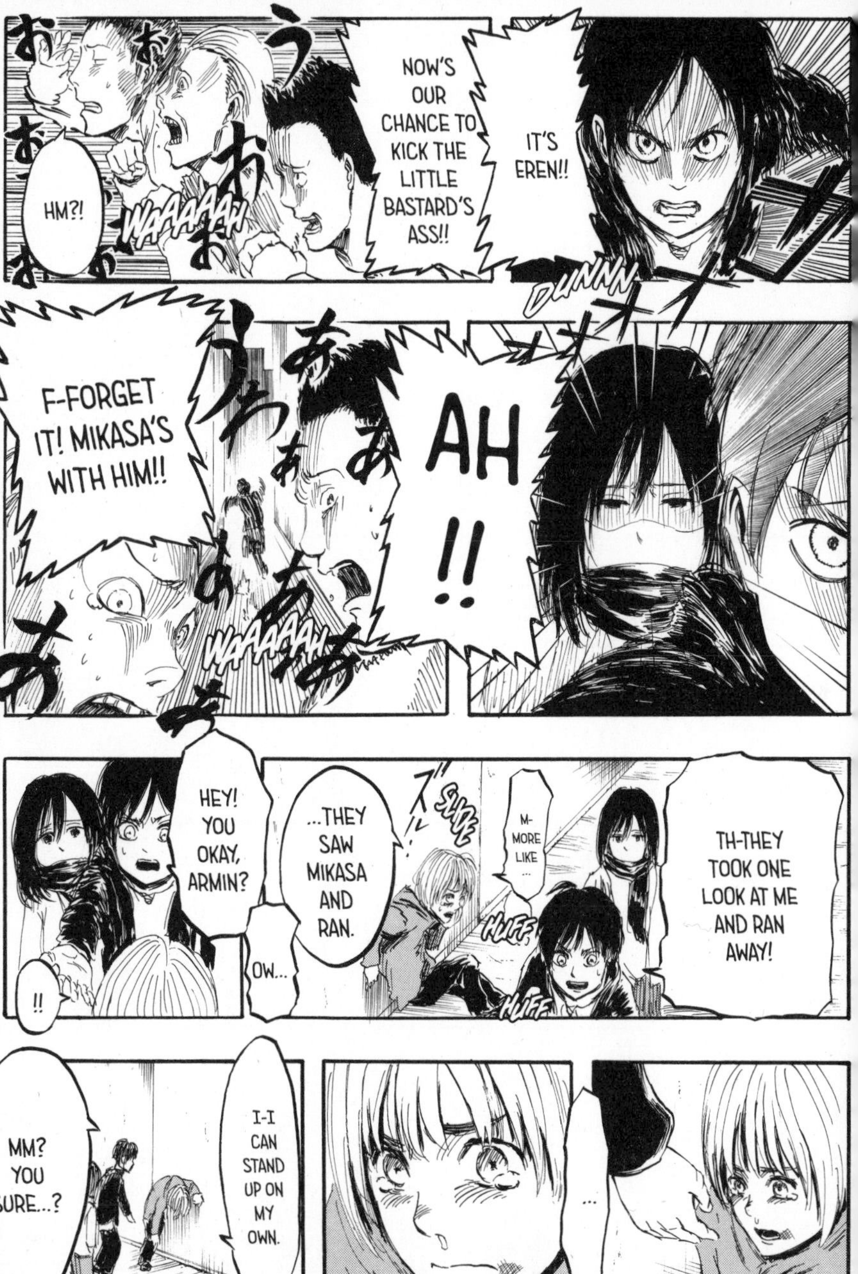
IT'S EREN!!
DUNNN
NOW'S OUR CHANCE TO KICK THE LITTLE BASTARD'S ASS!!
WAAAAAH
HM?!
AH !!
F-FORGET IT! MIKASA'S WITH HIM!!
WAAAAAH
TH-THEY TOOK ONE LOOK AT ME AND RAN AWAY!
M-MORE LIKE ...
HUFF
HUFF
SLIDE
...THEY SAW MIKASA AND RAN.
OW...
HEY! YOU OKAY, ARMIN?
!!
...
I-I CAN STAND UP ON MY OWN.
MM? YOU SURE...?

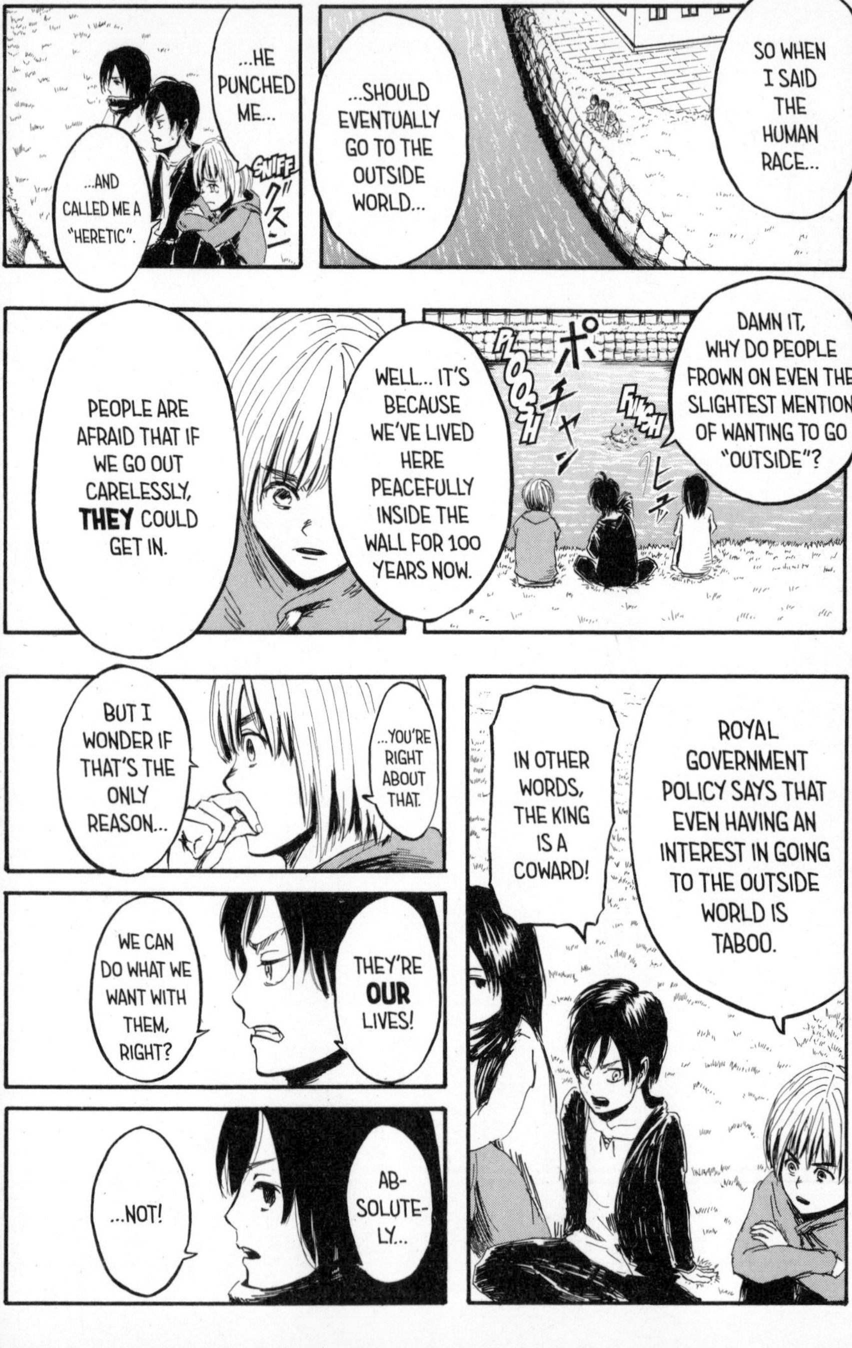
SO WHEN I SAID THE HUMAN RACE...
...SHOULD EVENTUALLY GO TO THE OUTSIDE WORLD...
...HE PUNCHED ME...
SNIFF
グスン
...AND CALLED ME A "HERETIC".
DAMN IT, WHY DO PEOPLE FROWN ON EVEN THE SLIGHTEST MENTION OF WANTING TO GO "OUTSIDE"?
FWISH
ヒュ
PLOOSH
ポチャン
WELL... IT'S BECAUSE WE'VE LIVED HERE PEACEFULLY INSIDE THE WALL FOR 100 YEARS NOW.
PEOPLE ARE AFRAID THAT IF WE GO OUT CARELESSLY, **THEY** COULD GET IN.
ROYAL GOVERNMENT POLICY SAYS THAT EVEN HAVING AN INTEREST IN GOING TO THE OUTSIDE WORLD IS TABOO.
IN OTHER WORDS, THE KING IS A COWARD!
...YOU'RE RIGHT ABOUT THAT.
BUT I WONDER IF THAT'S THE ONLY REASON...
THEY'RE **OUR** LIVES!
WE CAN DO WHAT WE WANT WITH THEM, RIGHT?
AB-SOLUTE-LY...
...NOT!

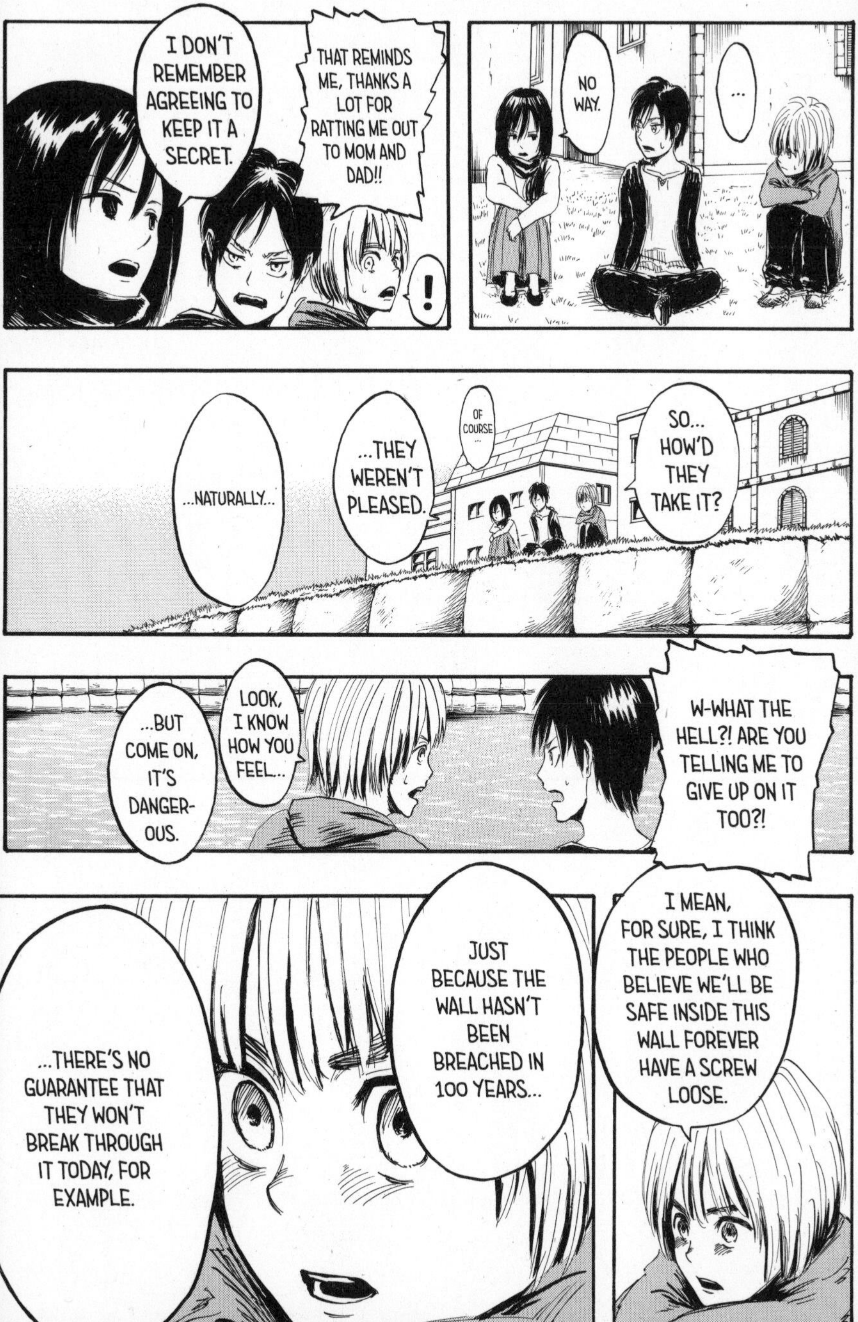
...
NO WAY.
THAT REMINDS ME, THANKS A LOT FOR RATTING ME OUT TO MOM AND DAD!!
I DON'T REMEMBER AGREEING TO KEEP IT A SECRET.
!
SO... HOW'D THEY TAKE IT?
OF COURSE...
...THEY WEREN'T PLEASED.
...NATURALLY...
W-WHAT THE HELL?! ARE YOU TELLING ME TO GIVE UP ON IT TOO?!
LOOK, I KNOW HOW YOU FEEL...
...BUT COME ON, IT'S DANGER-OUS.
I MEAN, FOR SURE, I THINK THE PEOPLE WHO BELIEVE WE'LL BE SAFE INSIDE THIS WALL FOREVER HAVE A SCREW LOOSE.
JUST BECAUSE THE WALL HASN'T BEEN BREACHED IN 100 YEARS...
...THERE'S NO GUARANTEE THAT THEY WON'T BREAK THROUGH IT TODAY, FOR EXAMPLE.

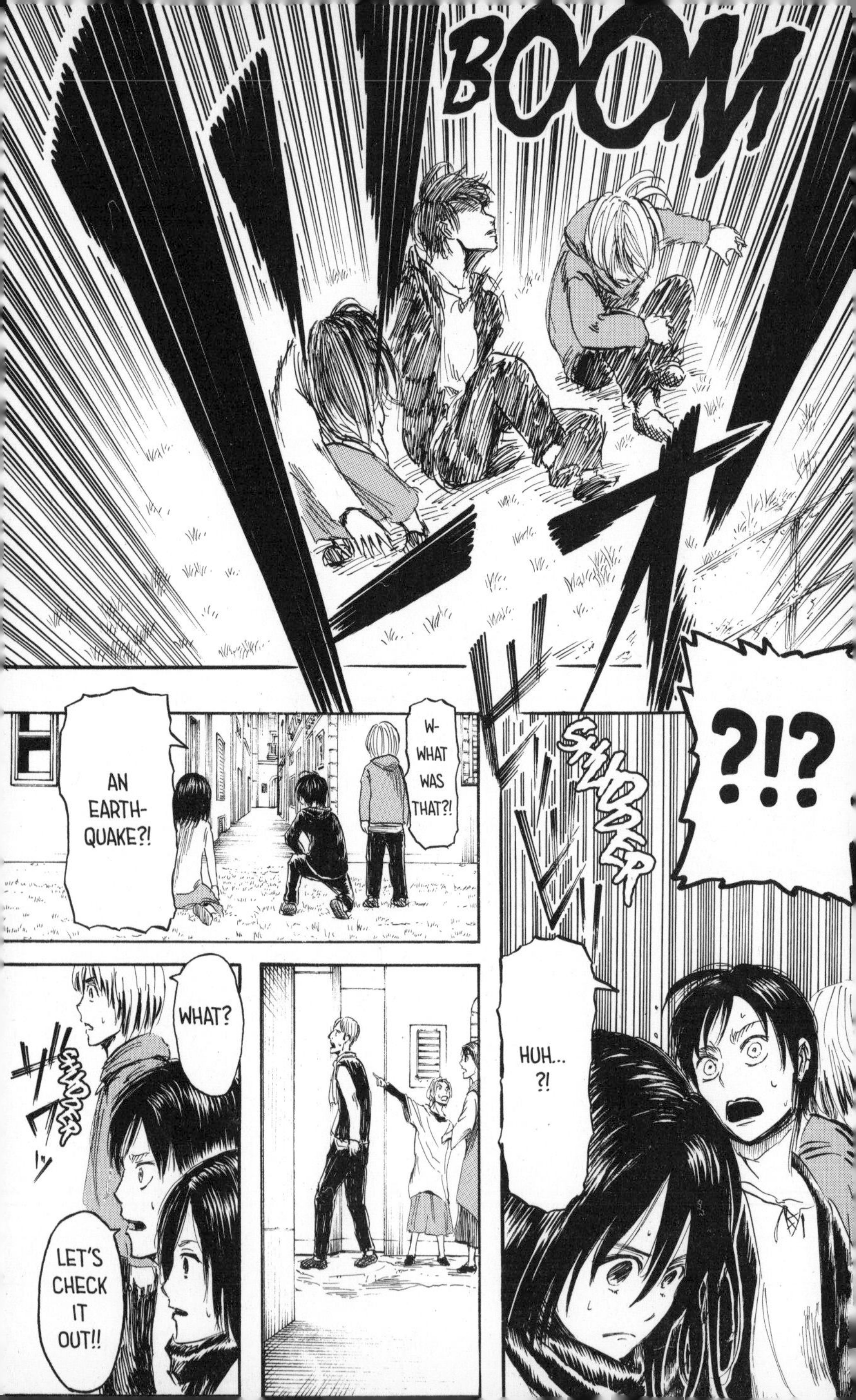
BOOM
SHUDDER
?!?
HUH... ?!
W-WHAT WAS THAT?!
AN EARTHQUAKE?!
WHAT?
SHUDDER
LET'S CHECK IT OUT!!

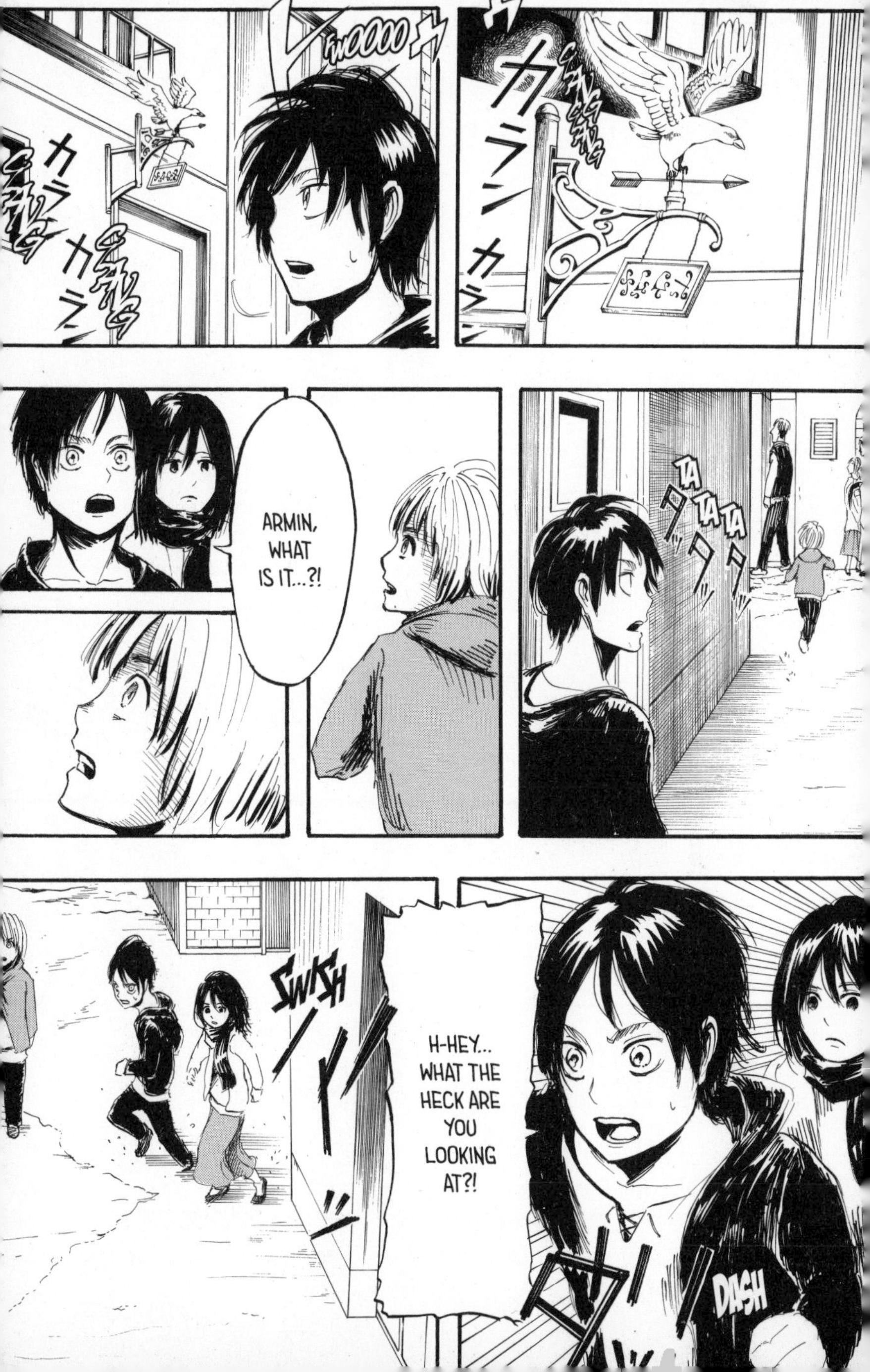

CLANG CLANG
FWOOOO
CLANG CLANG
TA TA TA
ARMIN, WHAT IS IT...?!
H-HEY... WHAT THE HECK ARE YOU LOOKING AT?!
DASH
SWISH

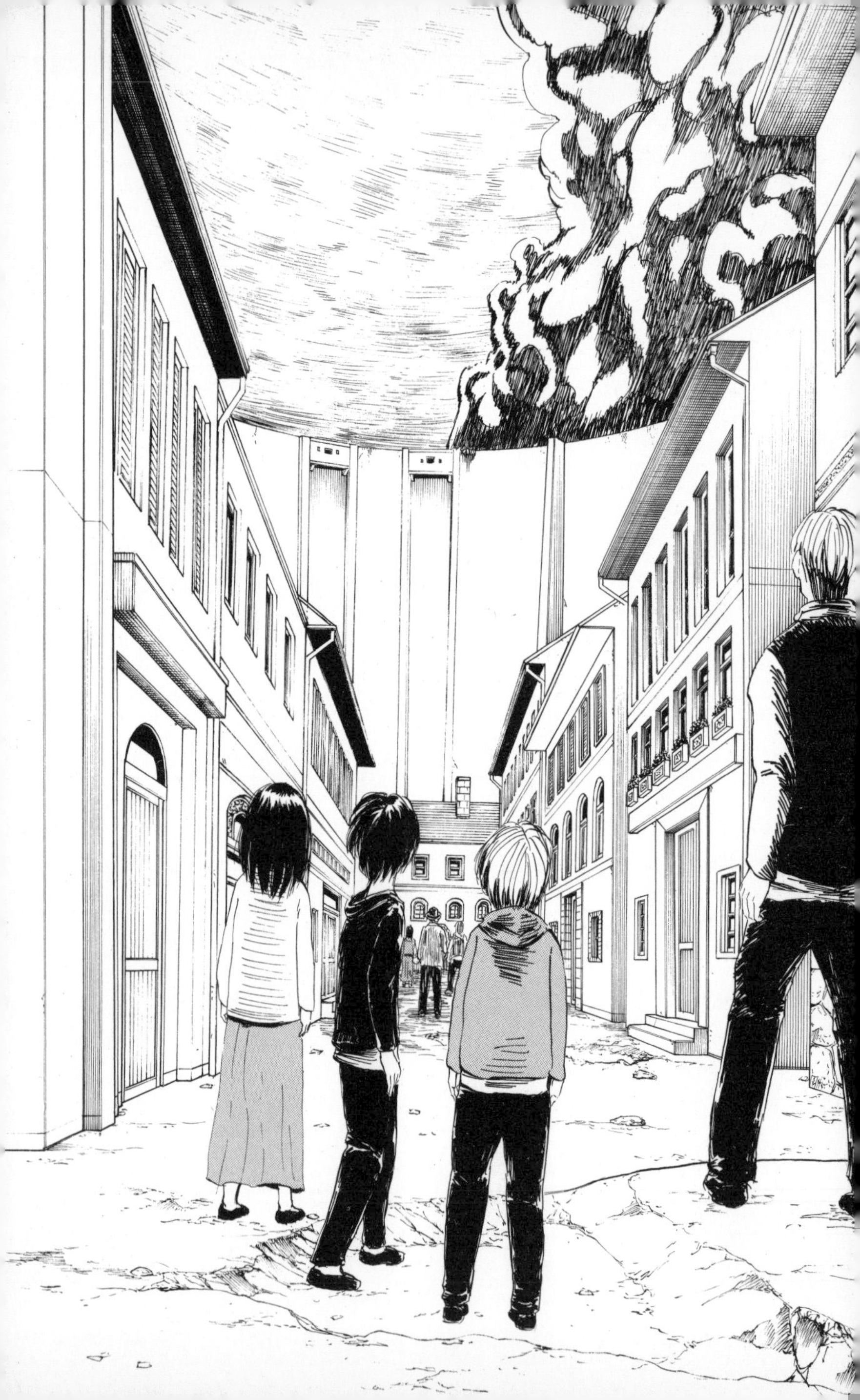

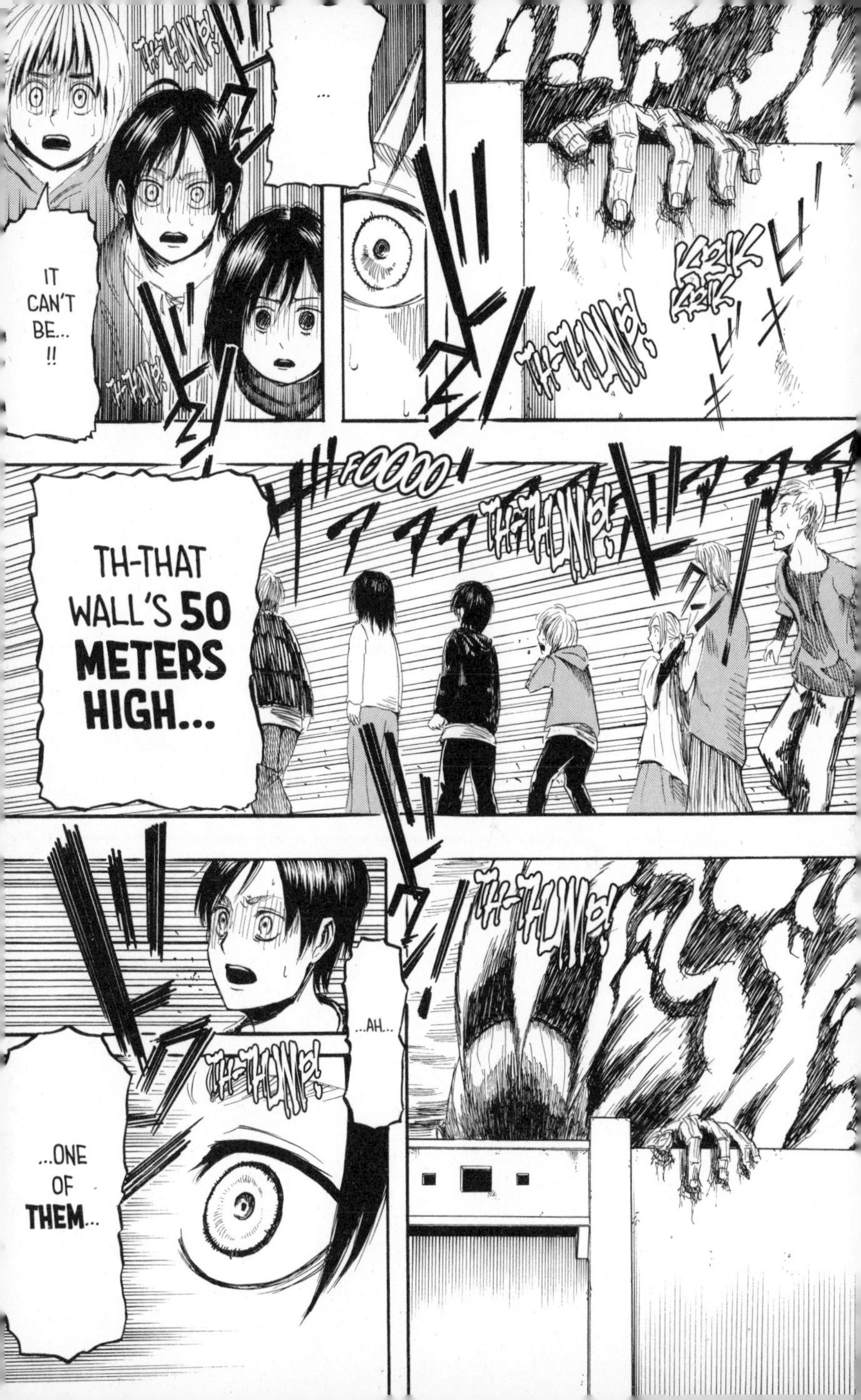
KRRK KRRK
TH-THUMP!
...
IT CAN'T BE...!!
TH-THUMP!
FOOOO
TH-THUMP!
TH-THAT WALL'S **50 METERS HIGH...**
TH-THUMP!
...AH...
TH-THUMP!
...ONE OF **THEM**...

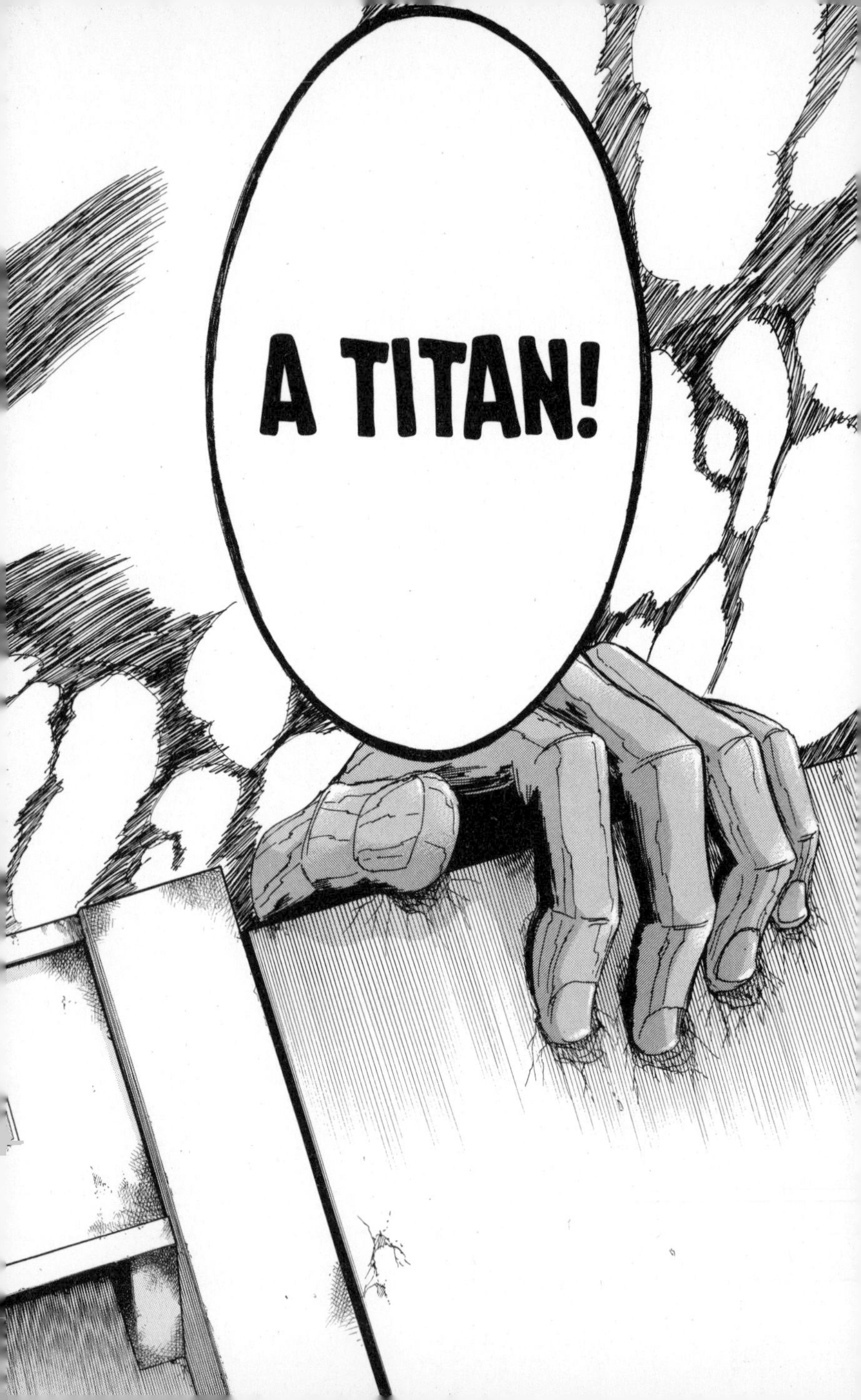
A TITAN!

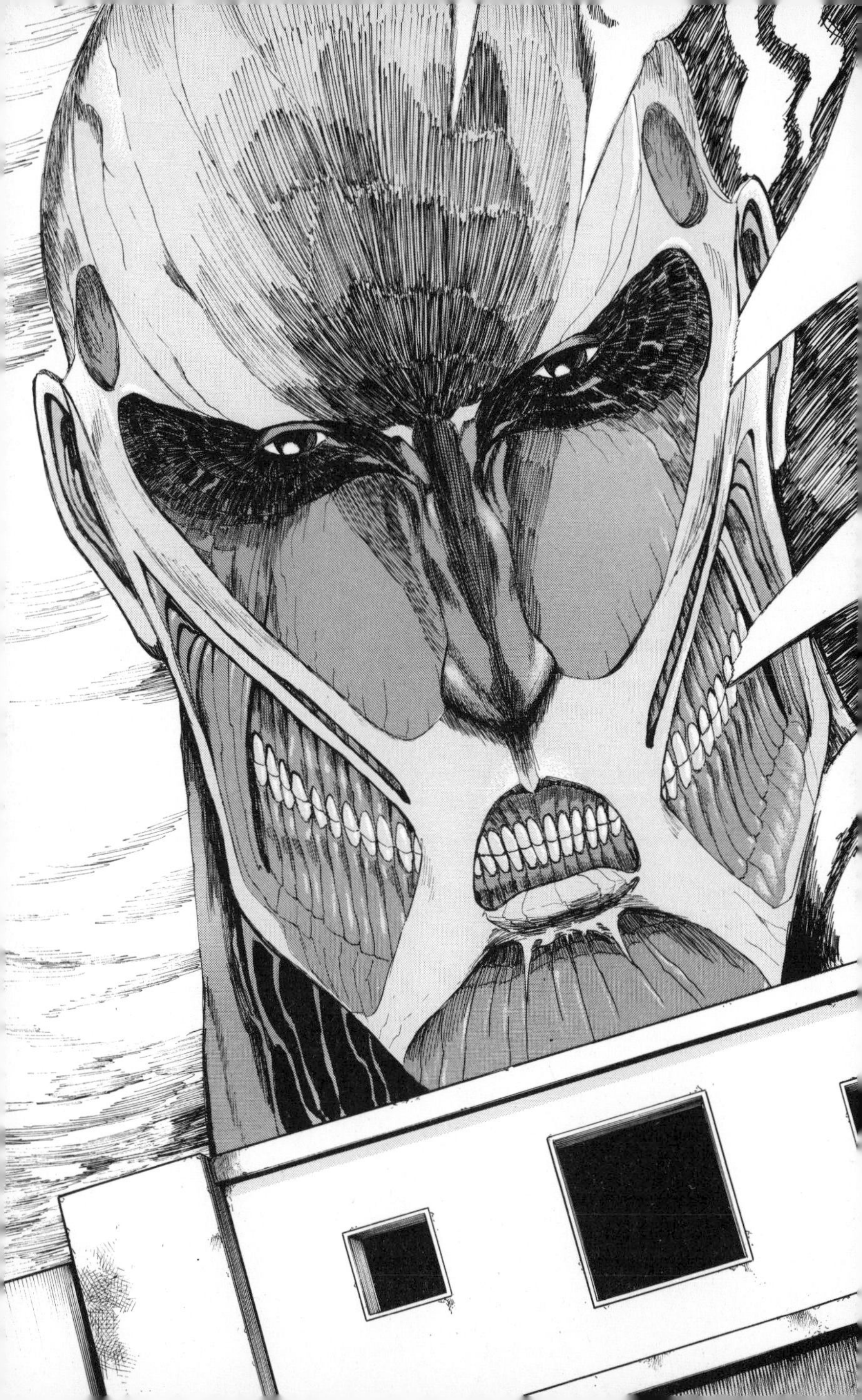

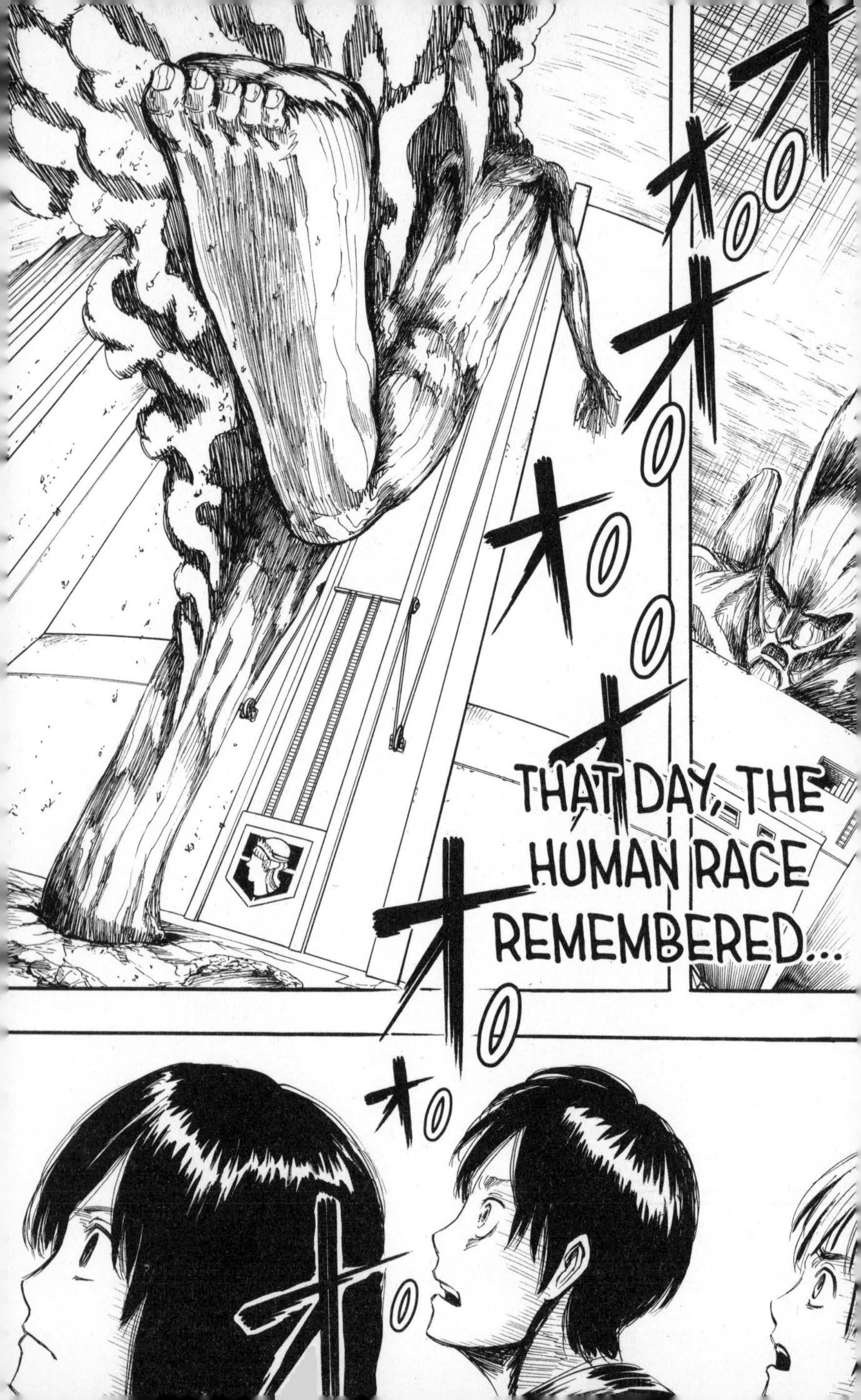
THAT DAY, THE HUMAN RACE REMEMBERED...

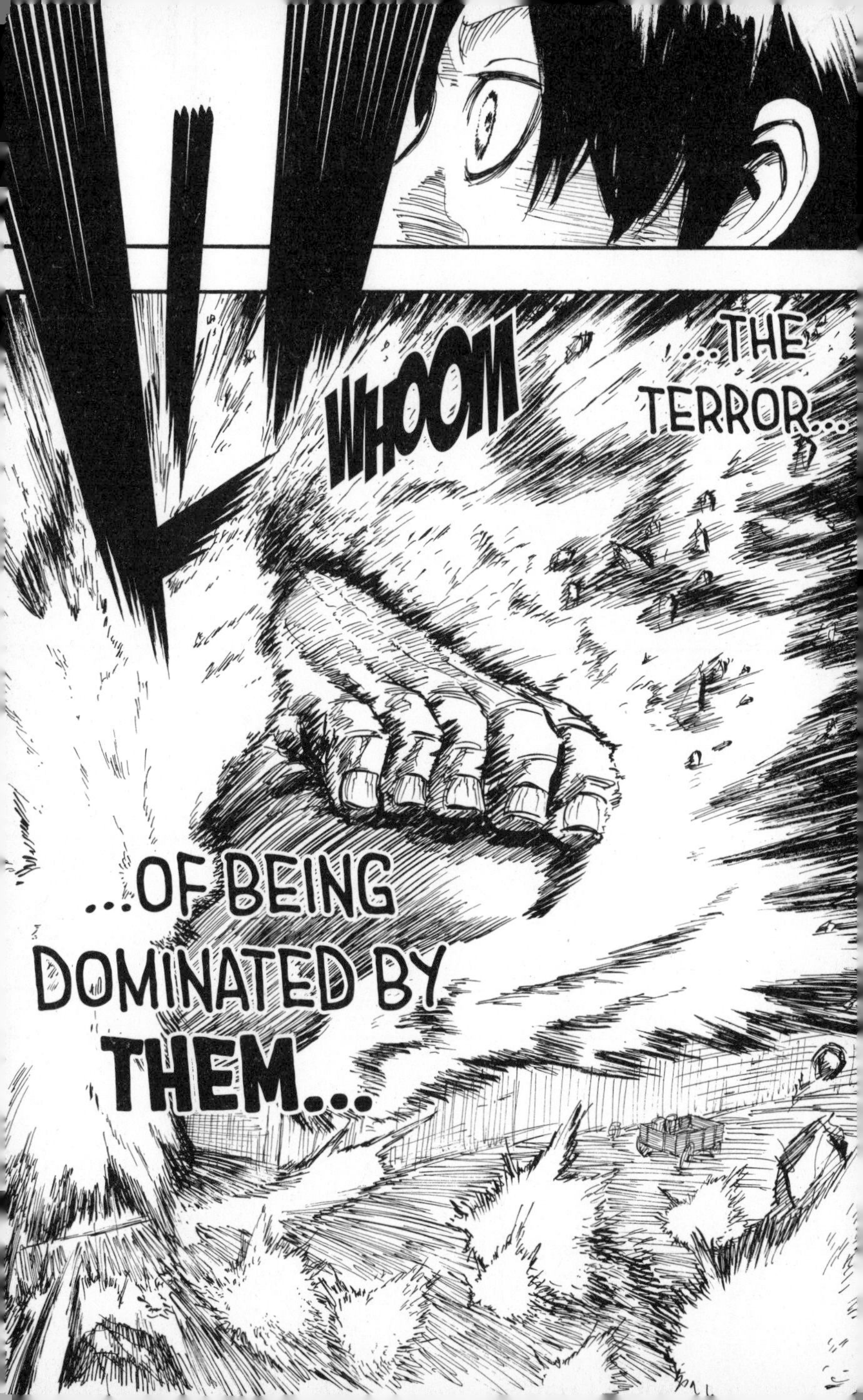
...THE TERROR...
WHOOM
...OF BEING DOMINATED BY THEM...

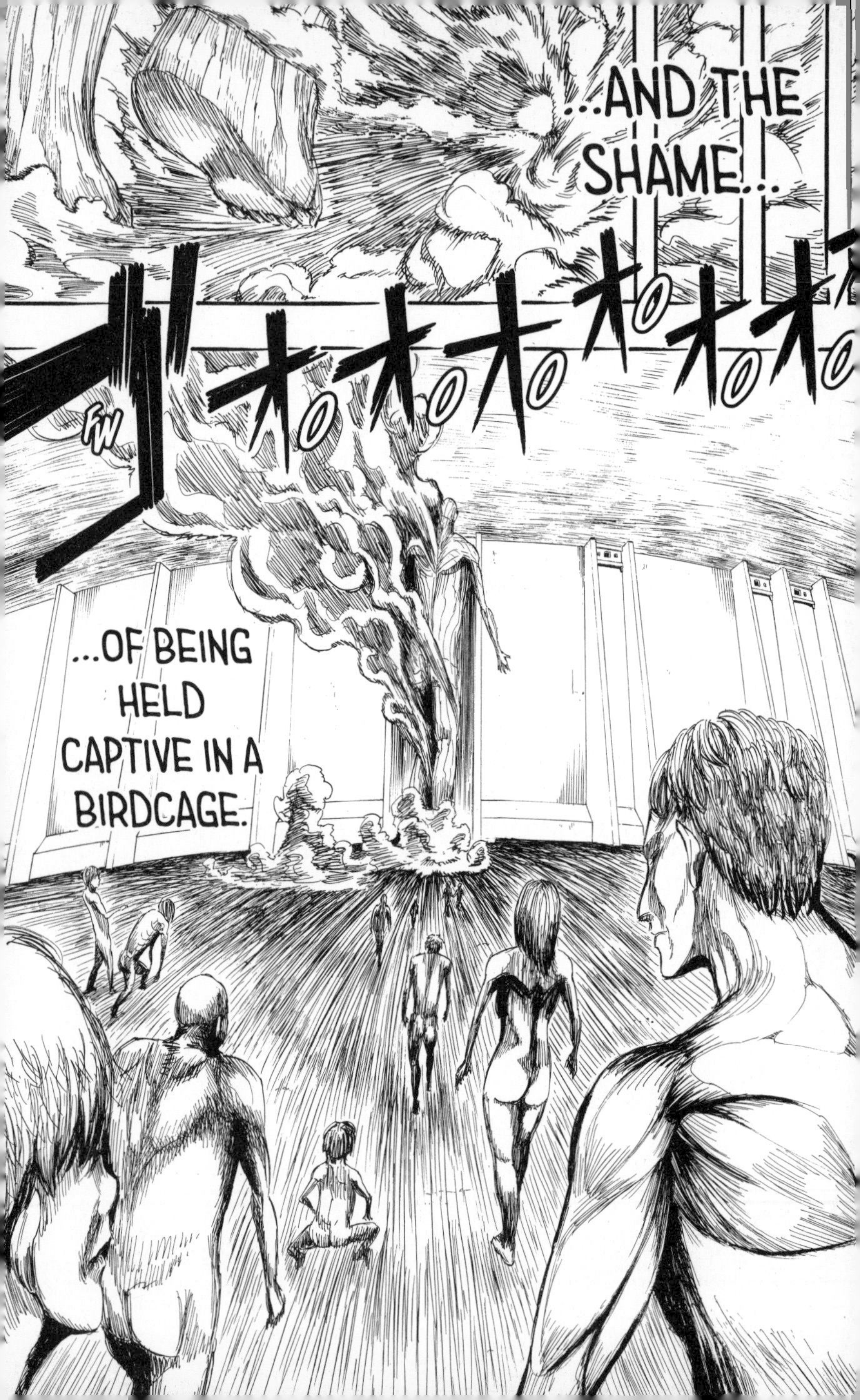
...AND THE SHAME...
...OF BEING HELD CAPTIVE IN A BIRDCAGE.

Episode 2: That Day

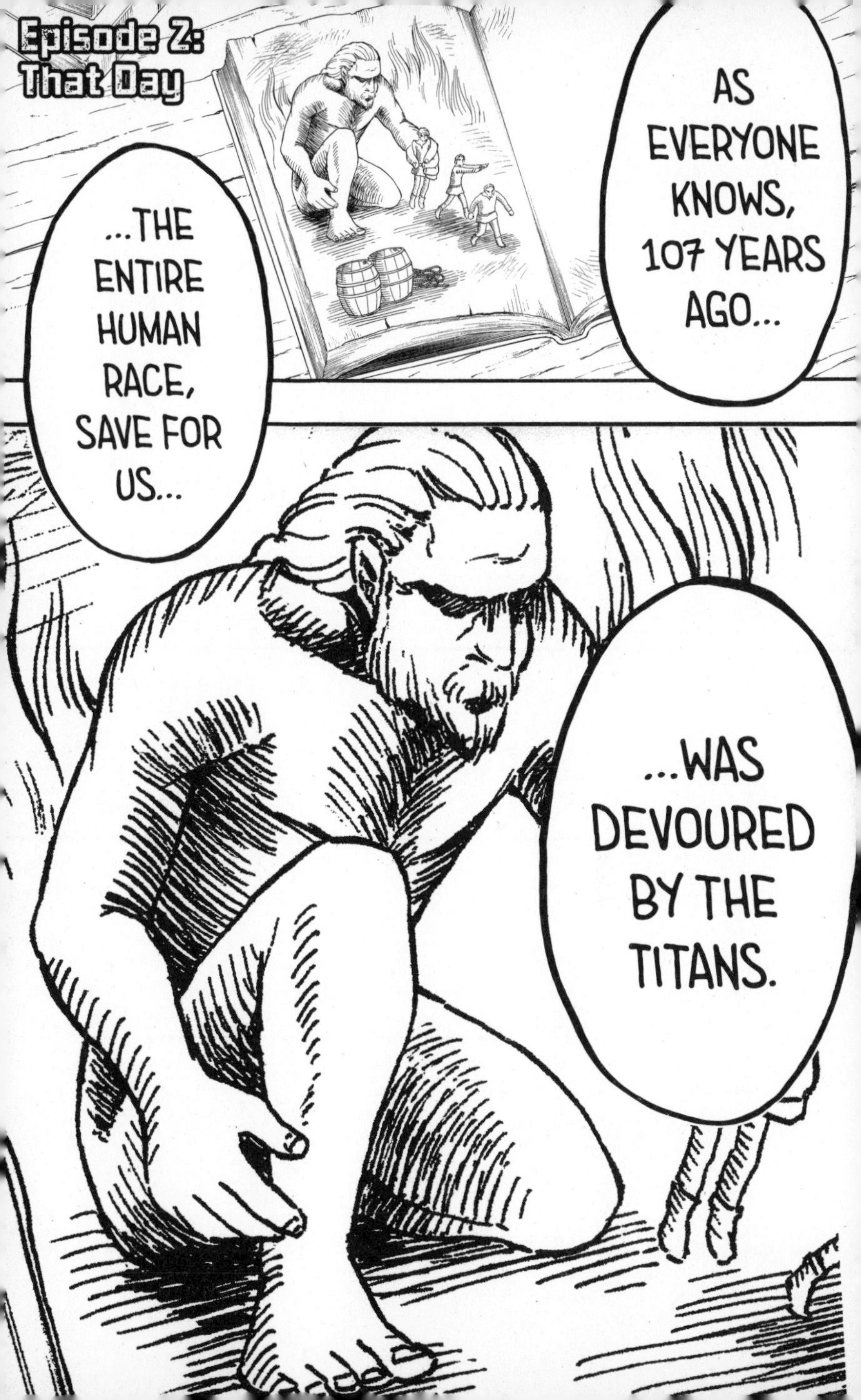
AS EVERYONE KNOWS, 107 YEARS AGO...
...THE ENTIRE HUMAN RACE, SAVE FOR US...
...WAS DEVOURED BY THE TITANS.

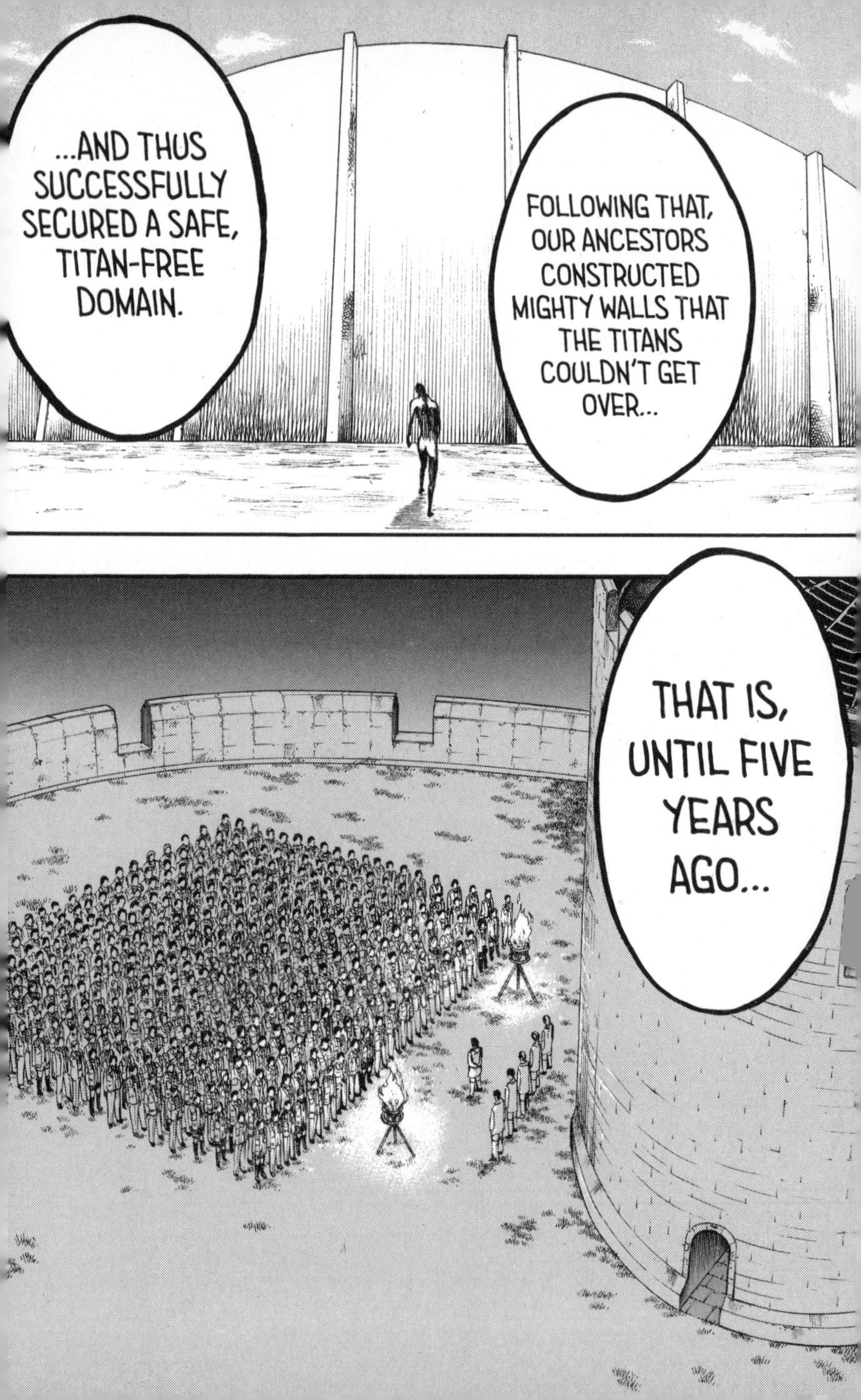
FOLLOWING THAT, OUR ANCESTORS CONSTRUCTED MIGHTY WALLS THAT THE TITANS COULDN'T GET OVER...
...AND THUS SUCCESSFULLY SECURED A SAFE, TITAN-FREE DOMAIN.
THAT IS, UNTIL FIVE YEARS AGO...

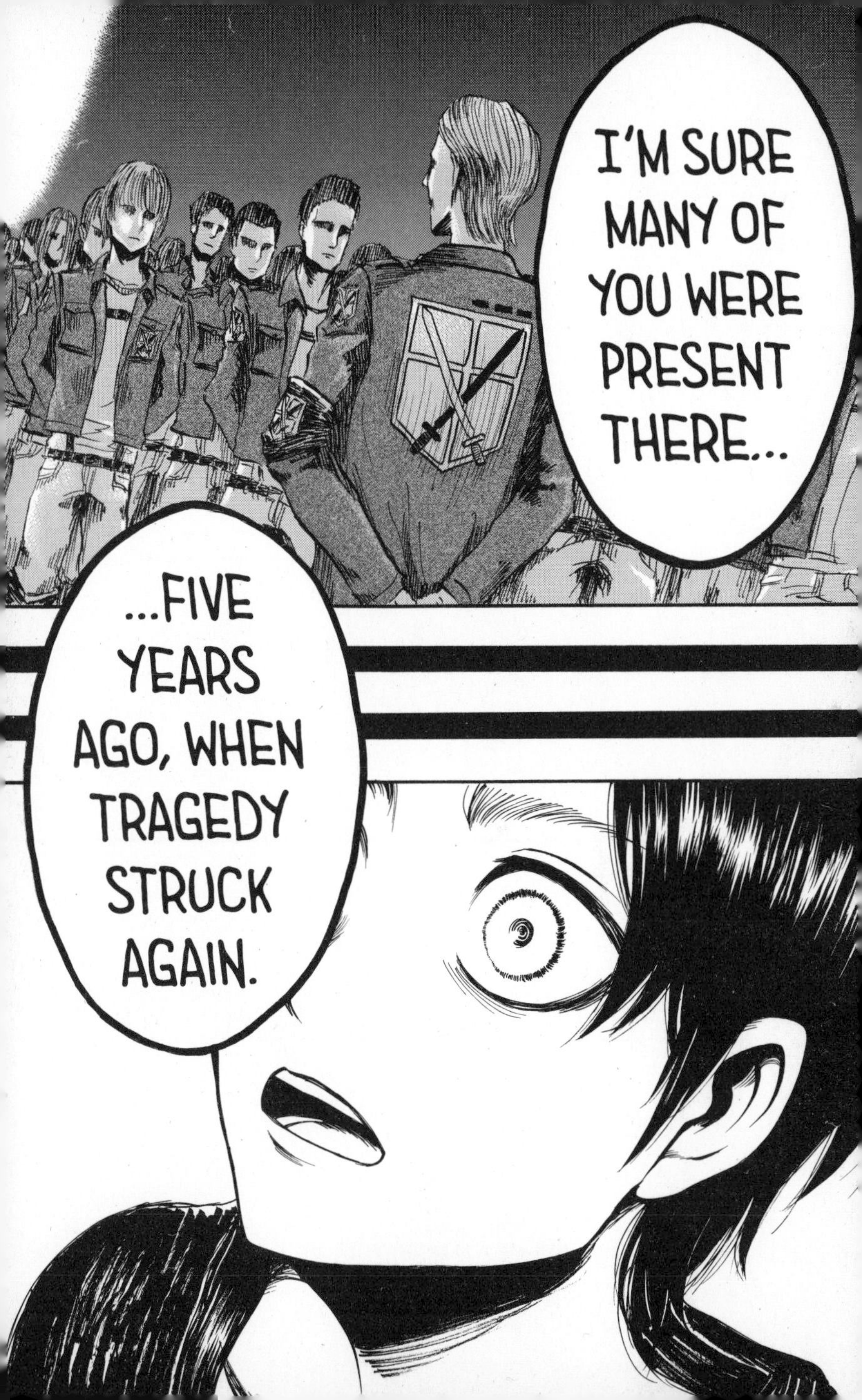
I'M SURE MANY OF YOU WERE PRESENT THERE...
...FIVE YEARS AGO, WHEN TRAGEDY STRUCK AGAIN.

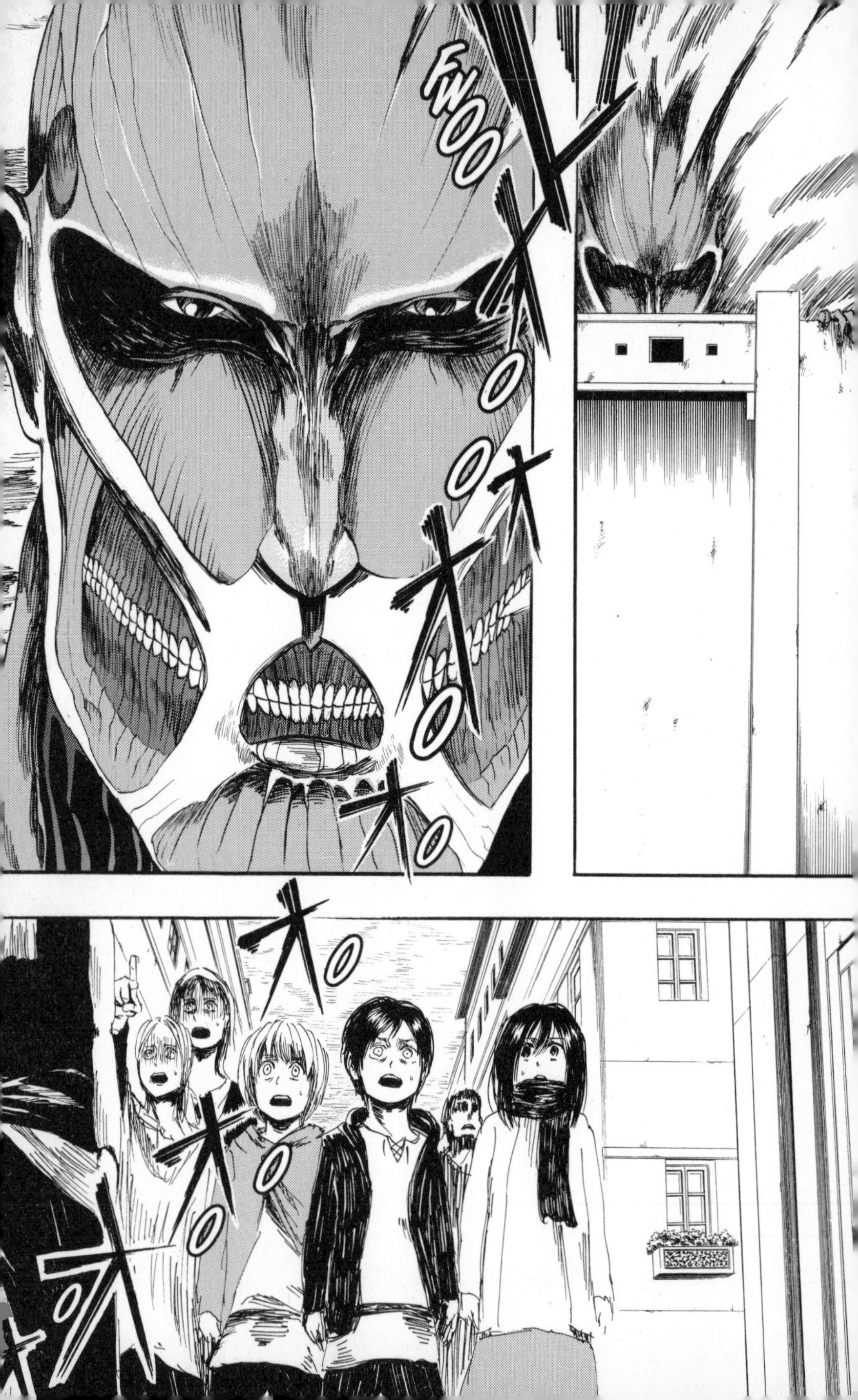
FWOOOOOOOOOO

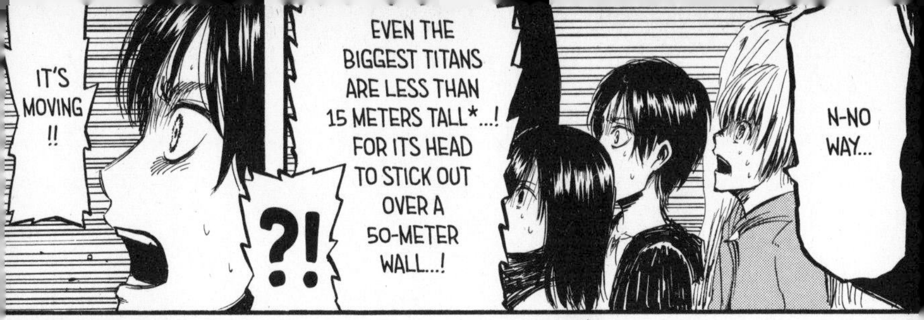
N-NO WAY...
EVEN THE BIGGEST TITANS ARE LESS THAN 15 METERS TALL*...! FOR ITS HEAD TO STICK OUT OVER A 50-METER WALL...!
?!
IT'S MOVING !!

*ABOUT 50 FEET

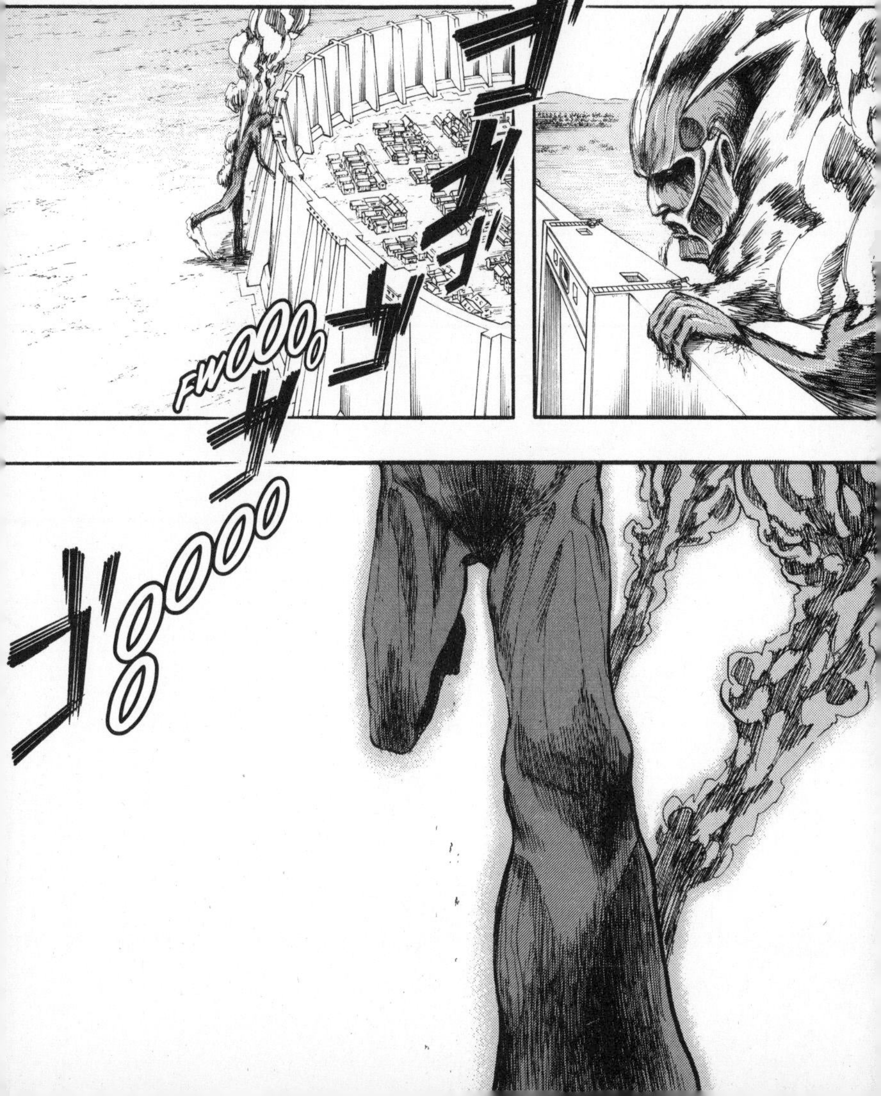
FWOOOO
OOOOO

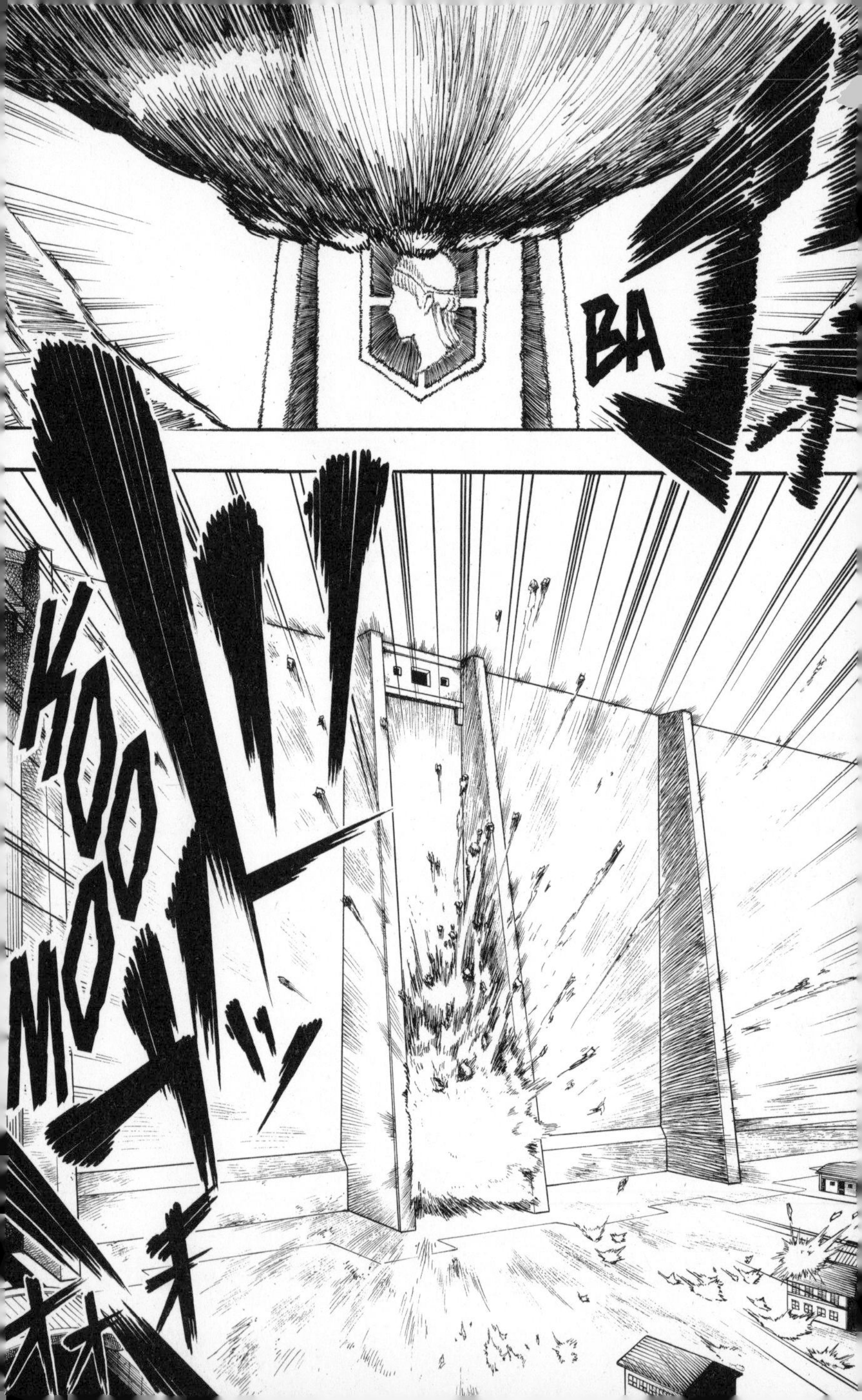
BA
KOOOM

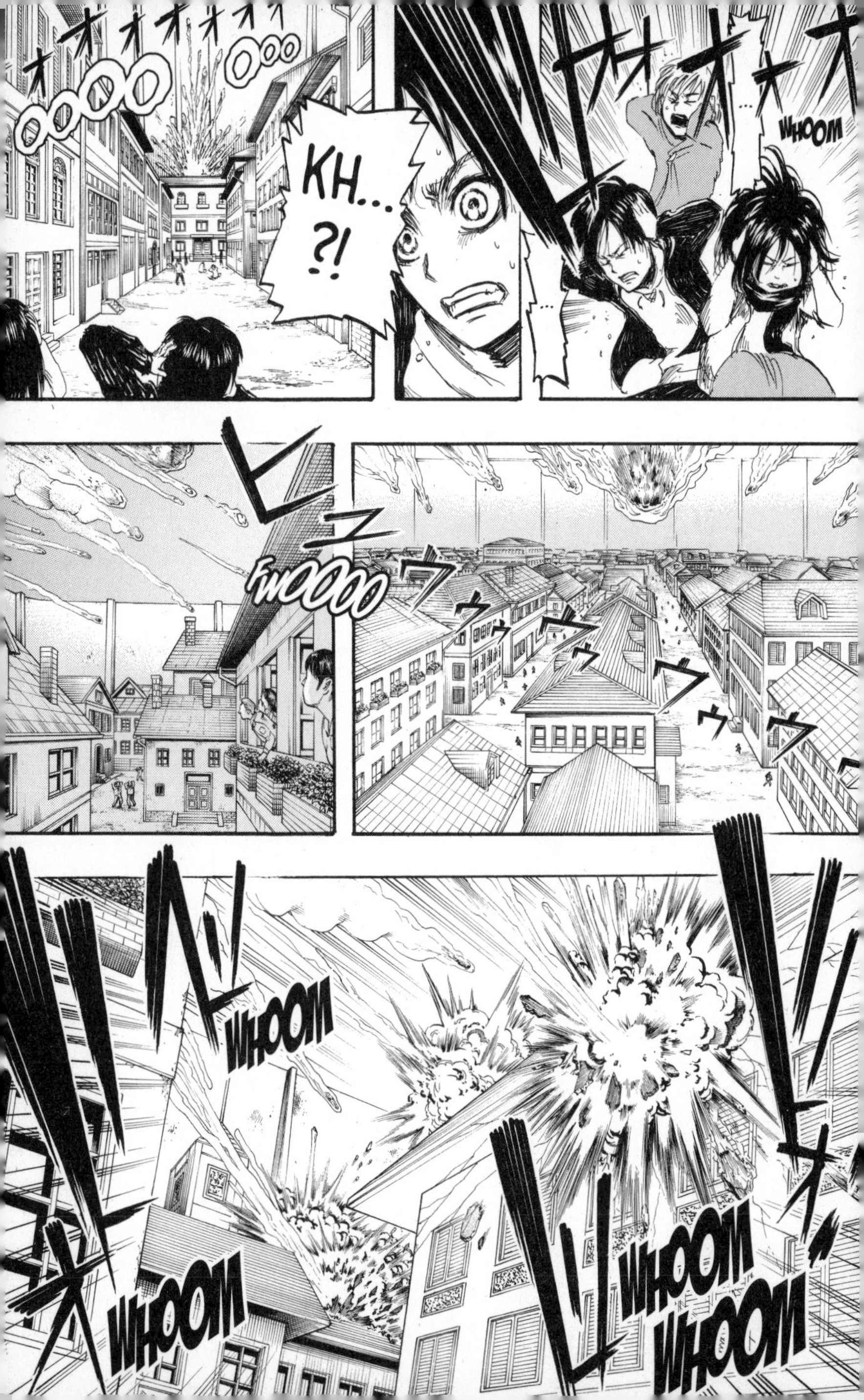
WHOOM
KH...
?!
OOOOO
Ooo
FWOOOO
WHOOM
WHOOM
WHOOM
WHOOM

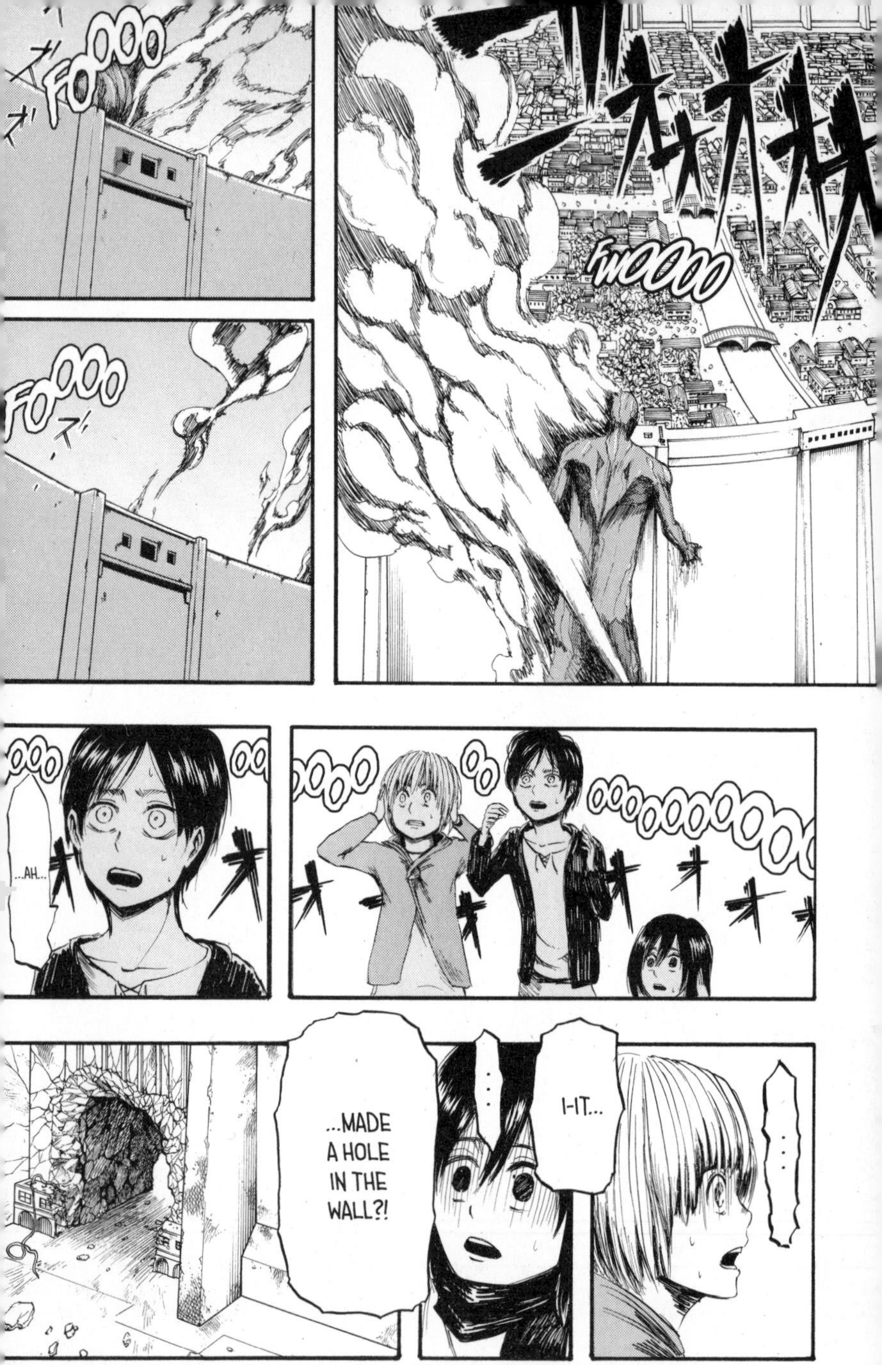
FWOOOOO
FOOOO
FOOOO
OOOOO
OO
OOOOOOOOOOOO
OOO
OO
...AH...
...
...
I-IT...
...MADE A HOLE IN THE WALL?!

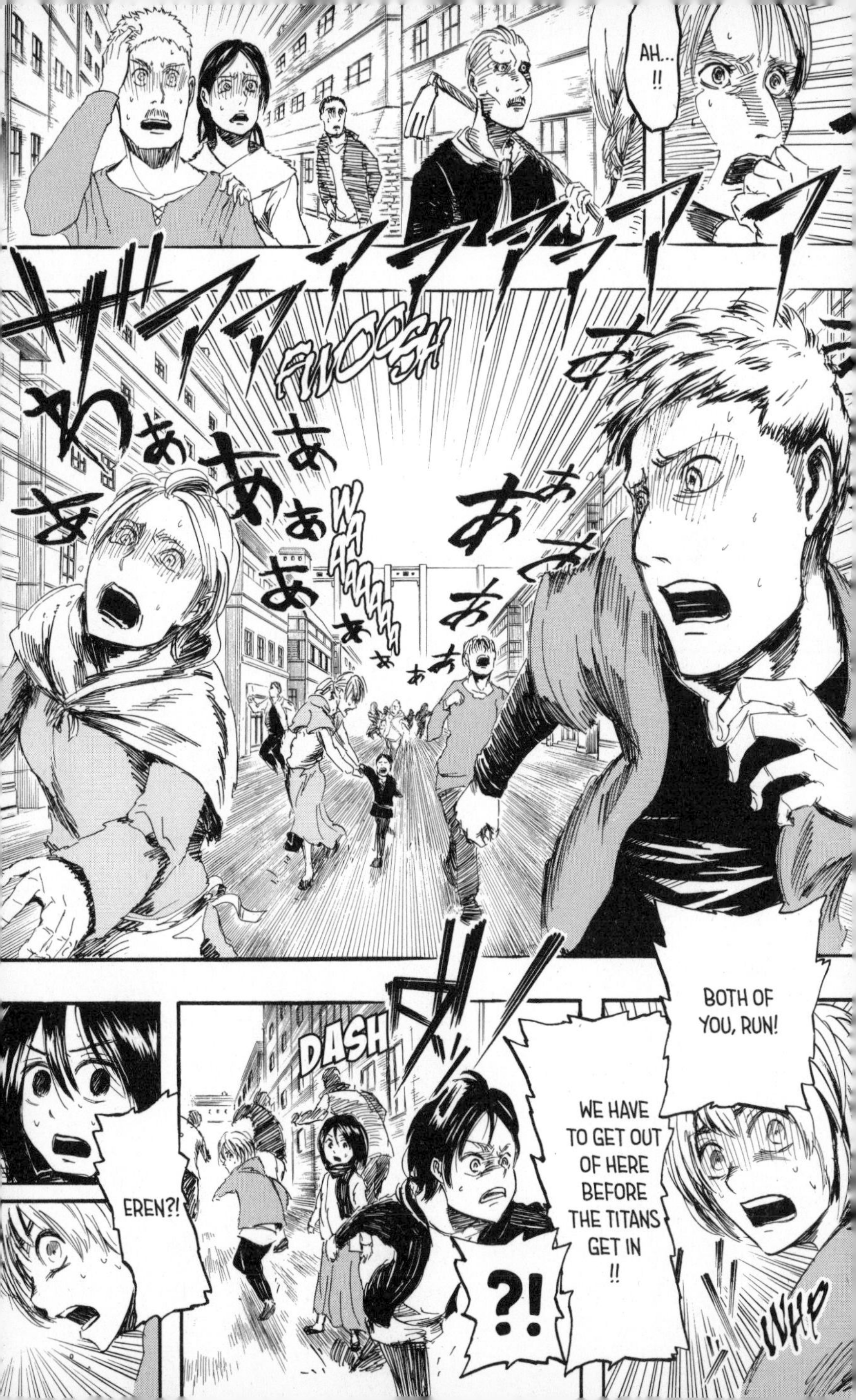
AH... !!
FLOOSH
WAAAAAAAA
BOTH OF YOU, RUN!
WE HAVE TO GET OUT OF HERE BEFORE THE TITANS GET IN !!
WHIP
?!
DASH
EREN?!

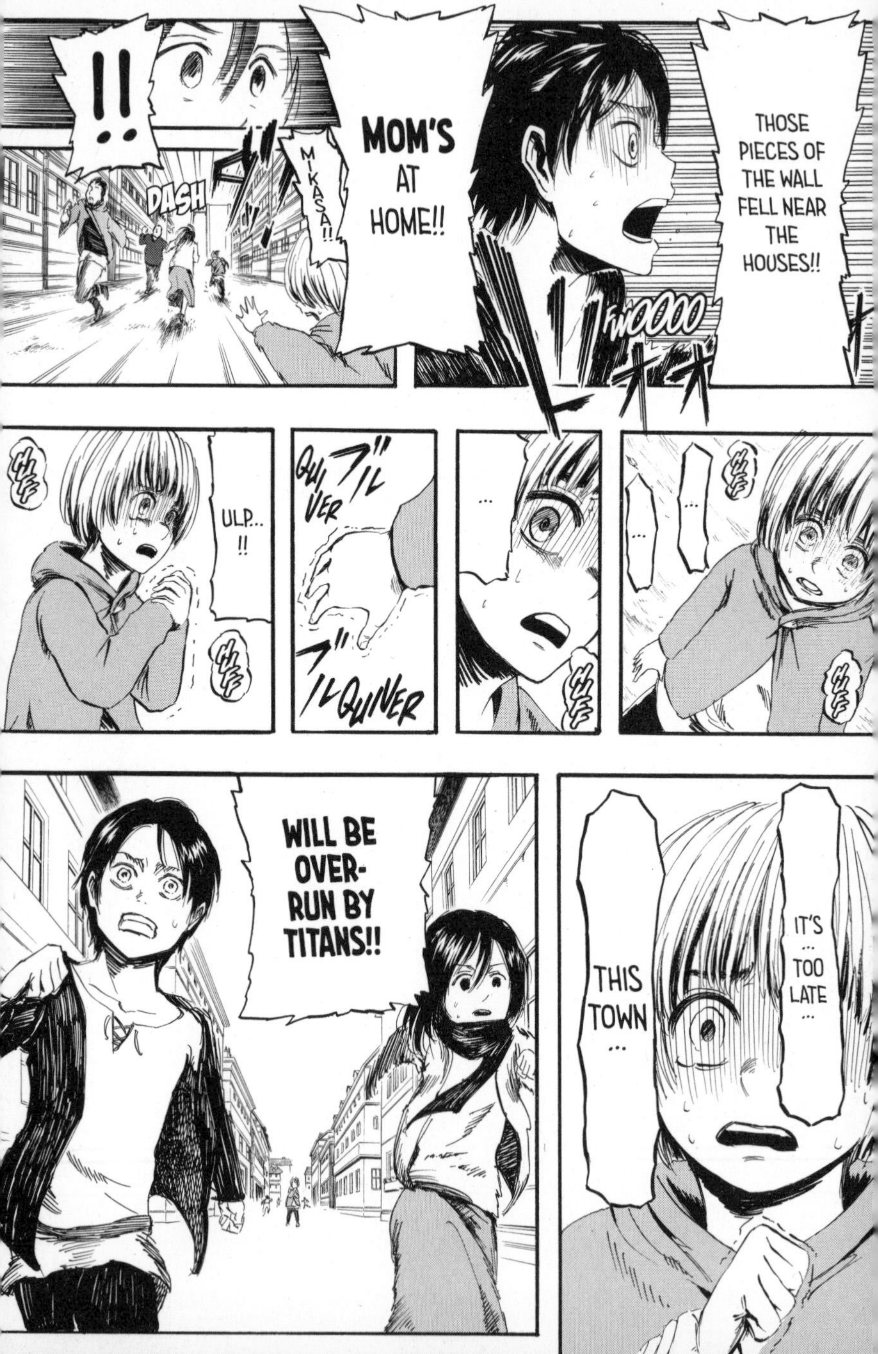
THOSE PIECES OF THE WALL FELL NEAR THE HOUSES!!
FWOOOO
MOM'S AT HOME!!
MIKASA!!
!!
DASH
...
...
HUF
HUF
...
HUF
QUIVER
QUIVER
ULP... !!
HUF
HUF
IT'S ... TOO LATE ...
THIS TOWN ...
WILL BE OVER-RUN BY TITANS!!

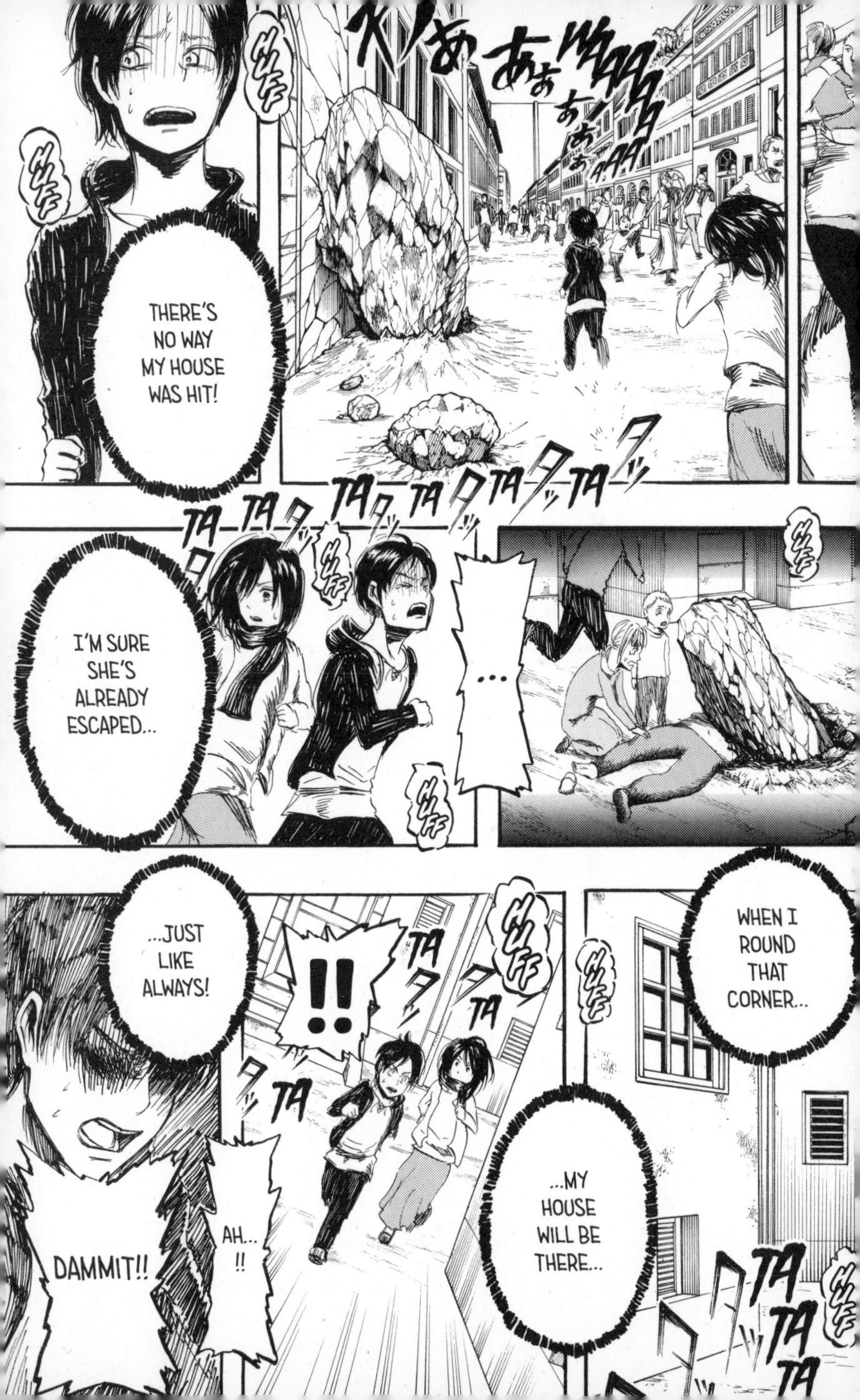
TA TA TA TA TA TA
HUFF
HUFF
THERE'S NO WAY MY HOUSE WAS HIT!
HUFF
...
HUFF
I'M SURE SHE'S ALREADY ESCAPED...
HUFF
WHEN I ROUND THAT CORNER...
...MY HOUSE WILL BE THERE...
HUFF
HUFF
TA TA TA
HUFF
TA TA
TA
!!
...JUST LIKE ALWAYS!
AH... !!
DAMMIT!!

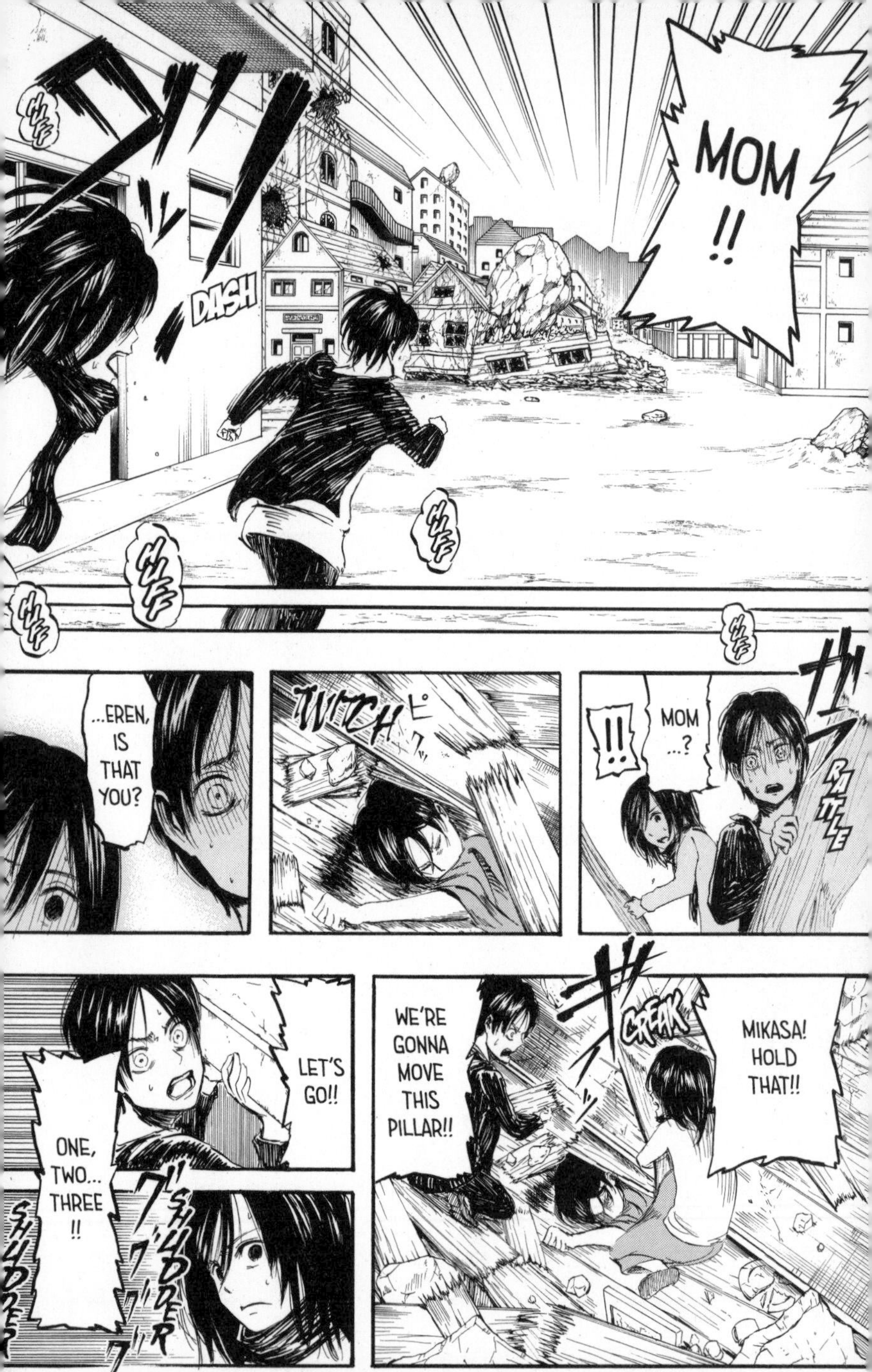
MOM!!
DASH
HUFF
HUFF
HUFF
HUFF
HUFF
HUFF
MOM ...?
!!
RATTLE
TWITCH
...EREN, IS THAT YOU?
MIKASA! HOLD THAT!!
CREAK
WE'RE GONNA MOVE THIS PILLAR!!
LET'S GO!!
ONE, TWO... THREE !!
SHUDDER
SHUDDER

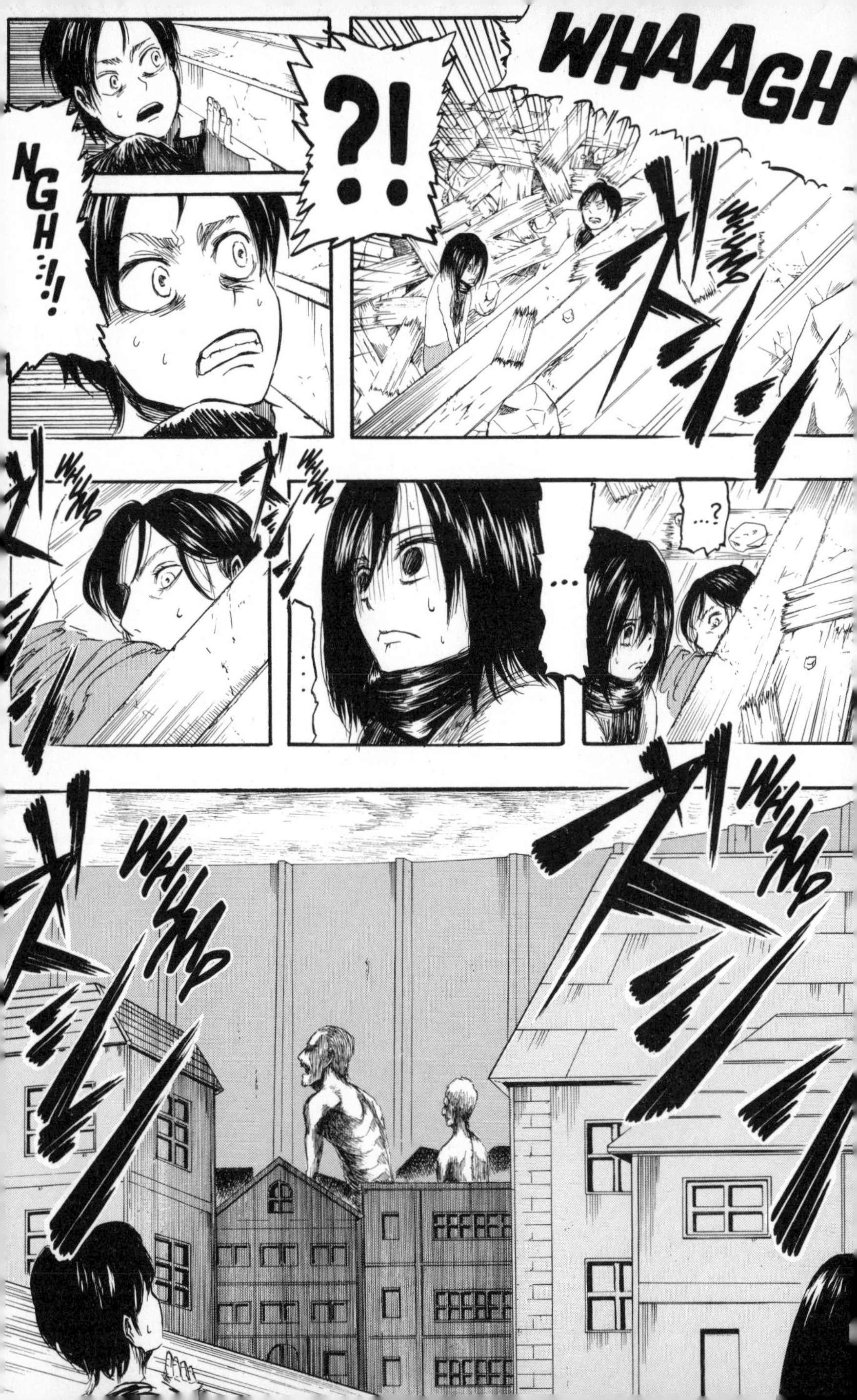
WHAAGH
WHUMP
?!
NGH...!!
...?
...
...
WHUMP
WHUMP
WHUMP
WHUMP

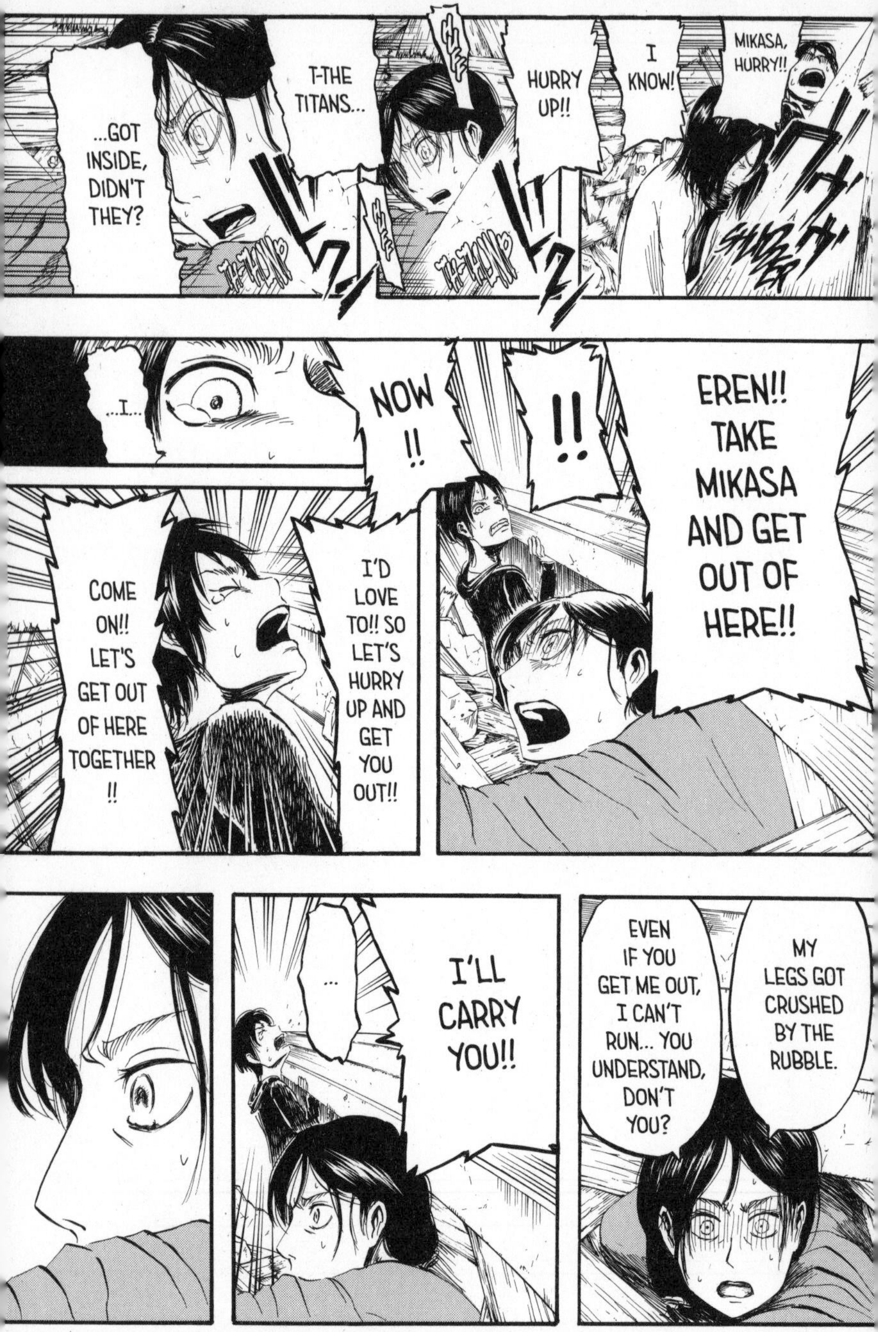
MIKASA, HURRY!!
I KNOW!
SHUDDER
HURRY UP!!
T-THE TITANS...
THA-THUMP
...GOT INSIDE, DIDN'T THEY?
THA-THUMP
EREN!! TAKE MIKASA AND GET OUT OF HERE!!
!!
NOW!!
...I...
I'D LOVE TO!! SO LET'S HURRY UP AND GET YOU OUT!!
COME ON!! LET'S GET OUT OF HERE TOGETHER!!
MY LEGS GOT CRUSHED BY THE RUBBLE.
EVEN IF YOU GET ME OUT, I CAN'T RUN... YOU UNDERSTAND, DON'T YOU?
I'LL CARRY YOU!!
...

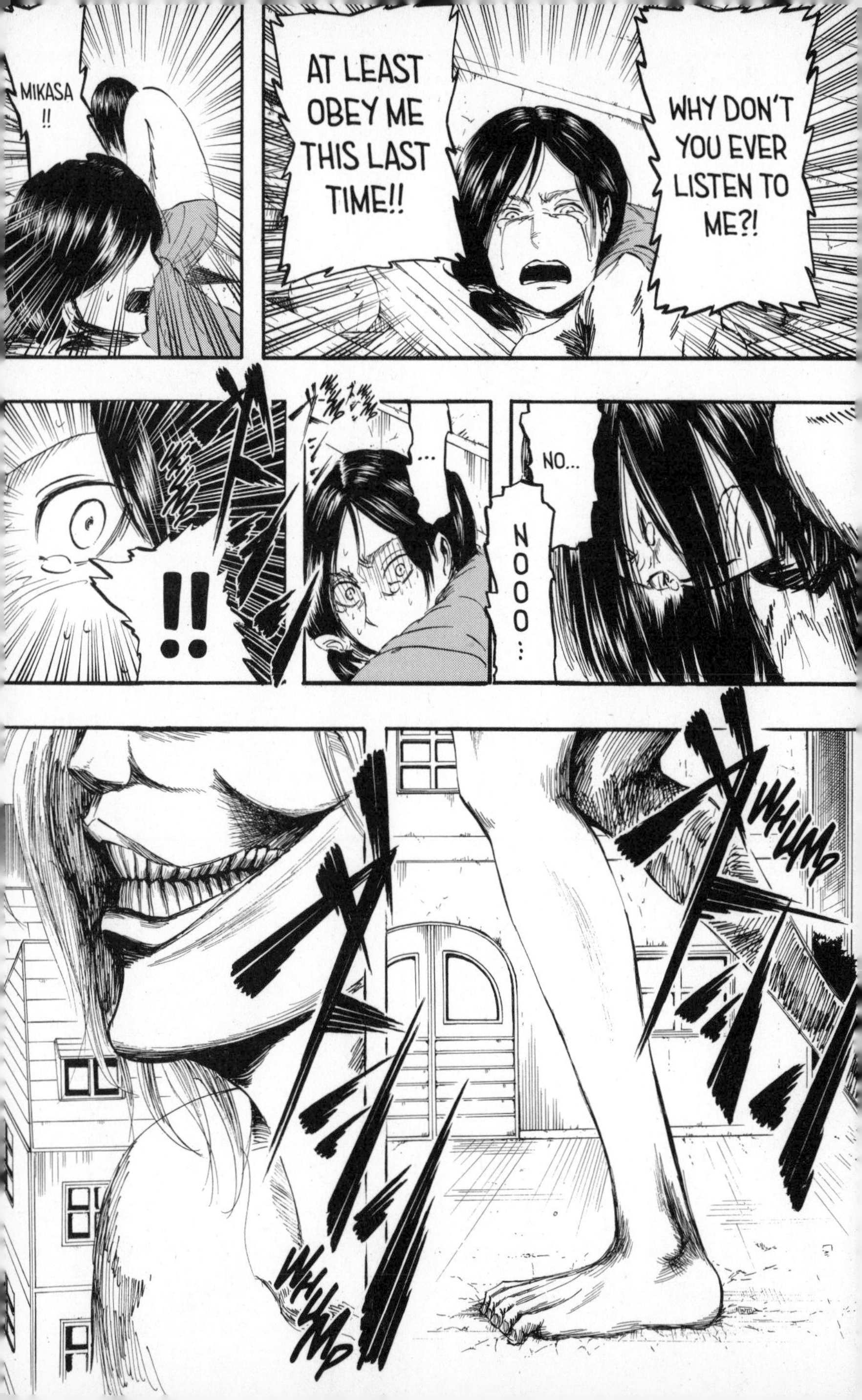
WHY DON'T YOU EVER LISTEN TO ME?!
AT LEAST OBEY ME THIS LAST TIME!!
MIKASA !!
NO...
NOOO...
...
!!
WHUMP
WHUMP

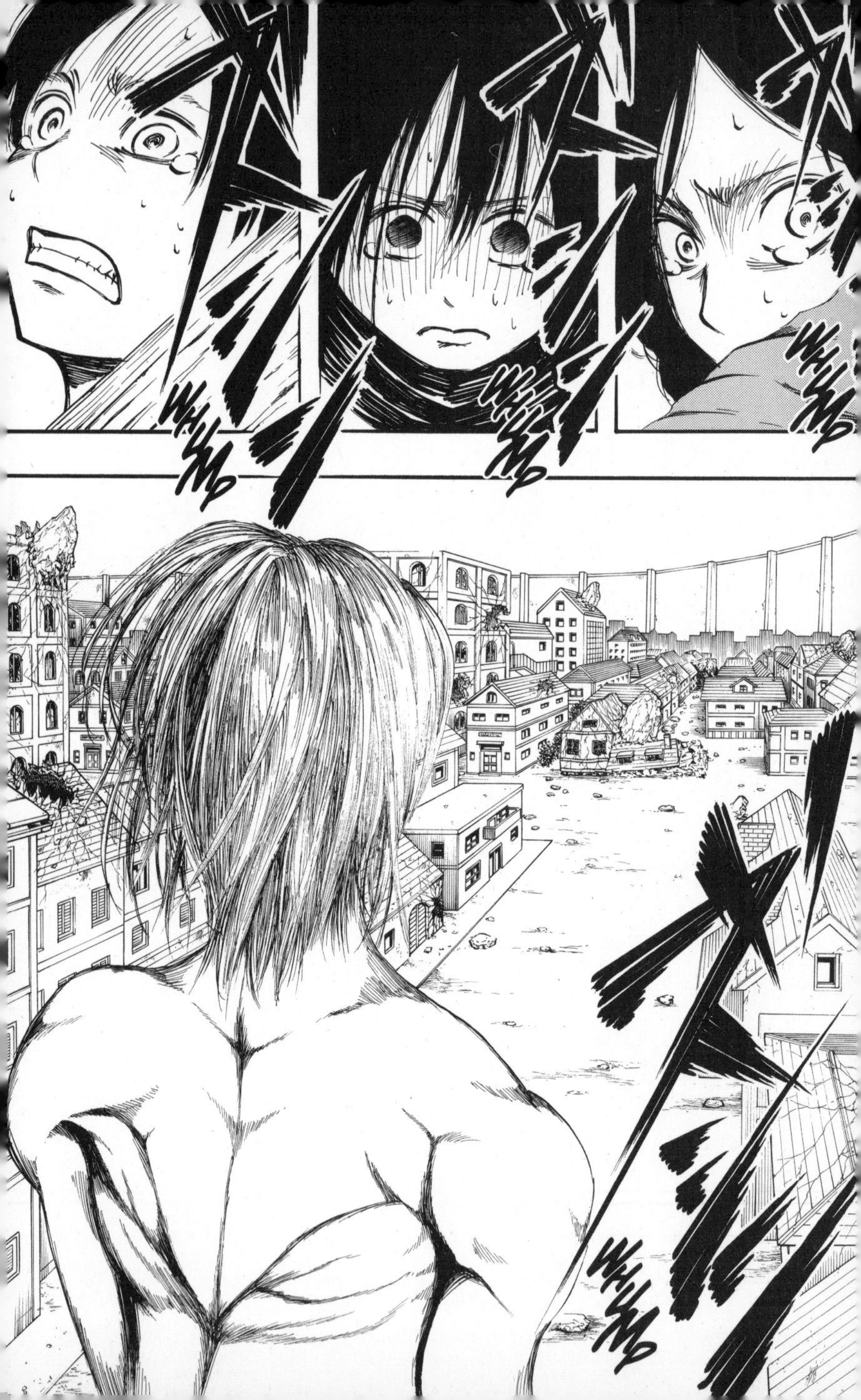
WHUMP
WHUMP
WHUMP
WHUMP

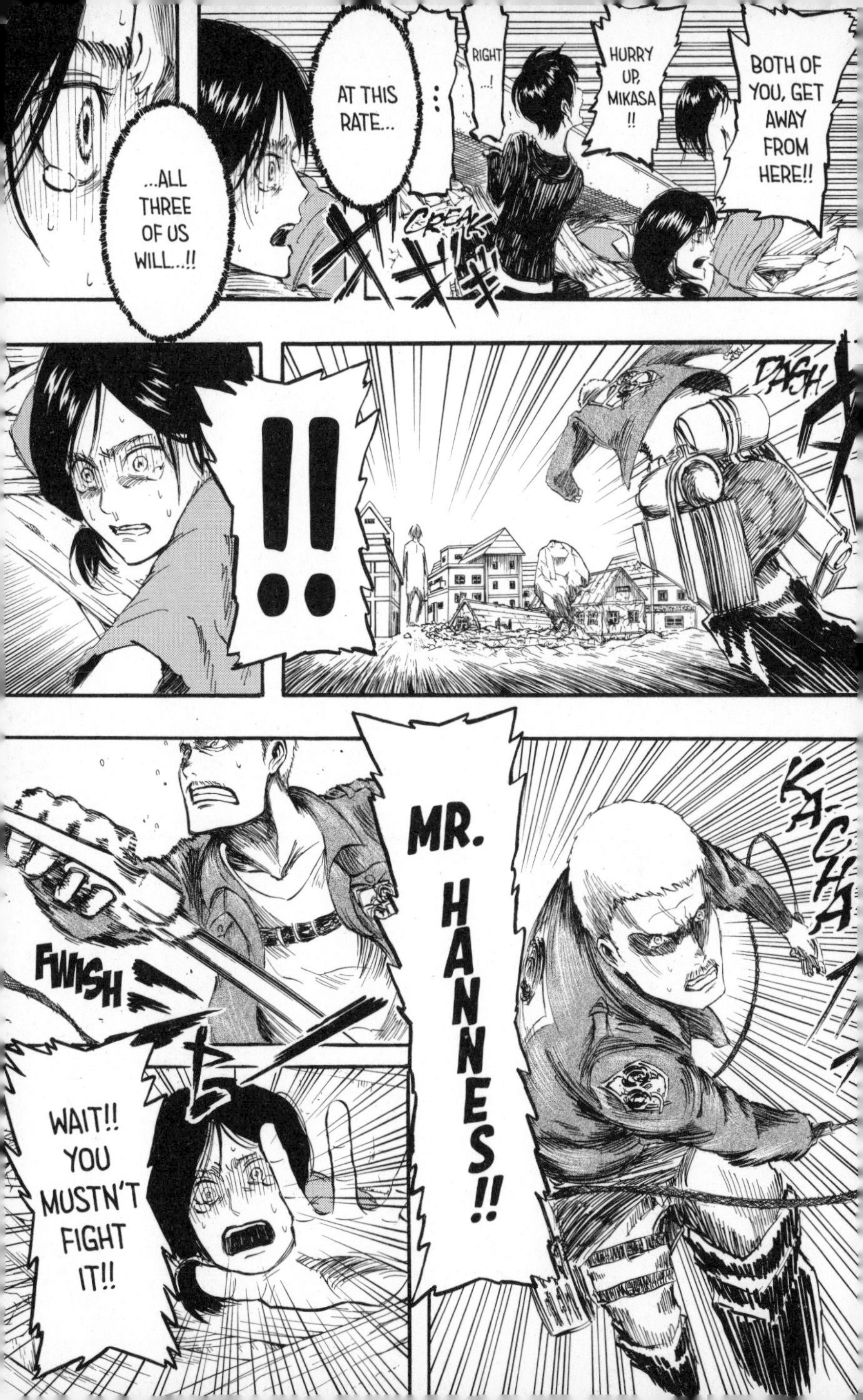
BOTH OF YOU, GET AWAY FROM HERE!!
HURRY UP, MIKASA !!
RIGHT ...!
CREAK
...
AT THIS RATE...
...ALL THREE OF US WILL...!!
DASH
!!
KA-CHA
MR. HANNES!!
FWISH
WAIT!! YOU MUSTN'T FIGHT IT!!

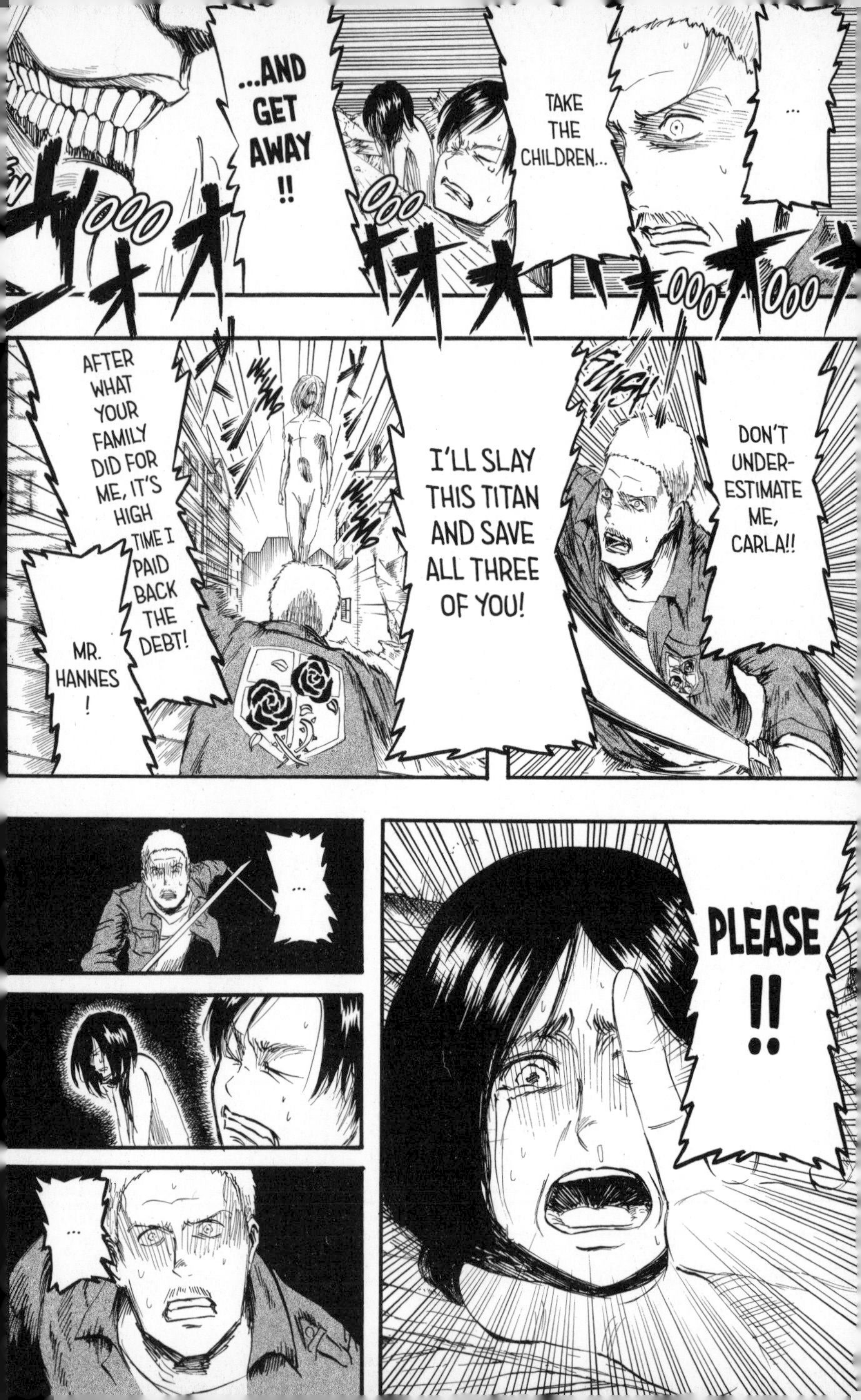
...
TAKE THE CHILDREN...
...AND GET AWAY !!
DON'T UNDER-ESTIMATE ME, CARLA!!
I'LL SLAY THIS TITAN AND SAVE ALL THREE OF YOU!
AFTER WHAT YOUR FAMILY DID FOR ME, IT'S HIGH TIME I PAID BACK THE DEBT!
MR. HANNES!
PLEASE !!
...
...

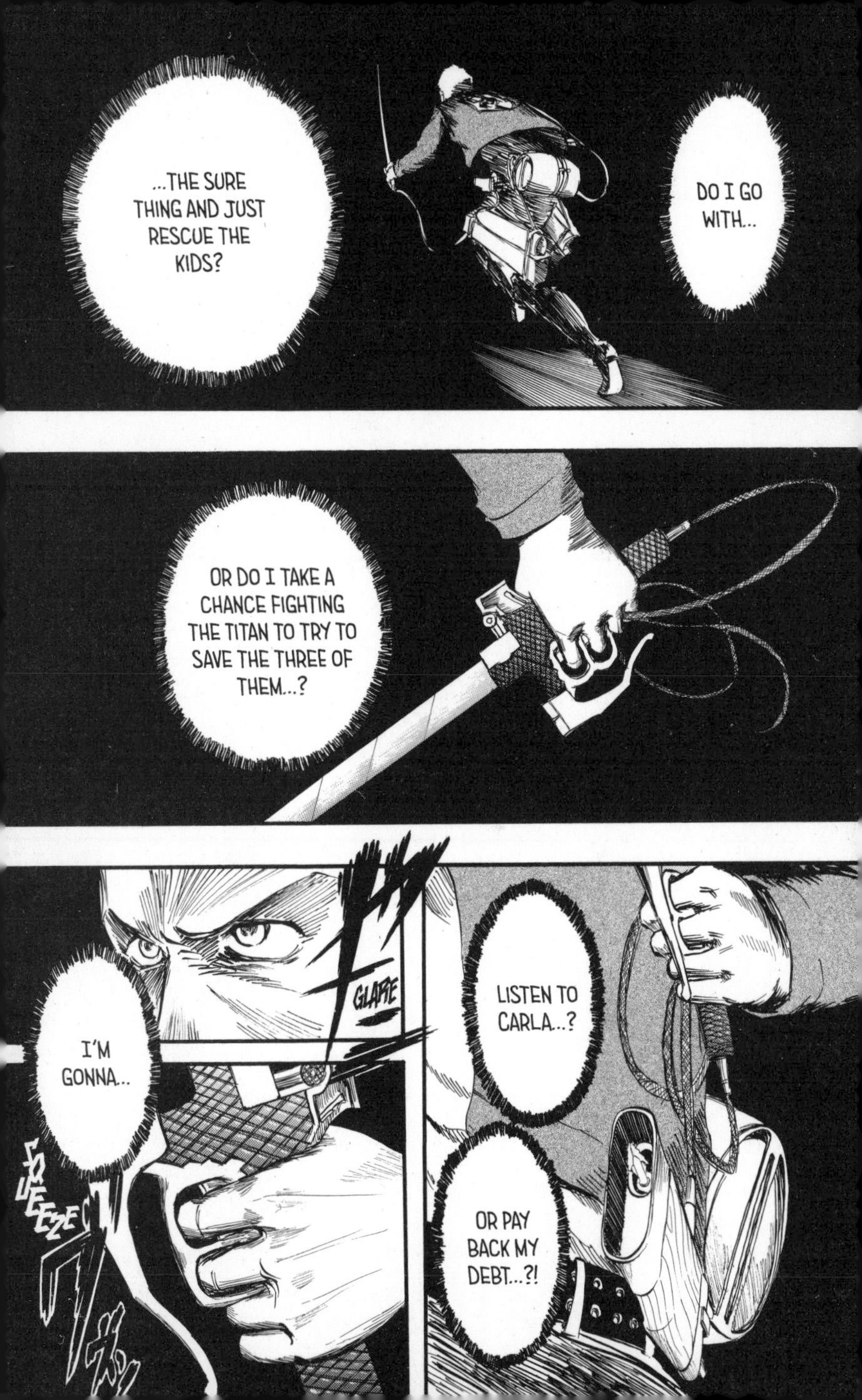
DO I GO WITH...
...THE SURE THING AND JUST RESCUE THE KIDS?
OR DO I TAKE A CHANCE FIGHTING THE TITAN TO TRY TO SAVE THE THREE OF THEM...?
LISTEN TO CARLA...?
OR PAY BACK MY DEBT...?!
GLARE
I'M GONNA...
SQUEEZE

I...
QUIVER
ブル

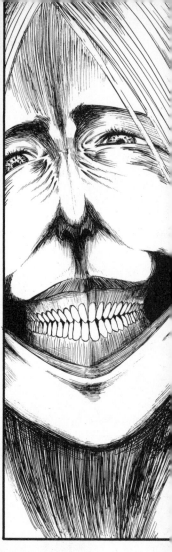

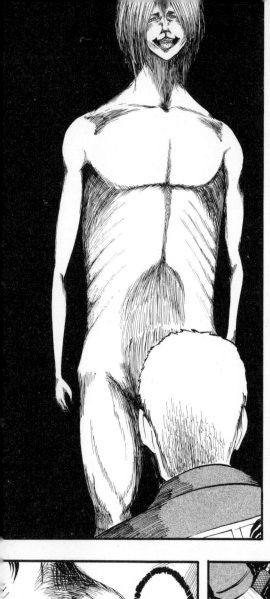

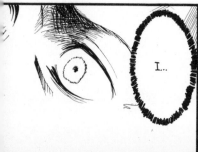

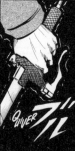

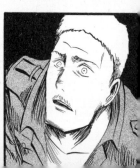

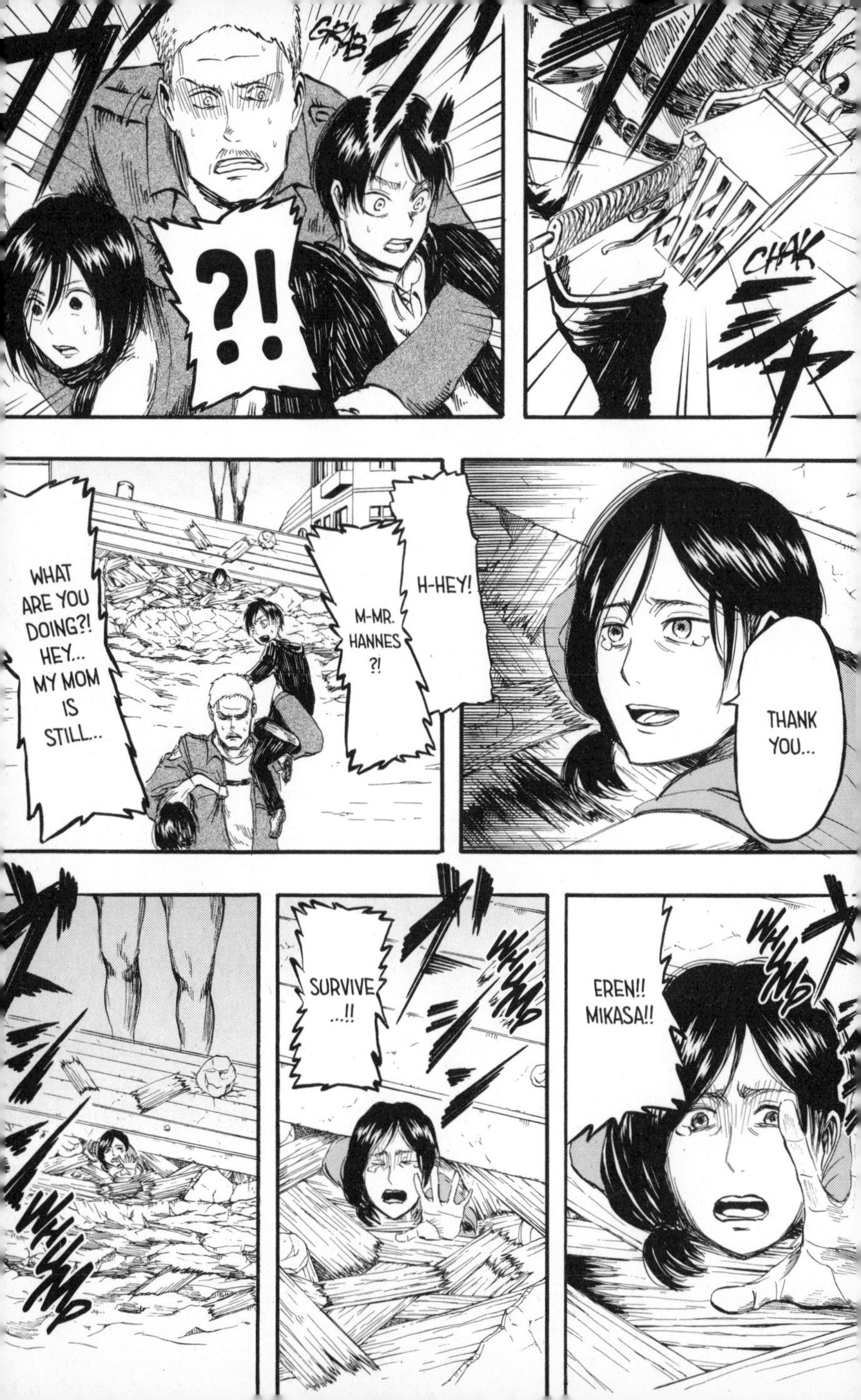
CHAK
GRAB
?!
THANK YOU...
H-HEY!
M-MR. HANNES ?!
WHAT ARE YOU DOING?! HEY... MY MOM IS STILL...
WHUMP
EREN!! MIKASA!!
WHUMP
SURVIVE ...!!
WHUMP

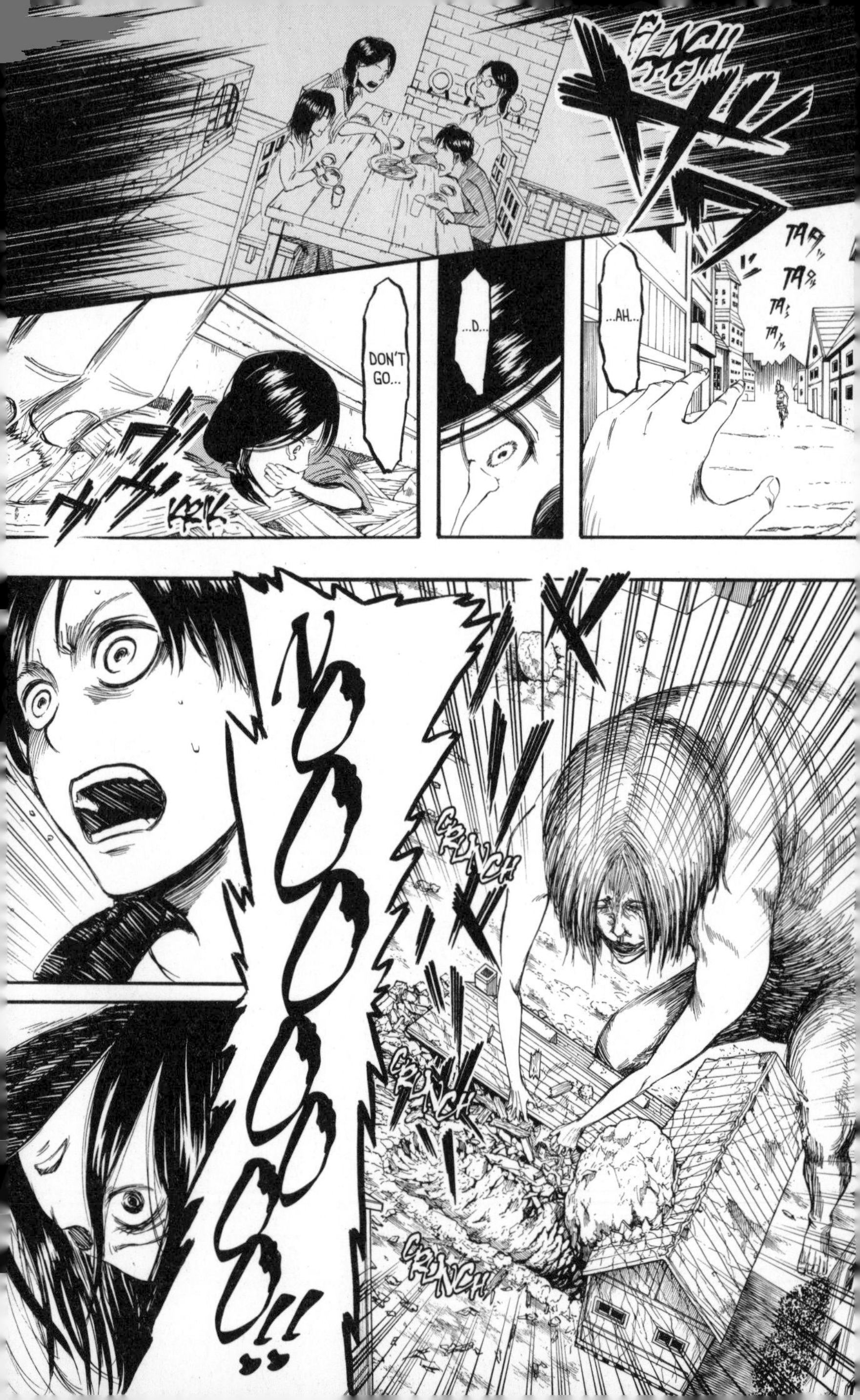

TA TA TA TA
...AH...
...D...
DON'T GO...
KRIK
NOOOOOOOOO!!
CRUNCH
CRUNCH
CRUNCH

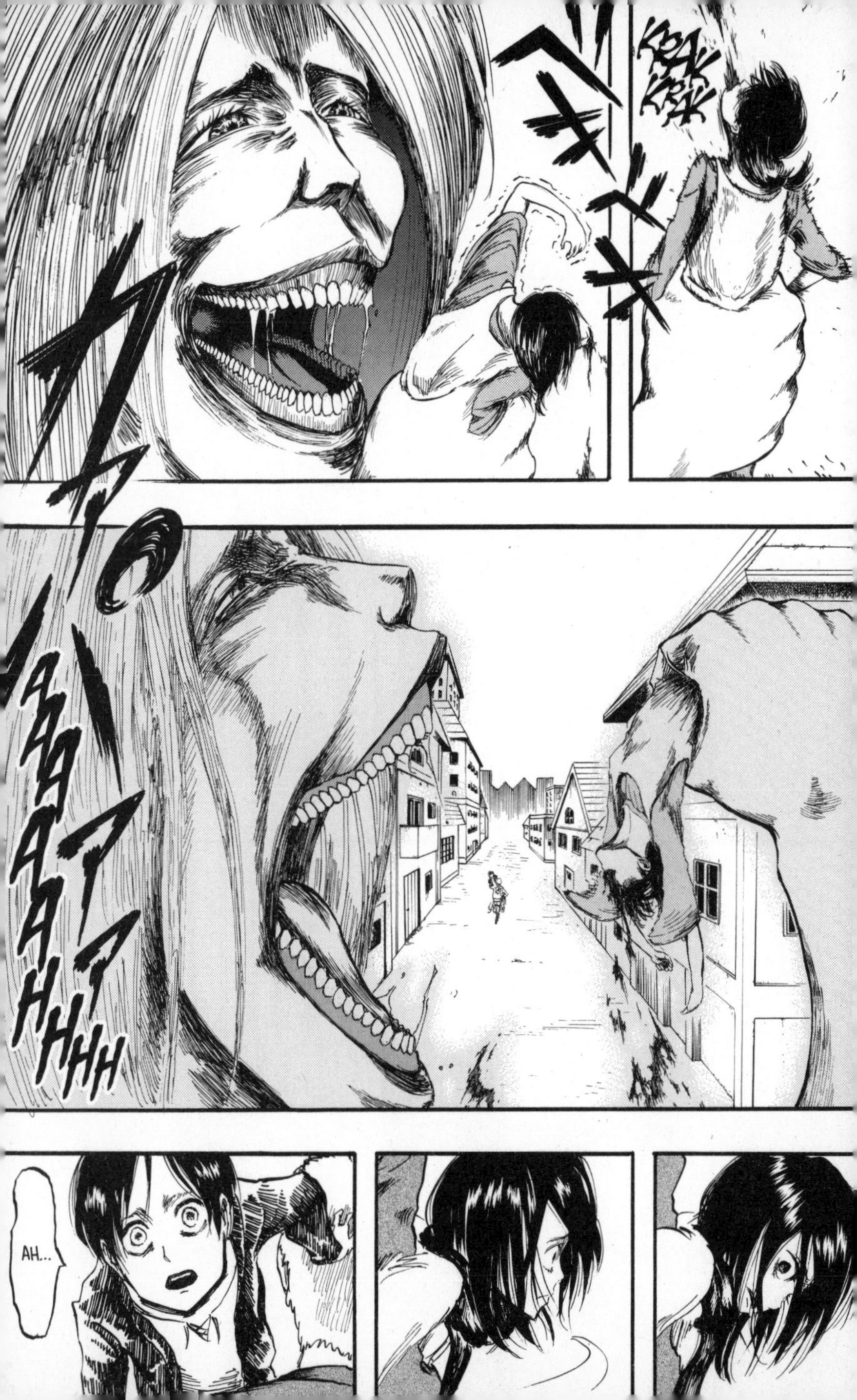
KRAK KRAK
AAAAAHHHH
AH...

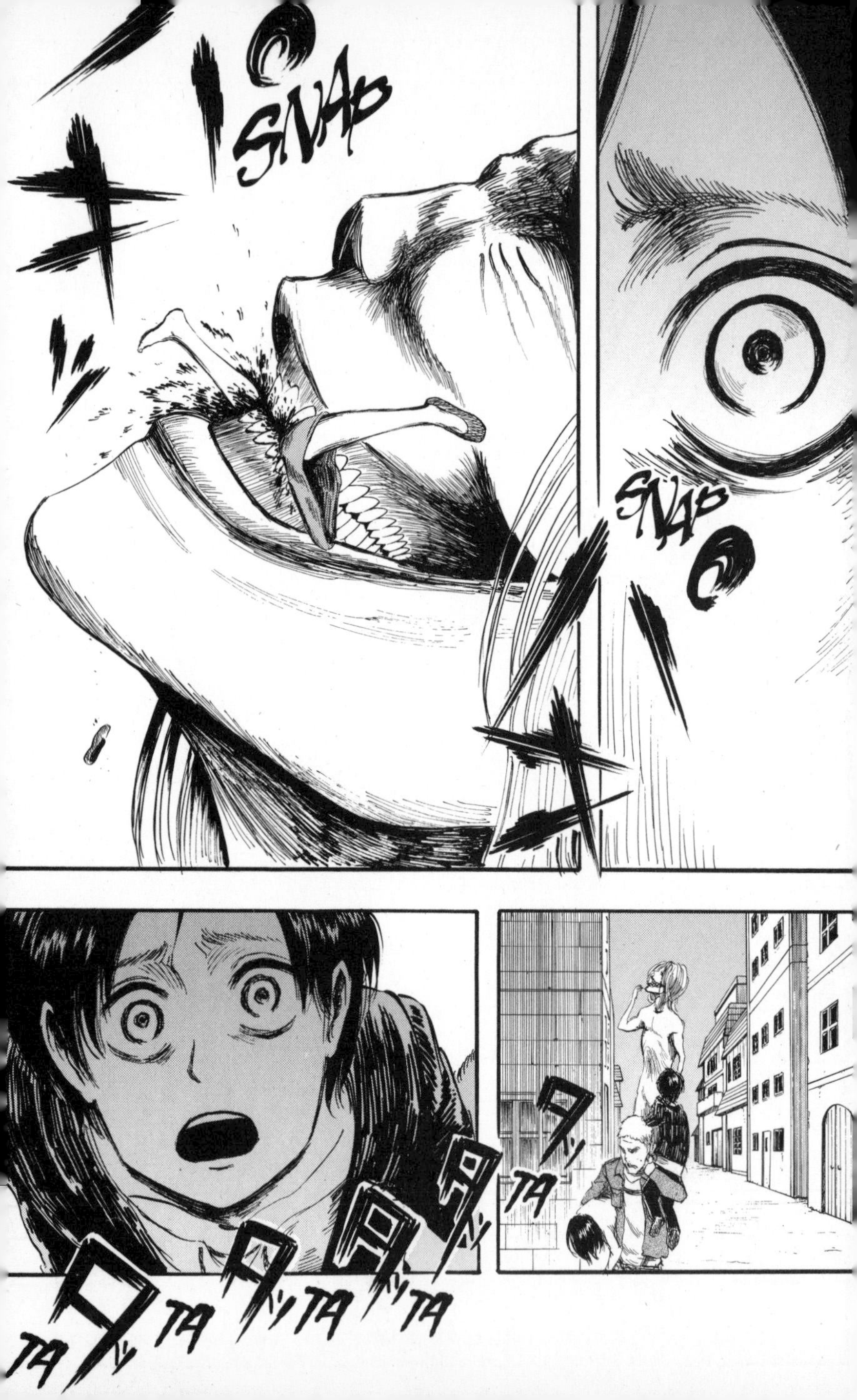
SNAP
SNAP
TA
TA
TA
TA
TA
TA

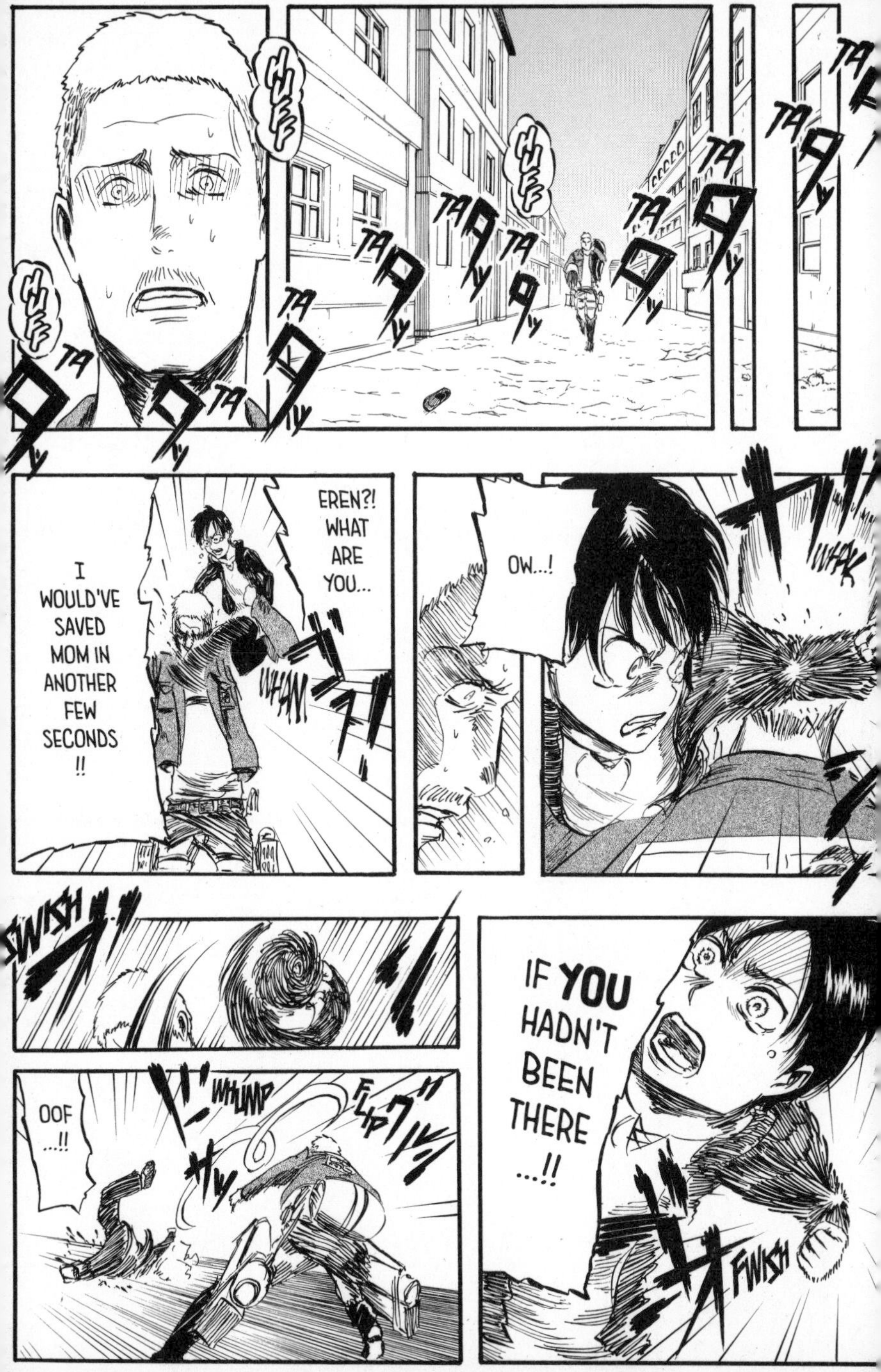
TA
TA
TA
TA
HUFF
TA
TA
TA
HUFF
HUFF
TA
TA
TA
WHAK
OW...!
EREN?! WHAT ARE YOU...
I WOULD'VE SAVED MOM IN ANOTHER FEW SECONDS !!
WHAM
IF YOU HADN'T BEEN THERE ...!!
FWISH
SWISH
FLIP
WHUMP
OOF ...!!

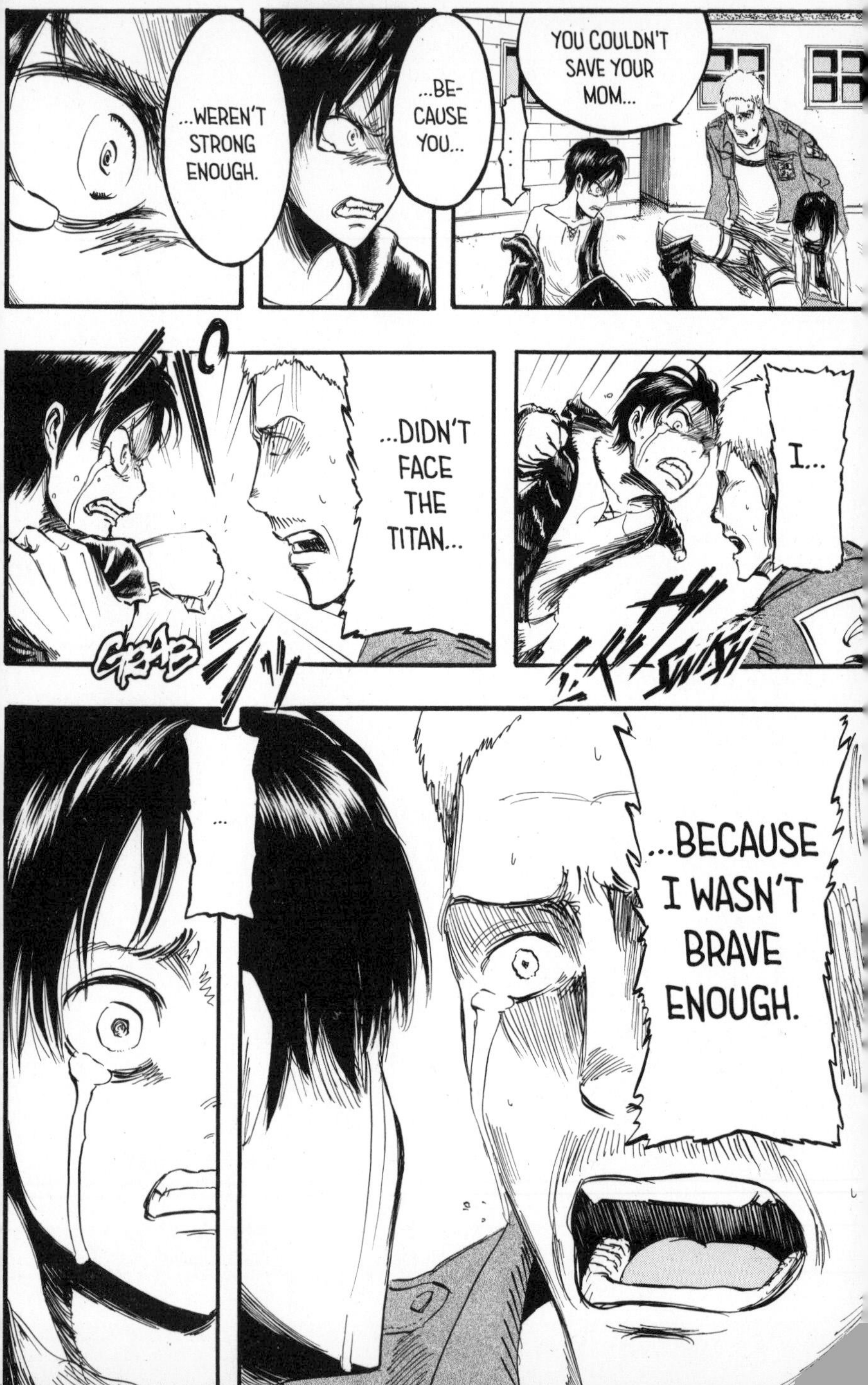
YOU COULDN'T SAVE YOUR MOM...
...
...BE-CAUSE YOU...
...WEREN'T STRONG ENOUGH.
I...
SWISH
...DIDN'T FACE THE TITAN...
GRAB
...BECAUSE I WASN'T BRAVE ENOUGH.
...

UHN...

...

I'M SORRY...

I'M SORRY...

FWOOOO

THIS AGAIN...

OH...

THROB

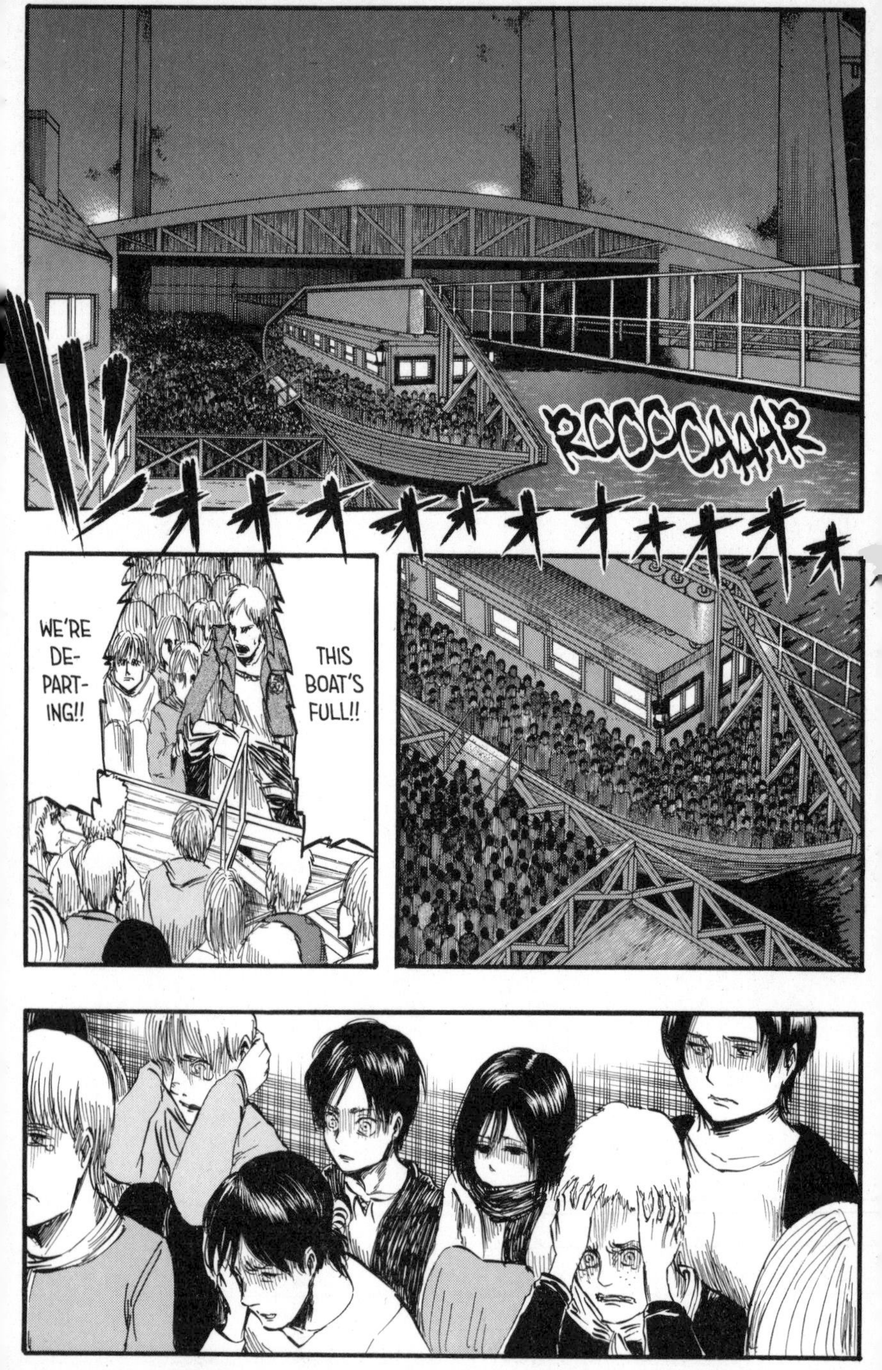
ROOOOAAAR
THIS BOAT'S FULL!!
WE'RE DE-PART-ING!!

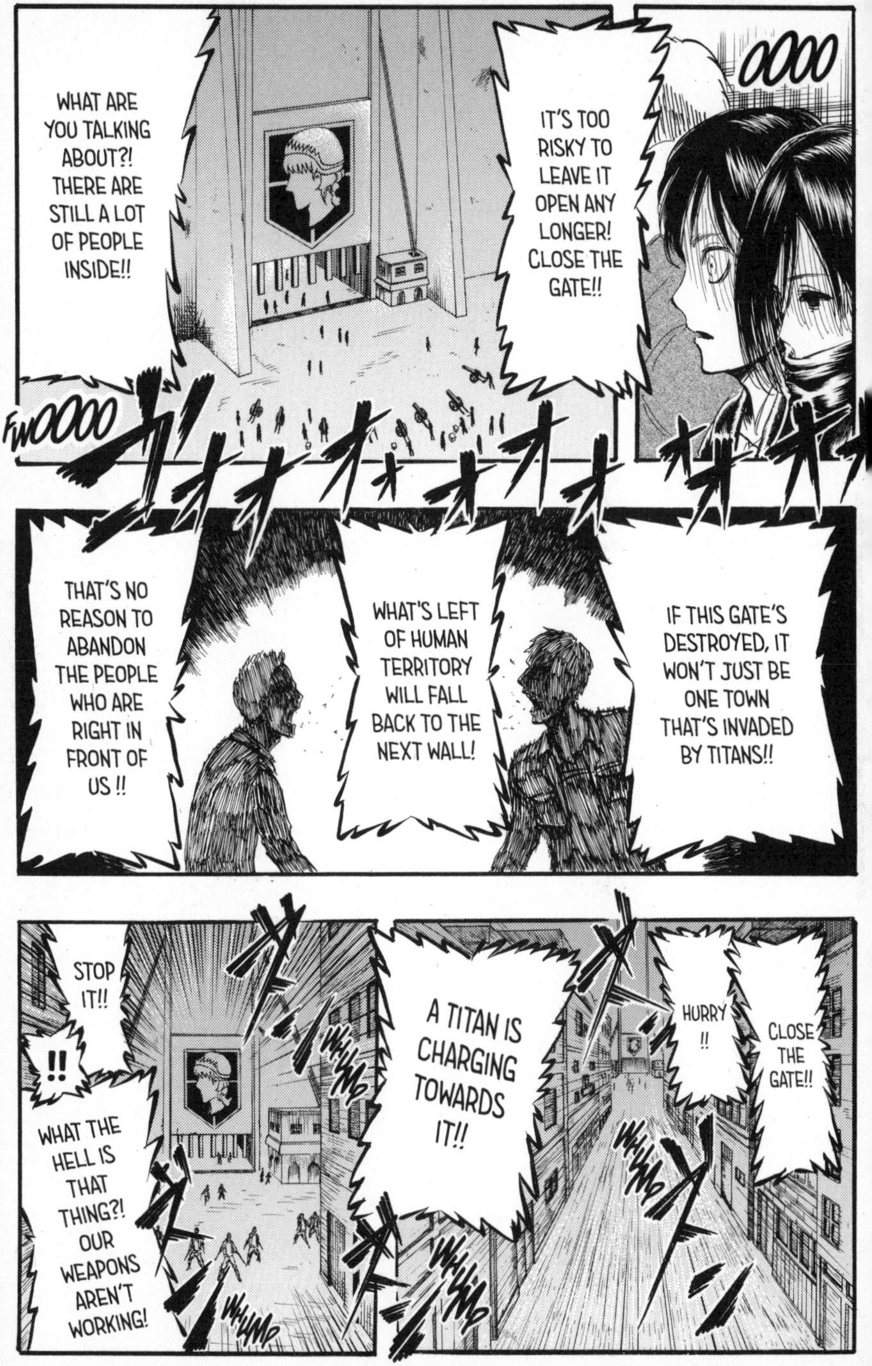
OOOO
IT'S TOO RISKY TO LEAVE IT OPEN ANY LONGER! CLOSE THE GATE!!
WHAT ARE YOU TALKING ABOUT?! THERE ARE STILL A LOT OF PEOPLE INSIDE!!
FWOOOO
IF THIS GATE'S DESTROYED, IT WON'T JUST BE ONE TOWN THAT'S INVADED BY TITANS!!
WHAT'S LEFT OF HUMAN TERRITORY WILL FALL BACK TO THE NEXT WALL!
THAT'S NO REASON TO ABANDON THE PEOPLE WHO ARE RIGHT IN FRONT OF US !!
CLOSE THE GATE!!
HURRY!!
A TITAN IS CHARGING TOWARDS IT!!
WHUMP
WHUMP
STOP IT!!
!!
WHAT THE HELL IS THAT THING?! OUR WEAPONS AREN'T WORKING!
WHUMP
WHUMP

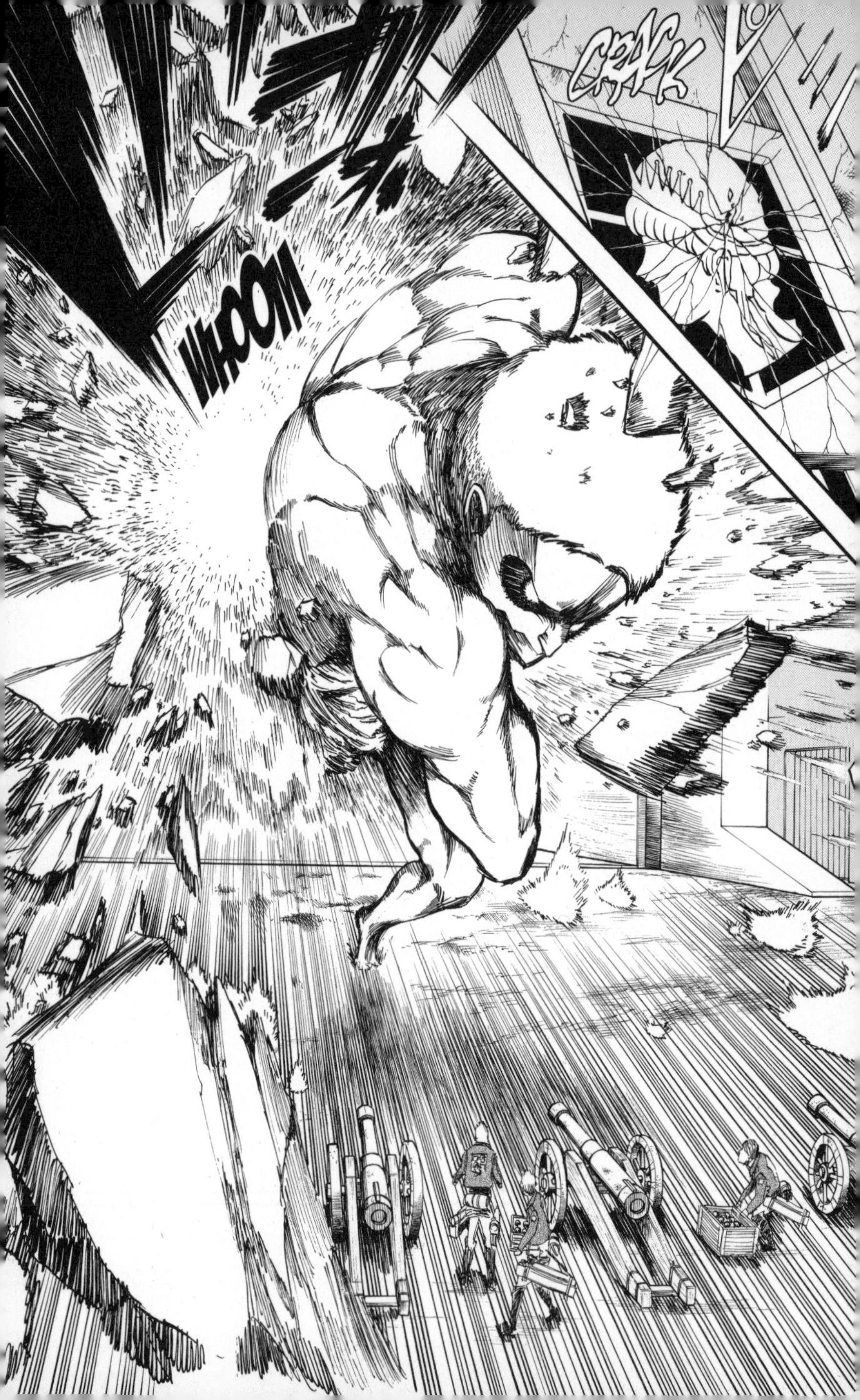
CRACK
WHOOM

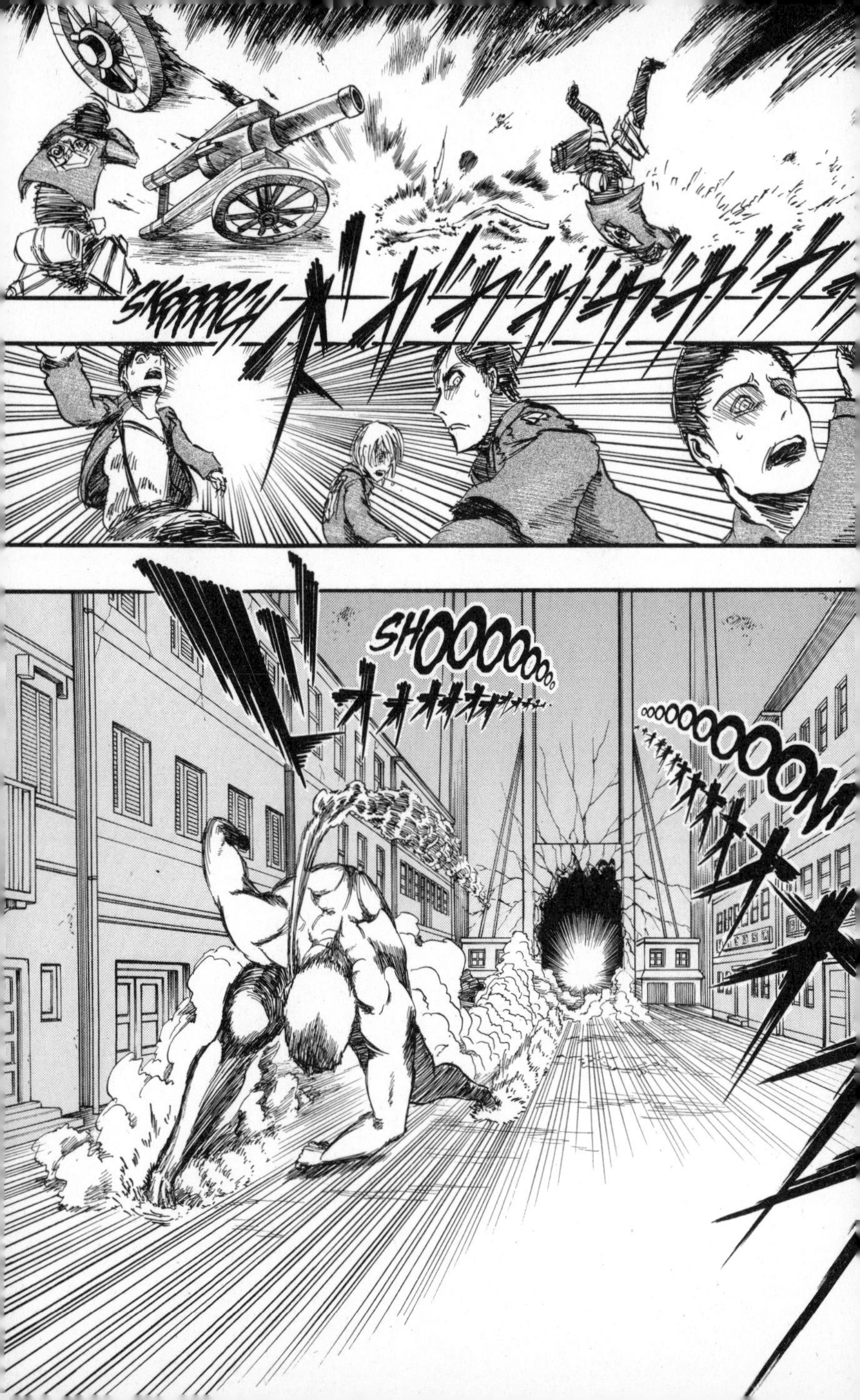
SKRRRRCH
SHOOOOOooo
oooOOOOOOOM

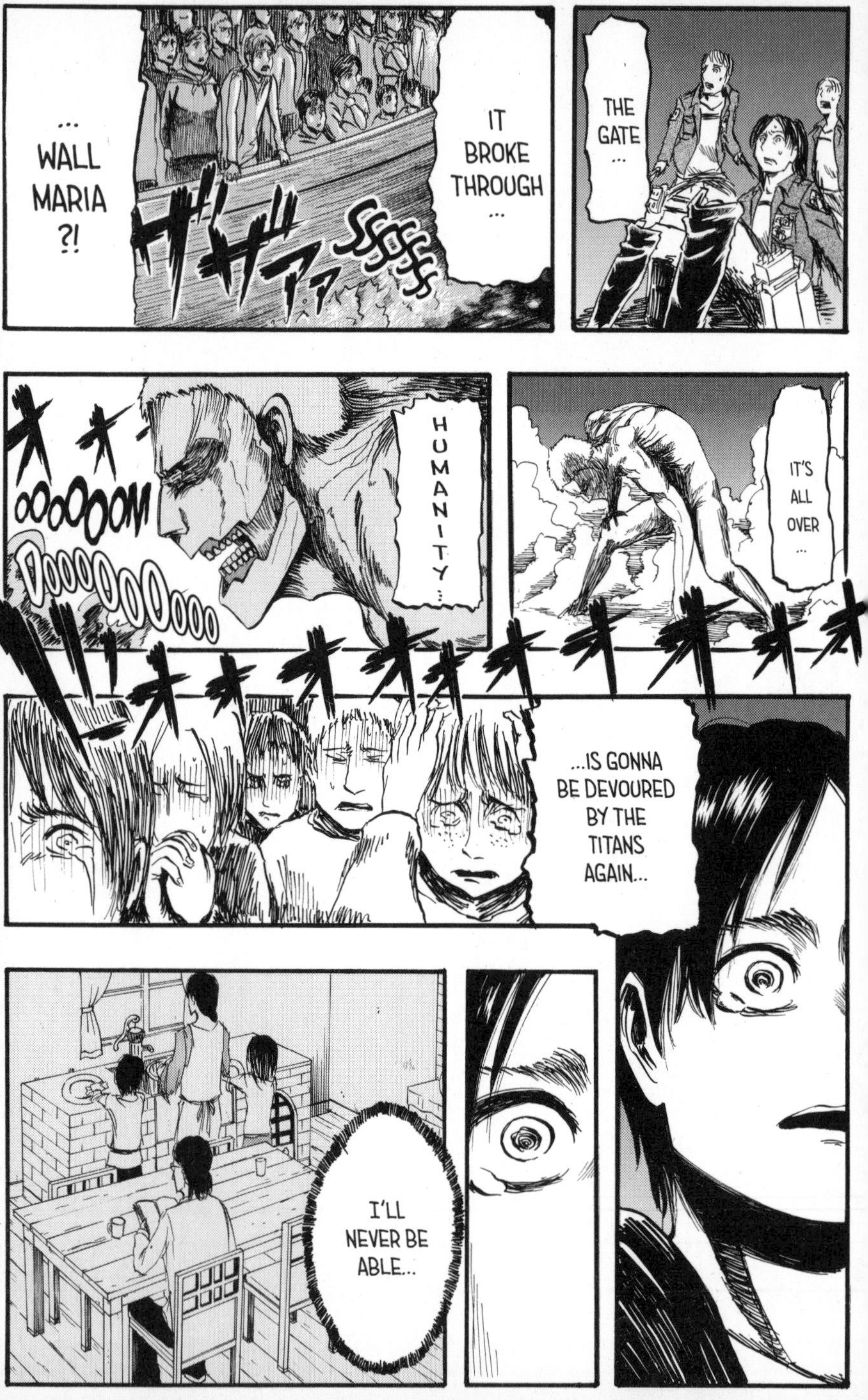
THE GATE ...
IT BROKE THROUGH ...
... WALL MARIA ?!
IT'S ALL OVER ...
HUMANITY...
...IS GONNA BE DEVOURED BY THE TITANS AGAIN...
I'LL NEVER BE ABLE...

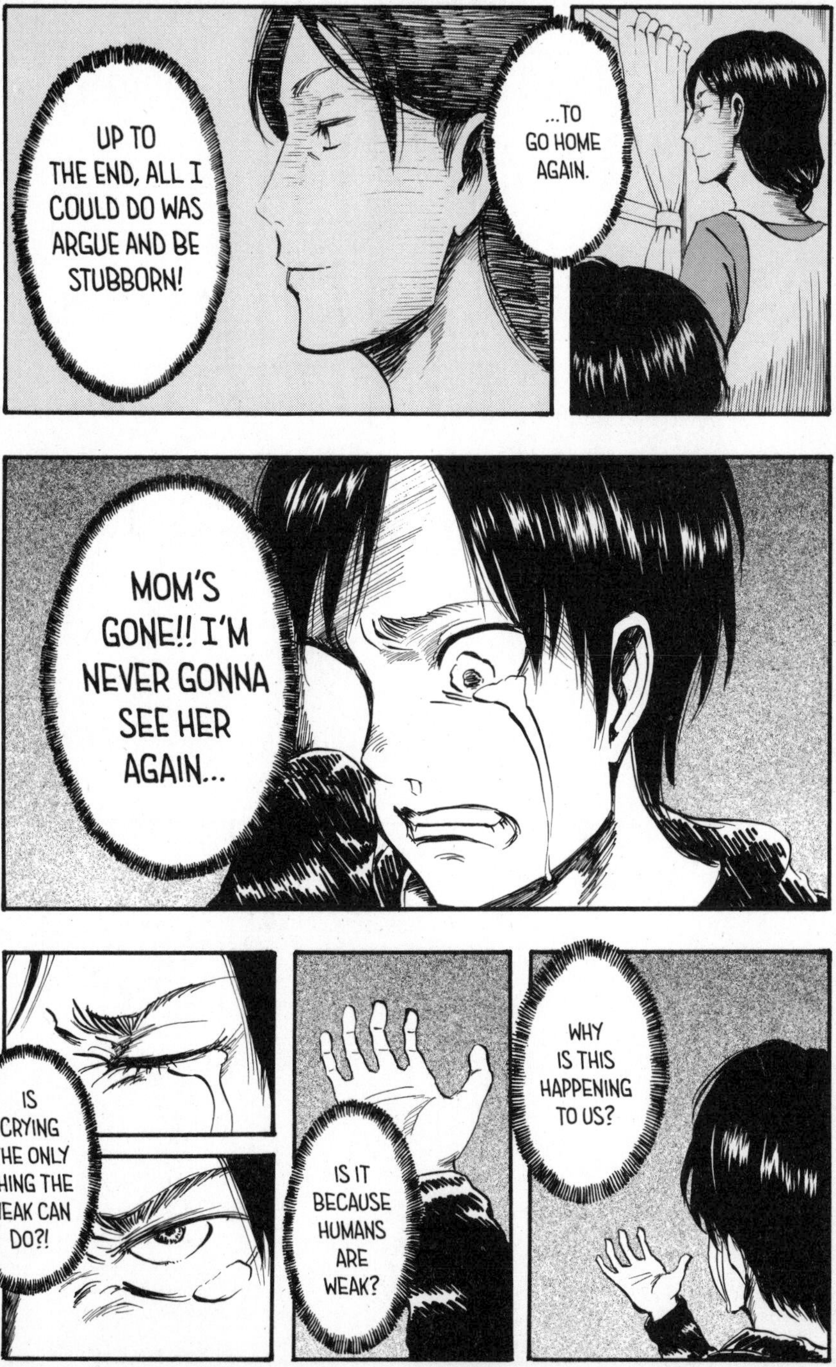
...TO GO HOME AGAIN.
UP TO THE END, ALL I COULD DO WAS ARGUE AND BE STUBBORN!
MOM'S GONE!! I'M NEVER GONNA SEE HER AGAIN...
WHY IS THIS HAPPENING TO US?
IS IT BECAUSE HUMANS ARE WEAK?
IS CRYING THE ONLY THING THE WEAK CAN DO?!

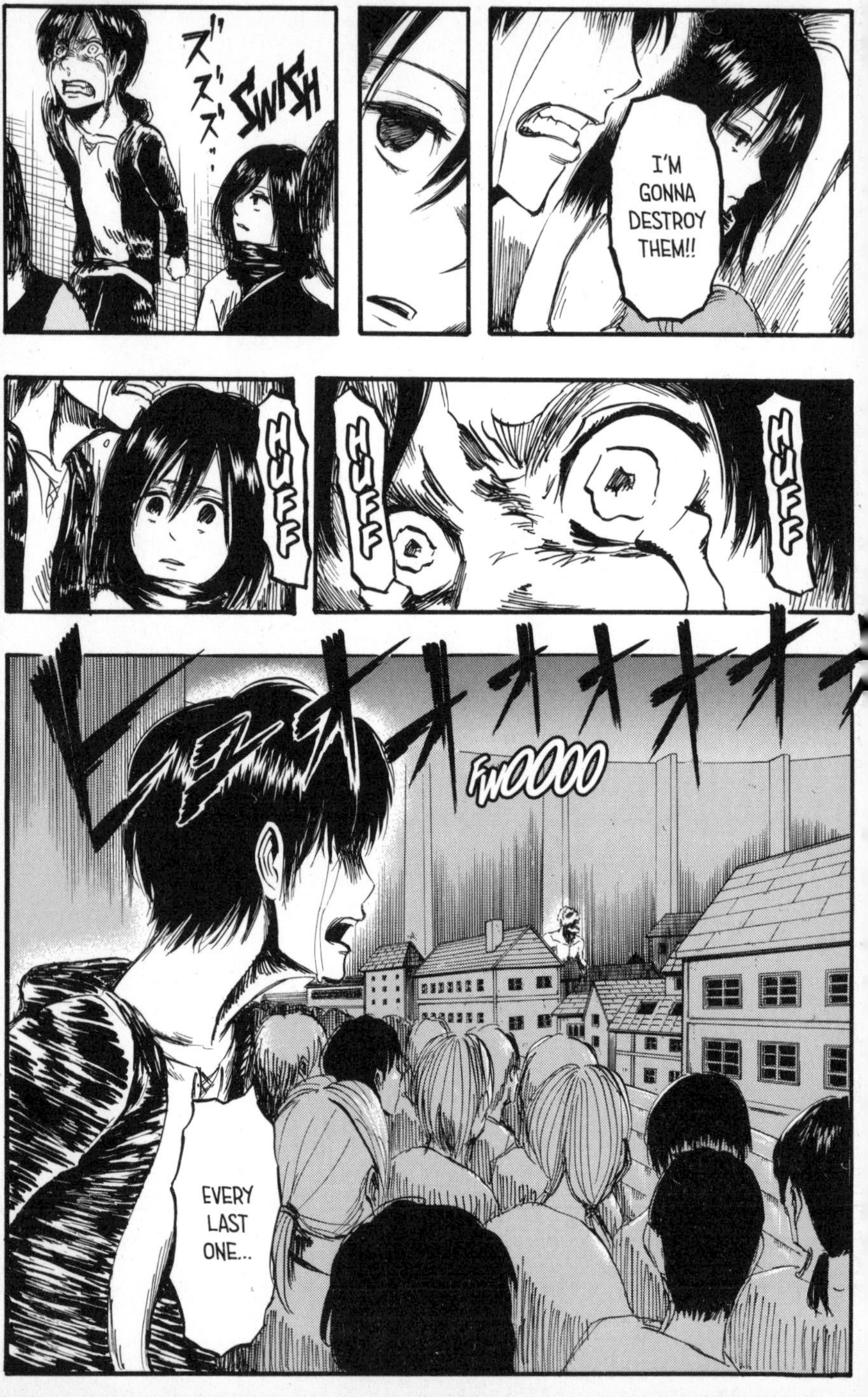
I'M GONNA DESTROY THEM!!
ズズズ‥
SWISH
HUFF
HUFF
HUFF
FWOOOO
EVERY LAST ONE...

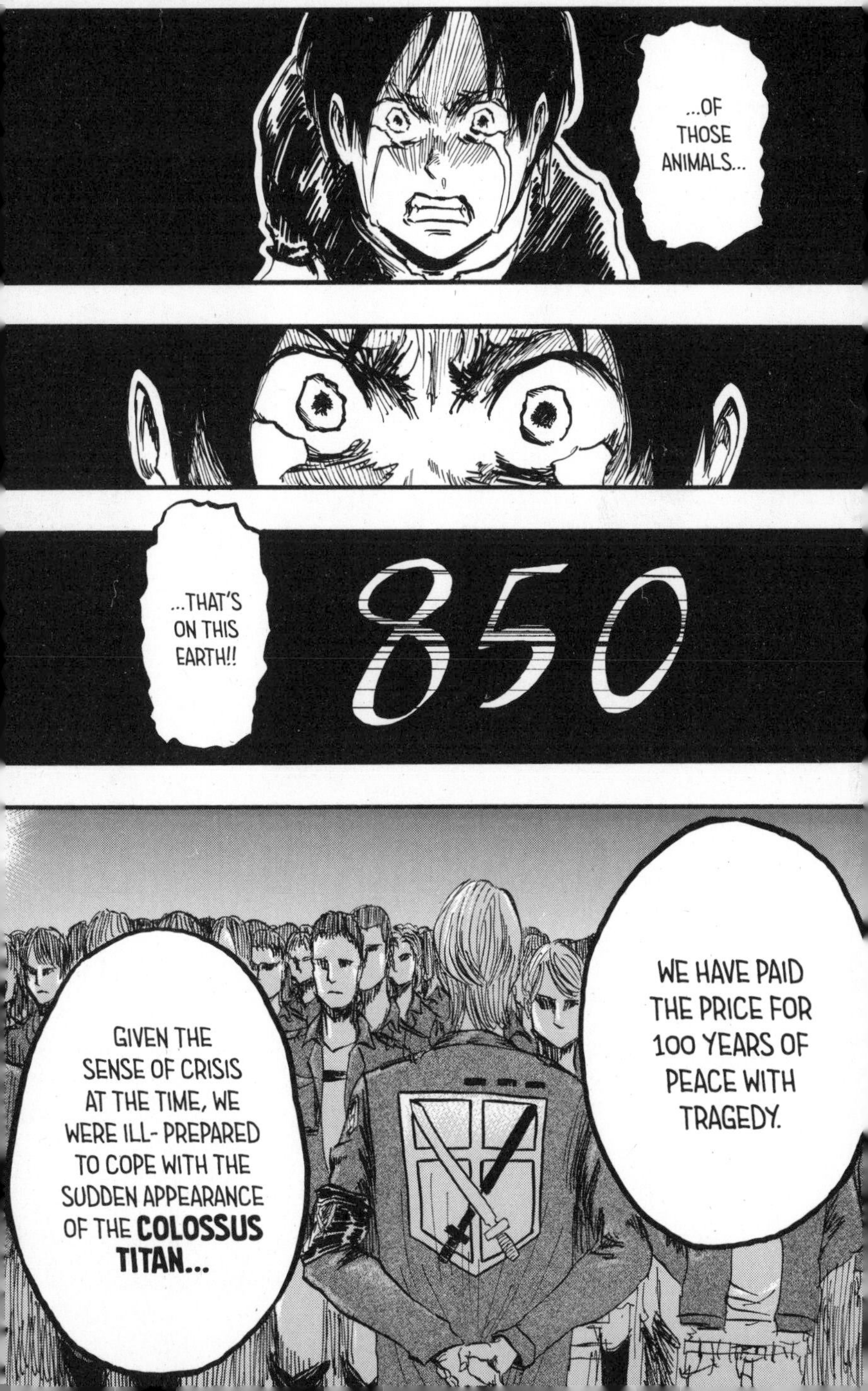
...OF THOSE ANIMALS...
...THAT'S ON THIS EARTH!!
850
WE HAVE PAID THE PRICE FOR 100 YEARS OF PEACE WITH TRAGEDY.
GIVEN THE SENSE OF CRISIS AT THE TIME, WE WERE ILL-PREPARED TO COPE WITH THE SUDDEN APPEARANCE OF THE **COLOSSUS TITAN...**

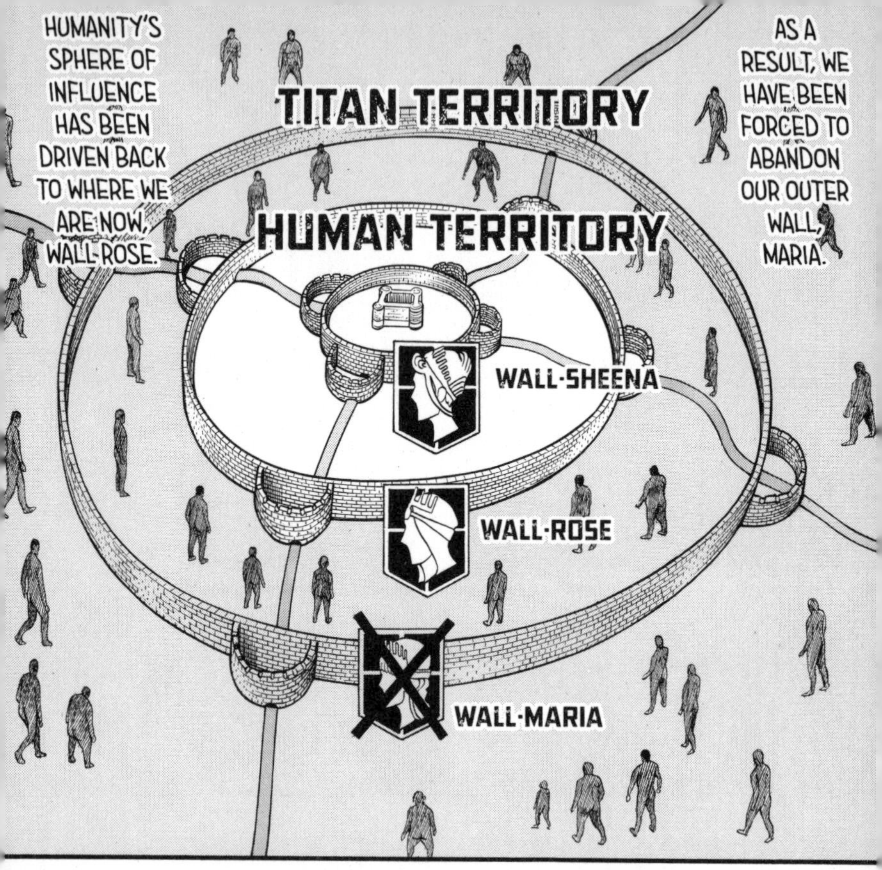
AS A RESULT, WE HAVE BEEN FORCED TO ABANDON OUR OUTER WALL, MARIA.
TITAN TERRITORY
HUMAN TERRITORY
WALL-SHEENA
WALL-ROSE
WALL-MARIA
HUMANITY'S SPHERE OF INFLUENCE HAS BEEN DRIVEN BACK TO WHERE WE ARE NOW, WALL-ROSE.

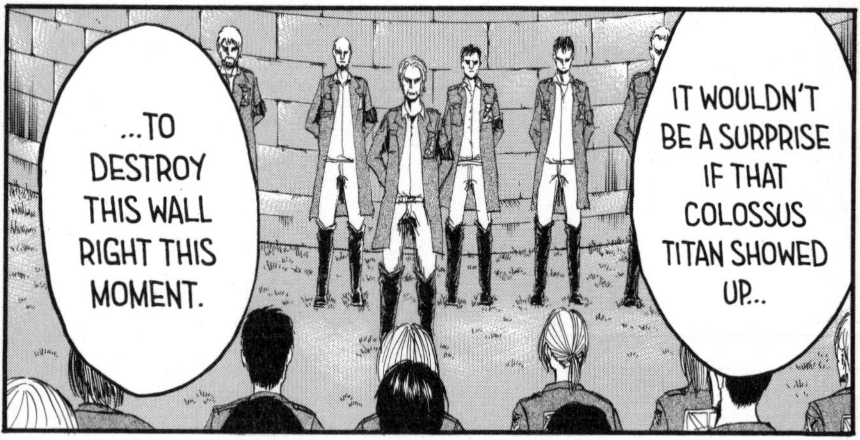
IT WOULDN'T BE A SURPRISE IF THAT COLOSSUS TITAN SHOWED UP...
...TO DESTROY THIS WALL RIGHT THIS MOMENT.

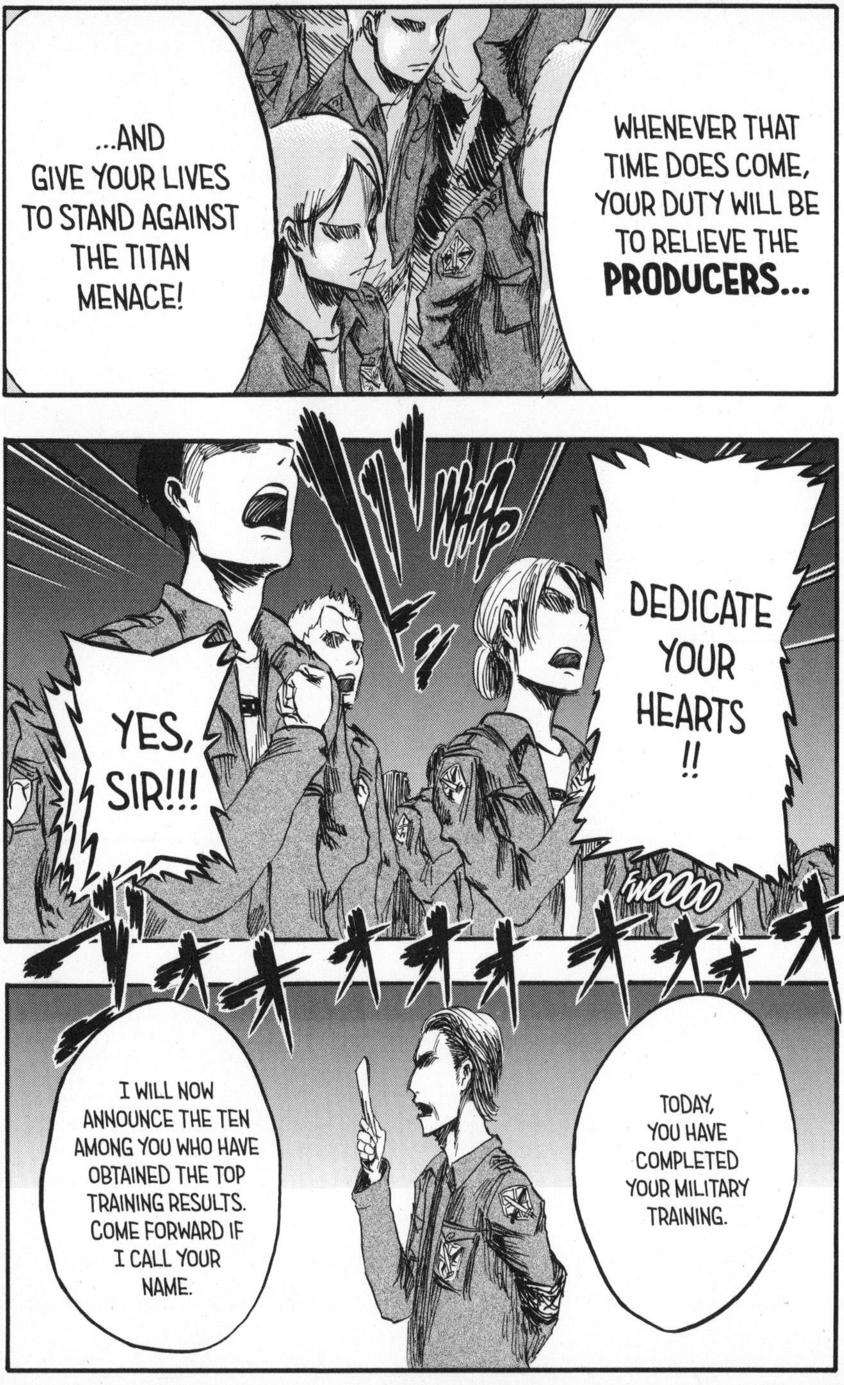
WHENEVER THAT TIME DOES COME, YOUR DUTY WILL BE TO RELIEVE THE **PRODUCERS...**
...AND GIVE YOUR LIVES TO STAND AGAINST THE TITAN MENACE!
DEDICATE YOUR HEARTS !!
YES, SIR!!!
FWOOOO
TODAY, YOU HAVE COMPLETED YOUR MILITARY TRAINING.
I WILL NOW ANNOUNCE THE TEN AMONG YOU WHO HAVE OBTAINED THE TOP TRAINING RESULTS. COME FORWARD IF I CALL YOUR NAME.

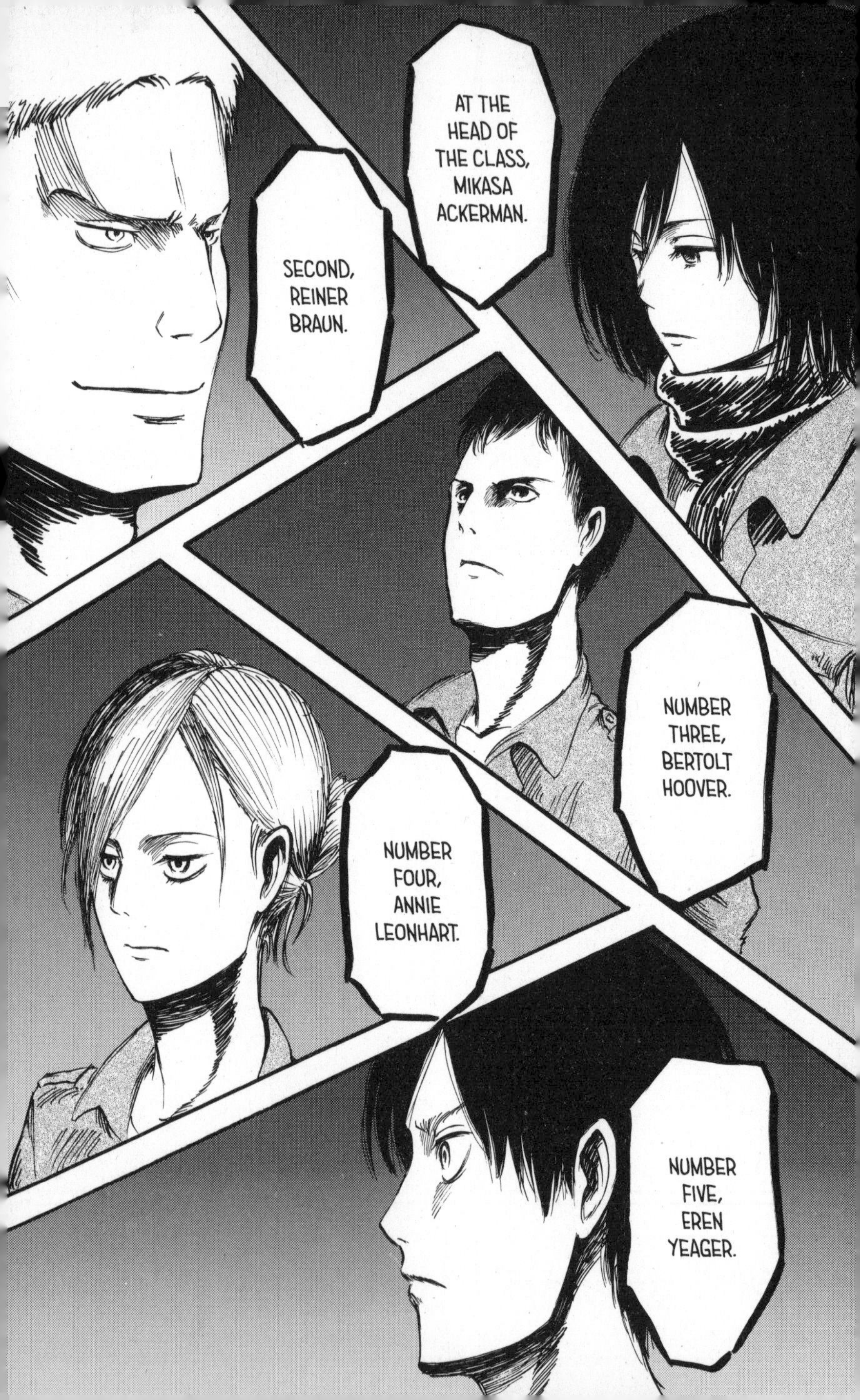
AT THE HEAD OF THE CLASS, MIKASA ACKERMAN.
SECOND, REINER BRAUN.
NUMBER THREE, BERTOLT HOOVER.
NUMBER FOUR, ANNIE LEONHART.
NUMBER FIVE, EREN YEAGER.

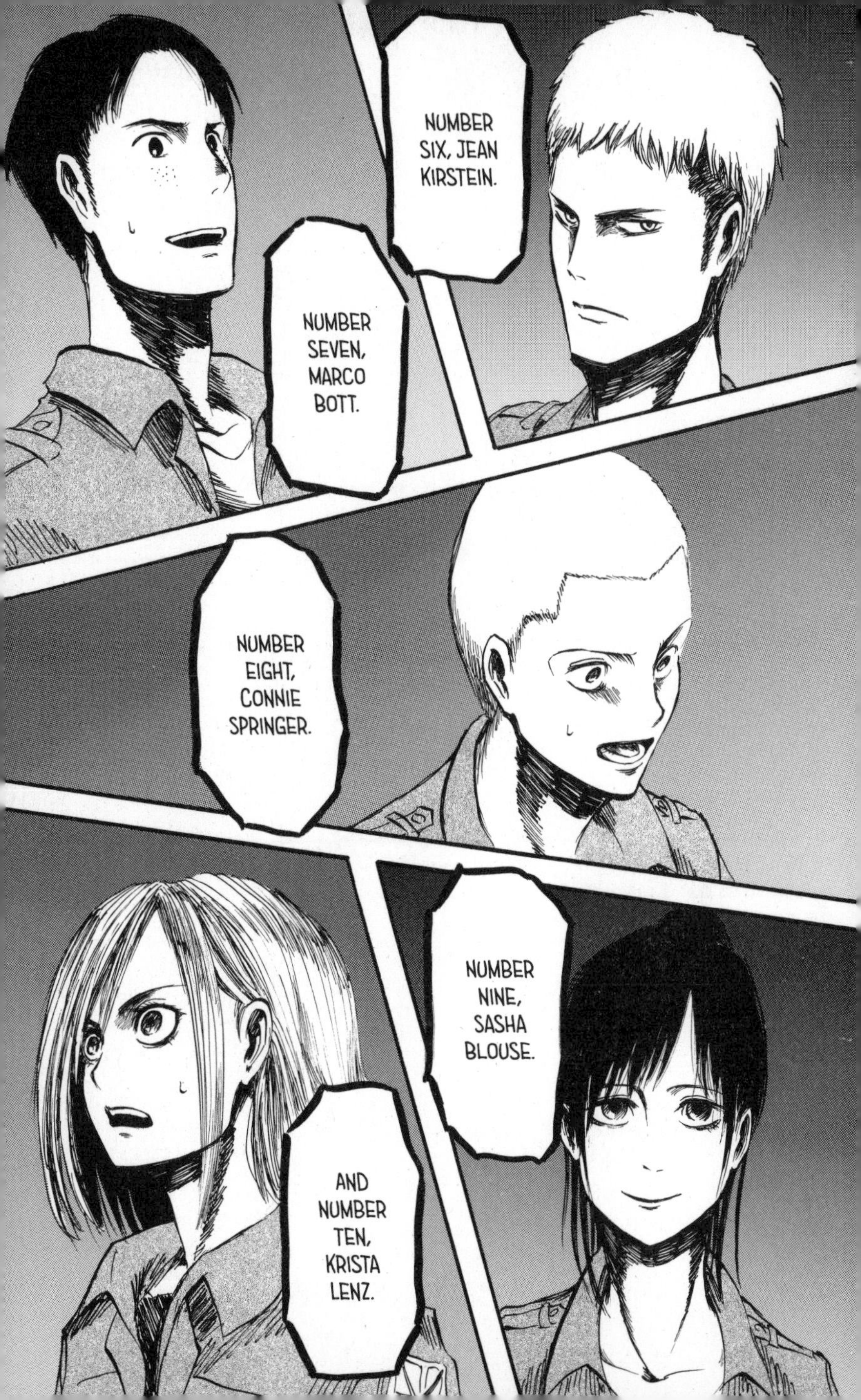
NUMBER SIX, JEAN KIRSTEIN.
NUMBER SEVEN, MARCO BOTT.
NUMBER EIGHT, CONNIE SPRINGER.
NUMBER NINE, SASHA BLOUSE.
AND NUMBER TEN, KRISTA LENZ.

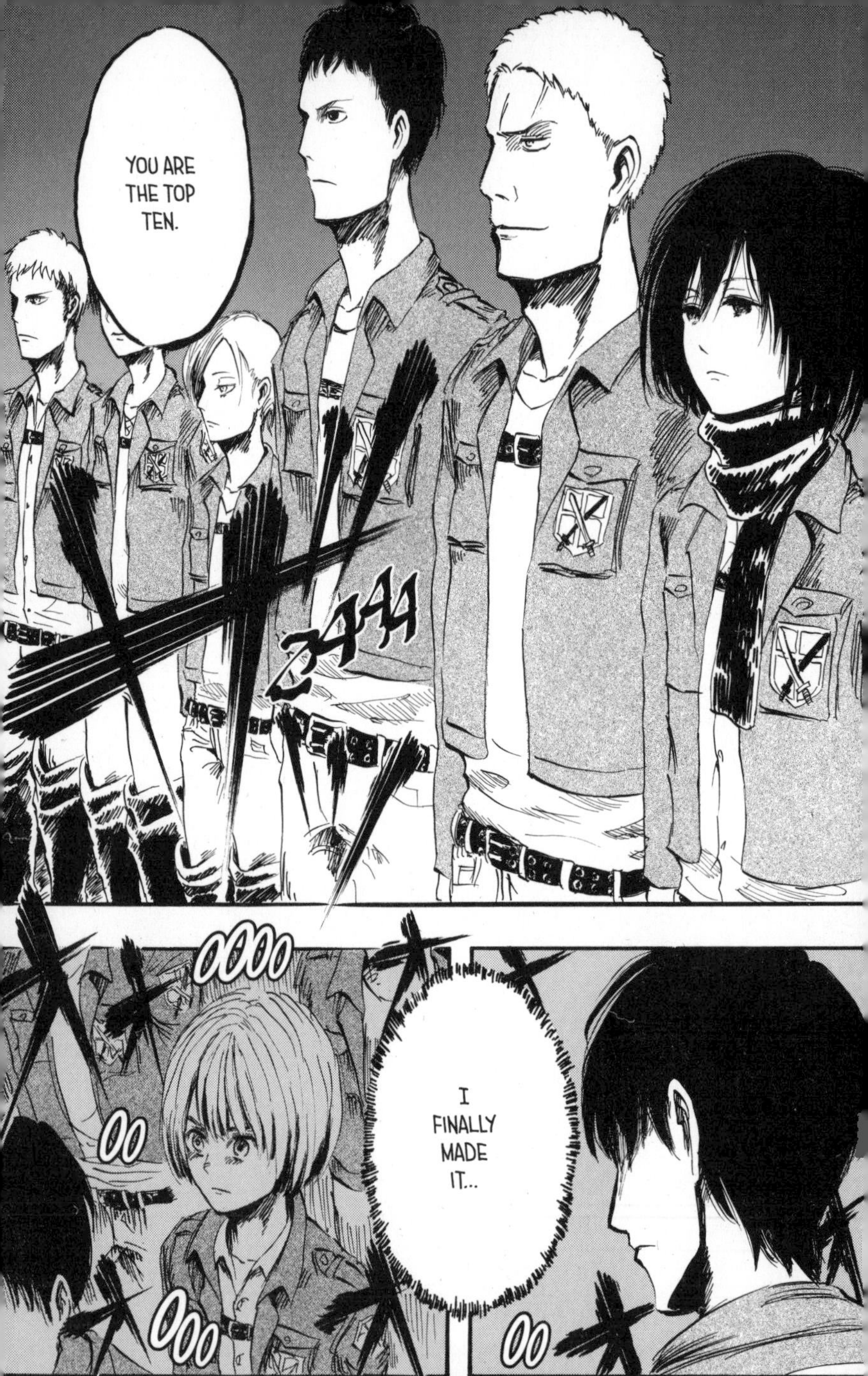
YOU ARE THE TOP TEN.
ZAAA
OO
I FINALLY MADE IT...
OOOO
OO
OOO

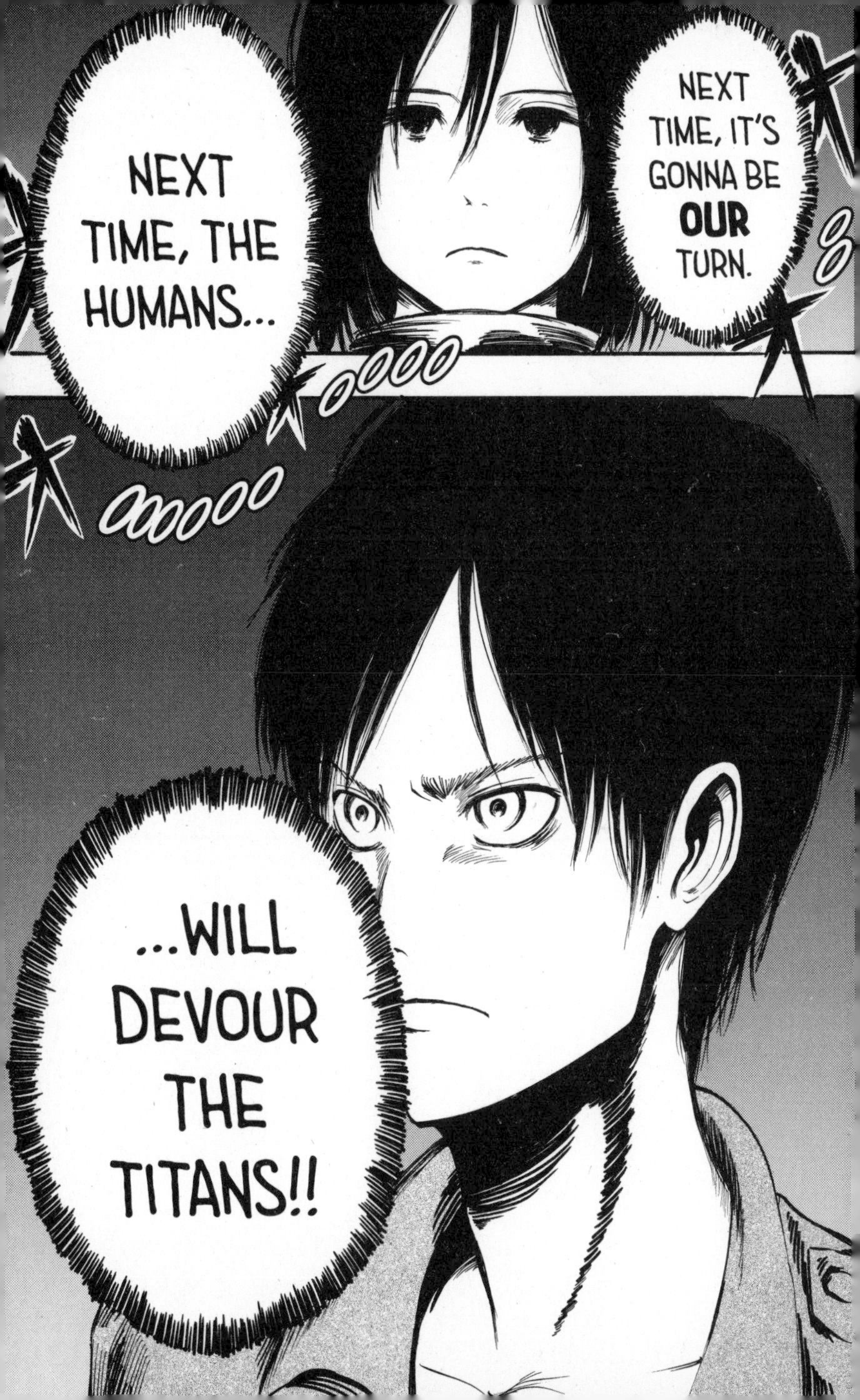
NEXT TIME, IT'S GONNA BE **OUR** TURN.
OO
NEXT TIME, THE HUMANS...
OOOO
OOOOOO
...WILL DEVOUR THE TITANS!!

Current Publicly Available Information

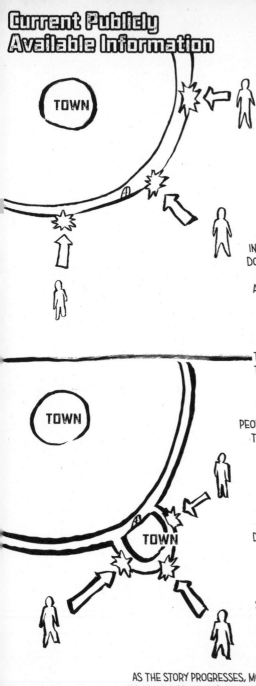

The reason for having a town jutting out of the main wall

IN THIS WORLD, WALL CONSTRUCTION IS A MATTER OF THE UTMOST IMPORTANCE.

AS ILLUSTRATED BY THE SIMPLE DIAGRAM ON THE LEFT, WITH A TOWN JUST BUILT INSIDE THE WALL, IN THE EVENT THAT THE TITANS BURST THROUGH, THE PEOPLE WOULD HAVE NO MEANS TO COPE WITH THE CRISIS. PUT SIMPLY, WITH SUCH A VAST CIRCUMFERENCE, PEOPLE WOULDN'T KNOW WHERE THE WALL WOULD BE BREACHED. AND NATURALLY, THERE AREN'T ENOUGH HUMANS TO SUPPORT A MILITARY FORCE THAT COULD MONITOR AND GUARD THE ENTIRE RINGED WALL.

IN OTHER WORDS, THE OBJECT IS TO NARROW DOWN THE TARGET. THIS STRATEGY KEEPS THE COST OF GUARDING THE WALL MANAGEABLE AND ALLOWS THE MILITARY TO CONSOLIDATE ITS FORCES. HOWEVER, WITHOUT HUMANS WITHIN THE WALL TO SERVE AS "BAIT" THAT WILL ATTRACT THE TITANS, THIS STRATEGY HAS NO CHANCE OF PAYING OFF. HAVING TROOPS GARRISONED AT THE TOWN GUARANTEES AN ECONOMIC BENEFIT FOR THE AREA, BUT THAT ECONOMIC ADVANTAGE FALLS SHORT WHEN COMPARED TO THE FEAR OF BEING EATEN BY A TITAN. THUS, NOT MANY PEOPLE ARE ENTHUSED ABOUT LIVING IN THESE TOWNS. THEREFORE, THE RULING MONARCHY PRAISES THE RESIDENTS OF THESE FRONT-LINE TOWNS AS "THE BRAVEST OF WARRIORS" IN AN ATTEMPT TO DRUM UP MORE VOLUNTEERS.

A BIT OF HISTORY: SINCE THE STRENGTH OF THE GATES THAT CONNECT THE HUMAN DOMAIN TO THE TITANS' TERRITORY OUTSIDE THE WALLS IS INFERIOR TO THAT OF THE WALL ITSELF, THERE WAS A PROPOSAL BY CONSERVATIVES TO SEAL THE GATES OFF ENTIRELY. HOWEVER, REFORMISTS SUCCESSFULLY ARGUED THAT "ABANDONING THE GATES TO THE OUTSIDE WORLD IS TANTAMOUNT TO ABANDONING THE WILL OF THE HUMAN RACE TO RECLAIM ITS DOMINION" AND THE PLAN WAS HALTED.

AS THE STORY PROGRESSES, MORE LIGHT WILL BE SHED ON HOW THE WALL WAS INITIALLY BUILT AND THE SITUATION AT THE TIME OF ITS CONSTRUCTION.

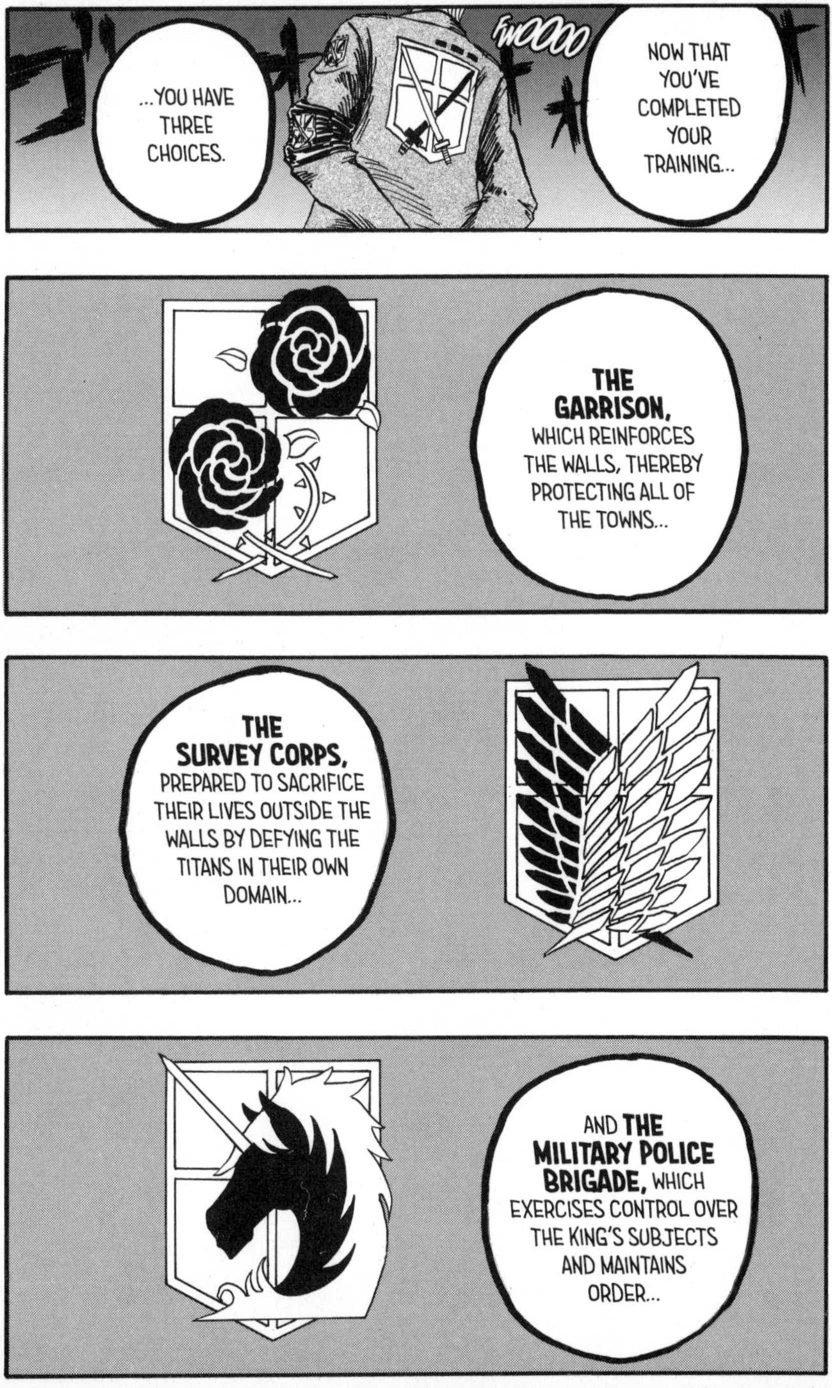
NOW THAT YOU'VE COMPLETED YOUR TRAINING...
FWOOOO
...YOU HAVE THREE CHOICES.
THE GARRISON, WHICH REINFORCES THE WALLS, THEREBY PROTECTING ALL OF THE TOWNS...
THE SURVEY CORPS, PREPARED TO SACRIFICE THEIR LIVES OUTSIDE THE WALLS BY DEFYING THE TITANS IN THEIR OWN DOMAIN...
AND THE MILITARY POLICE BRIGADE, WHICH EXERCISES CONTROL OVER THE KING'S SUBJECTS AND MAINTAINS ORDER...

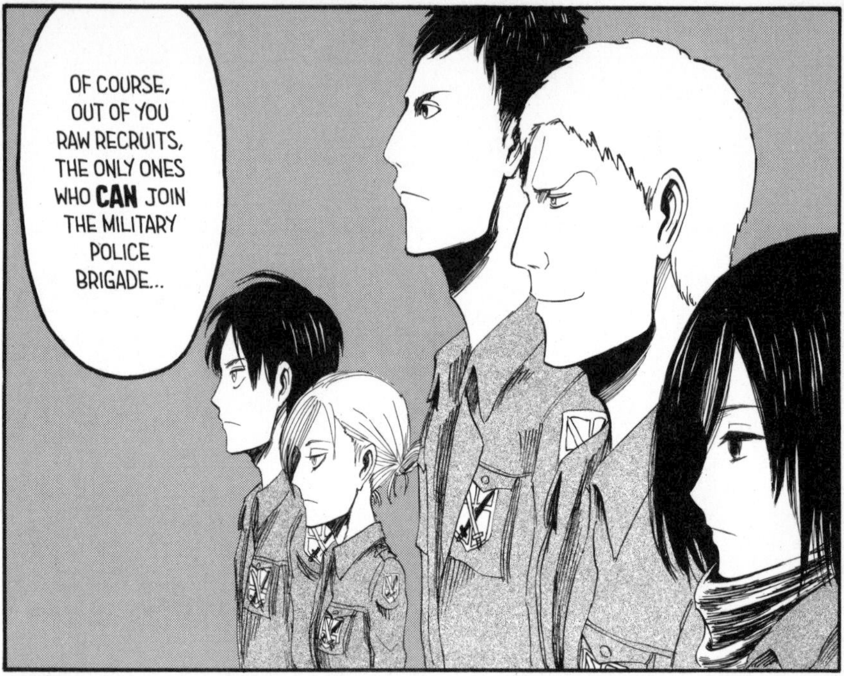
OF COURSE, OUT OF YOU RAW RECRUITS, THE ONLY ONES WHO CAN JOIN THE MILITARY POLICE BRIGADE...
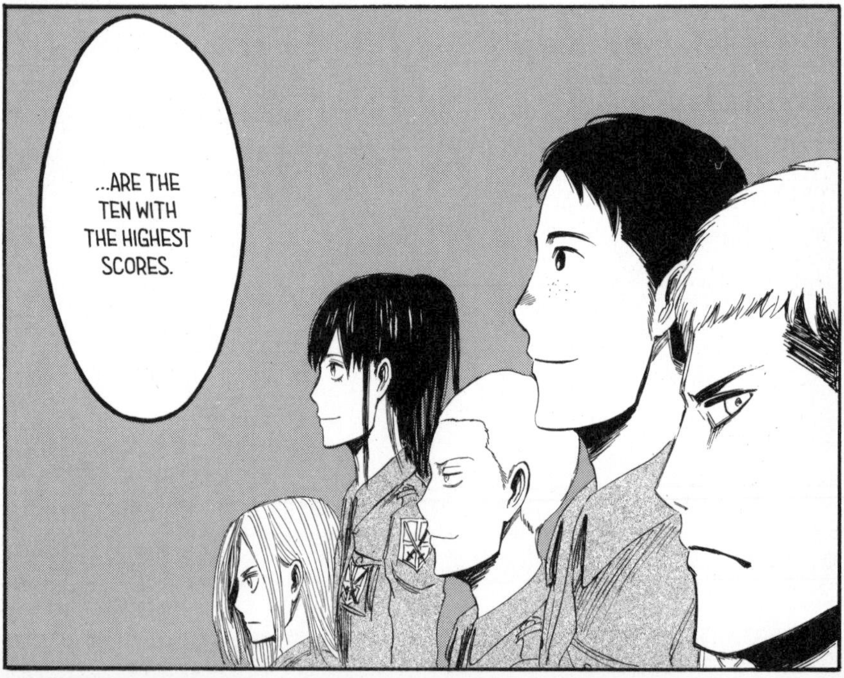
...ARE THE TEN WITH THE HIGHEST SCORES.

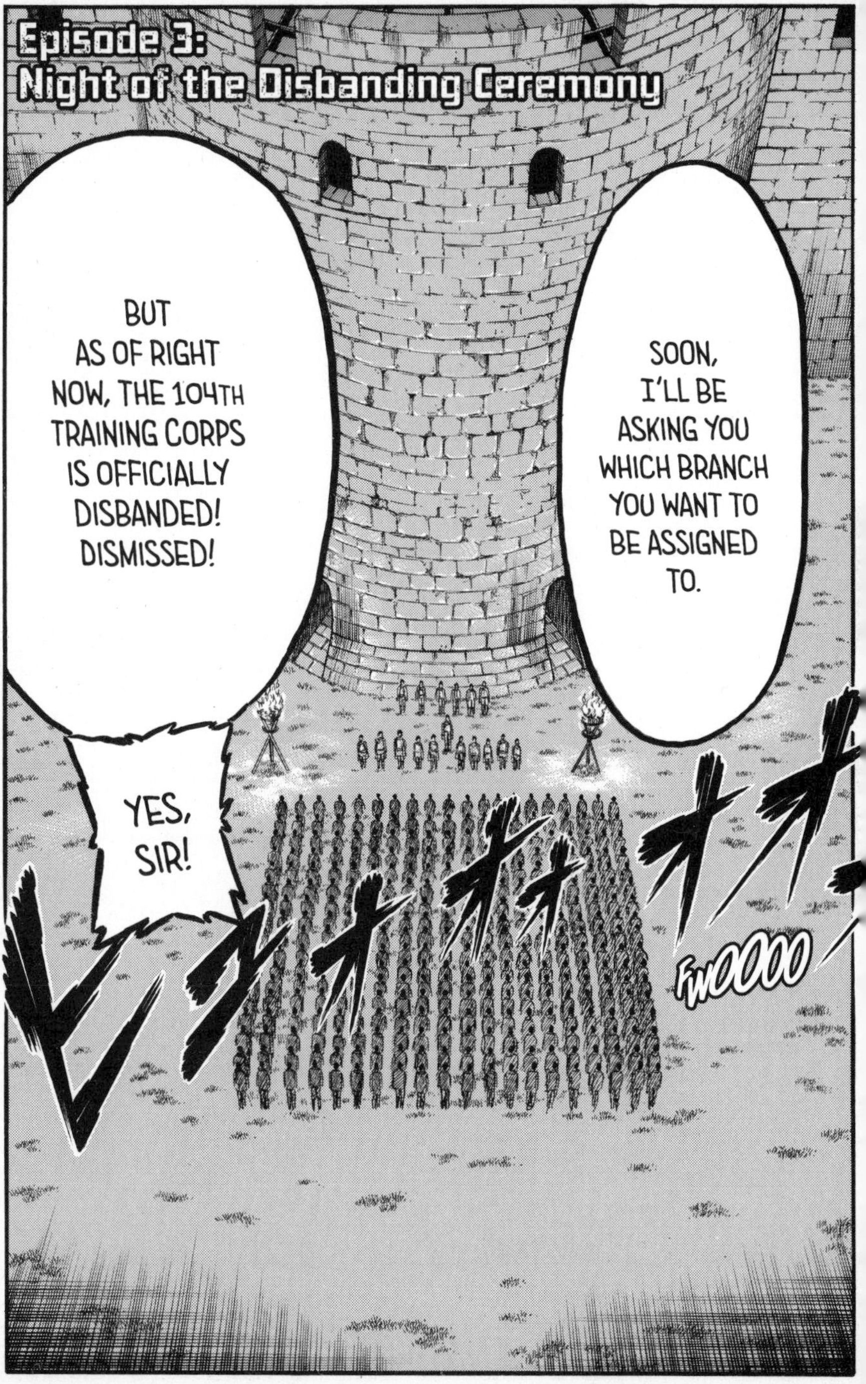
Episode 3:
Night of the Disbanding Ceremony
SOON, I'LL BE ASKING YOU WHICH BRANCH YOU WANT TO BE ASSIGNED TO.
BUT AS OF RIGHT NOW, THE 104TH TRAINING CORPS IS OFFICIALLY DISBANDED! DISMISSED!
YES, SIR!
FWOOOO

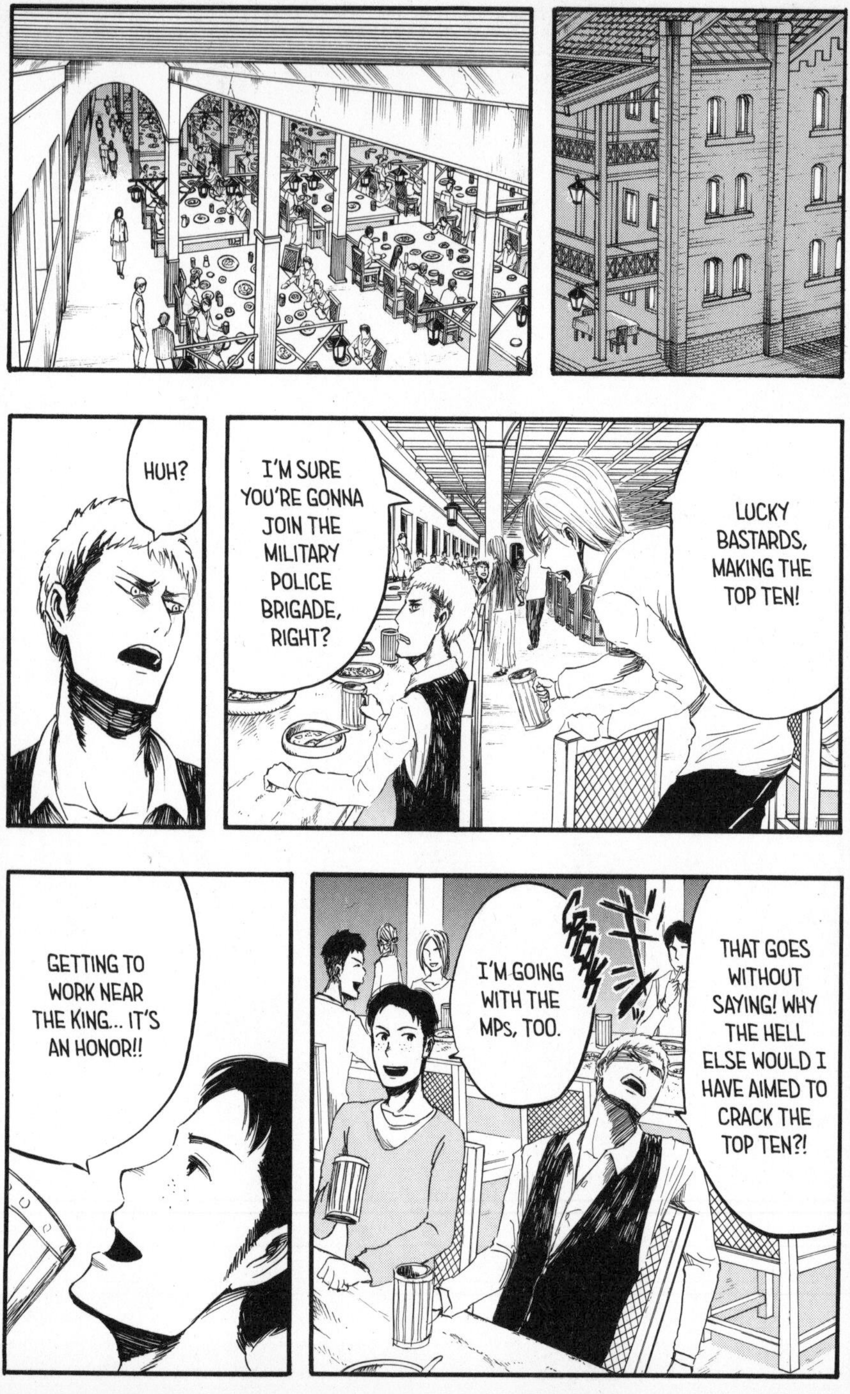
LUCKY BASTARDS, MAKING THE TOP TEN!
I'M SURE YOU'RE GONNA JOIN THE MILITARY POLICE BRIGADE, RIGHT?
HUH?
THAT GOES WITHOUT SAYING! WHY THE HELL ELSE WOULD I HAVE AIMED TO CRACK THE TOP TEN?!
CREAK
I'M GOING WITH THE MPs, TOO.
GETTING TO WORK NEAR THE KING... IT'S AN HONOR!!

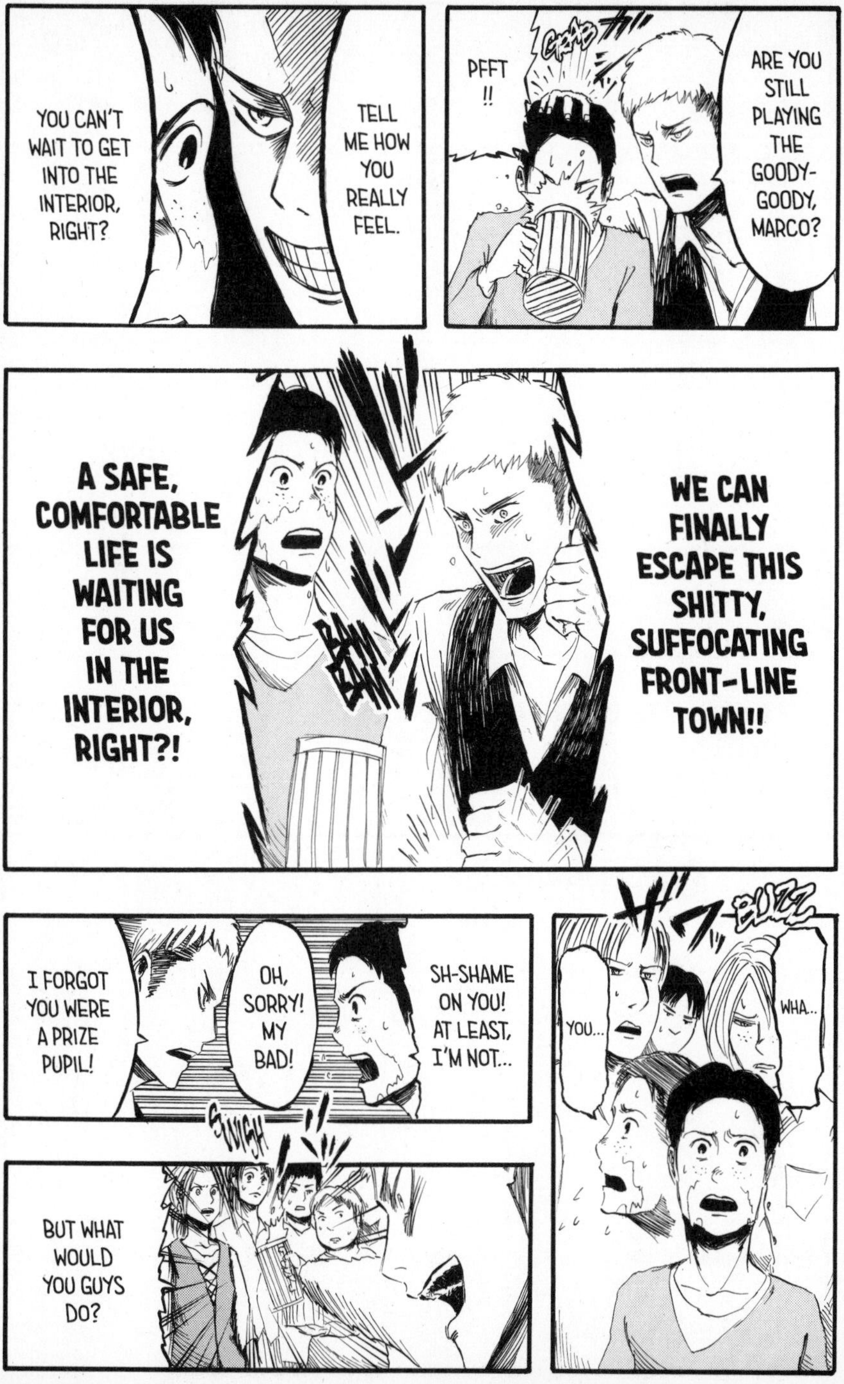
ARE YOU STILL PLAYING THE GOODY-GOODY, MARCO?
GRAB
PFFT !!
TELL ME HOW YOU REALLY FEEL.
YOU CAN'T WAIT TO GET INTO THE INTERIOR, RIGHT?
WE CAN FINALLY ESCAPE THIS SHITTY, SUFFOCATING FRONT-LINE TOWN!!
BAM BAM
A SAFE, COMFORTABLE LIFE IS WAITING FOR US IN THE INTERIOR, RIGHT?!
BUZZ
WHA...
YOU...
SH-SHAME ON YOU! AT LEAST, I'M NOT...
OH, SORRY! MY BAD!
I FORGOT YOU WERE A PRIZE PUPIL!
BUT WHAT WOULD YOU GUYS DO?

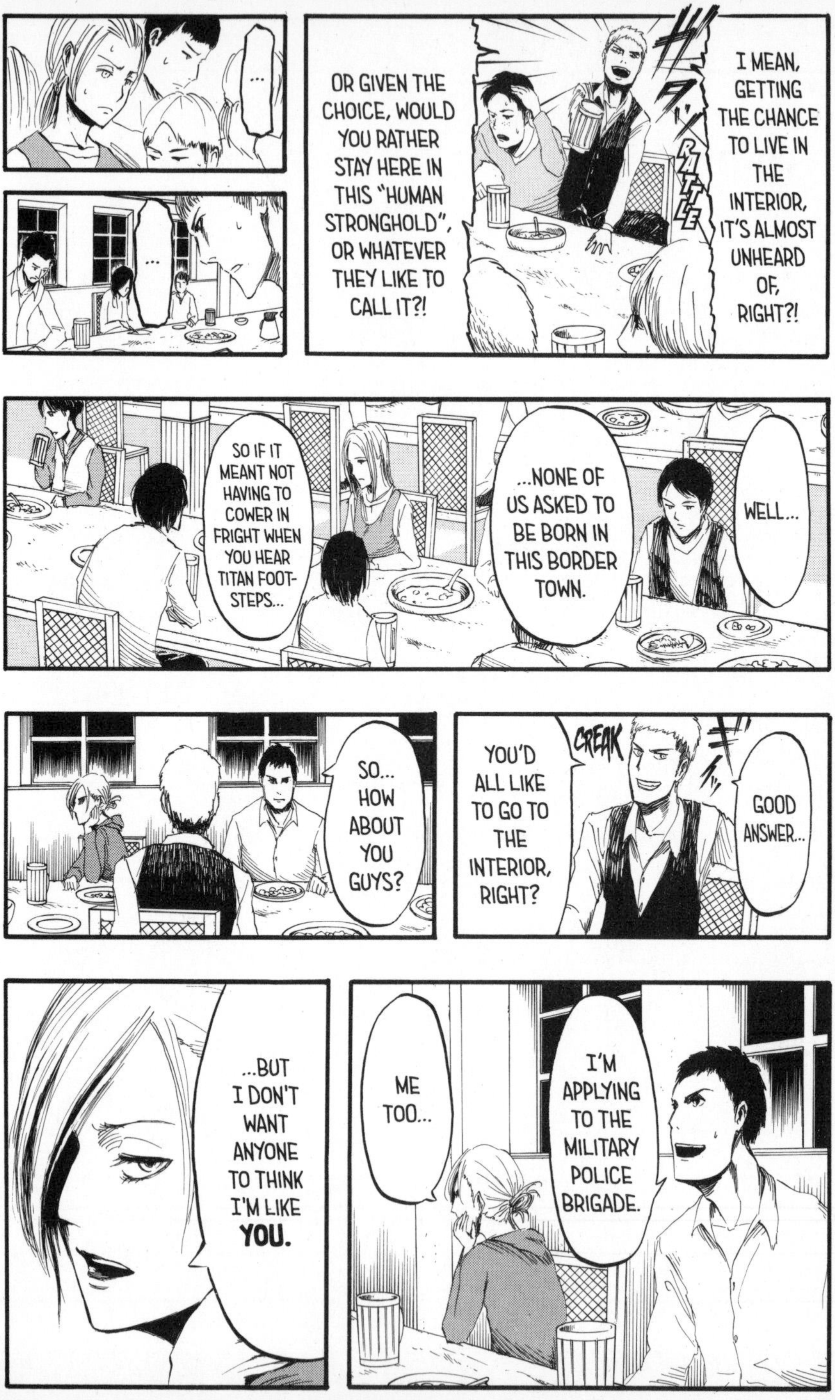
I MEAN, GETTING THE CHANCE TO LIVE IN THE INTERIOR, IT'S ALMOST UNHEARD OF, RIGHT?!
RATTLE
OR GIVEN THE CHOICE, WOULD YOU RATHER STAY HERE IN THIS "HUMAN STRONGHOLD", OR WHATEVER THEY LIKE TO CALL IT?!
...
...
WELL...
...NONE OF US ASKED TO BE BORN IN THIS BORDER TOWN.
SO IF IT MEANT NOT HAVING TO COWER IN FRIGHT WHEN YOU HEAR TITAN FOOT-STEPS...
GOOD ANSWER...
CREAK
YOU'D ALL LIKE TO GO TO THE INTERIOR, RIGHT?
SO... HOW ABOUT YOU GUYS?
I'M APPLYING TO THE MILITARY POLICE BRIGADE.
ME TOO...
...BUT I DON'T WANT ANYONE TO THINK I'M LIKE **YOU.**

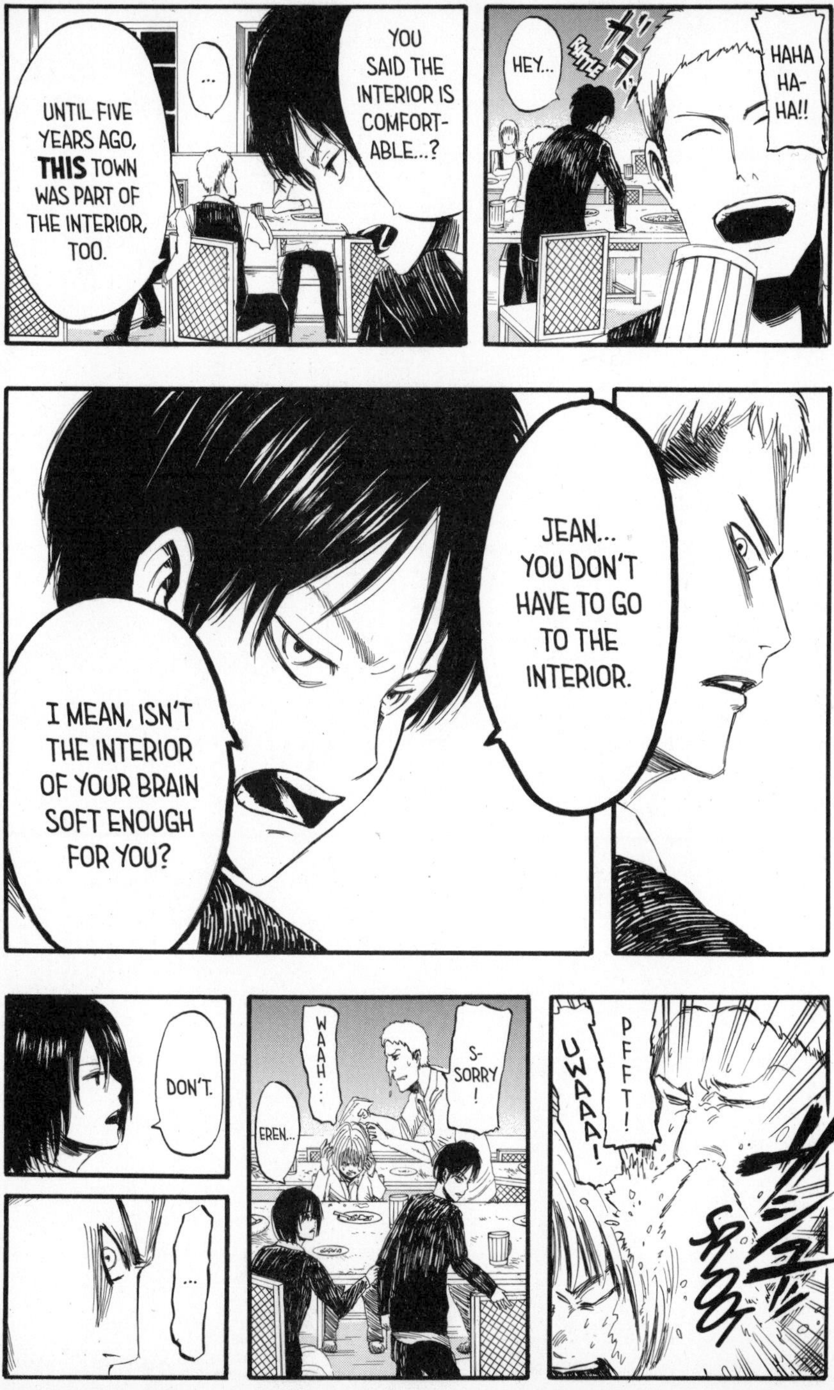
HAHA HA-HA!!
RATTLE
HEY...
YOU SAID THE INTERIOR IS COMFORT-ABLE...?
...
UNTIL FIVE YEARS AGO, **THIS** TOWN WAS PART OF THE INTERIOR, TOO.
JEAN... YOU DON'T HAVE TO GO TO THE INTERIOR.
I MEAN, ISN'T THE INTERIOR OF YOUR BRAIN SOFT ENOUGH FOR YOU?
PFFT!
UWAAA!
S-SORRY!
WAAH...
EREN...
DON'T.
...

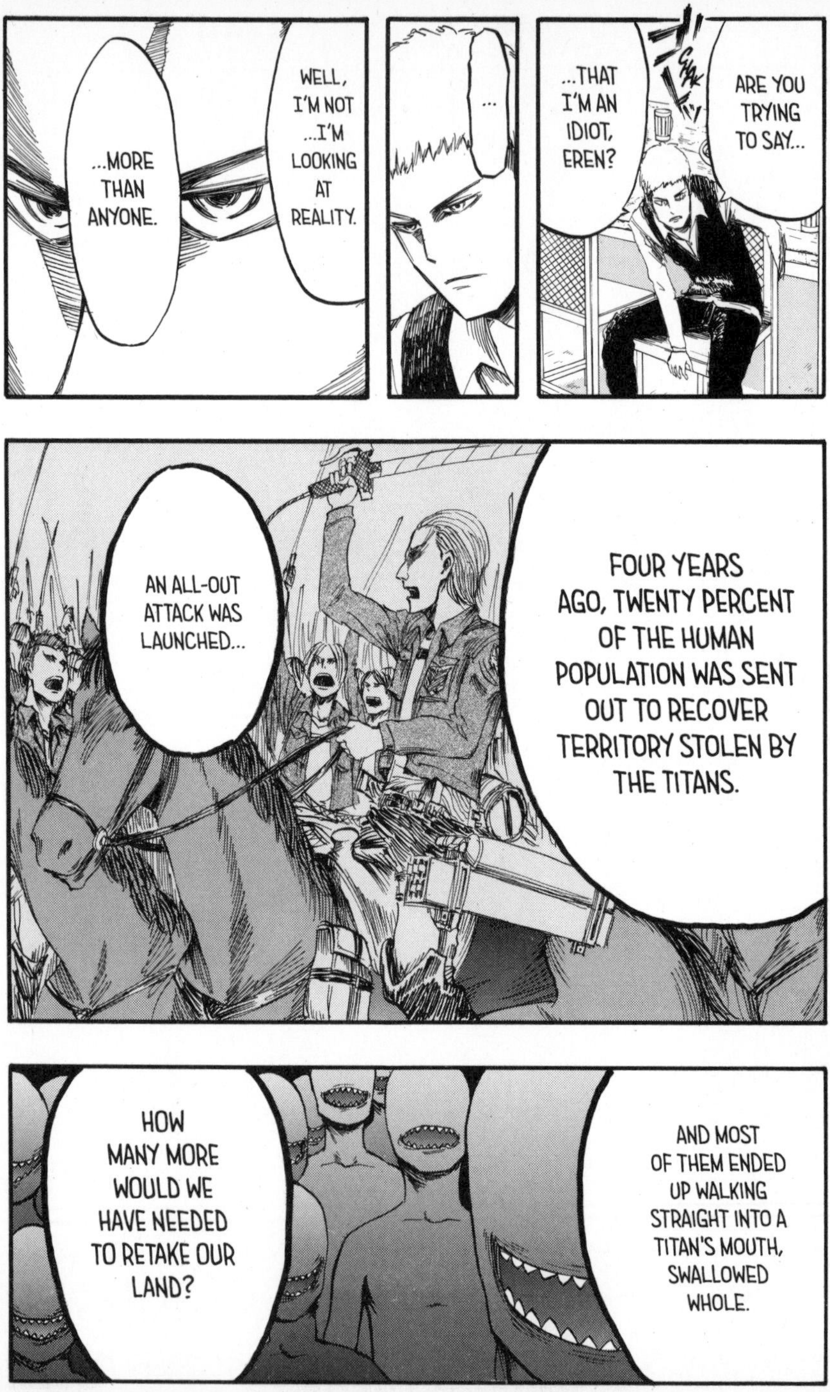
ARE YOU TRYING TO SAY...
...THAT I'M AN IDIOT, EREN?
...
WELL, I'M NOT ...I'M LOOKING AT REALITY.
...MORE THAN ANYONE.
FOUR YEARS AGO, TWENTY PERCENT OF THE HUMAN POPULATION WAS SENT OUT TO RECOVER TERRITORY STOLEN BY THE TITANS.
AN ALL-OUT ATTACK WAS LAUNCHED...
AND MOST OF THEM ENDED UP WALKING STRAIGHT INTO A TITAN'S MOUTH, SWALLOWED WHOLE.
HOW MANY MORE WOULD WE HAVE NEEDED TO RETAKE OUR LAND?

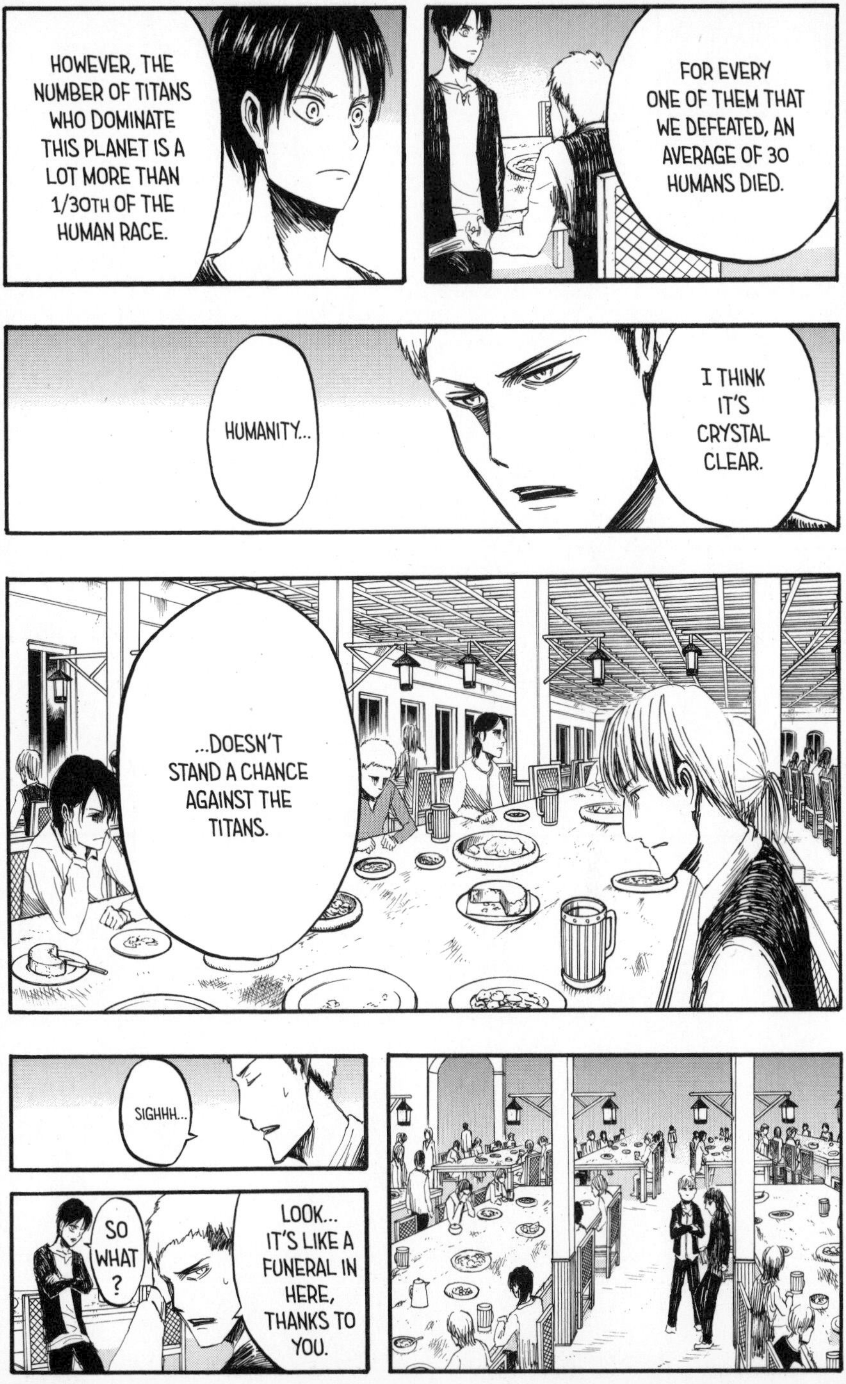
FOR EVERY ONE OF THEM THAT WE DEFEATED, AN AVERAGE OF 30 HUMANS DIED.
HOWEVER, THE NUMBER OF TITANS WHO DOMINATE THIS PLANET IS A LOT MORE THAN 1/30TH OF THE HUMAN RACE.
I THINK IT'S CRYSTAL CLEAR.
HUMANITY...
...DOESN'T STAND A CHANCE AGAINST THE TITANS.
SIGHHH...
LOOK... IT'S LIKE A FUNERAL IN HERE, THANKS TO YOU.
SO WHAT?

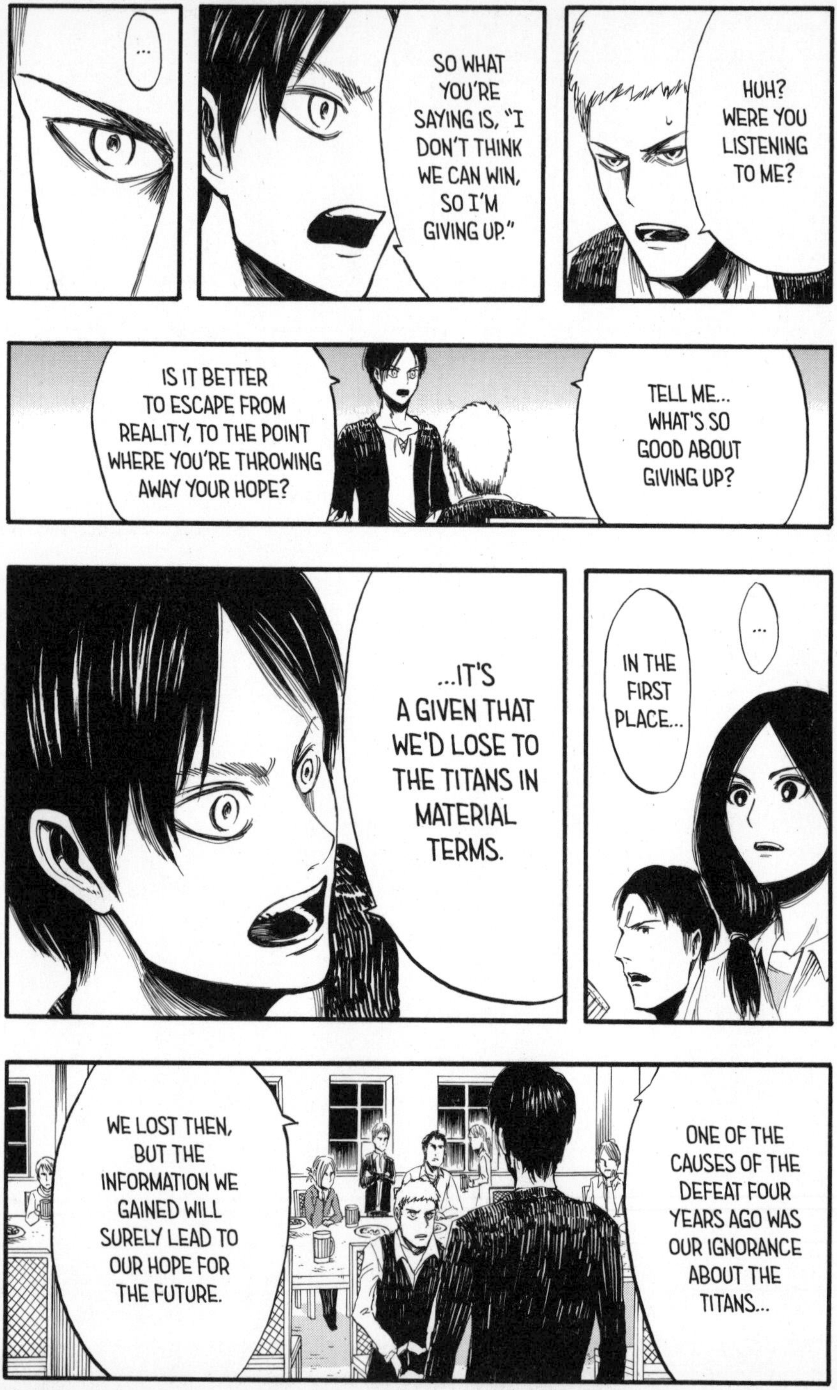
HUH? WERE YOU LISTENING TO ME?
SO WHAT YOU'RE SAYING IS, "I DON'T THINK WE CAN WIN, SO I'M GIVING UP."
...
TELL ME... WHAT'S SO GOOD ABOUT GIVING UP?
IS IT BETTER TO ESCAPE FROM REALITY, TO THE POINT WHERE YOU'RE THROWING AWAY YOUR HOPE?
...
IN THE FIRST PLACE...
...IT'S A GIVEN THAT WE'D LOSE TO THE TITANS IN MATERIAL TERMS.
ONE OF THE CAUSES OF THE DEFEAT FOUR YEARS AGO WAS OUR IGNORANCE ABOUT THE TITANS...
WE LOST THEN, BUT THE INFORMATION WE GAINED WILL SURELY LEAD TO OUR HOPE FOR THE FUTURE.

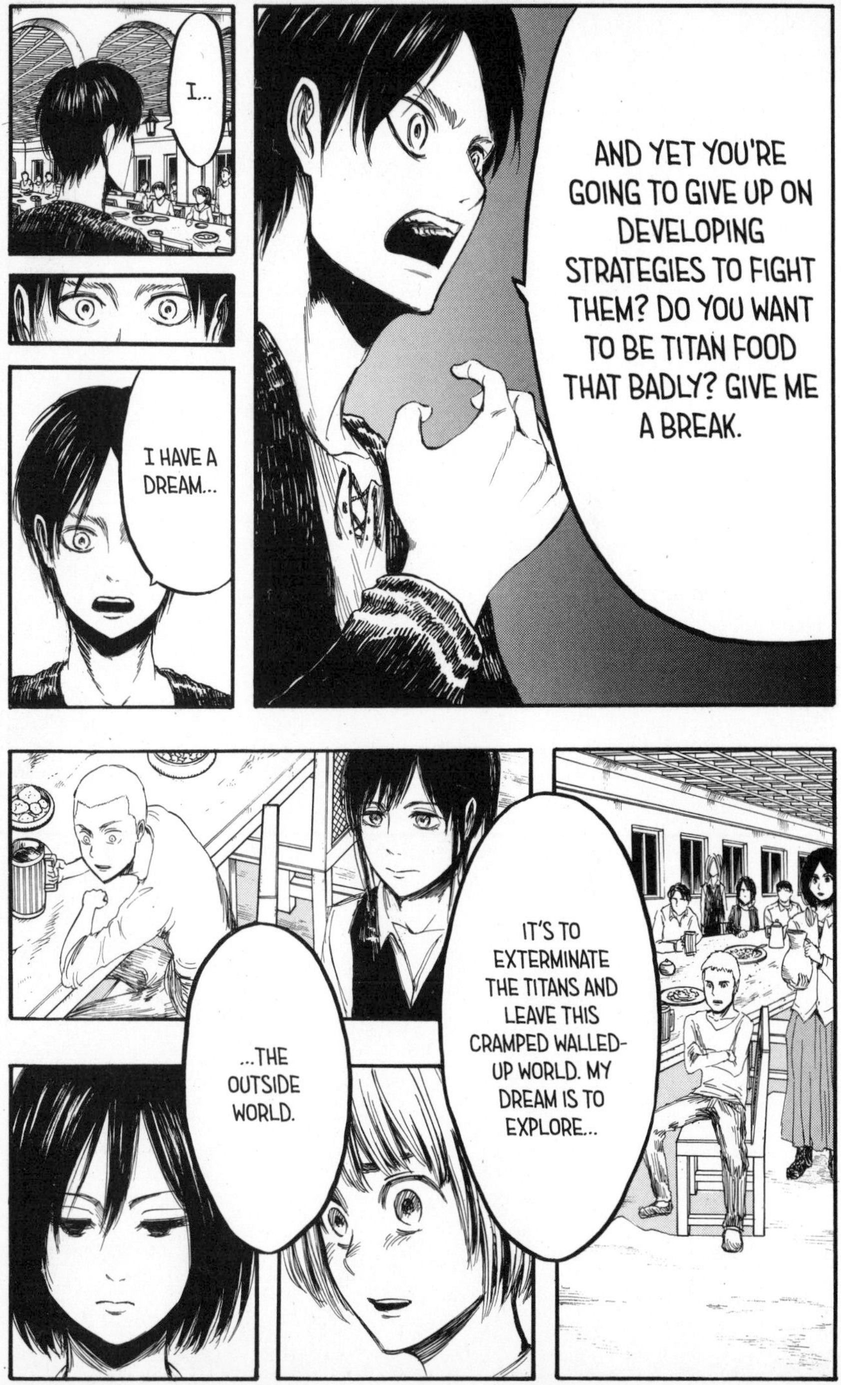
AND YET YOU'RE GOING TO GIVE UP ON DEVELOPING STRATEGIES TO FIGHT THEM? DO YOU WANT TO BE TITAN FOOD THAT BADLY? GIVE ME A BREAK.
I...
I HAVE A DREAM...
IT'S TO EXTERMINATE THE TITANS AND LEAVE THIS CRAMPED WALLED-UP WORLD. MY DREAM IS TO EXPLORE...
...THE OUTSIDE WORLD.

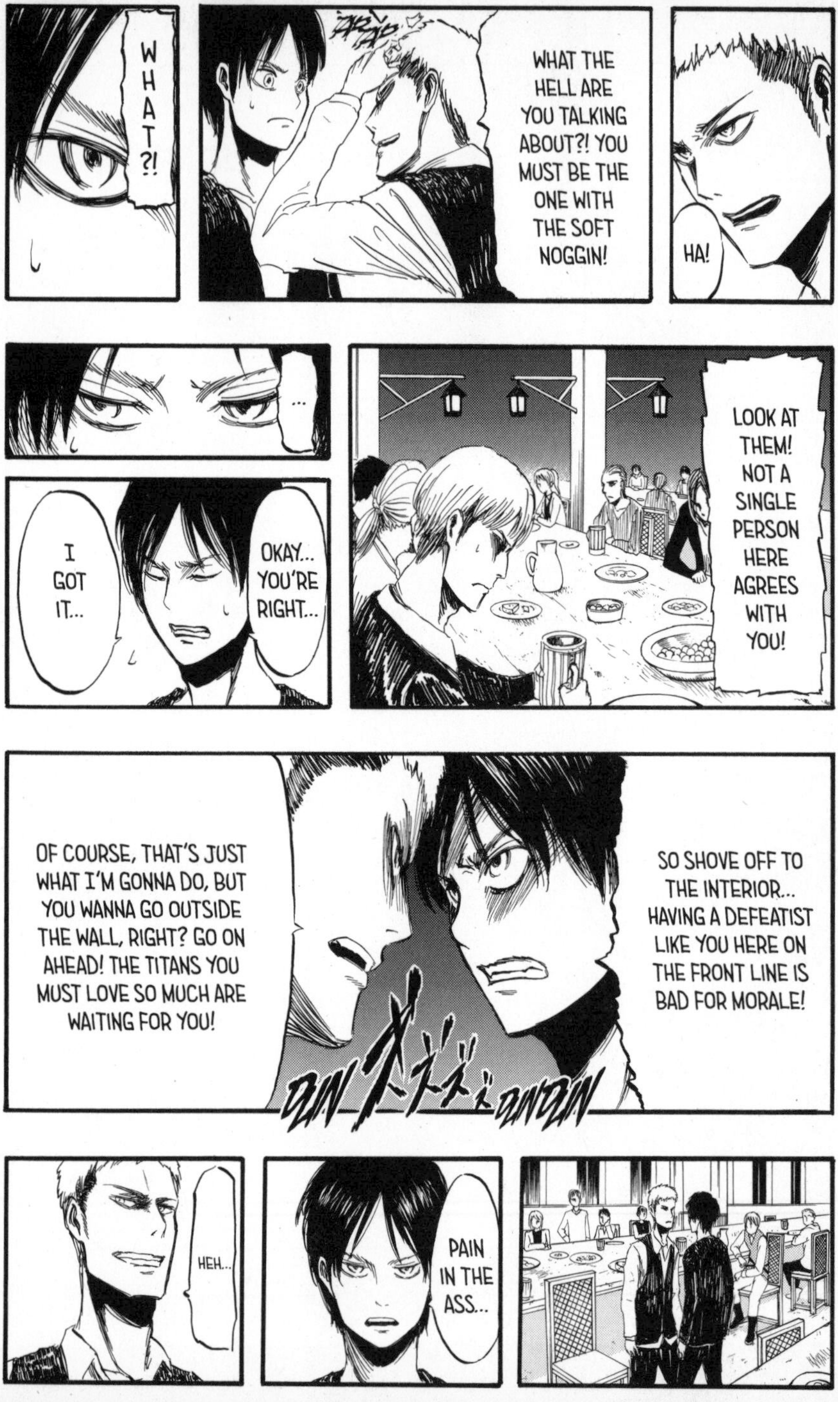
HA!
WHAT THE HELL ARE YOU TALKING ABOUT?! YOU MUST BE THE ONE WITH THE SOFT NOGGIN!
WHAT?!
LOOK AT THEM! NOT A SINGLE PERSON HERE AGREES WITH YOU!
...
OKAY... YOU'RE RIGHT...
I GOT IT...
SO SHOVE OFF TO THE INTERIOR... HAVING A DEFEATIST LIKE YOU HERE ON THE FRONT LINE IS BAD FOR MORALE!
OF COURSE, THAT'S JUST WHAT I'M GONNA DO, BUT YOU WANNA GO OUTSIDE THE WALL, RIGHT? GO ON AHEAD! THE TITANS YOU MUST LOVE SO MUCH ARE WAITING FOR YOU!
DUN
DUNDUN
PAIN IN THE ASS...
HEH...

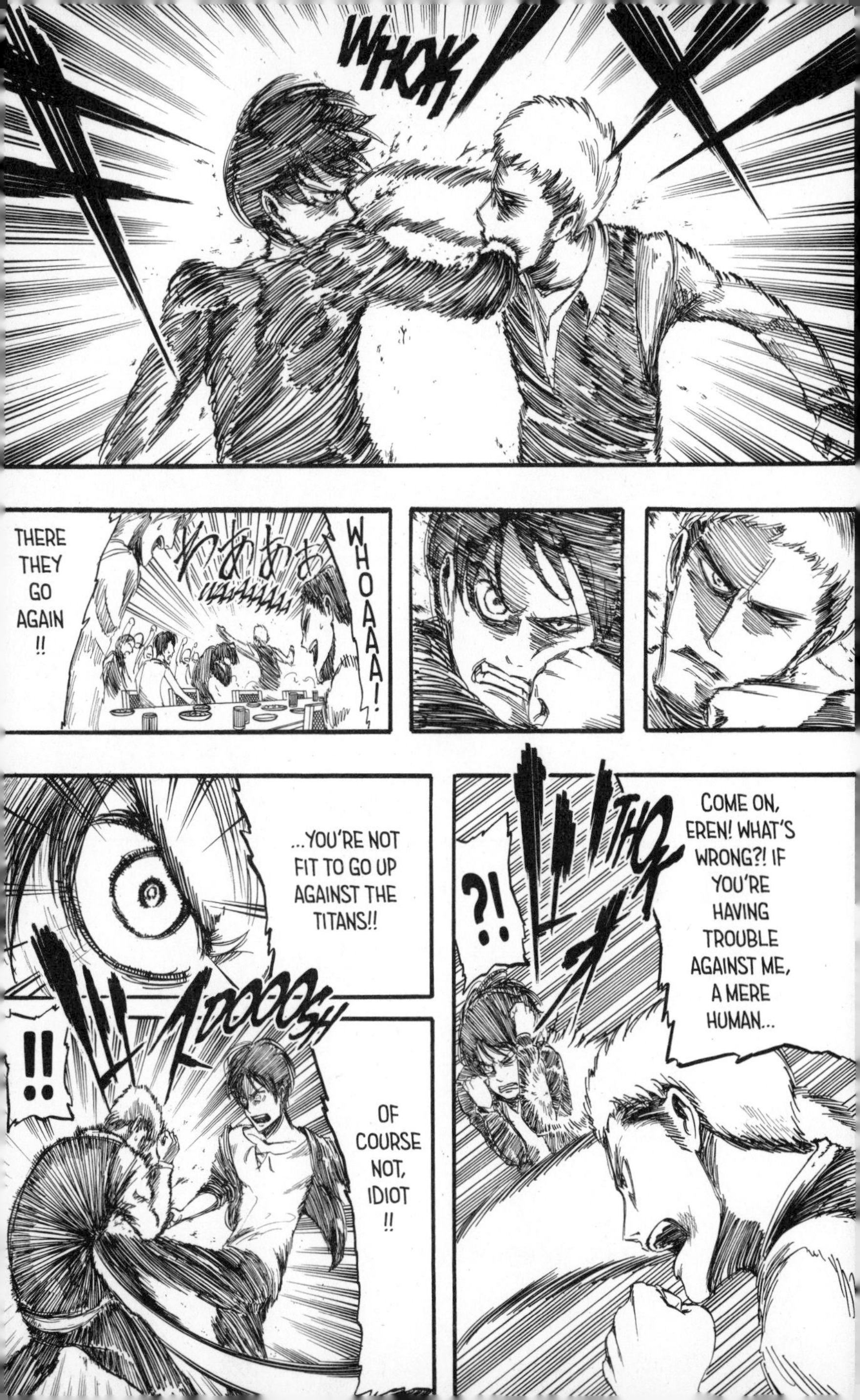
WHOK
WHOAAAA!
わあああ
THERE THEY GO AGAIN!!
COME ON, EREN! WHAT'S WRONG?! IF YOU'RE HAVING TROUBLE AGAINST ME, A MERE HUMAN...
THOK
?!
...YOU'RE NOT FIT TO GO UP AGAINST THE TITANS!!
DOOOSH
!!
OF COURSE NOT, IDIOT!!

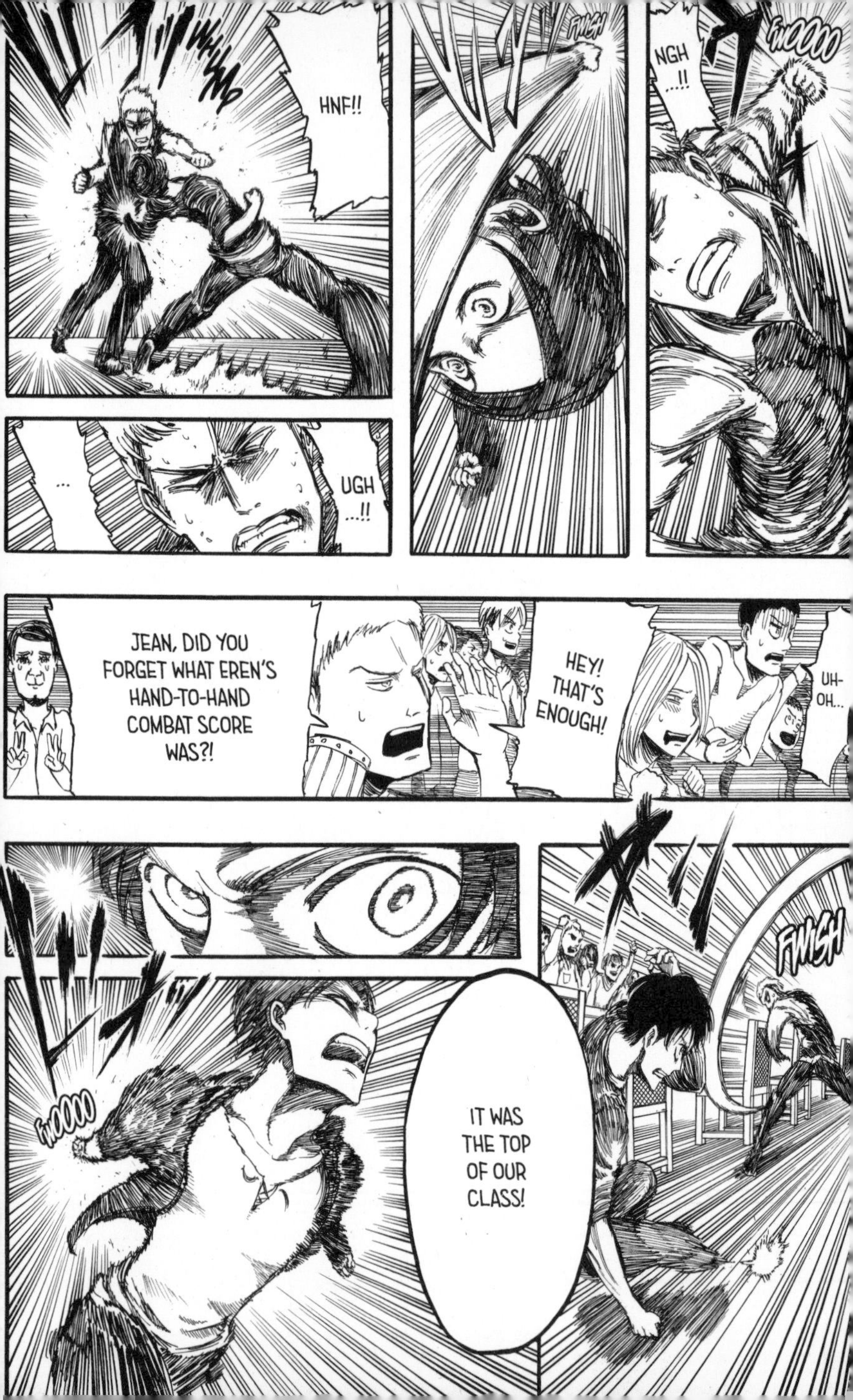
FWOOOO
NGH ...!!
FWISH
HNF!!
UGH ...!!
...
UH-OH...
HEY! THAT'S ENOUGH!
JEAN, DID YOU FORGET WHAT EREN'S HAND-TO-HAND COMBAT SCORE WAS?!
FWISH
FWOOOO
IT WAS THE TOP OF OUR CLASS!

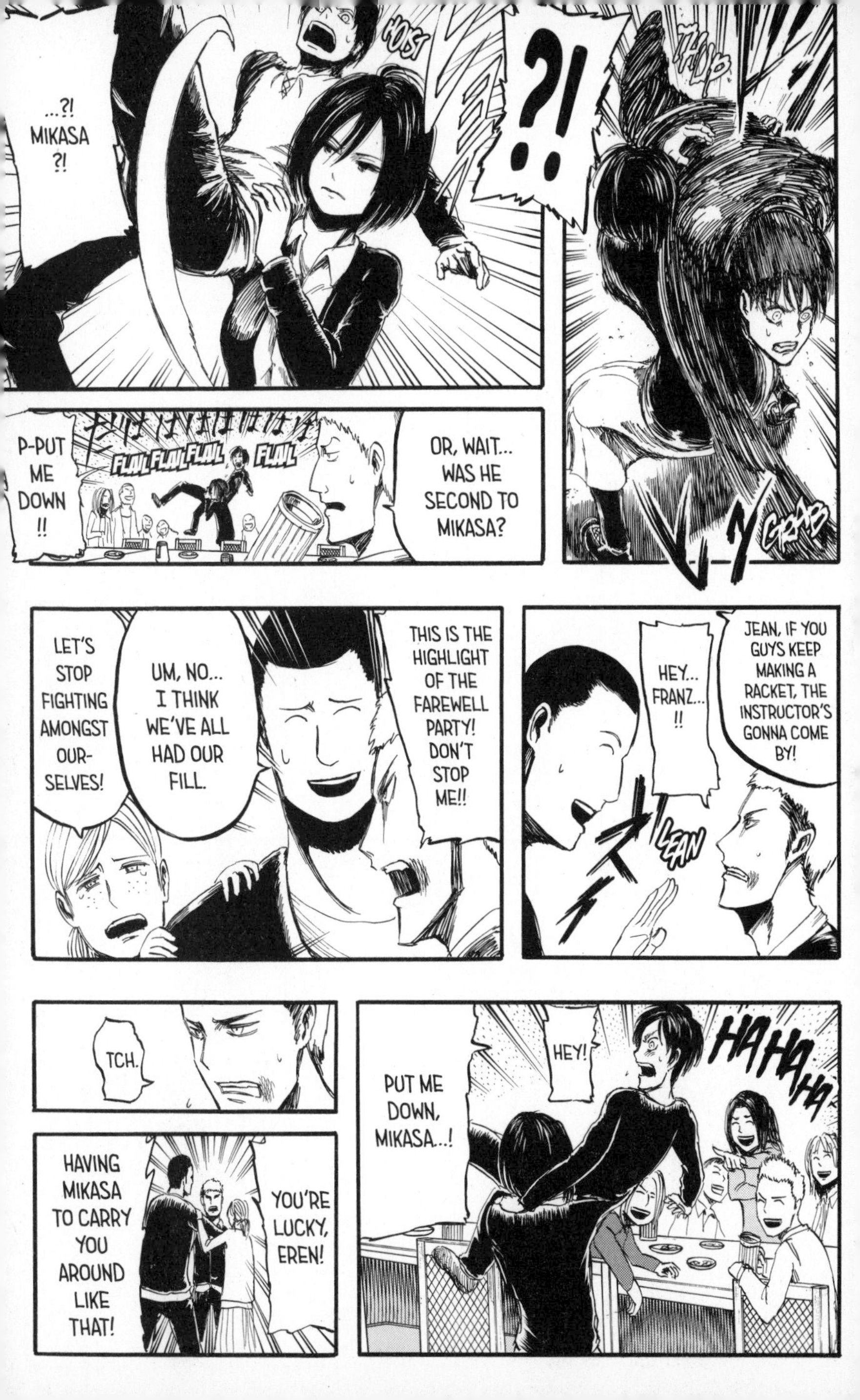

THUD
?!
GRAB
HOIST
...?! MIKASA ?!
OR, WAIT... WAS HE SECOND TO MIKASA?
FLAIL FLAIL FLAIL FLAIL
P-PUT ME DOWN !!
JEAN, IF YOU GUYS KEEP MAKING A RACKET, THE INSTRUCTOR'S GONNA COME BY!
HEY... FRANZ... !!
LEAN
THIS IS THE HIGHLIGHT OF THE FAREWELL PARTY! DON'T STOP ME!!
UM, NO... I THINK WE'VE ALL HAD OUR FILL.
LET'S STOP FIGHTING AMONGST OUR-SELVES!
HEY!
HA HA HA HA
PUT ME DOWN, MIKASA...!
TCH.
YOU'RE LUCKY, EREN!
HAVING MIKASA TO CARRY YOU AROUND LIKE THAT!

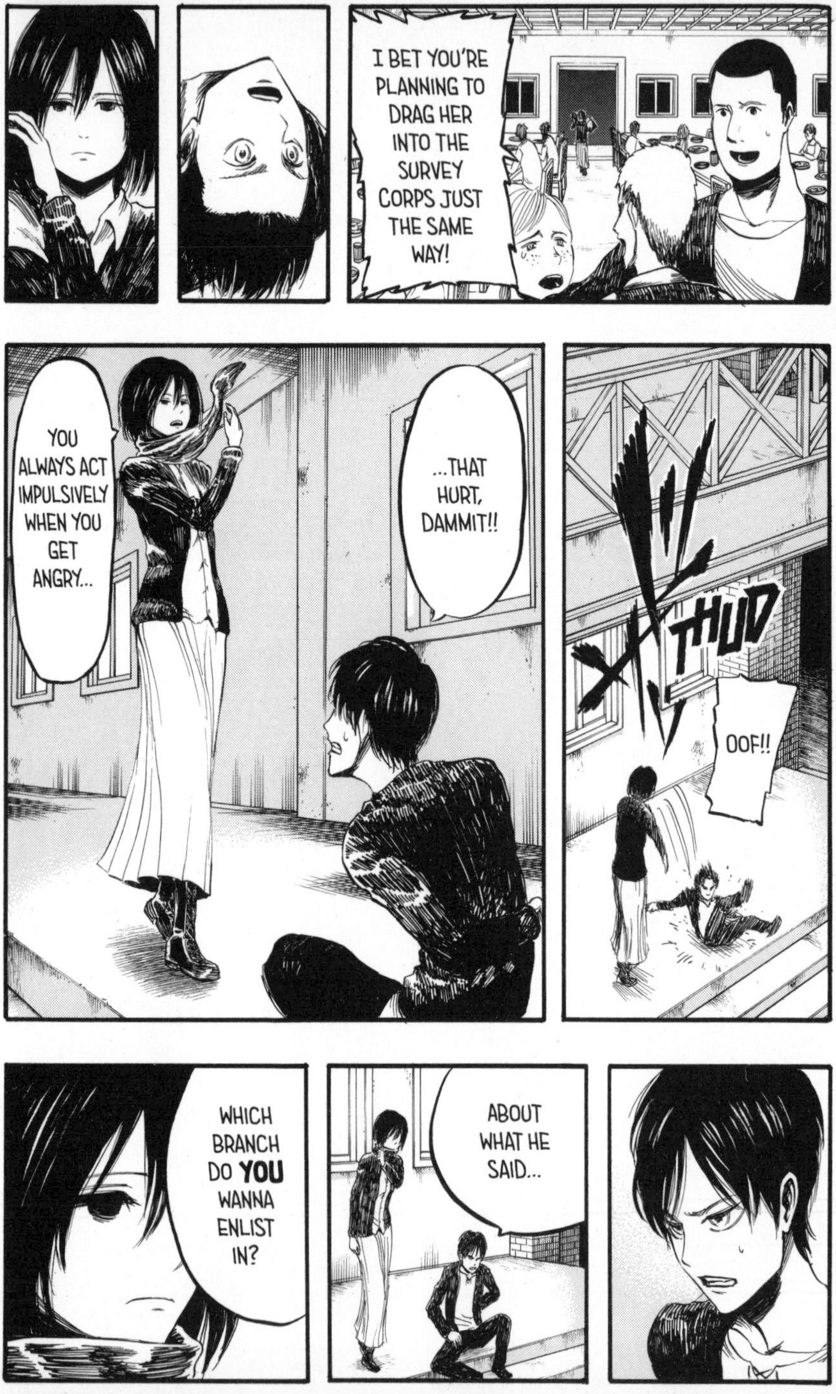
I BET YOU'RE PLANNING TO DRAG HER INTO THE SURVEY CORPS JUST THE SAME WAY!
THUD
OOF!!
...THAT HURT, DAMMIT!!
YOU ALWAYS ACT IMPULSIVELY WHEN YOU GET ANGRY...
ABOUT WHAT HE SAID...
WHICH BRANCH DO **YOU** WANNA ENLIST IN?

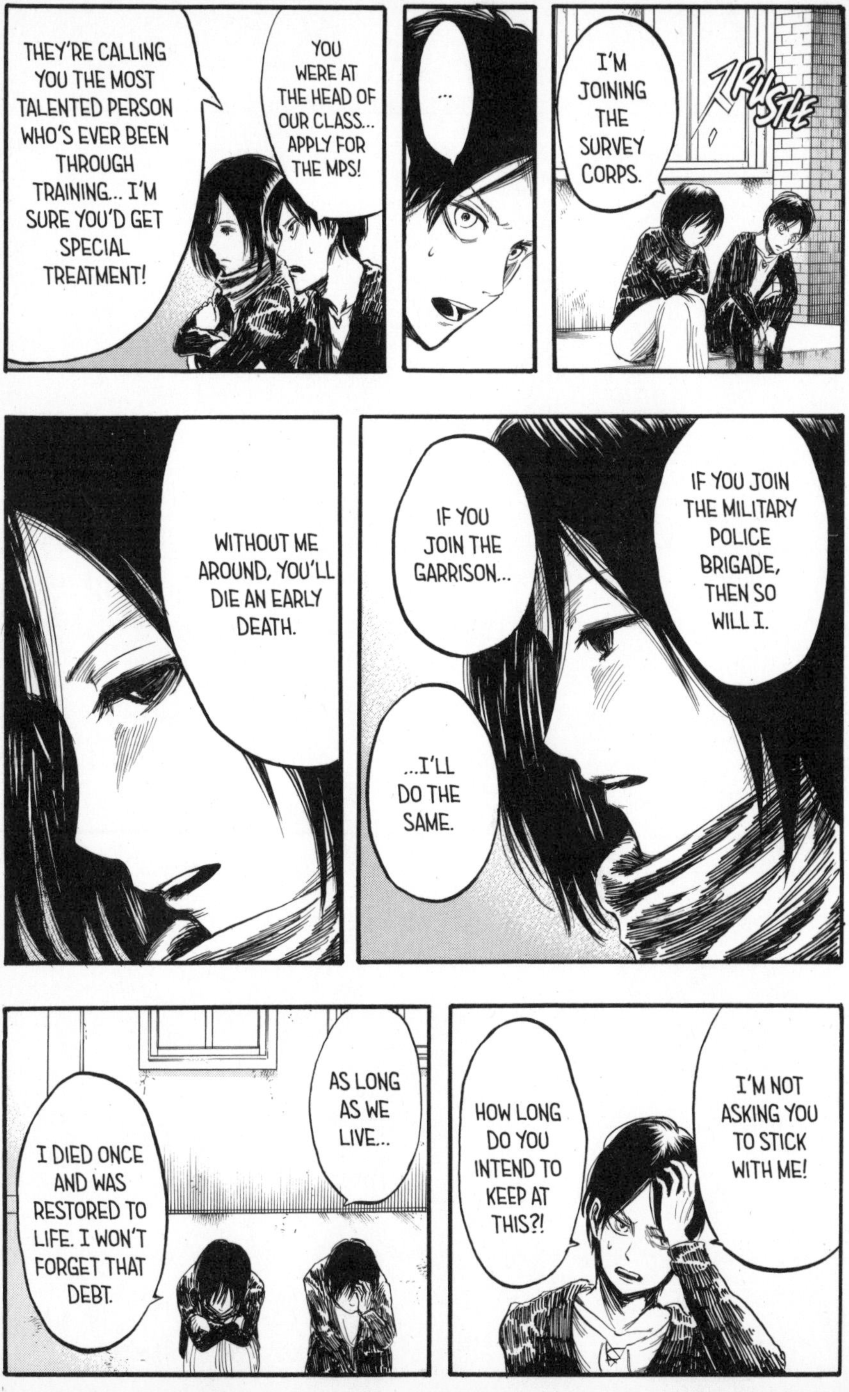
RUSTLE
I'M JOINING THE SURVEY CORPS.
...
YOU WERE AT THE HEAD OF OUR CLASS... APPLY FOR THE MPS!
THEY'RE CALLING YOU THE MOST TALENTED PERSON WHO'S EVER BEEN THROUGH TRAINING... I'M SURE YOU'D GET SPECIAL TREATMENT!
IF YOU JOIN THE MILITARY POLICE BRIGADE, THEN SO WILL I.
IF YOU JOIN THE GARRISON...
...I'LL DO THE SAME.
WITHOUT ME AROUND, YOU'LL DIE AN EARLY DEATH.
I'M NOT ASKING YOU TO STICK WITH ME!
HOW LONG DO YOU INTEND TO KEEP AT THIS?!
AS LONG AS WE LIVE...
I DIED ONCE AND WAS RESTORED TO LIFE. I WON'T FORGET THAT DEBT.

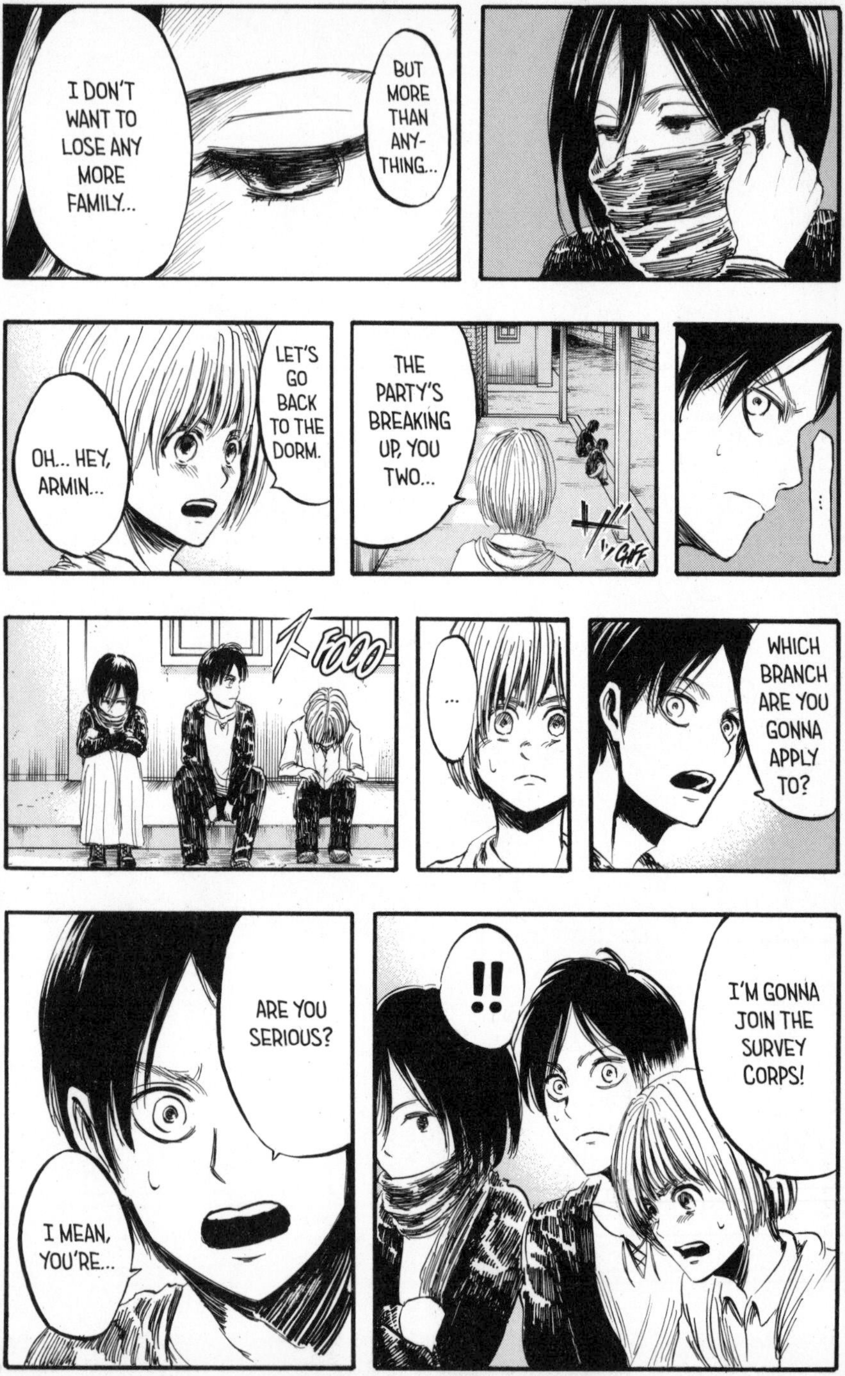
BUT MORE THAN ANY-THING...
I DON'T WANT TO LOSE ANY MORE FAMILY...
...
THE PARTY'S BREAKING UP, YOU TWO...
GUFF
LET'S GO BACK TO THE DORM.
OH... HEY, ARMIN...
WHICH BRANCH ARE YOU GONNA APPLY TO?
...
FOOO
I'M GONNA JOIN THE SURVEY CORPS!
!!
ARE YOU SERIOUS?
I MEAN, YOU'RE...

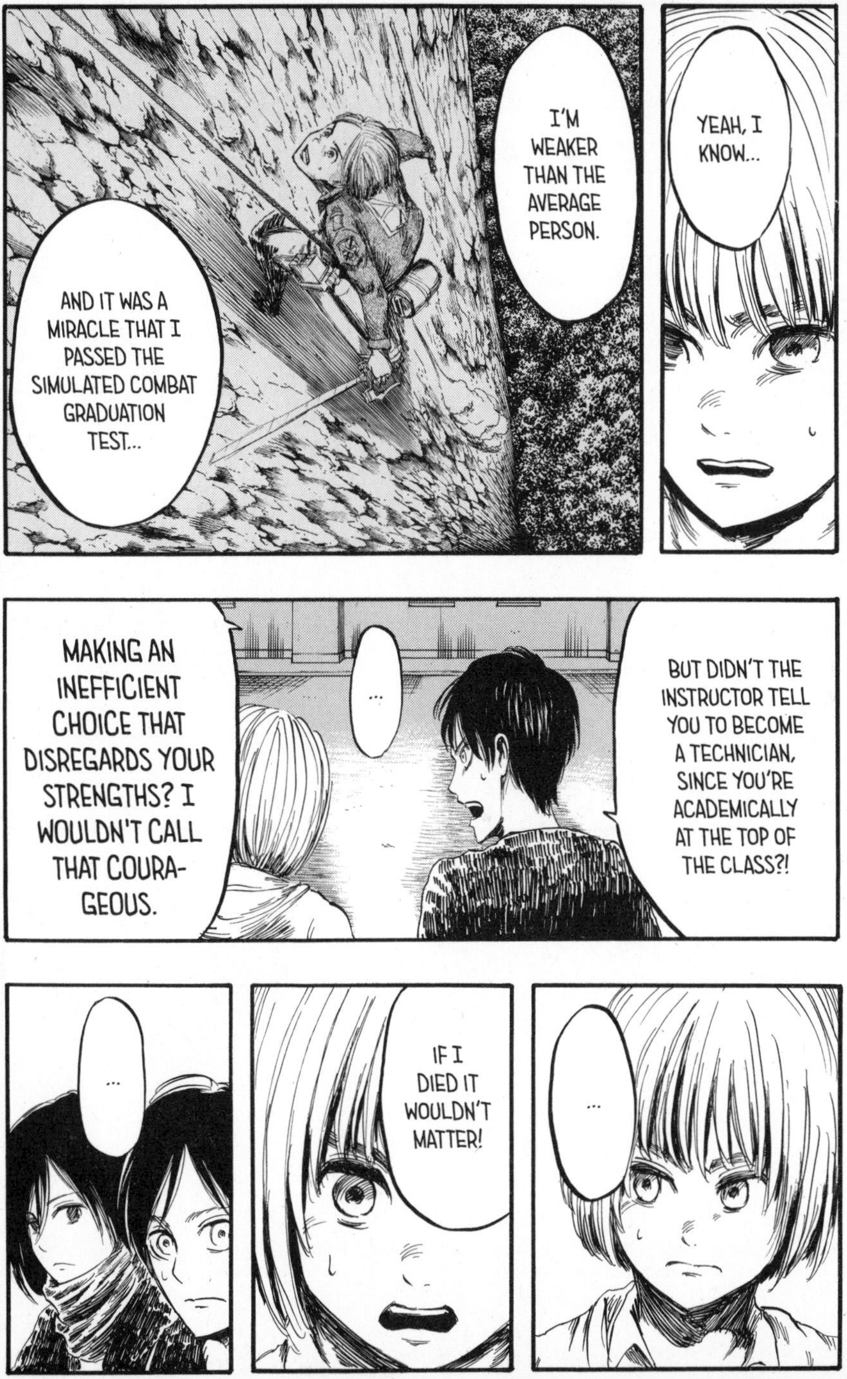
YEAH, I KNOW...
I'M WEAKER THAN THE AVERAGE PERSON.
AND IT WAS A MIRACLE THAT I PASSED THE SIMULATED COMBAT GRADUATION TEST...
BUT DIDN'T THE INSTRUCTOR TELL YOU TO BECOME A TECHNICIAN, SINCE YOU'RE ACADEMICALLY AT THE TOP OF THE CLASS?!
...
MAKING AN INEFFICIENT CHOICE THAT DISREGARDS YOUR STRENGTHS? I WOULDN'T CALL THAT COURAGEOUS.
...
IF I DIED IT WOULDN'T MATTER!
...

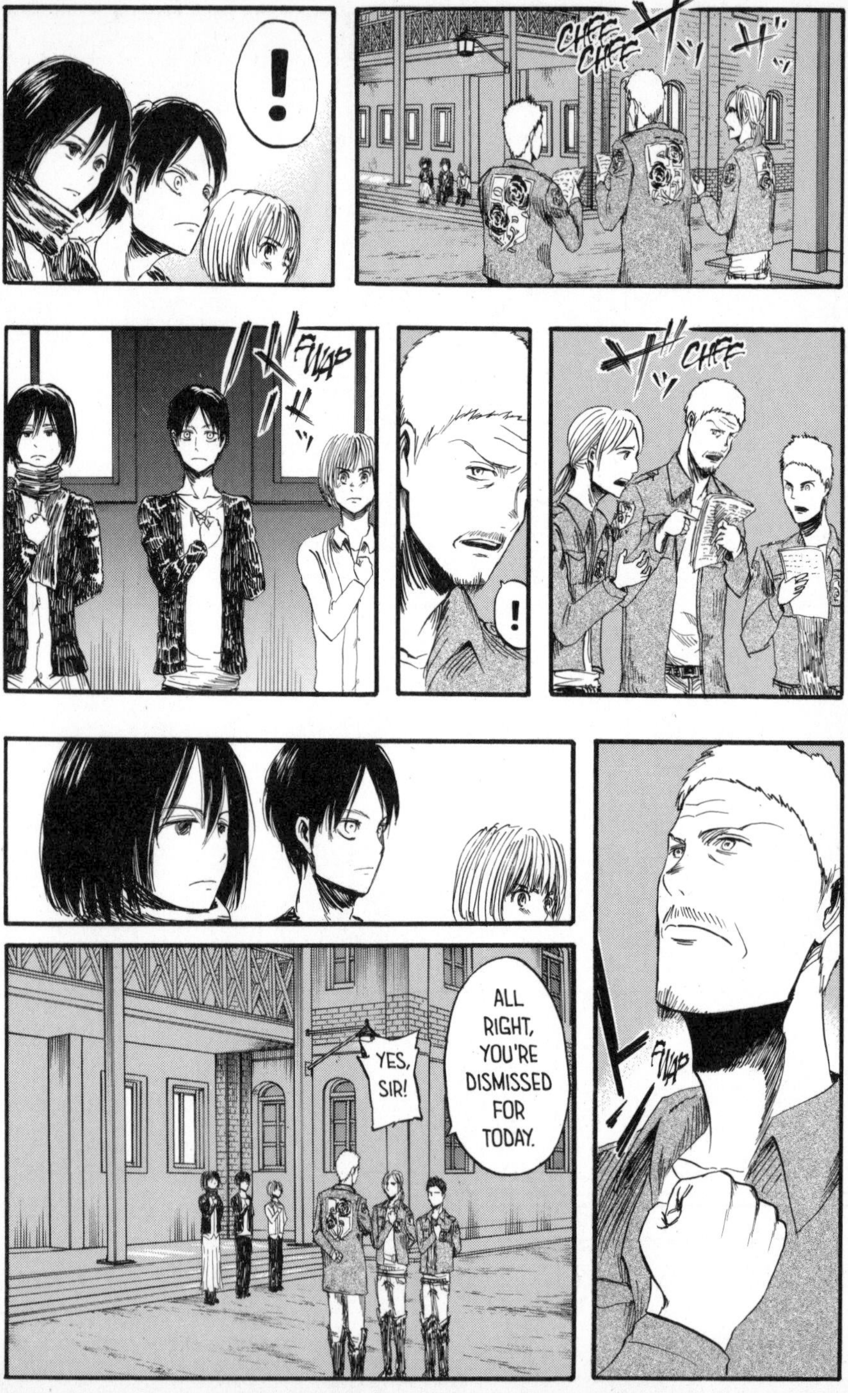
CHFF CHFF
!
CHFF
!
FWAP
FWAP
ALL RIGHT, YOU'RE DISMISSED FOR TODAY.
YES, SIR!

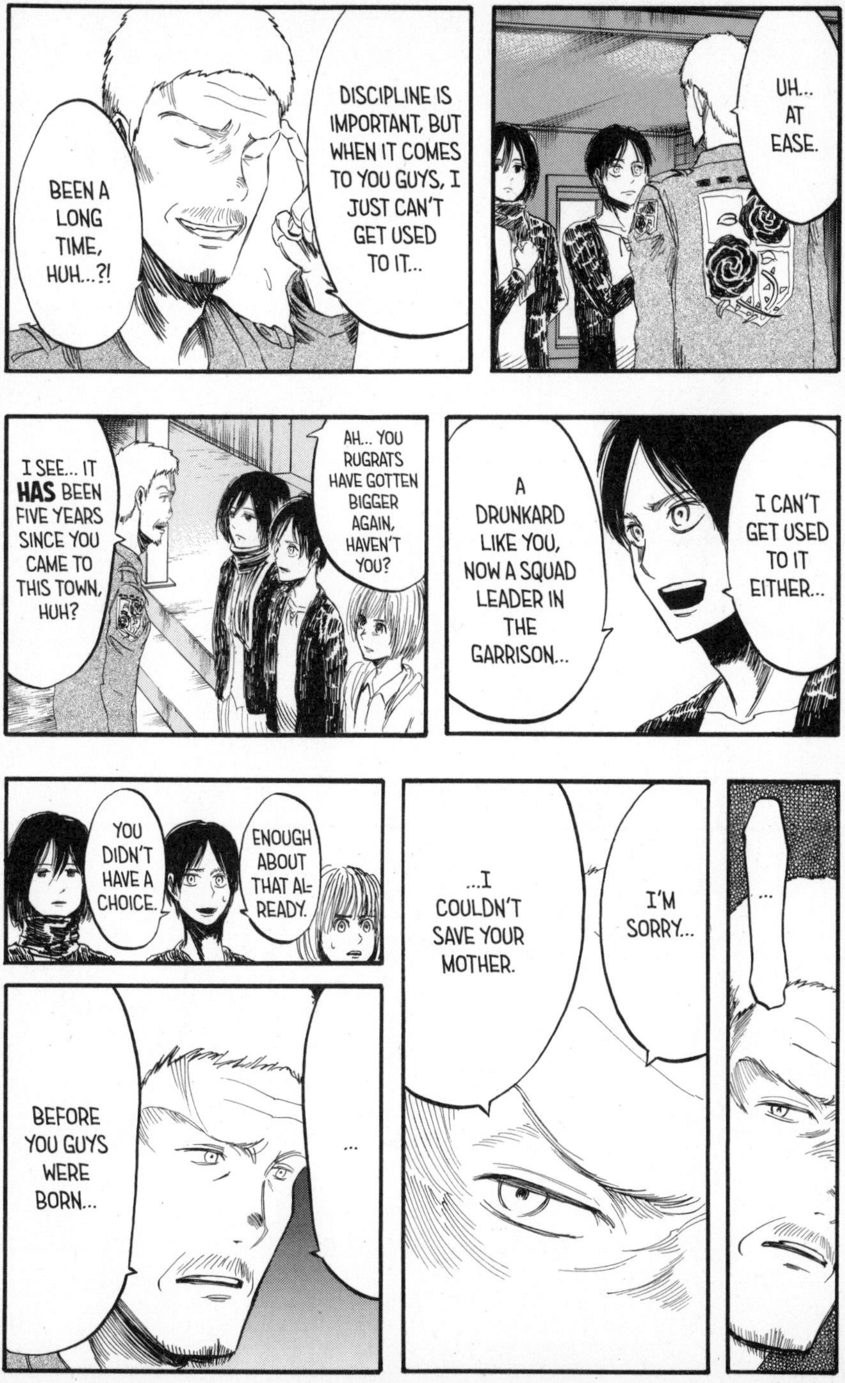
UH... AT EASE.
DISCIPLINE IS IMPORTANT, BUT WHEN IT COMES TO YOU GUYS, I JUST CAN'T GET USED TO IT...
BEEN A LONG TIME, HUH...?!
I CAN'T GET USED TO IT EITHER...
A DRUNKARD LIKE YOU, NOW A SQUAD LEADER IN THE GARRISON...
AH... YOU RUGRATS HAVE GOTTEN BIGGER AGAIN, HAVEN'T YOU?
I SEE... IT **HAS** BEEN FIVE YEARS SINCE YOU CAME TO THIS TOWN, HUH?
...
I'M SORRY...
...I COULDN'T SAVE YOUR MOTHER.
ENOUGH ABOUT THAT AL-READY.
YOU DIDN'T HAVE A CHOICE.
...
BEFORE YOU GUYS WERE BORN...

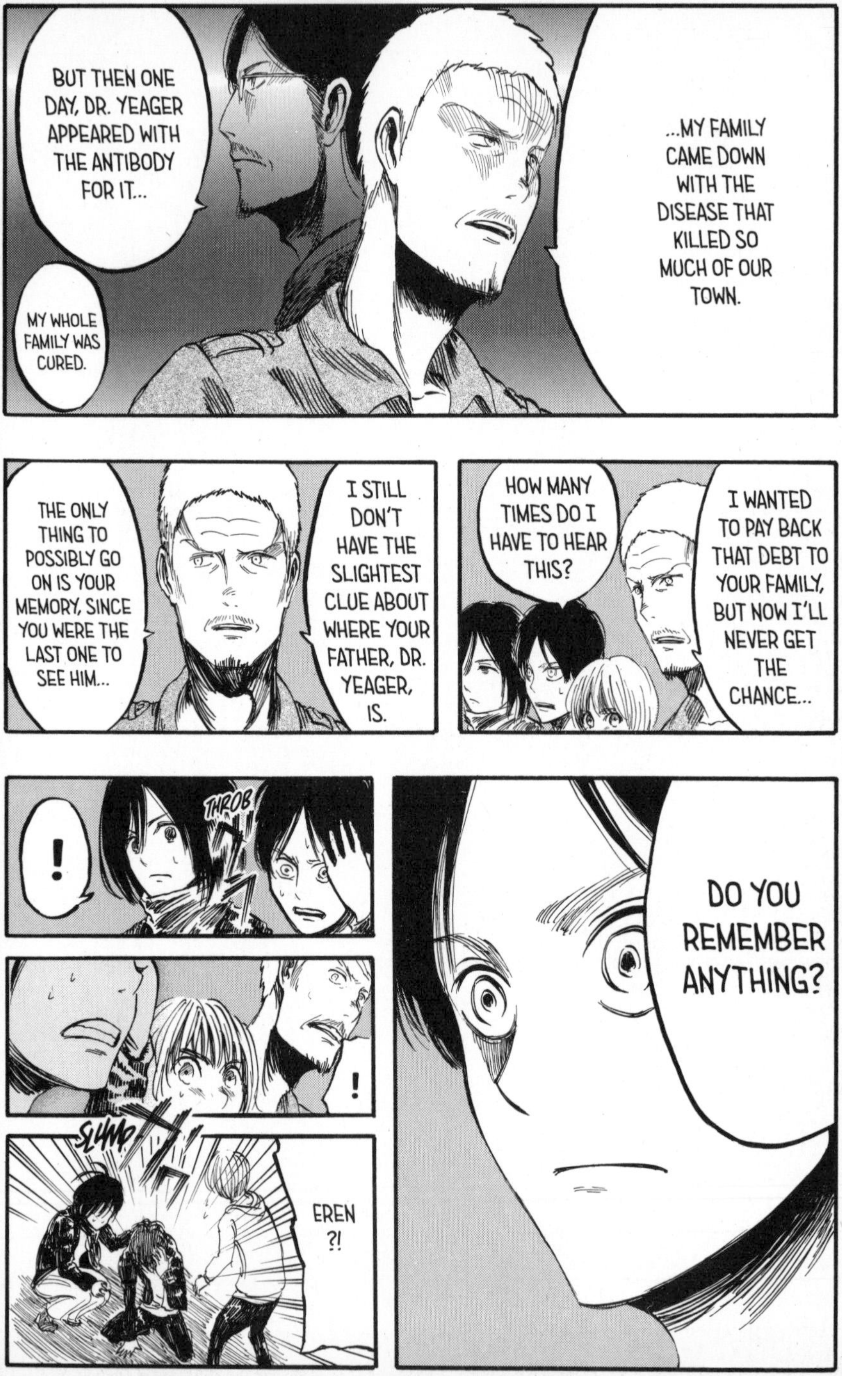
...MY FAMILY CAME DOWN WITH THE DISEASE THAT KILLED SO MUCH OF OUR TOWN.
BUT THEN ONE DAY, DR. YEAGER APPEARED WITH THE ANTIBODY FOR IT...
MY WHOLE FAMILY WAS CURED.
I WANTED TO PAY BACK THAT DEBT TO YOUR FAMILY, BUT NOW I'LL NEVER GET THE CHANCE...
HOW MANY TIMES DO I HAVE TO HEAR THIS?
I STILL DON'T HAVE THE SLIGHTEST CLUE ABOUT WHERE YOUR FATHER, DR. YEAGER, IS.
THE ONLY THING TO POSSIBLY GO ON IS YOUR MEMORY, SINCE YOU WERE THE LAST ONE TO SEE HIM...
DO YOU REMEMBER ANYTHING?
THROB
!
!
SLUMP
EREN ?!

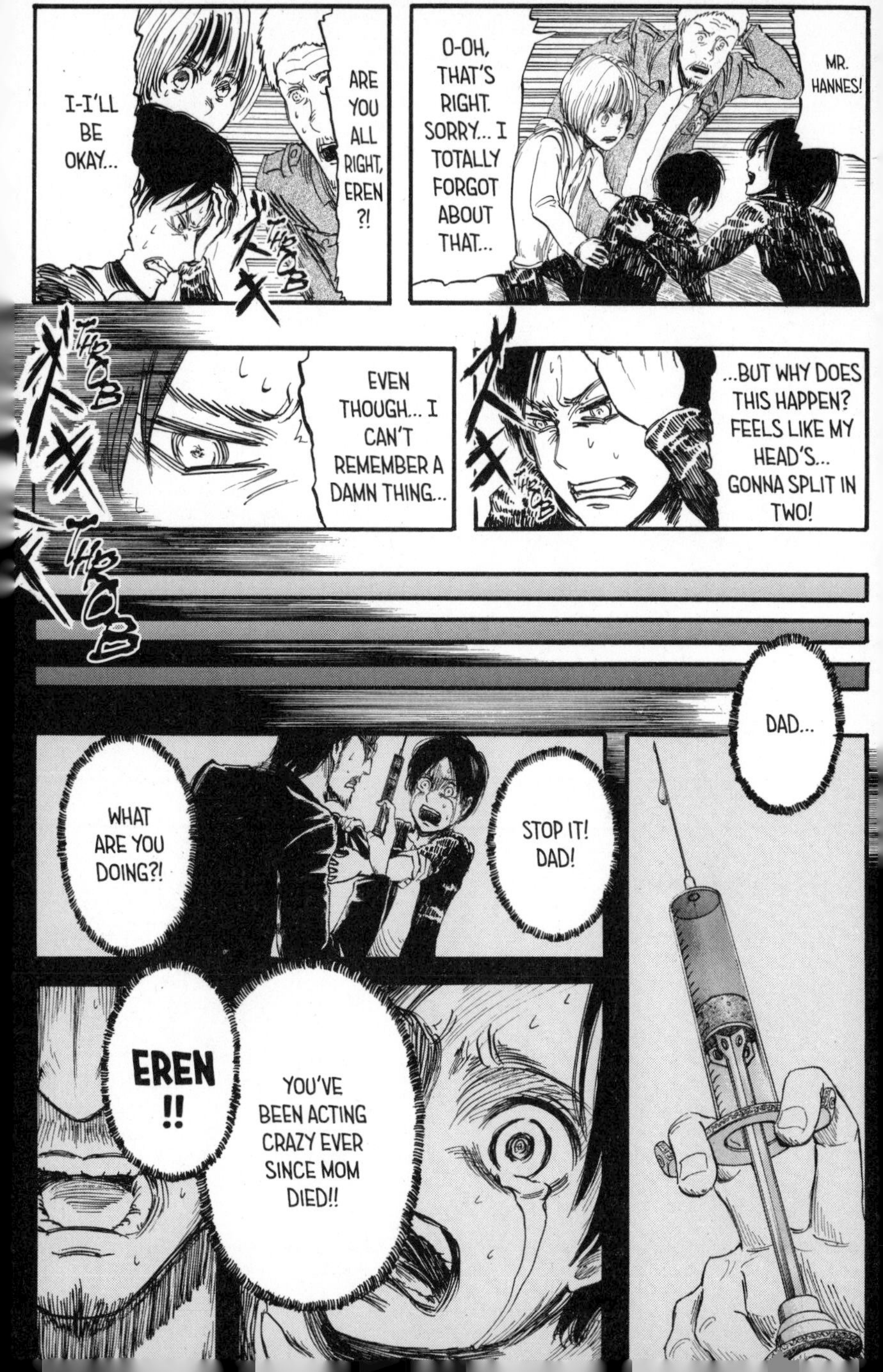
MR. HANNES!
O-OH, THAT'S RIGHT. SORRY... I TOTALLY FORGOT ABOUT THAT...
ARE YOU ALL RIGHT, EREN?!
THROB
I-I'LL BE OKAY...
...BUT WHY DOES THIS HAPPEN? FEELS LIKE MY HEAD'S... GONNA SPLIT IN TWO!
THROB
EVEN THOUGH... I CAN'T REMEMBER A DAMN THING...
THROB
THROB
DAD...
STOP IT! DAD!
WHAT ARE YOU DOING?!
YOU'VE BEEN ACTING CRAZY EVER SINCE MOM DIED!!
EREN !!

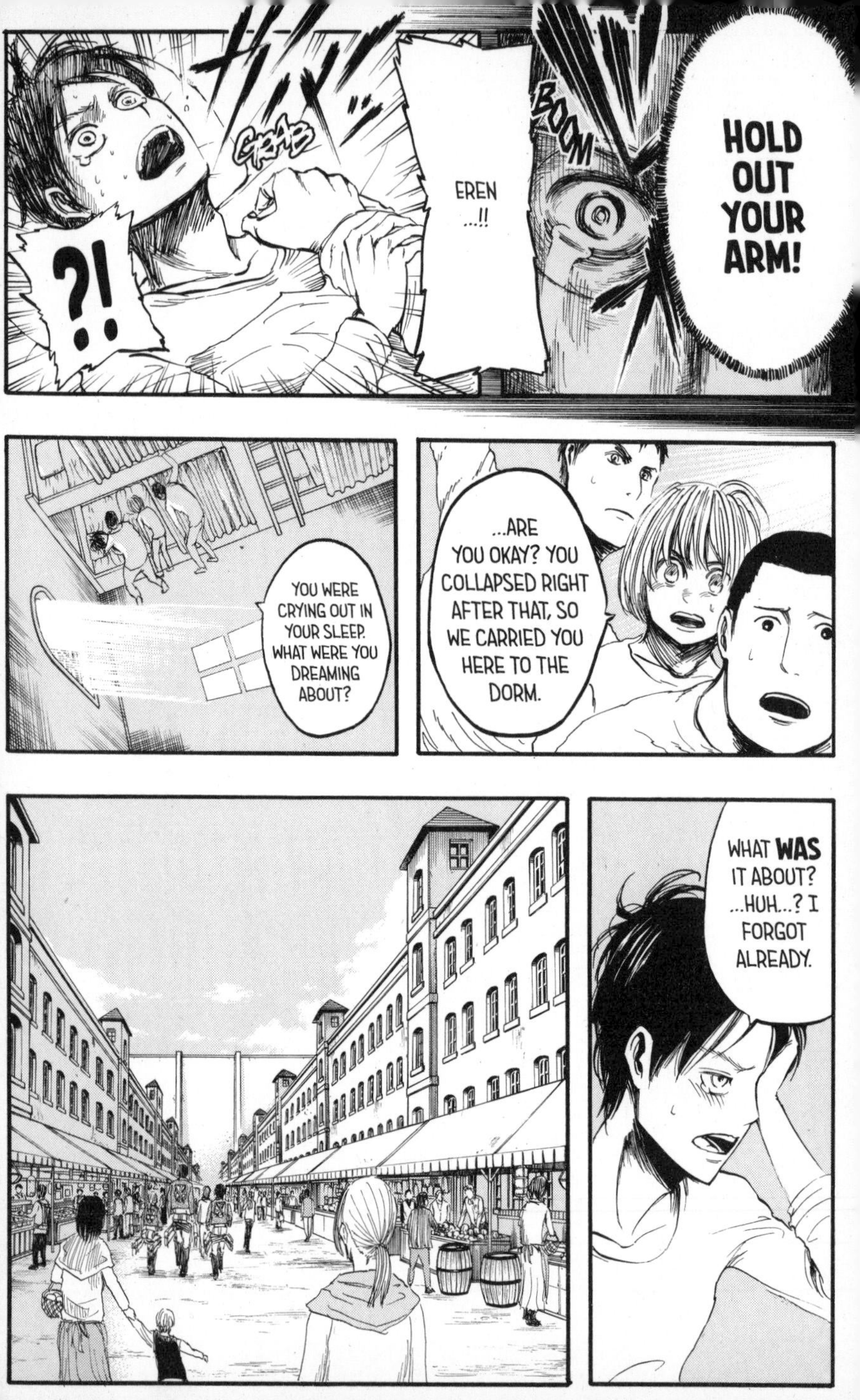
HOLD OUT YOUR ARM!
BOOM
EREN ...!!
GRAB
?!
...ARE YOU OKAY? YOU COLLAPSED RIGHT AFTER THAT, SO WE CARRIED YOU HERE TO THE DORM.
YOU WERE CRYING OUT IN YOUR SLEEP. WHAT WERE YOU DREAMING ABOUT?
WHAT **WAS** IT ABOUT? ...HUH...? I FORGOT ALREADY.

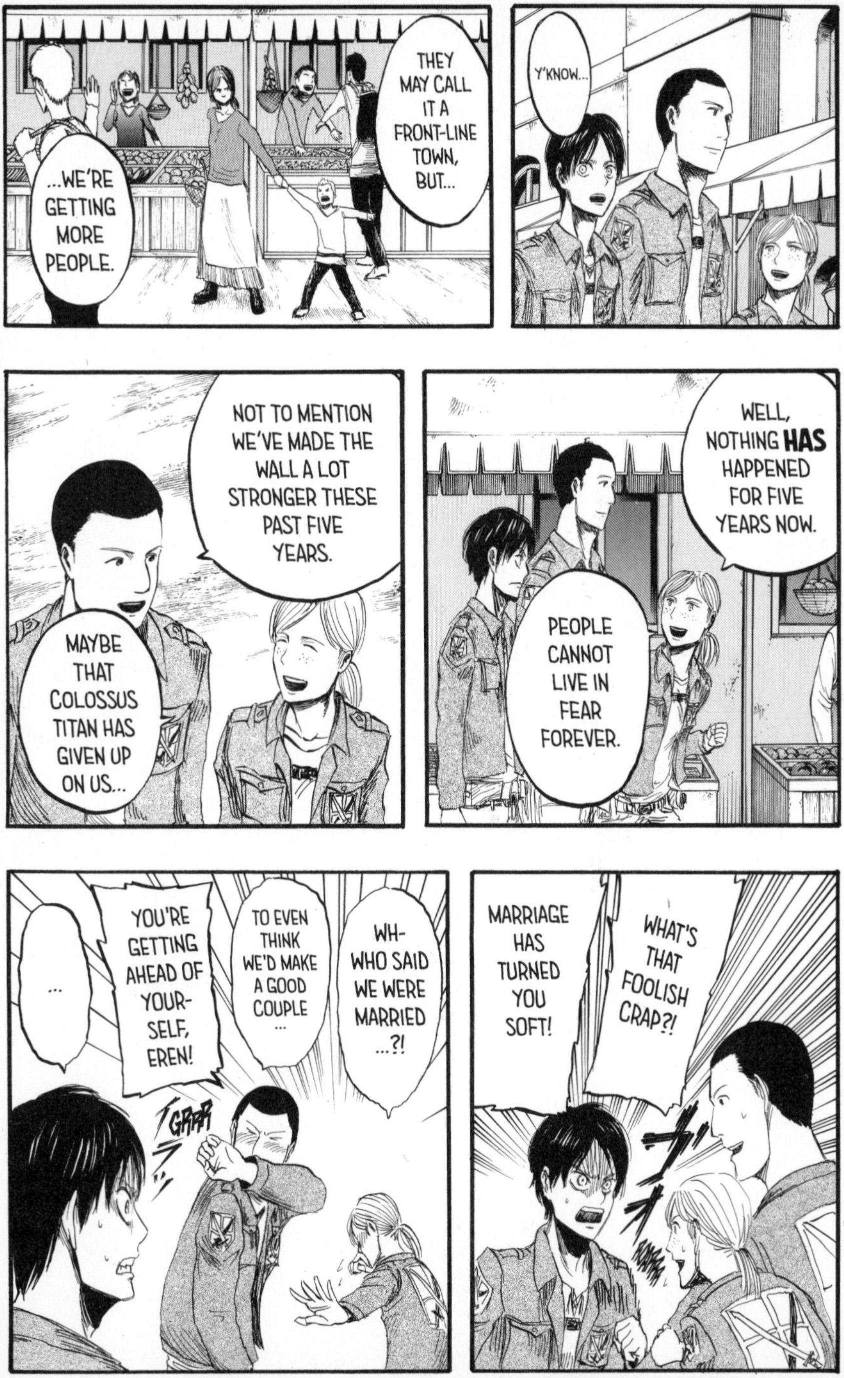
Y'KNOW...
THEY MAY CALL IT A FRONT-LINE TOWN, BUT...
...WE'RE GETTING MORE PEOPLE.
WELL, NOTHING **HAS** HAPPENED FOR FIVE YEARS NOW.
PEOPLE CANNOT LIVE IN FEAR FOREVER.
NOT TO MENTION WE'VE MADE THE WALL A LOT STRONGER THESE PAST FIVE YEARS.
MAYBE THAT COLOSSUS TITAN HAS GIVEN UP ON US...
WHAT'S THAT FOOLISH CRAP?!
MARRIAGE HAS TURNED YOU SOFT!
WH- WHO SAID WE WERE MARRIED ...?!
TO EVEN THINK WE'D MAKE A GOOD COUPLE ...
YOU'RE GETTING AHEAD OF YOUR-SELF, EREN!
GRRR
...

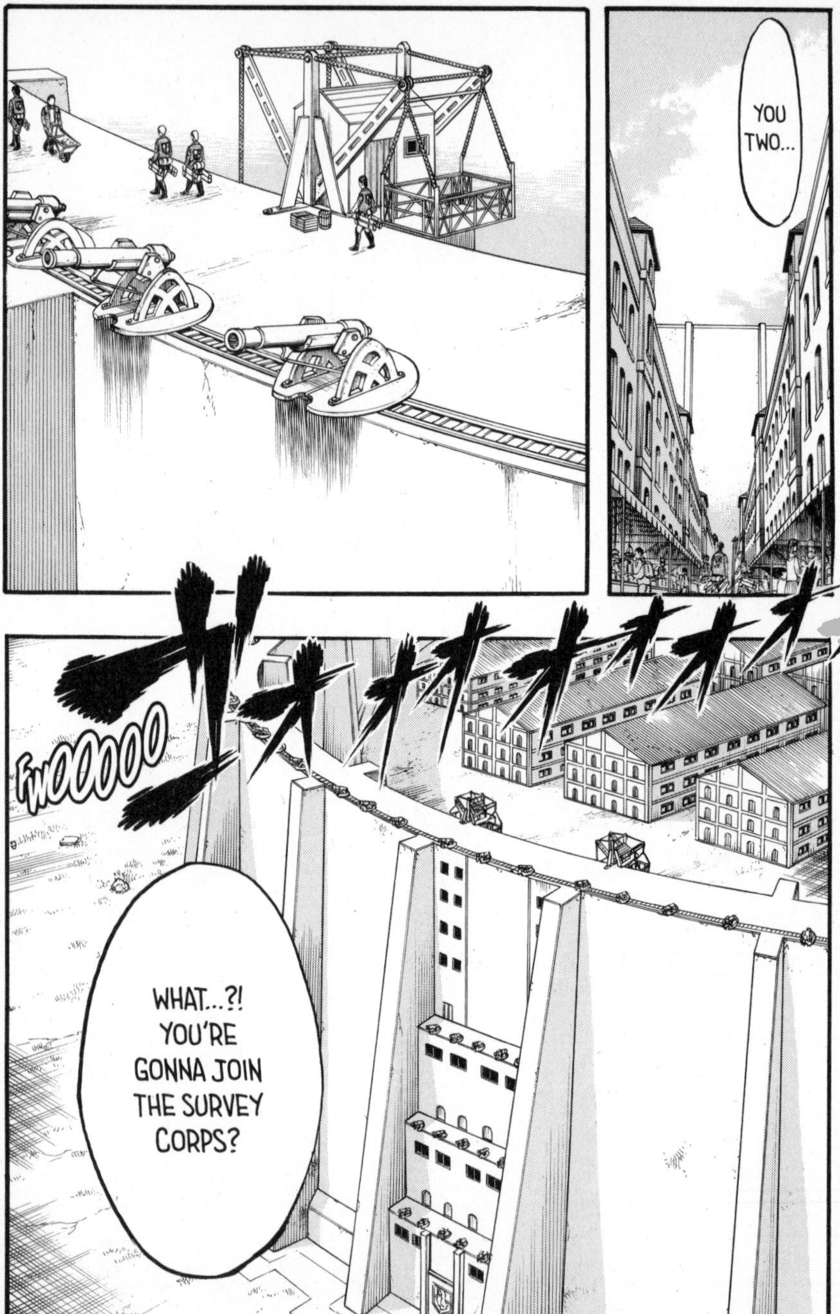
YOU TWO...
FWOOOOO
WHAT...?! YOU'RE GONNA JOIN THE SURVEY CORPS?

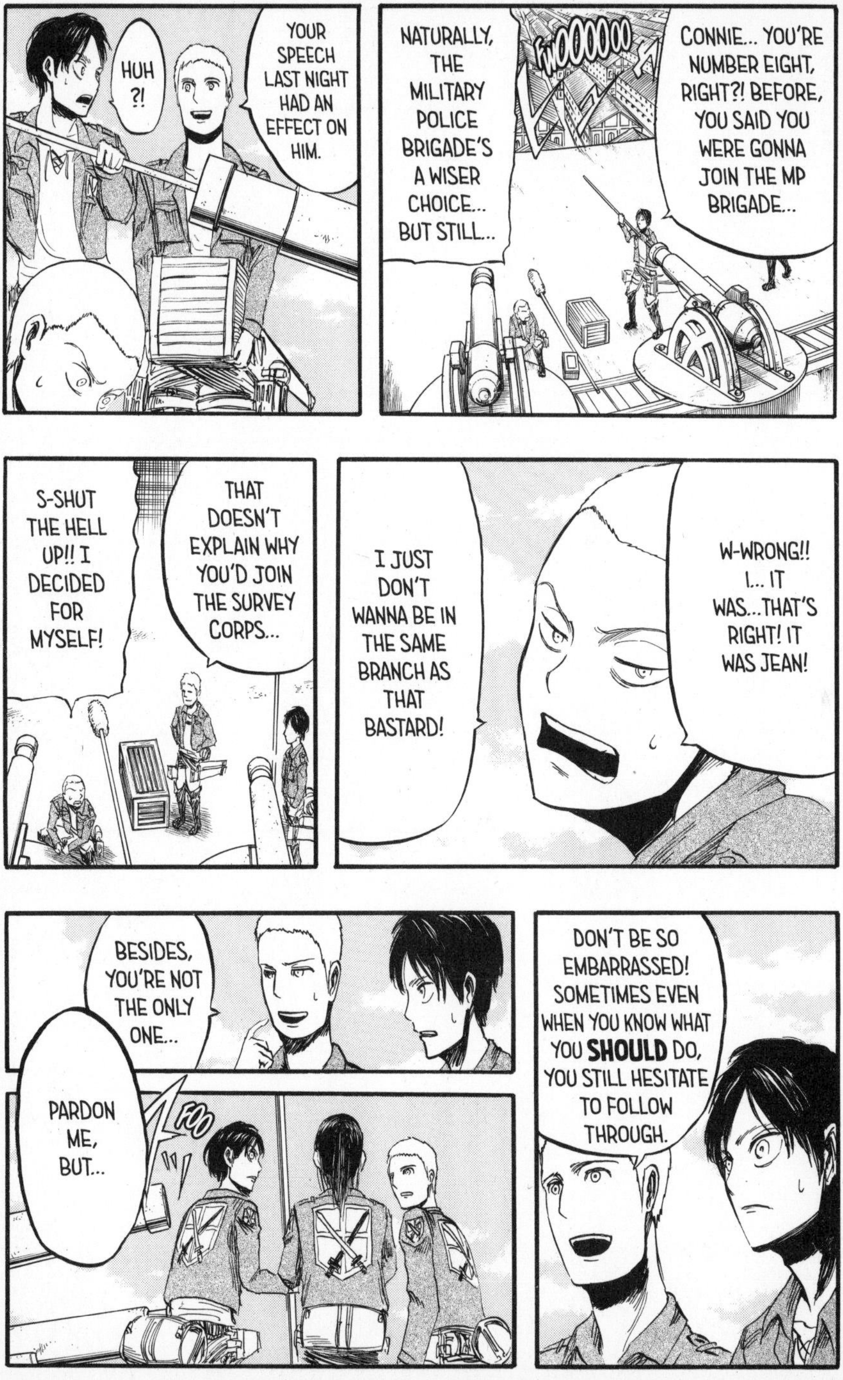
CONNIE... YOU'RE NUMBER EIGHT, RIGHT?! BEFORE, YOU SAID YOU WERE GONNA JOIN THE MP BRIGADE...
FWOOOOOO
NATURALLY, THE MILITARY POLICE BRIGADE'S A WISER CHOICE... BUT STILL...
YOUR SPEECH LAST NIGHT HAD AN EFFECT ON HIM.
HUH ?!
W-WRONG!! I... IT WAS...THAT'S RIGHT! IT WAS JEAN!
I JUST DON'T WANNA BE IN THE SAME BRANCH AS THAT BASTARD!
THAT DOESN'T EXPLAIN WHY YOU'D JOIN THE SURVEY CORPS...
S-SHUT THE HELL UP!! I DECIDED FOR MYSELF!
DON'T BE SO EMBARRASSED! SOMETIMES EVEN WHEN YOU KNOW WHAT YOU **SHOULD** DO, YOU STILL HESITATE TO FOLLOW THROUGH.
BESIDES, YOU'RE NOT THE ONLY ONE...
FOO
PARDON ME, BUT...

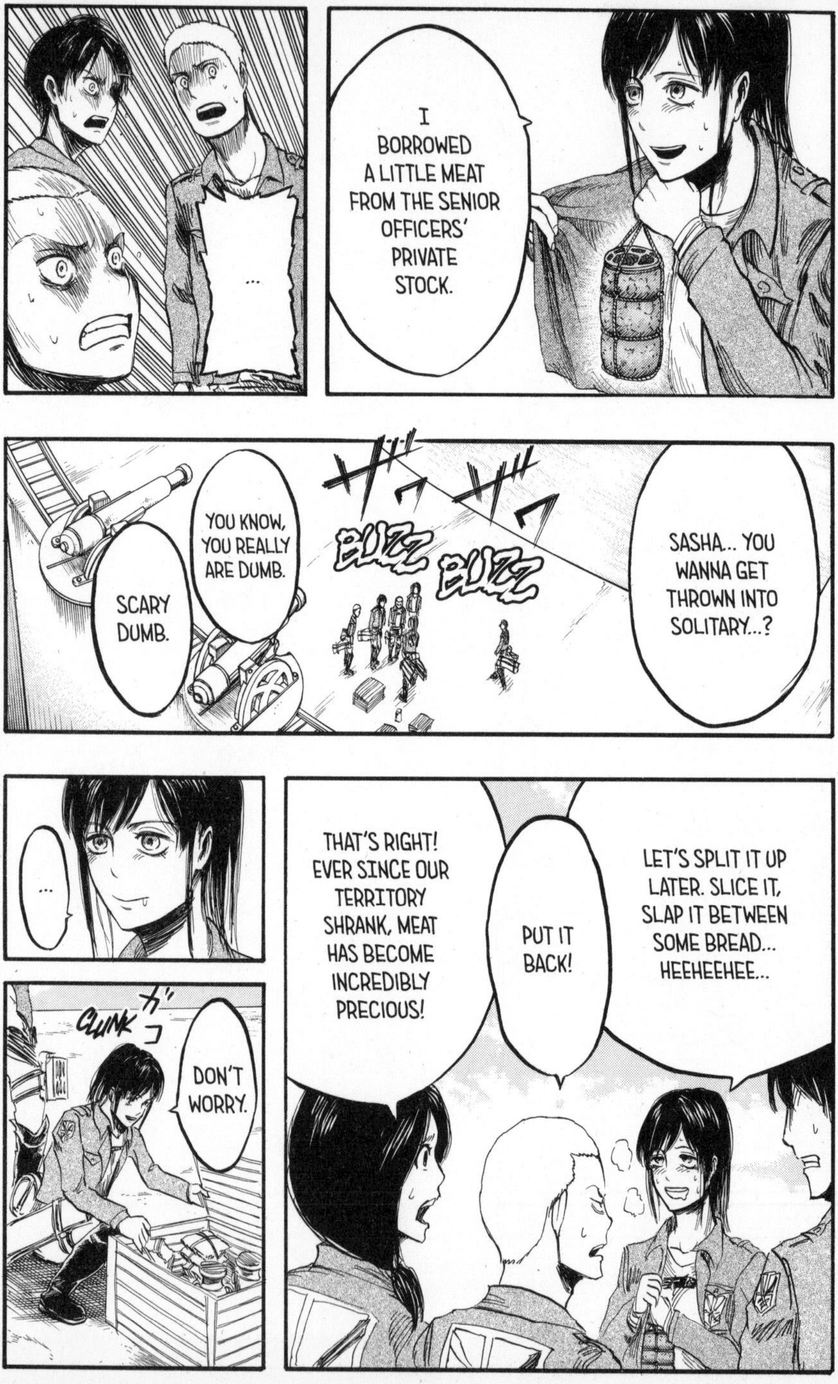
I BORROWED A LITTLE MEAT FROM THE SENIOR OFFICERS' PRIVATE STOCK.
...
SASHA... YOU WANNA GET THROWN INTO SOLITARY...?
ザワ ザワ
BUZZ BUZZ
YOU KNOW, YOU REALLY ARE DUMB.
SCARY DUMB.
LET'S SPLIT IT UP LATER. SLICE IT, SLAP IT BETWEEN SOME BREAD... HEEHEEHEE...
PUT IT BACK!
THAT'S RIGHT! EVER SINCE OUR TERRITORY SHRANK, MEAT HAS BECOME INCREDIBLY PRECIOUS!
...
ガコ
CLUNK
DON'T WORRY.

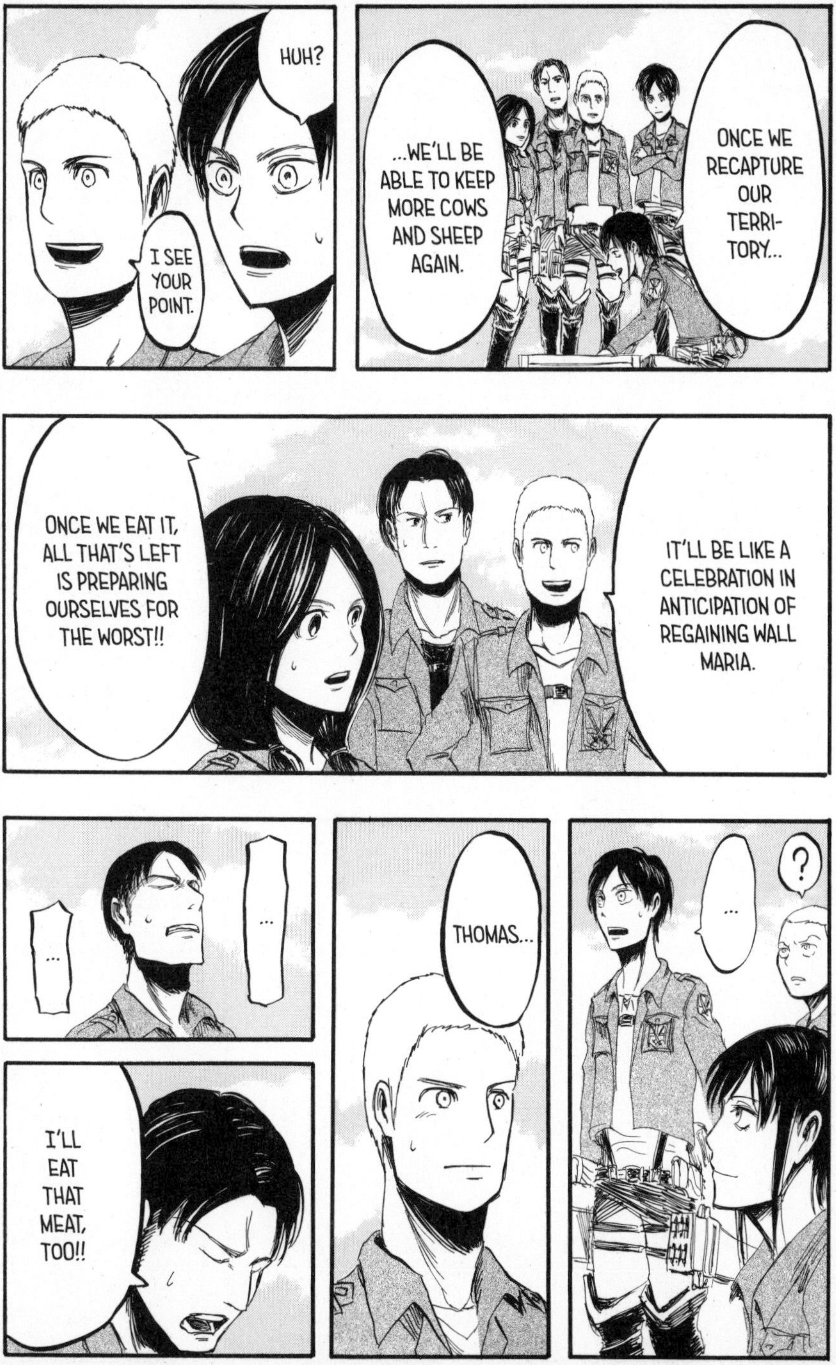
ONCE WE RECAPTURE OUR TERRI-TORY...
...WE'LL BE ABLE TO KEEP MORE COWS AND SHEEP AGAIN.
HUH?
I SEE YOUR POINT.
IT'LL BE LIKE A CELEBRATION IN ANTICIPATION OF REGAINING WALL MARIA.
ONCE WE EAT IT, ALL THAT'S LEFT IS PREPARING OURSELVES FOR THE WORST!!
?
...
THOMAS...
...
...
I'LL EAT THAT MEAT, TOO!!

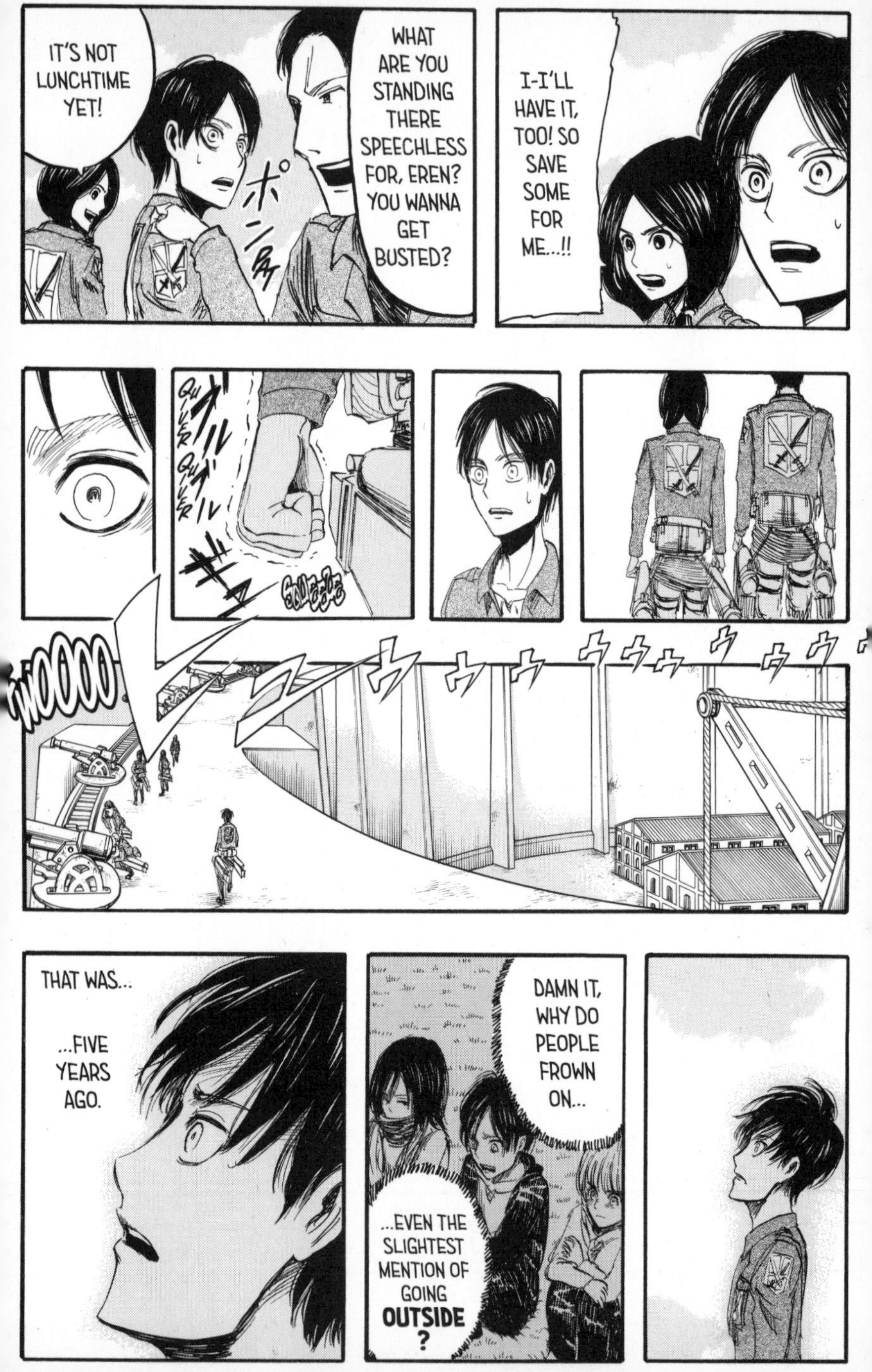
I-I'LL HAVE IT, TOO! SO SAVE SOME FOR ME...!!
WHAT ARE YOU STANDING THERE SPEECHLESS FOR, EREN? YOU WANNA GET BUSTED?
IT'S NOT LUNCHTIME YET!
QUIVER QUIVER
WOOOO
DAMN IT, WHY DO PEOPLE FROWN ON...
...EVEN THE SLIGHTEST MENTION OF GOING **OUTSIDE**?
THAT WAS...
...FIVE YEARS AGO.

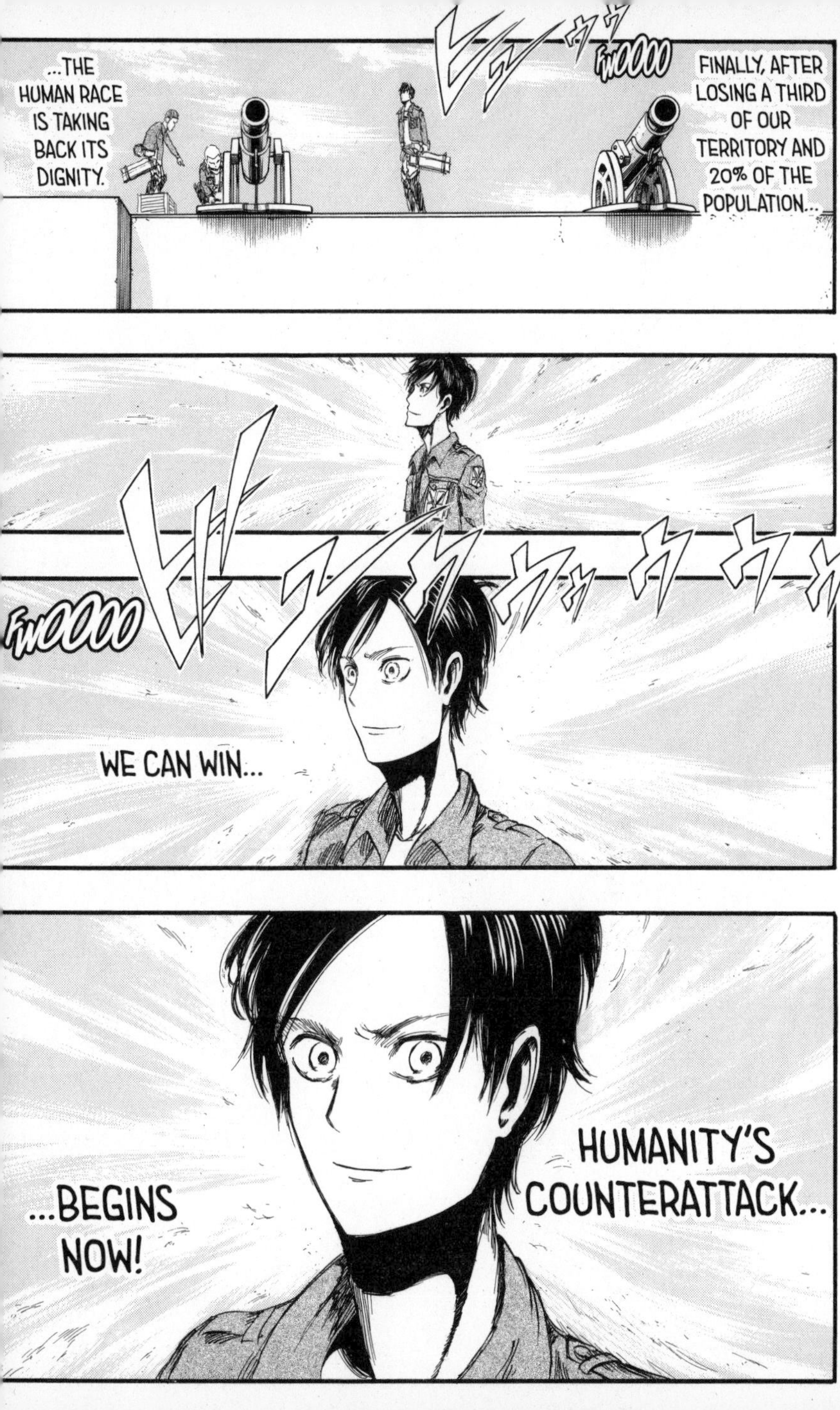
FINALLY, AFTER LOSING A THIRD OF OUR TERRITORY AND 20% OF THE POPULATION...
FWOOOO
...THE HUMAN RACE IS TAKING BACK ITS DIGNITY.
FWOOOO
WE CAN WIN...
HUMANITY'S COUNTERATTACK...
...BEGINS NOW!

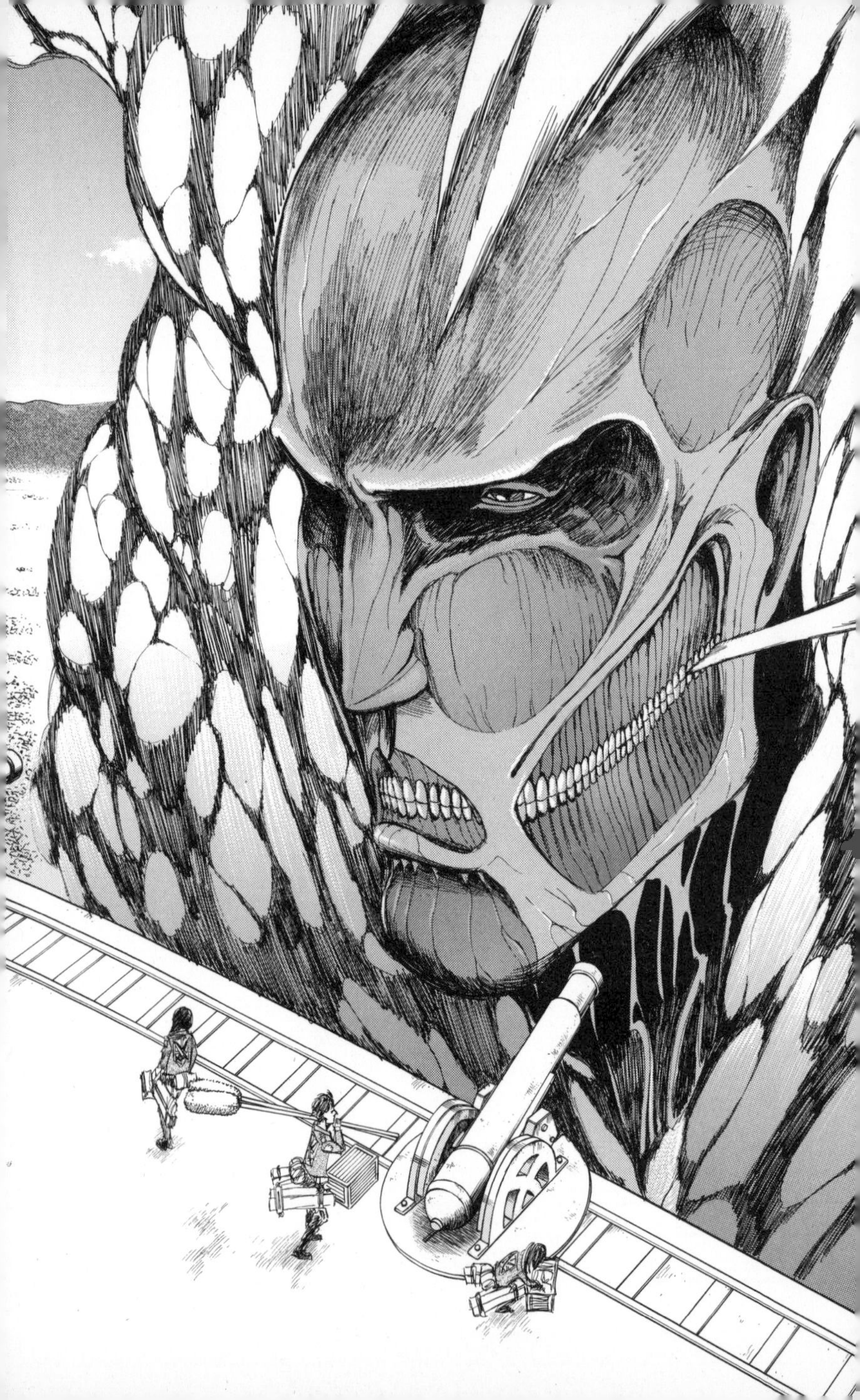

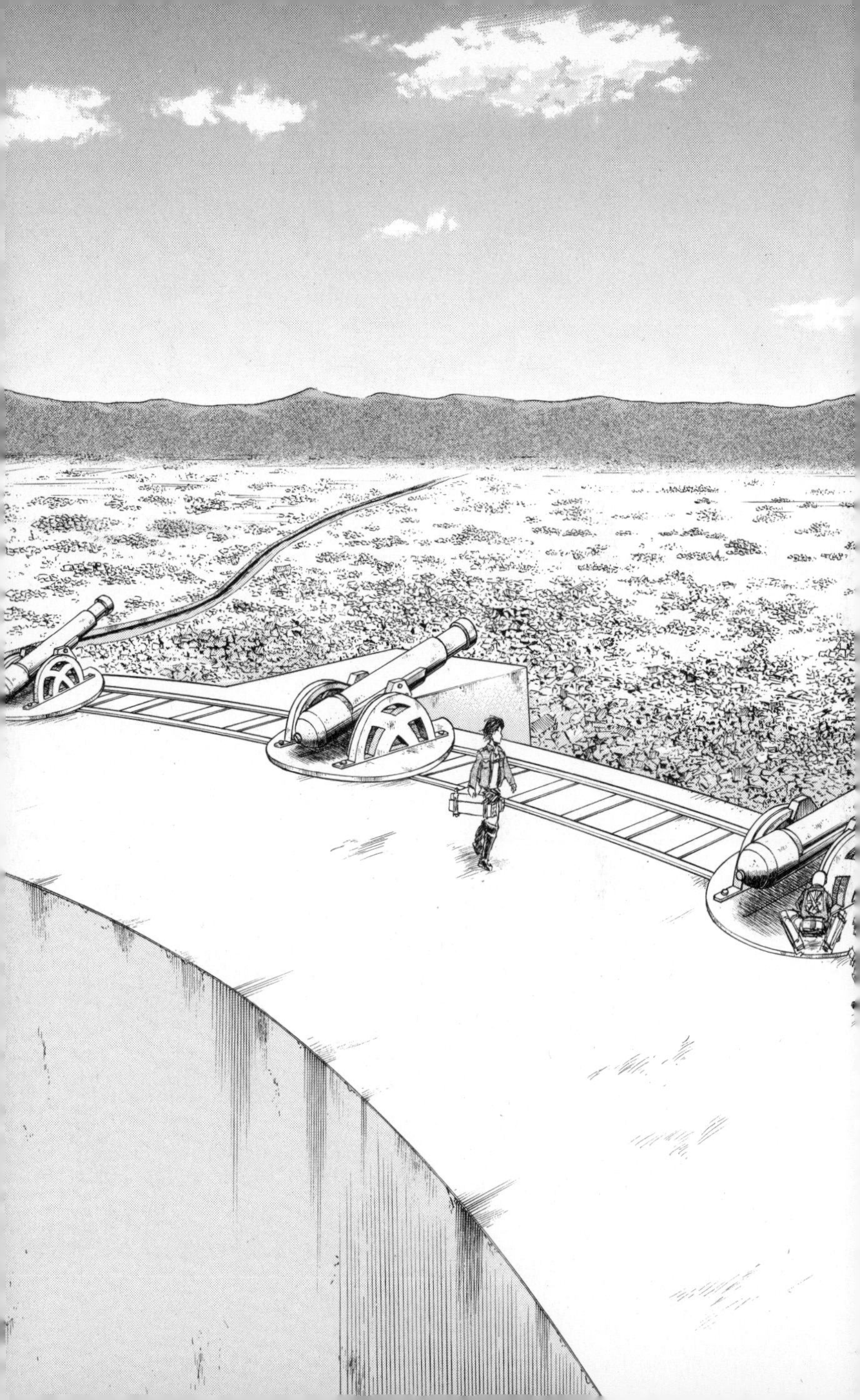

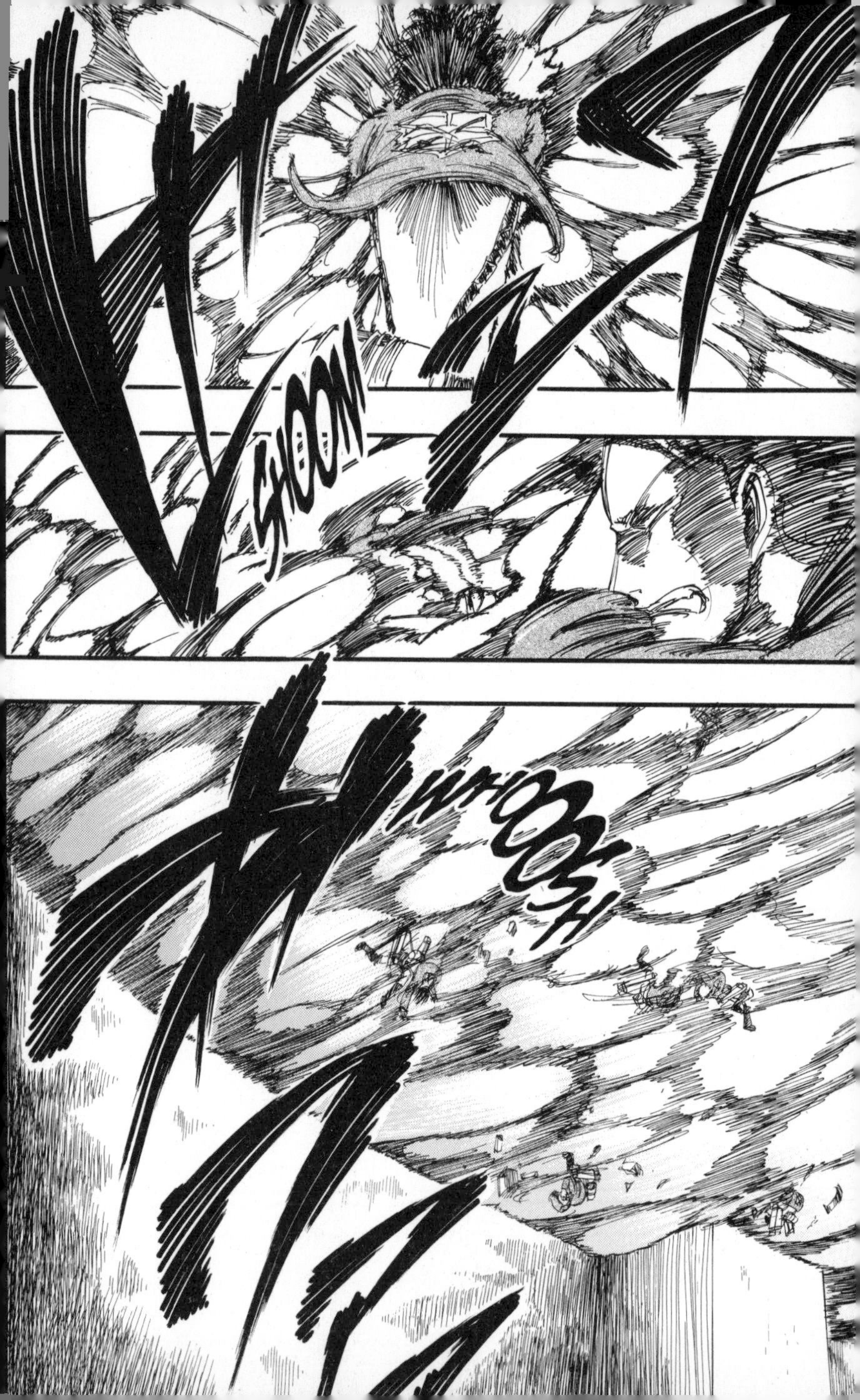
SHOOM
WHOOOSH

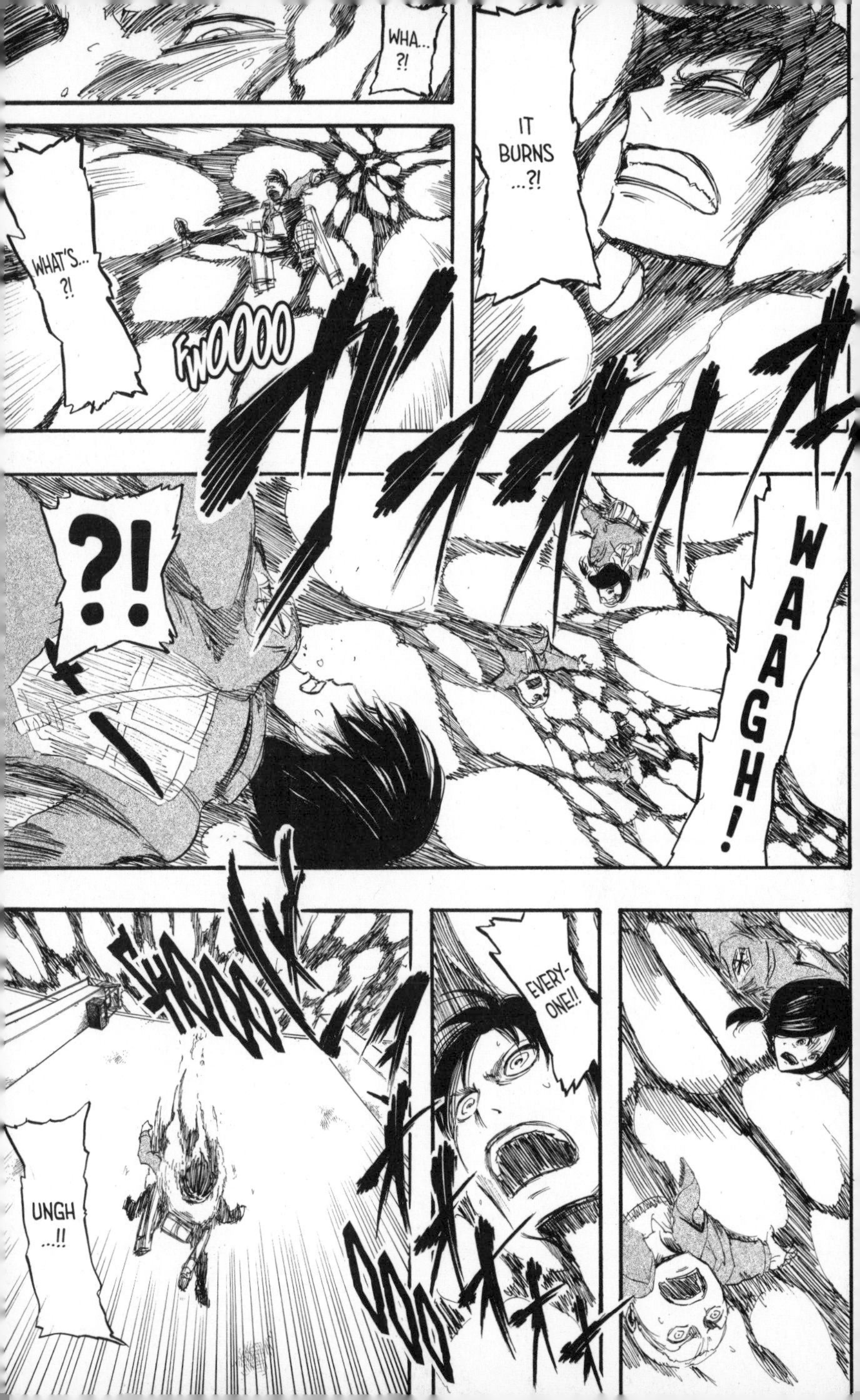
WHA... ?!
IT BURNS ...?!
WHAT'S... ?!
FWOOOO
WAAAGH!
?!
EVERY-ONE!!
UNGH ...!!

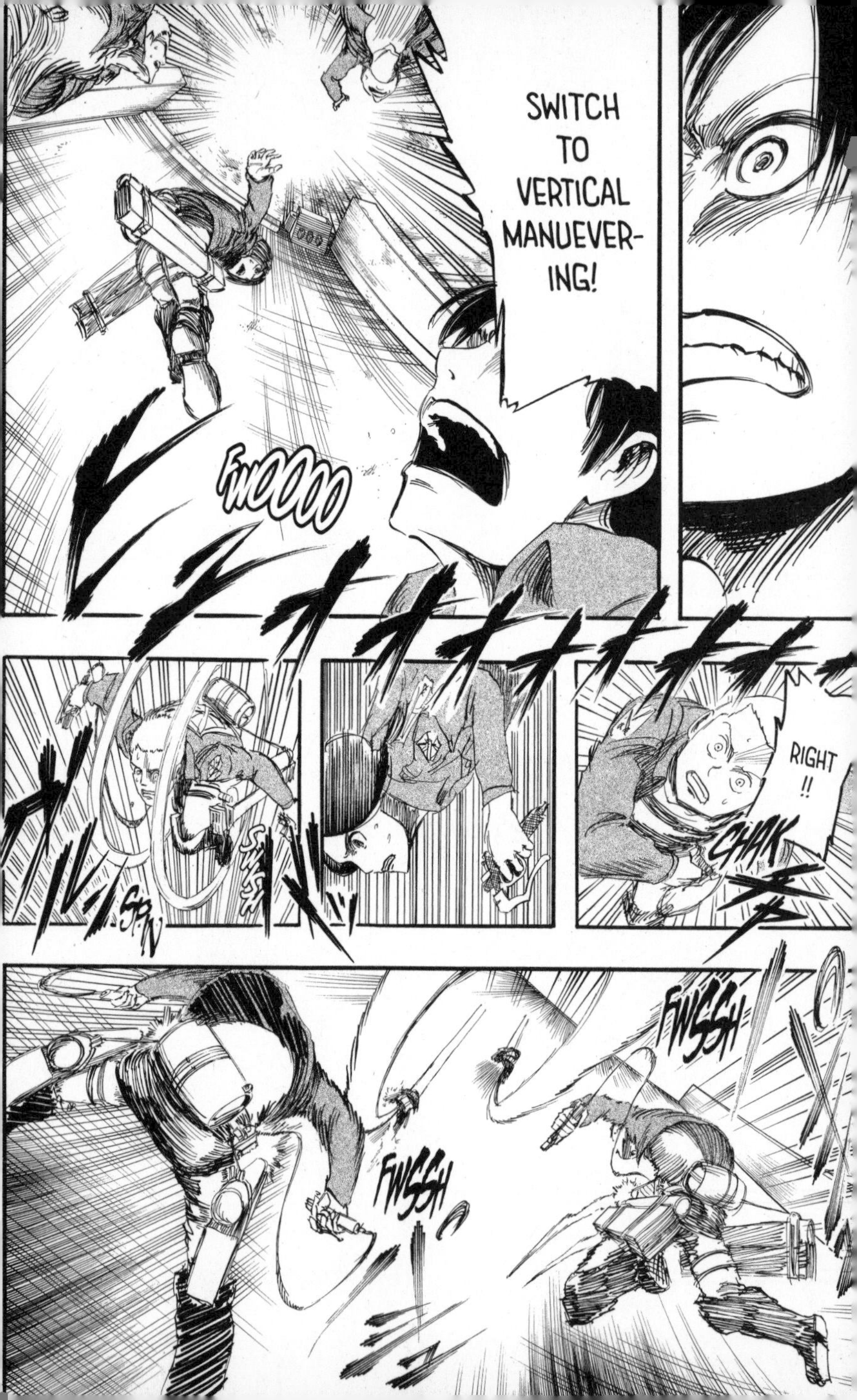
SWITCH TO VERTICAL MANUEVER-ING!
FWOOOO
RIGHT !!
CHAK
SWISH
SPIN
FWSSH
FWSSH

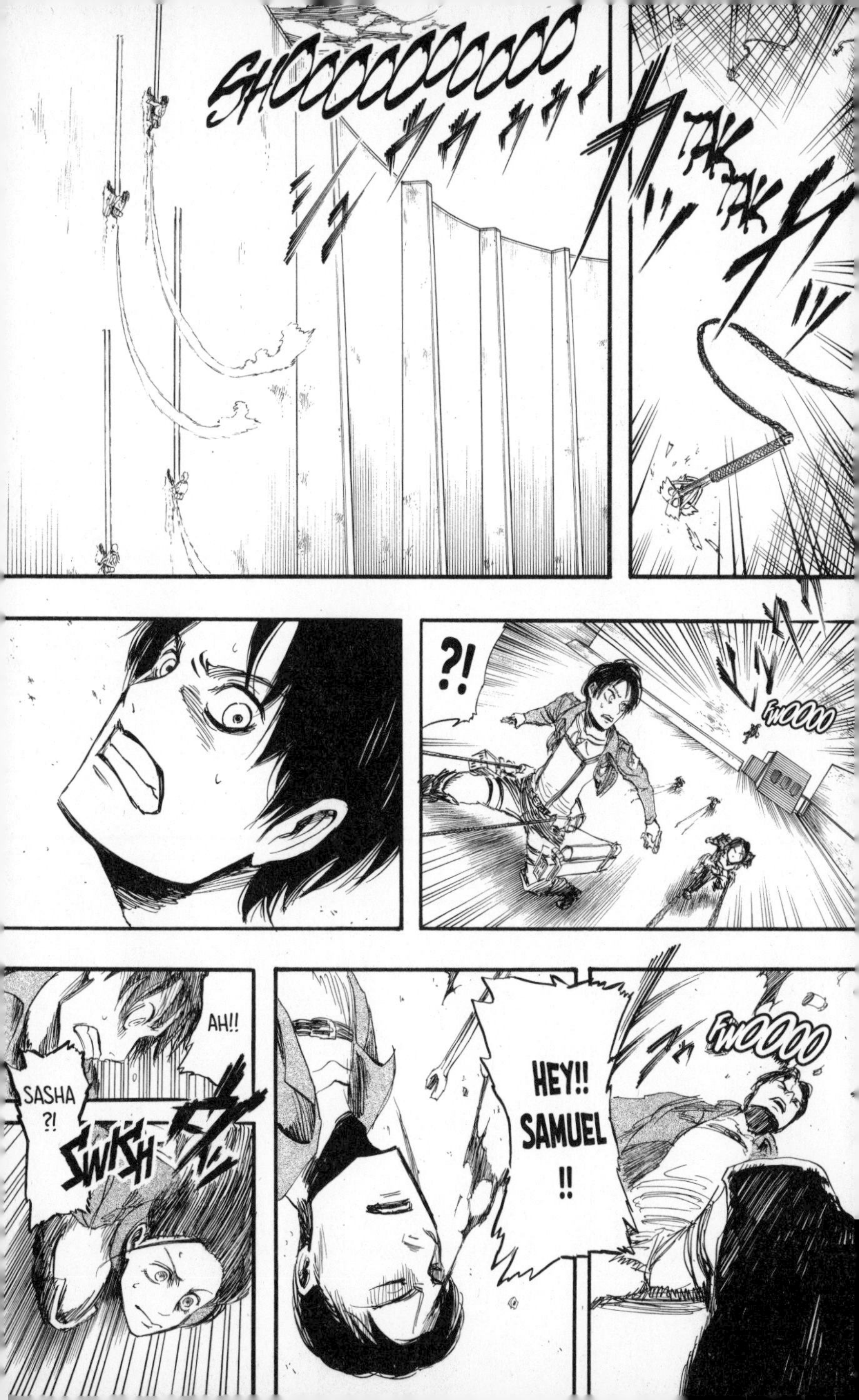
TAK TAK
SHOOOOOOOOOO
?!
FWOOOO
FWOOOO
HEY!! SAMUEL !!
AH!!
SASHA ?!
SWISH

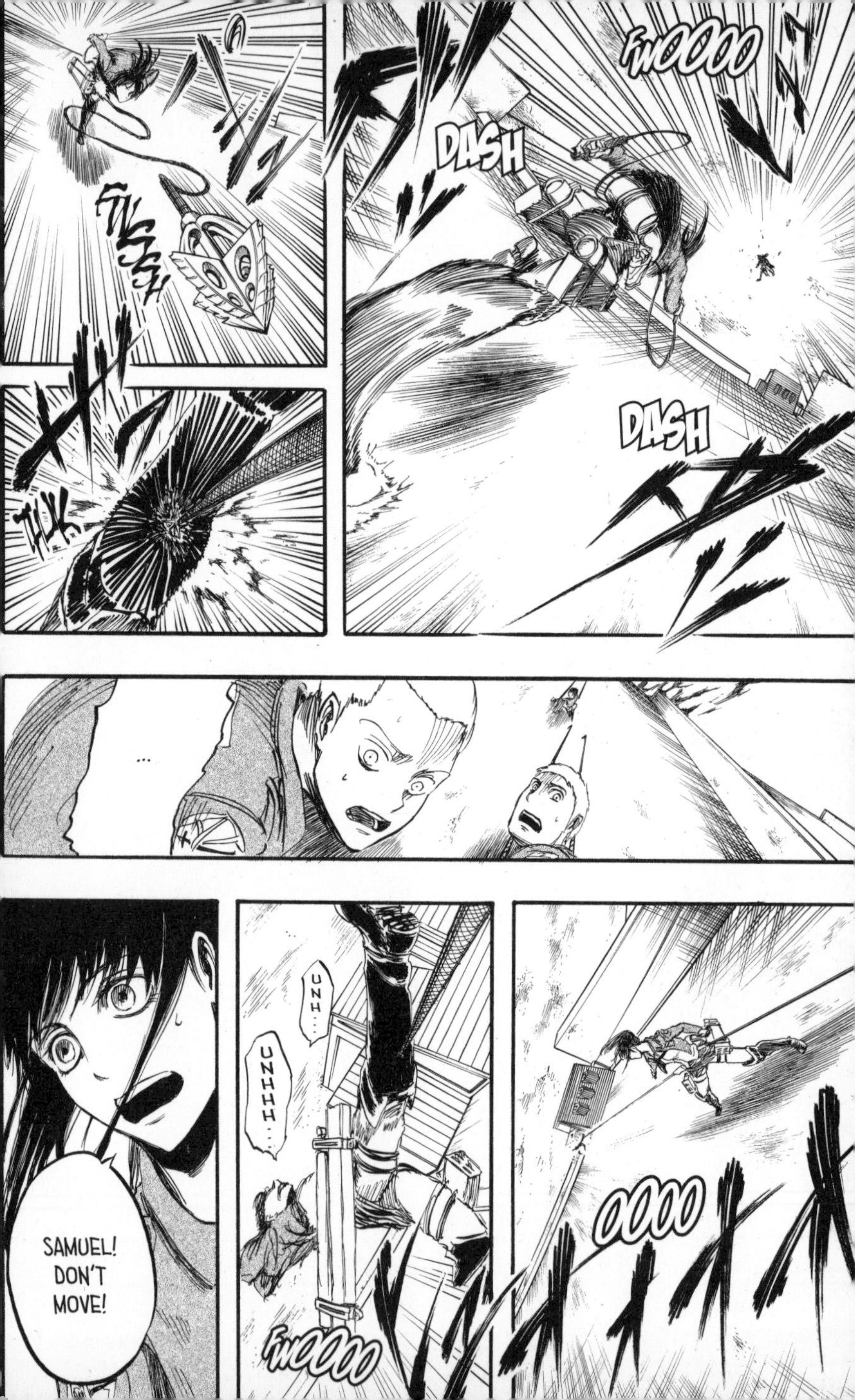
FWOOOO
DASH
DASH
FWSSSH
THUK
...
OOOO
UNH...
UNHHH...
FWOOOO
SAMUEL! DON'T MOVE!

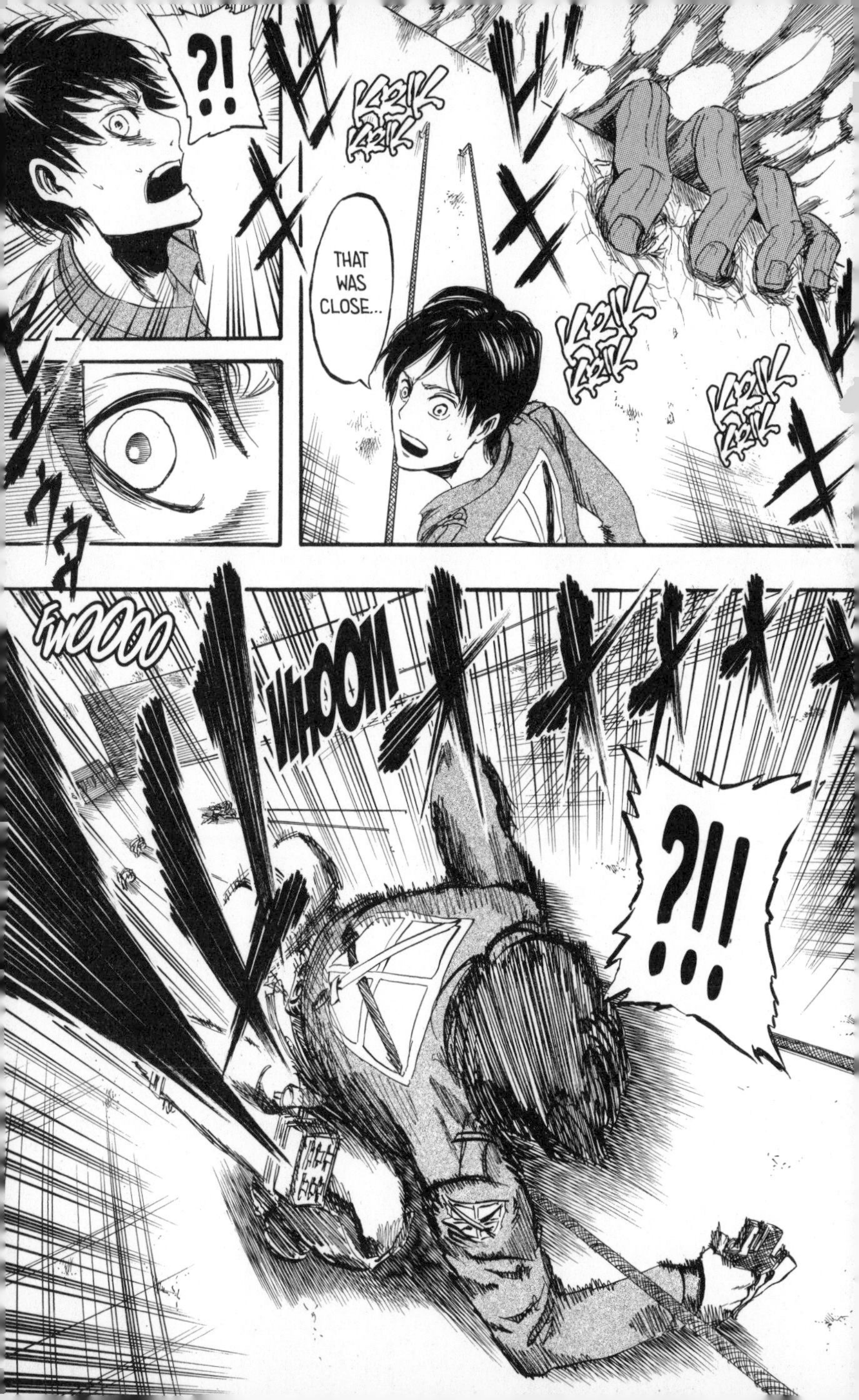
KRAK KRAK
KRAK KRAK
KRAK KRAK
THAT WAS CLOSE...
?!
WHOOM
?!!
FWOOOO

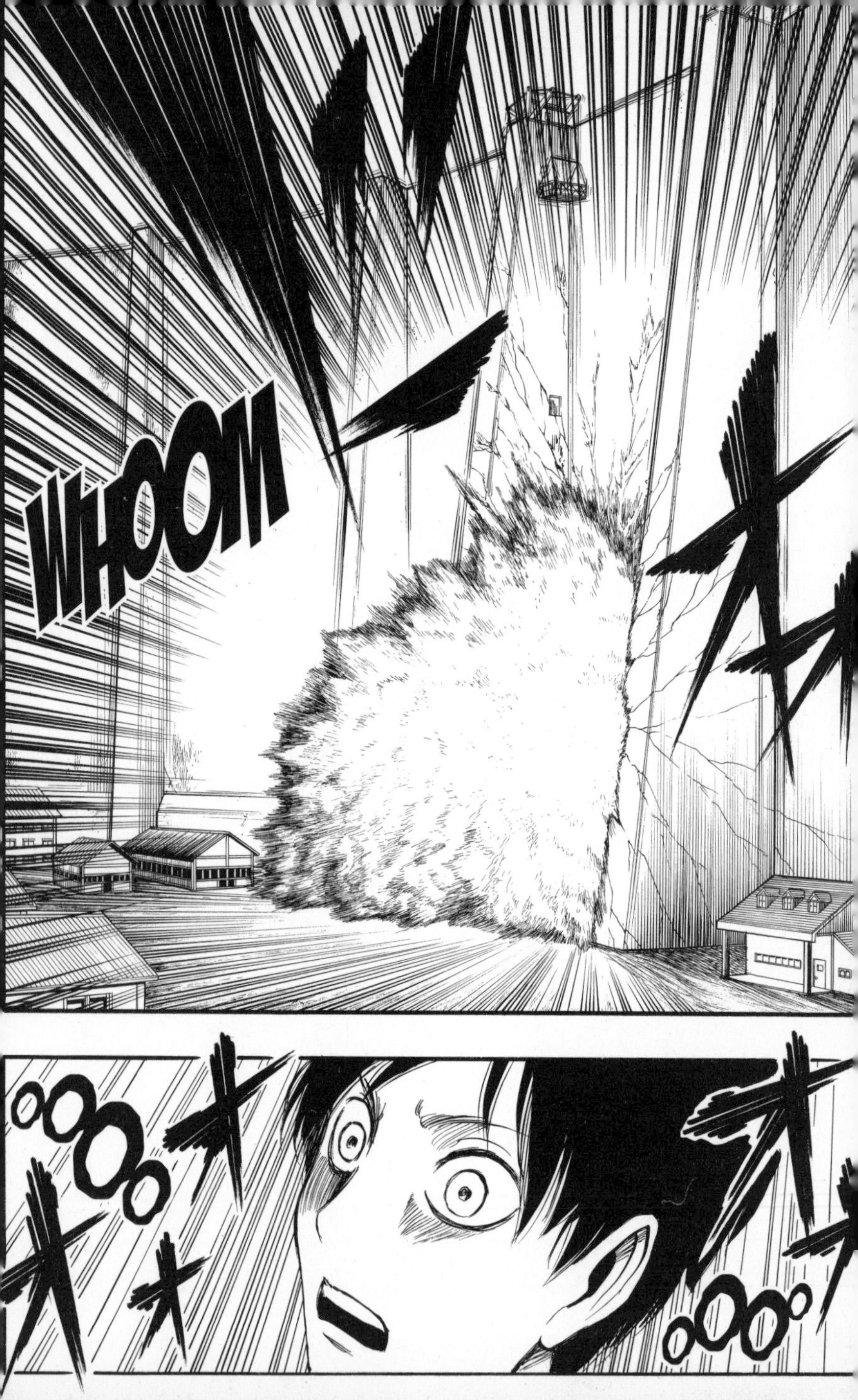
WHOOM

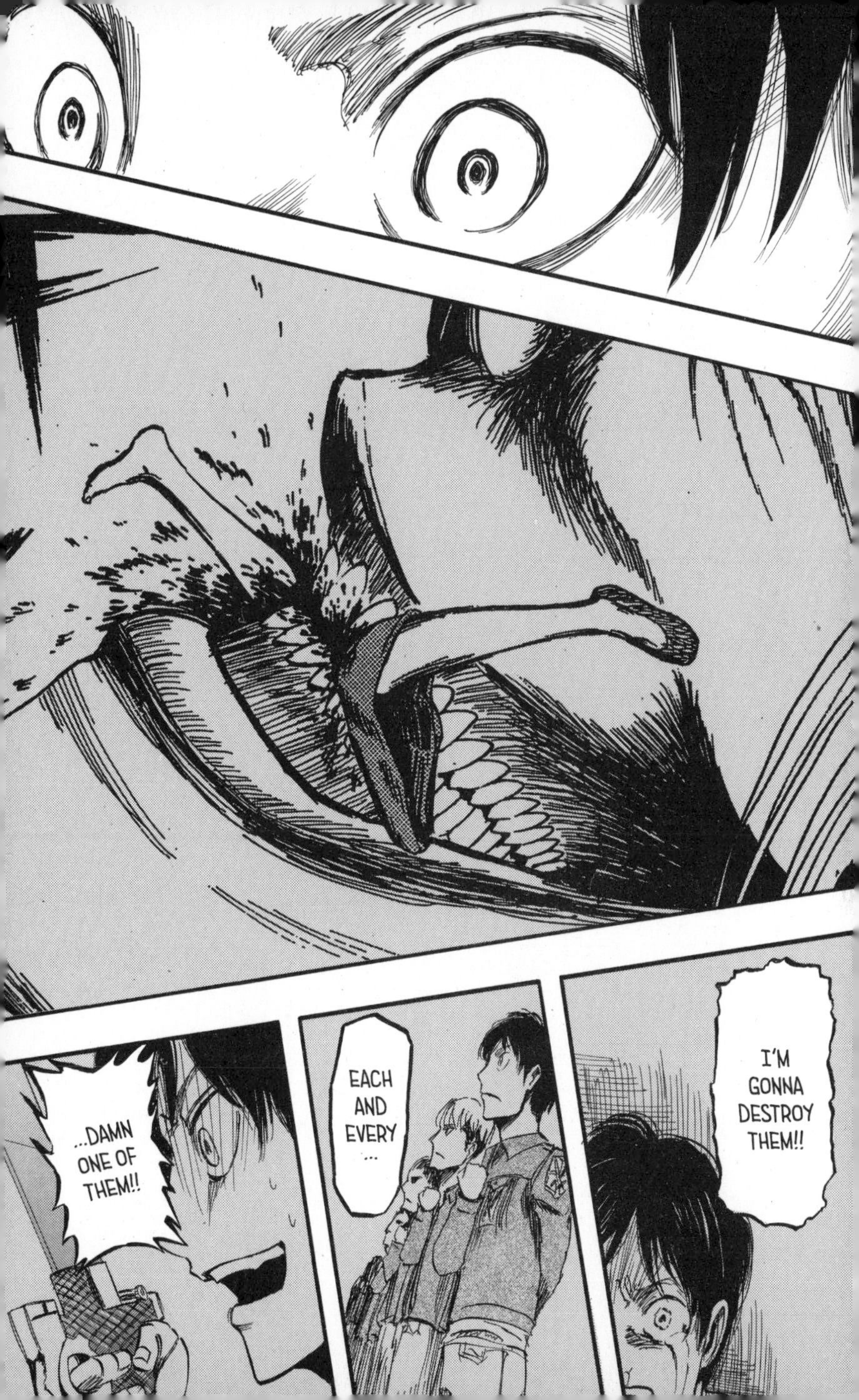
I'M GONNA DESTROY THEM!!
EACH AND EVERY ...
...DAMN ONE OF THEM!!

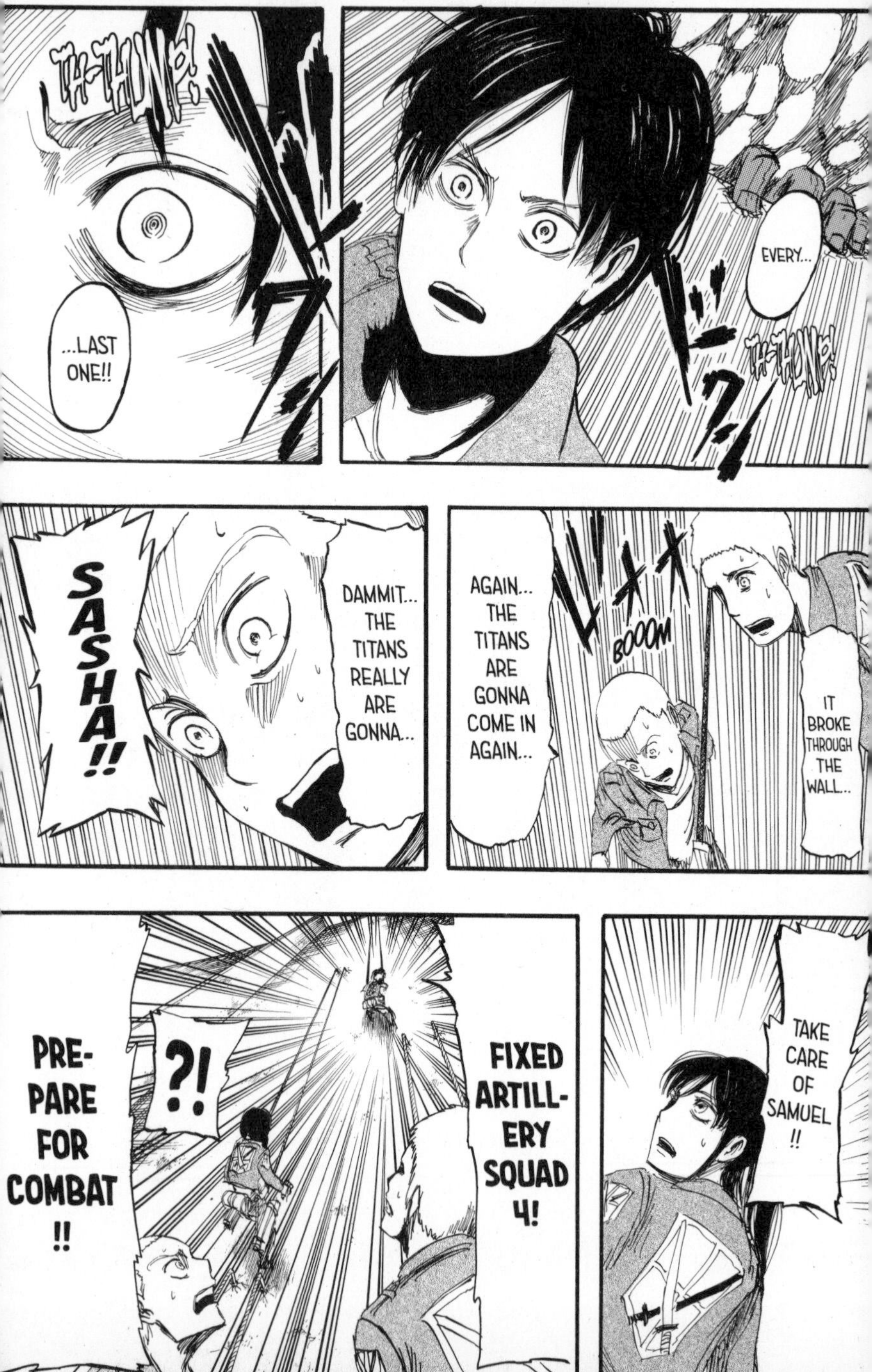
EVERY...
TH-THUNK!
TH-THUNK!
...LAST ONE!!
IT BROKE THROUGH THE WALL...
BOOOM
AGAIN... THE TITANS ARE GONNA COME IN AGAIN...
DAMMIT... THE TITANS REALLY ARE GONNA...
SASHA!!
TAKE CARE OF SAMUEL!!
FIXED ARTILL-ERY SQUAD 4!
?!
PRE-PARE FOR COMBAT!!

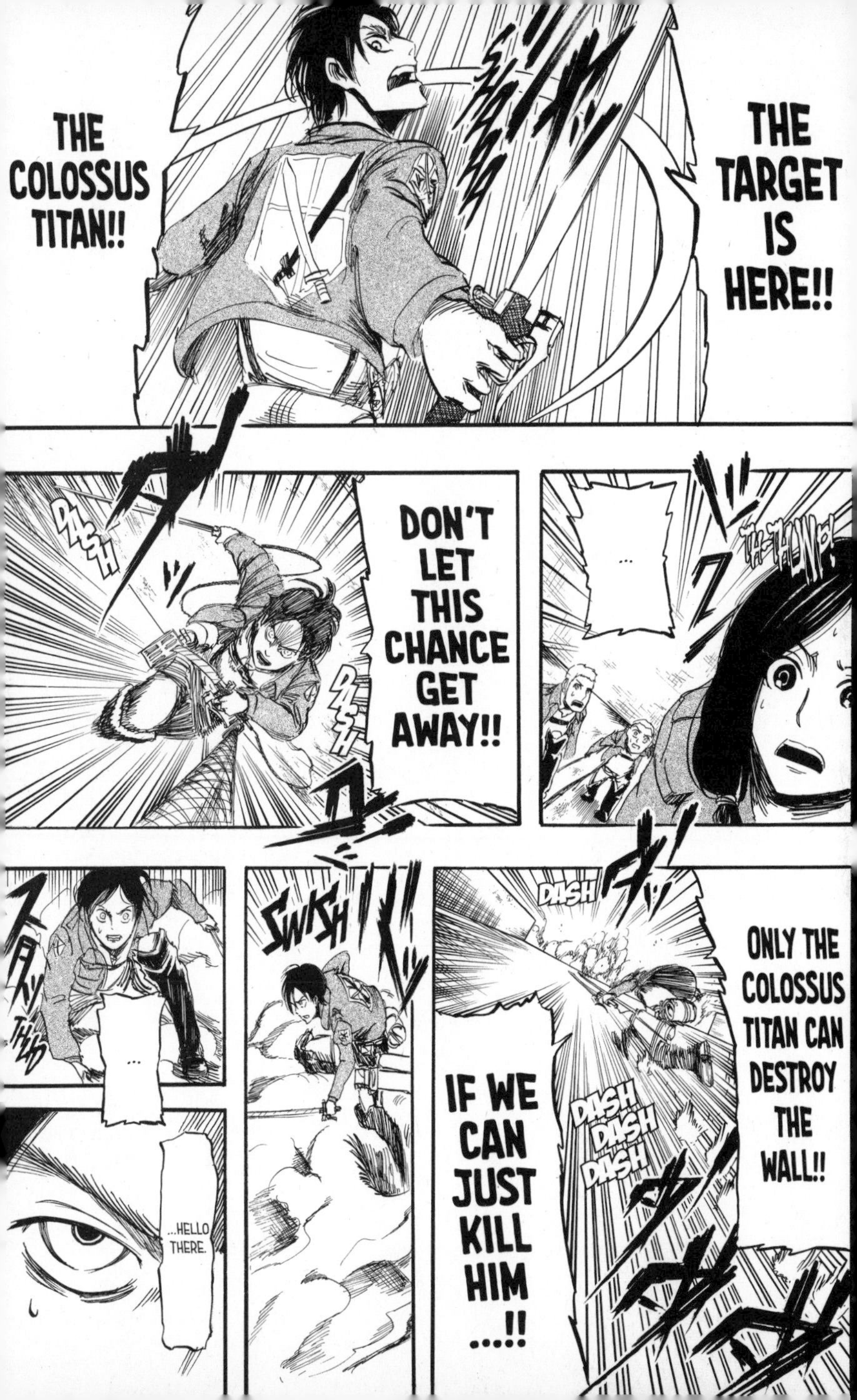
THE TARGET IS HERE!!
THE COLOSSUS TITAN!!
TH-THUMP!
...
DASH
DON'T LET THIS CHANCE GET AWAY!!
DASH
DASH
ONLY THE COLOSSUS TITAN CAN DESTROY THE WALL!!
IF WE CAN JUST KILL HIM ...!!
DASH DASH DASH
SWISH
...
...HELLO THERE.

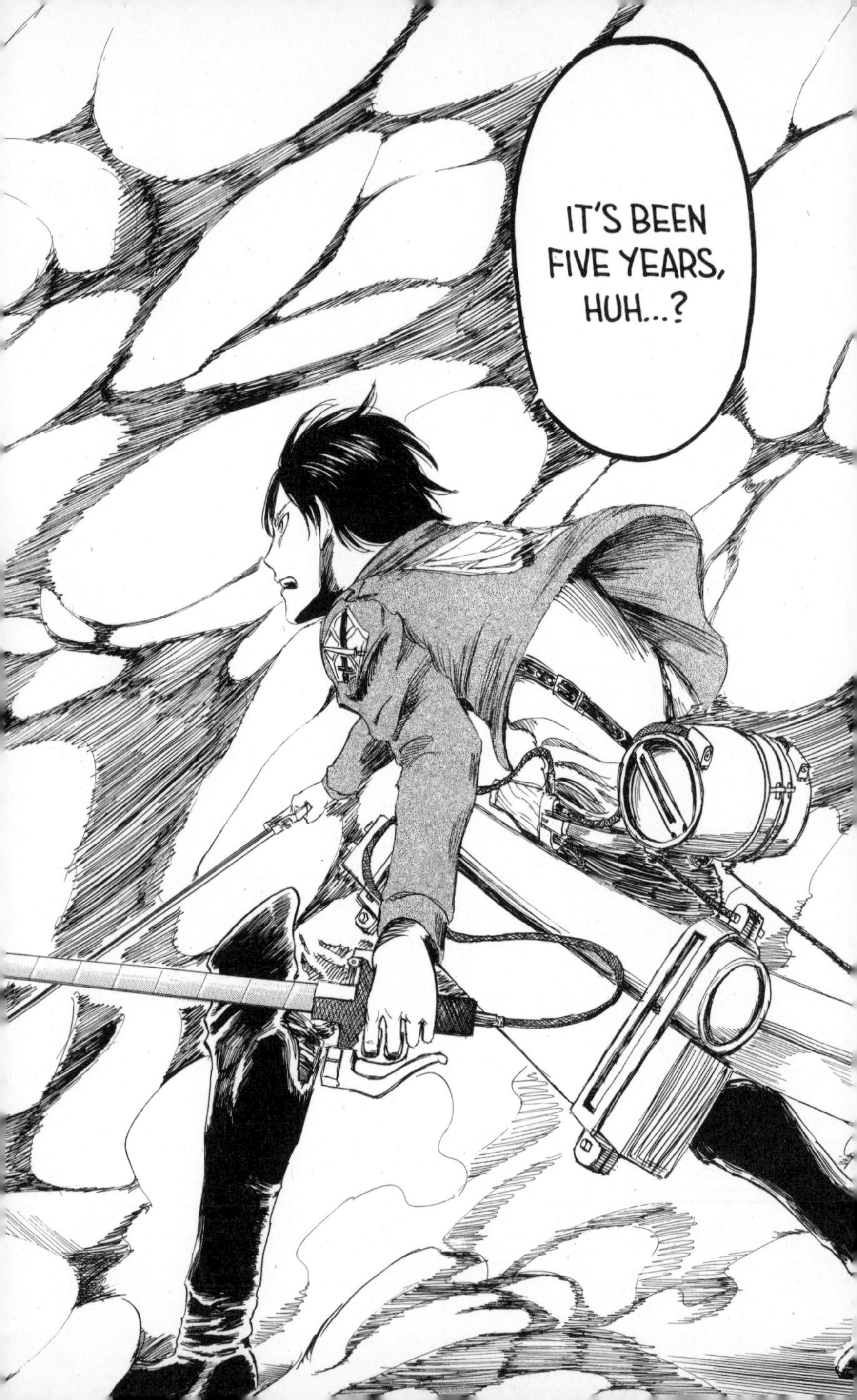
IT'S BEEN FIVE YEARS, HUH...?

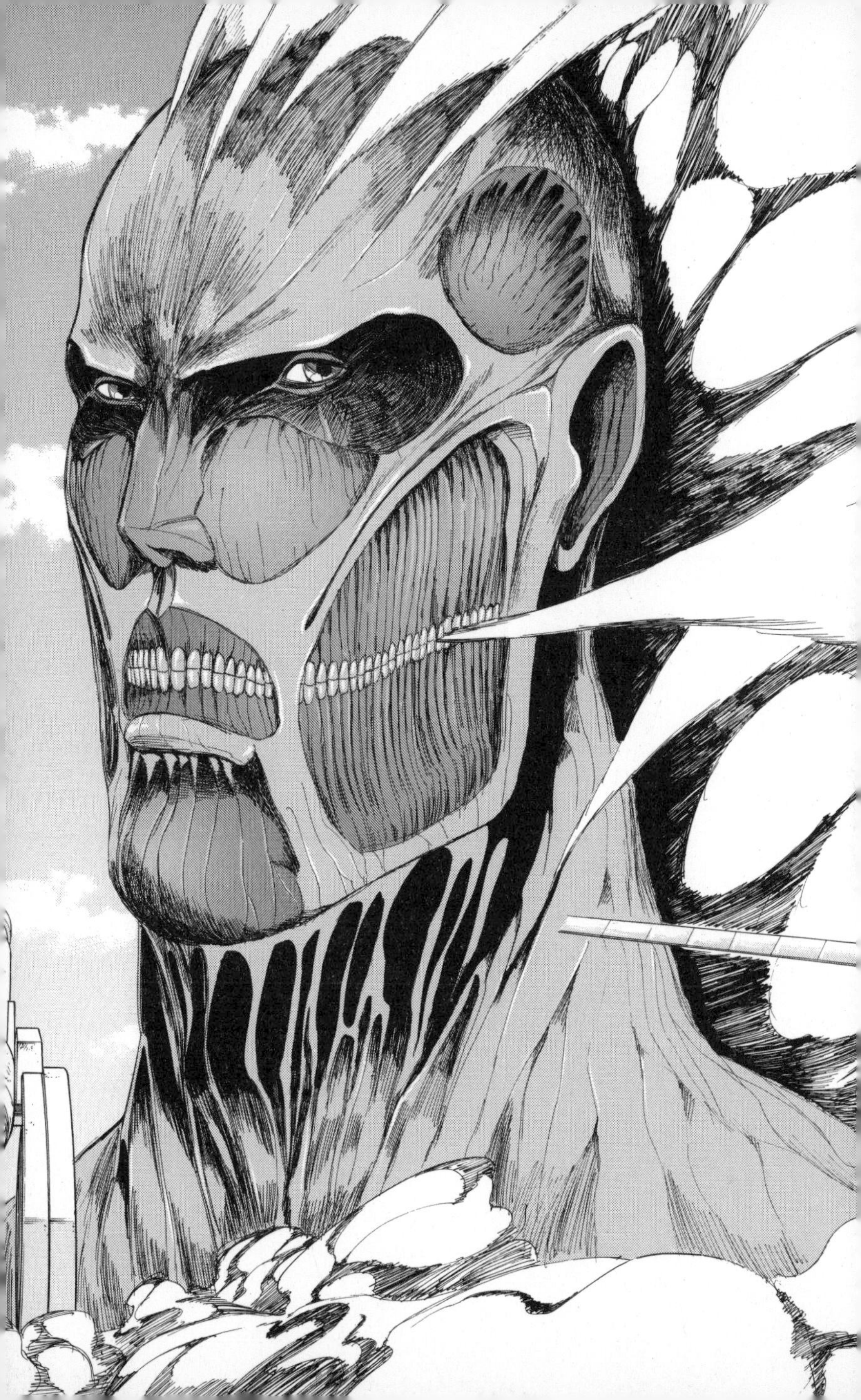

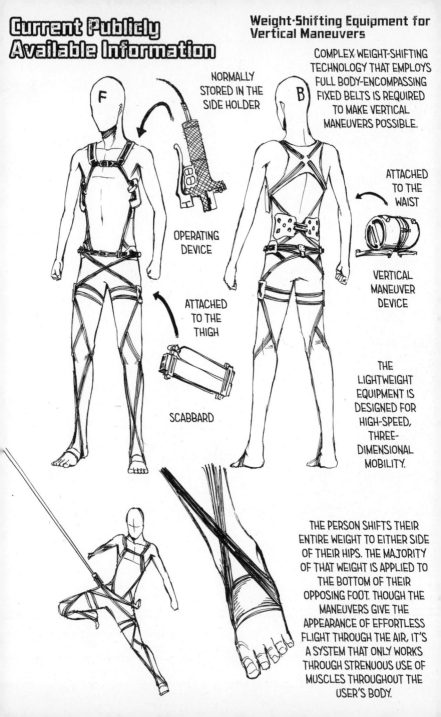

Current Publicly Available Information

Weight-Shifting Equipment for Vertical Maneuvers

COMPLEX WEIGHT-SHIFTING TECHNOLOGY THAT EMPLOYS FULL BODY-ENCOMPASSING FIXED BELTS IS REQUIRED TO MAKE VERTICAL MANEUVERS POSSIBLE.

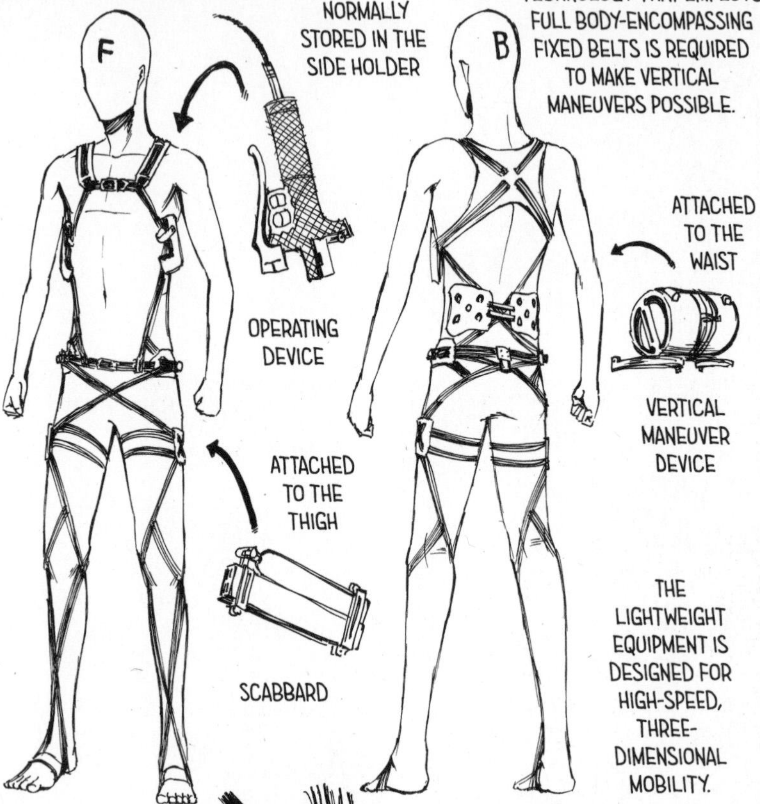
F
NORMALLY STORED IN THE SIDE HOLDER
B
ATTACHED TO THE WAIST
OPERATING DEVICE
VERTICAL MANEUVER DEVICE
ATTACHED TO THE THIGH
SCABBARD

THE LIGHTWEIGHT EQUIPMENT IS DESIGNED FOR HIGH-SPEED, THREE-DIMENSIONAL MOBILITY.

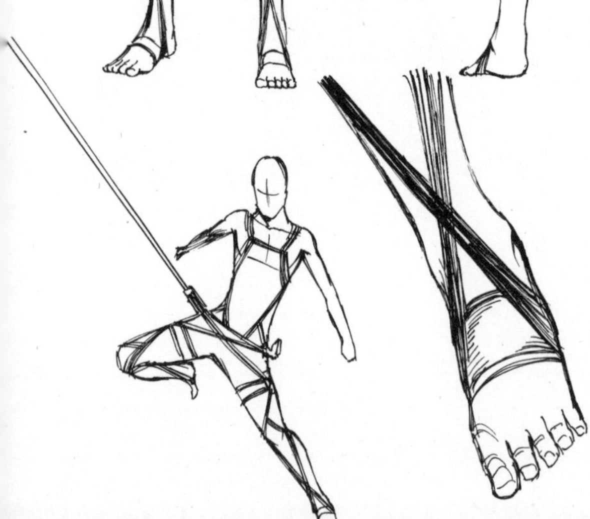

THE PERSON SHIFTS THEIR ENTIRE WEIGHT TO EITHER SIDE OF THEIR HIPS. THE MAJORITY OF THAT WEIGHT IS APPLIED TO THE BOTTOM OF THEIR OPPOSING FOOT. THOUGH THE MANEUVERS GIVE THE APPEARANCE OF EFFORTLESS FLIGHT THROUGH THE AIR, IT'S A SYSTEM THAT ONLY WORKS THROUGH STRENUOUS USE OF MUSCLES THROUGHOUT THE USER'S BODY.

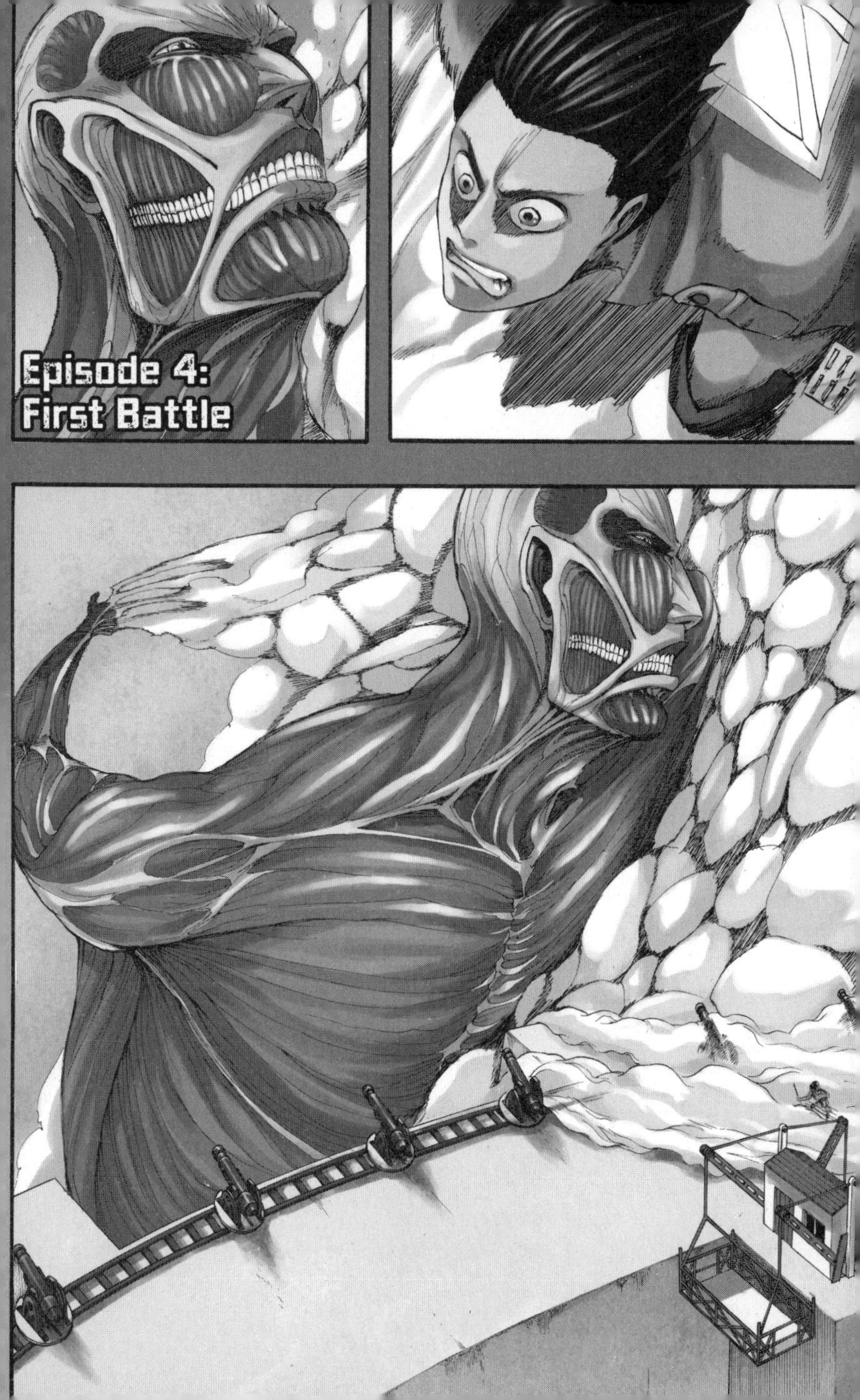
Episode 4:
First Battle

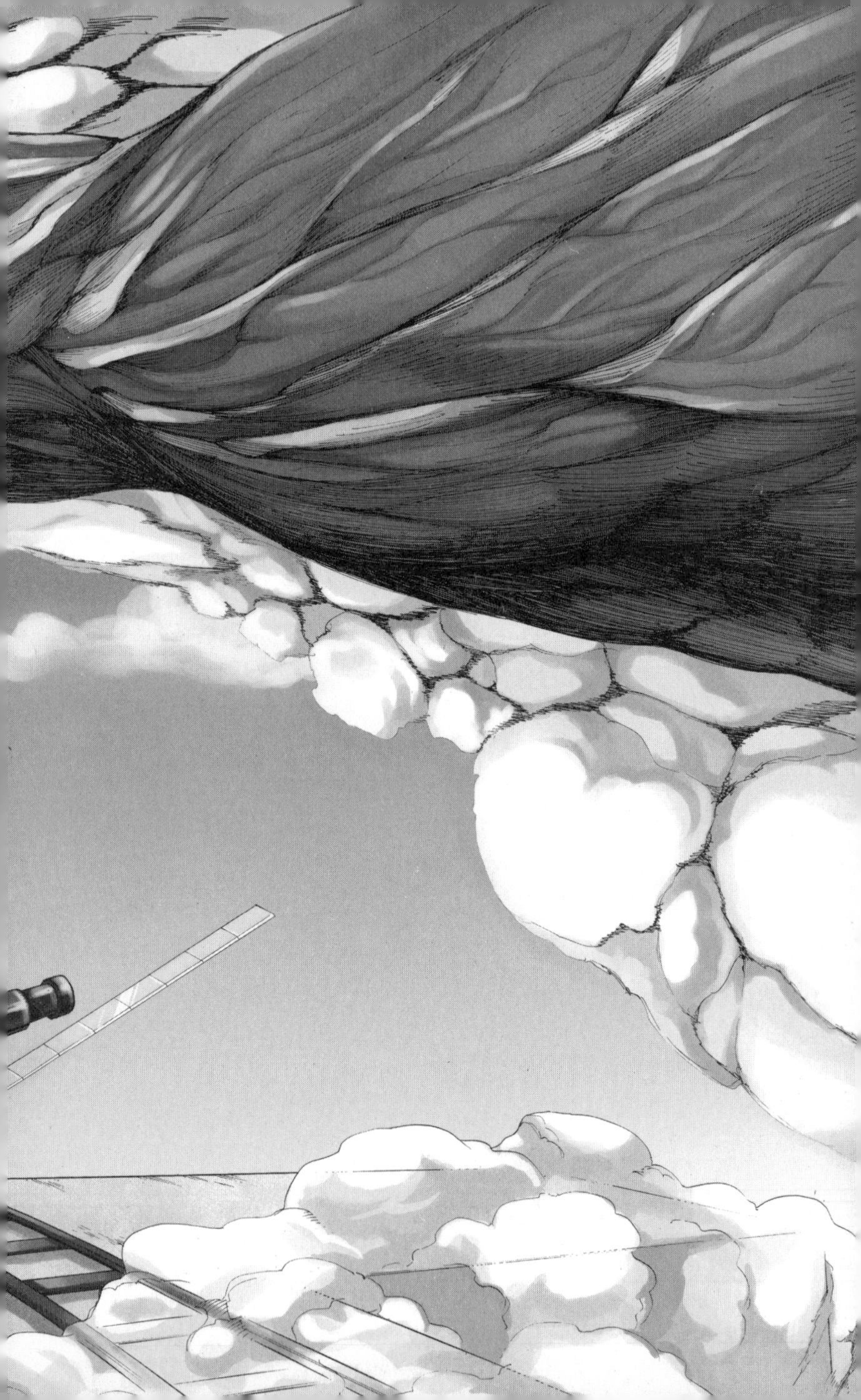

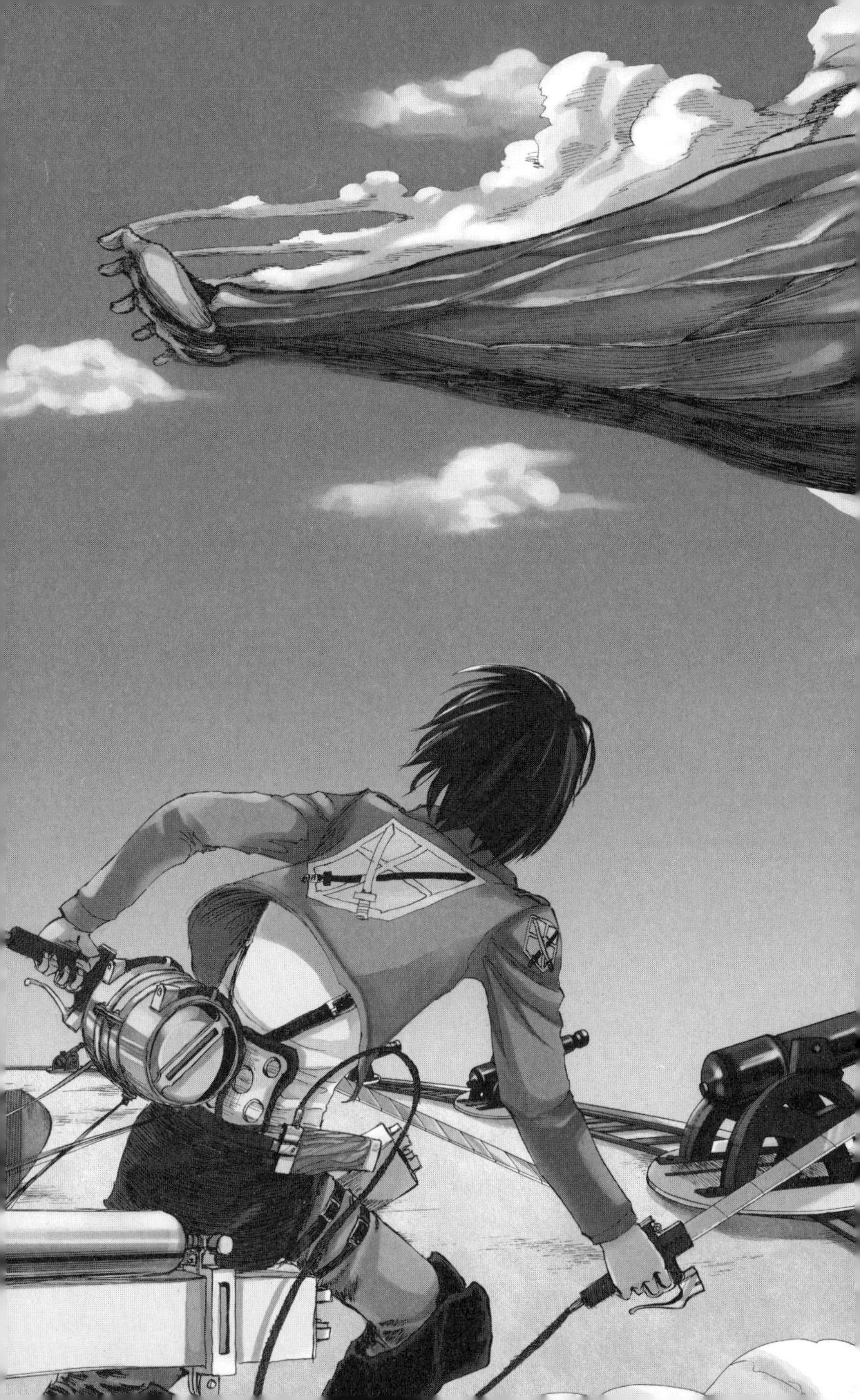

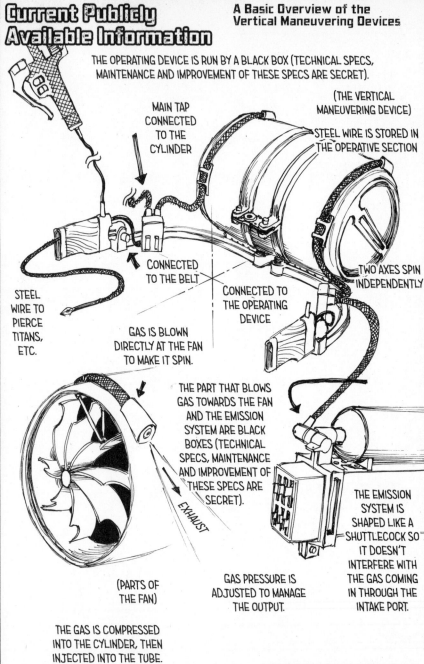

Current Publicly Available Information

A Basic Overview of the Vertical Maneuvering Devices

THE OPERATING DEVICE IS RUN BY A BLACK BOX (TECHNICAL SPECS, MAINTENANCE AND IMPROVEMENT OF THESE SPECS ARE SECRET).

MAIN TAP CONNECTED TO THE CYLINDER

(THE VERTICAL MANEUVERING DEVICE)

STEEL WIRE IS STORED IN THE OPERATIVE SECTION

CONNECTED TO THE BELT

CONNECTED TO THE OPERATING DEVICE

TWO AXES SPIN INDEPENDENTLY

STEEL WIRE TO PIERCE TITANS, ETC.

GAS IS BLOWN DIRECTLY AT THE FAN TO MAKE IT SPIN.

THE PART THAT BLOWS GAS TOWARDS THE FAN AND THE EMISSION SYSTEM ARE BLACK BOXES (TECHNICAL SPECS, MAINTENANCE AND IMPROVEMENT OF THESE SPECS ARE SECRET).

EXHAUST

THE EMISSION SYSTEM IS SHAPED LIKE A SHUTTLECOCK SO IT DOESN'T INTERFERE WITH THE GAS COMING IN THROUGH THE INTAKE PORT.

(PARTS OF THE FAN)

GAS PRESSURE IS ADJUSTED TO MANAGE THE OUTPUT.

THE GAS IS COMPRESSED INTO THE CYLINDER, THEN INJECTED INTO THE TUBE.

THANKS TO MY SCIENTIST FRIEND WHO HELPED ME COME UP WITH THIS!

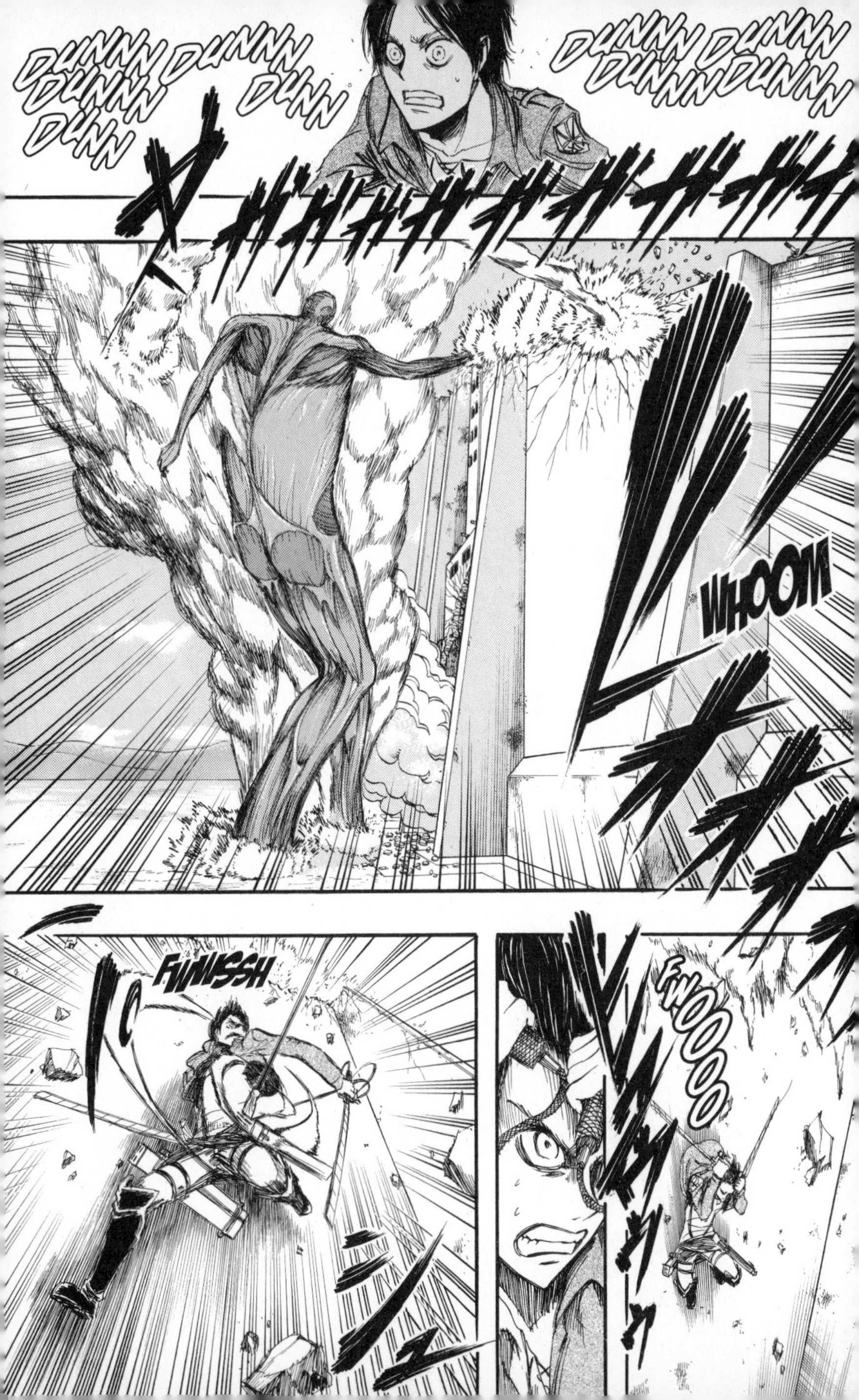
DUNNN DUNNN
DUNNN DUNNN
DUNNN
DUNN
DUNNN
DUNNN
DUNN
WHOOM
FWOOOO
FWUSSH

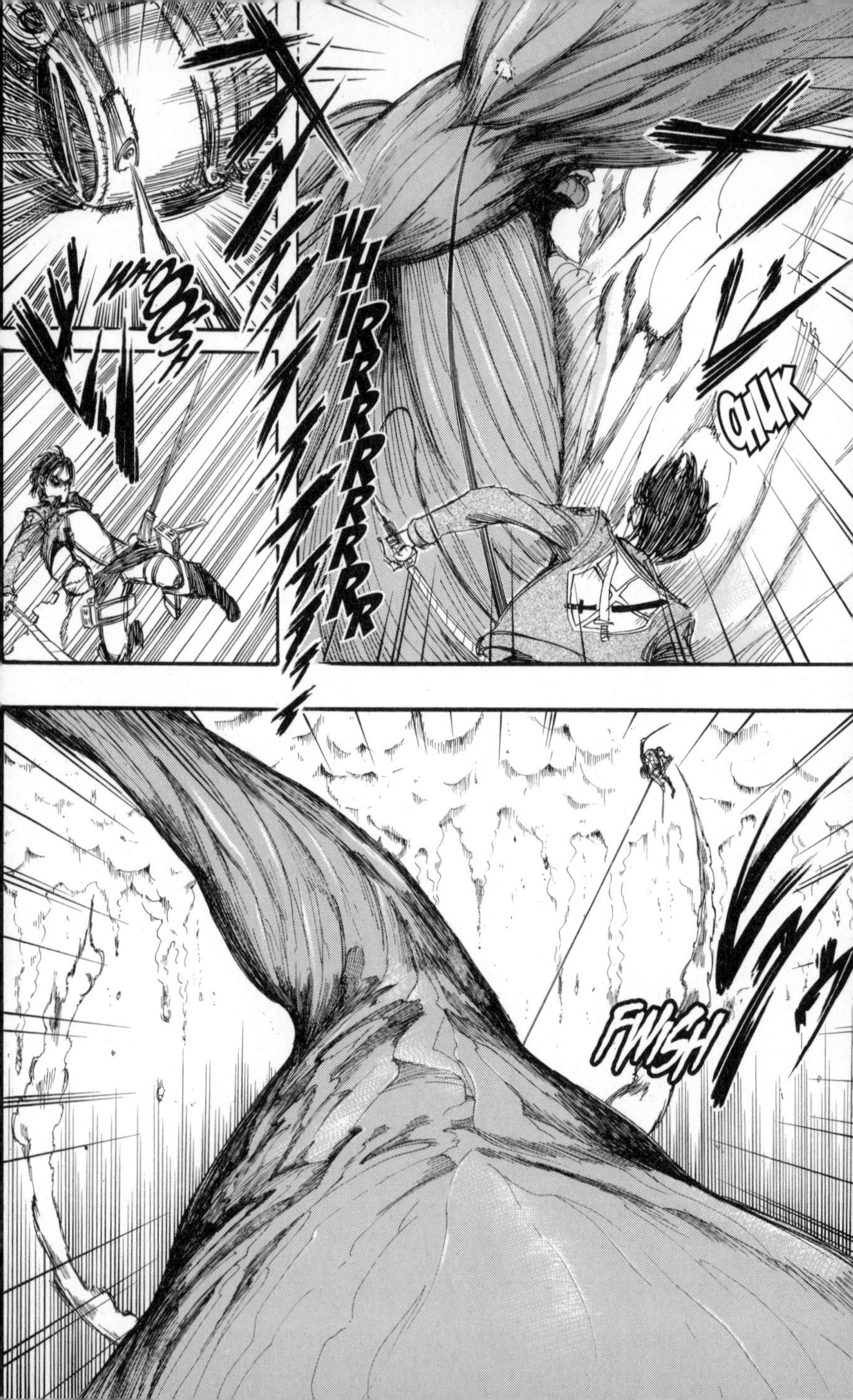
CHUK
WHIRRRRRRRRR
WHOOOSH
FWISH

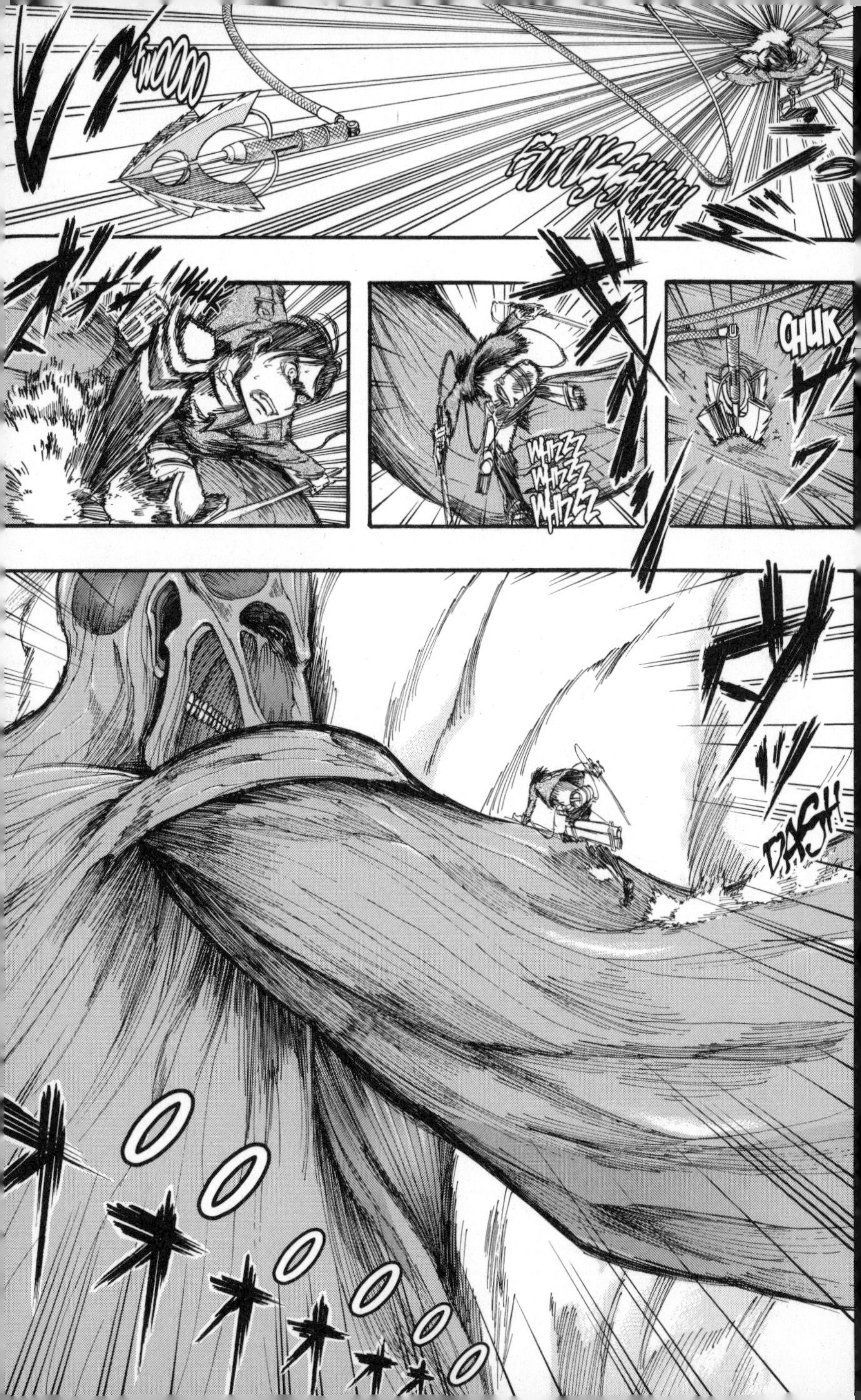
FWOOOO
FWSHHHH
CHUK
WHIZZZ
WHIZZZ
WHIZZZ
DASH

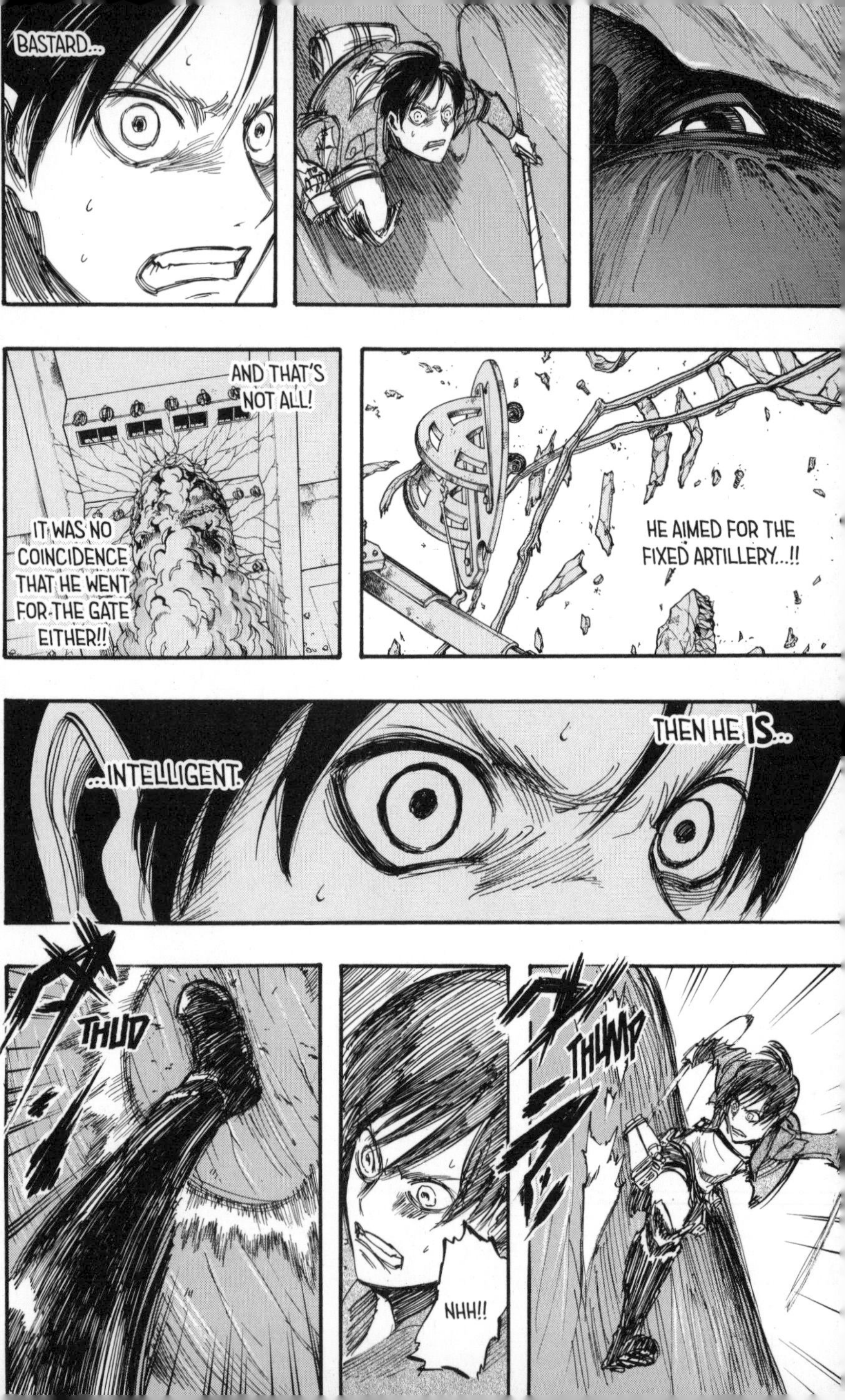
BASTARD...
HE AIMED FOR THE FIXED ARTILLERY...!!
AND THAT'S NOT ALL!
IT WAS NO COINCIDENCE THAT HE WENT FOR THE GATE EITHER!!
THEN HE IS...
...INTELLIGENT.
THUMP
NHH!!
THUD

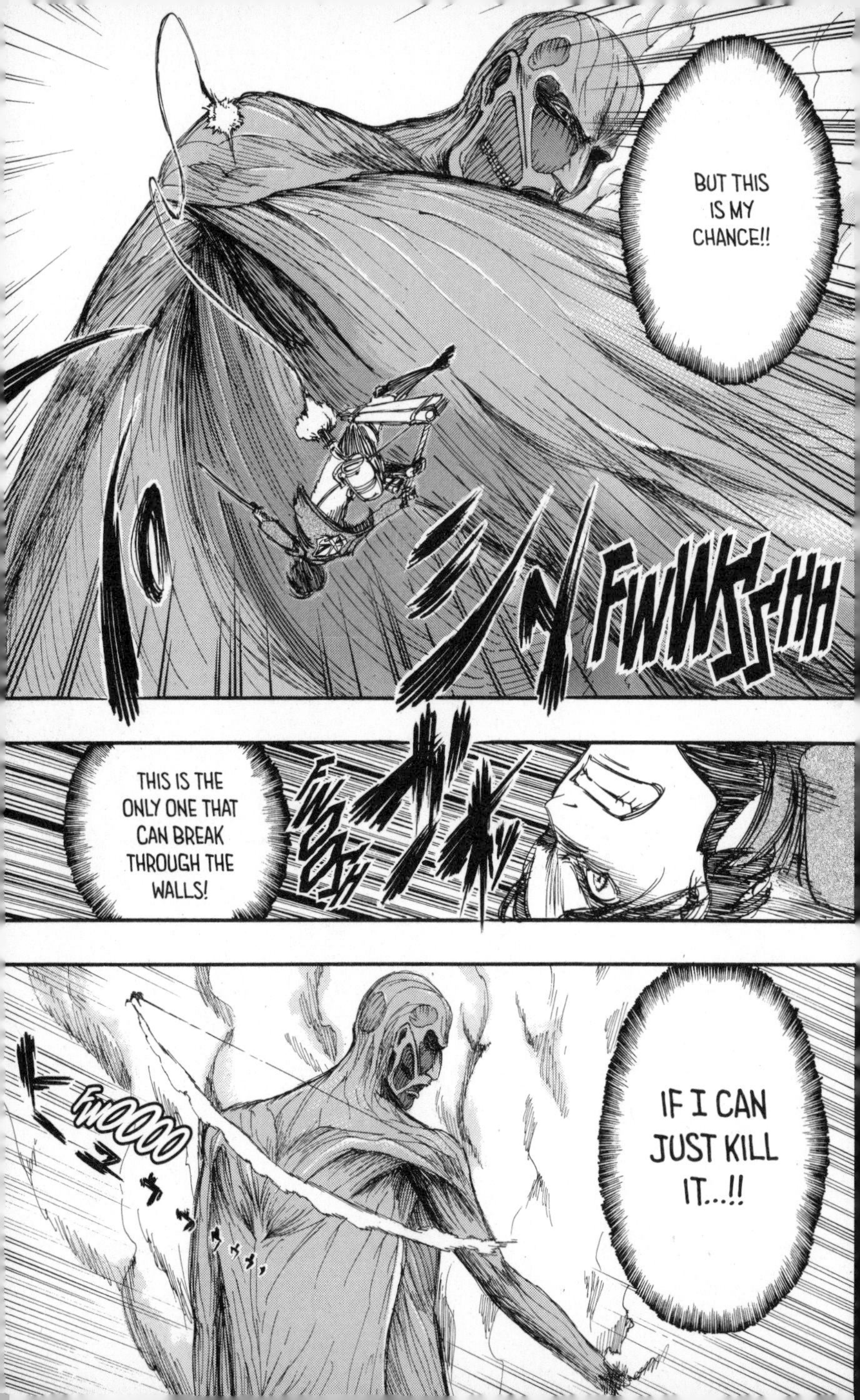
BUT THIS IS MY CHANCE!!
FWWSHH
FWOOSH
THIS IS THE ONLY ONE THAT CAN BREAK THROUGH THE WALLS!
IF I CAN JUST KILL IT...!!
FWOOOO

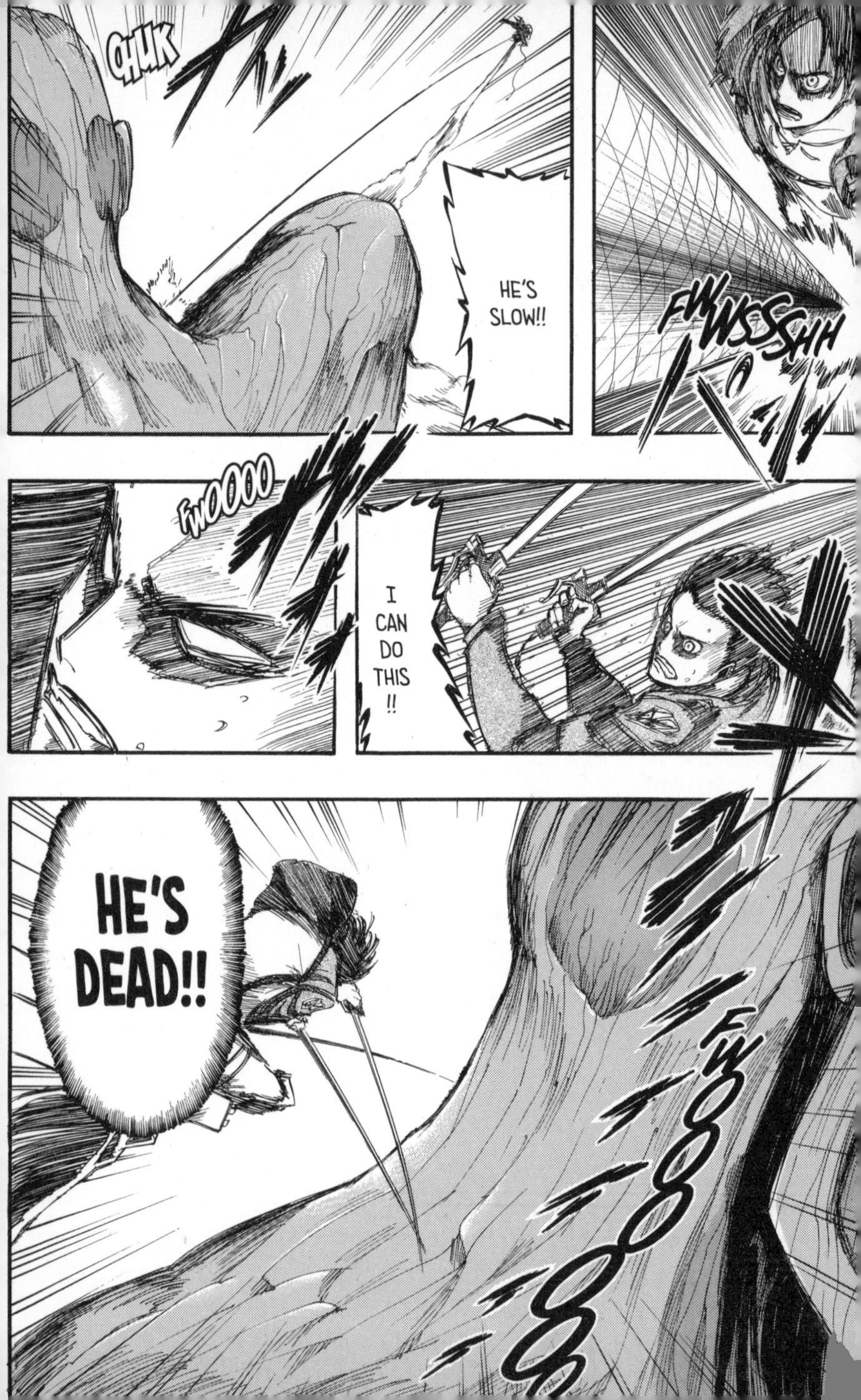
FWWSSSHH
CHUK
HE'S SLOW!!
I CAN DO THIS!!
FWOOOO
HE'S DEAD!!
FWOOOOOOO

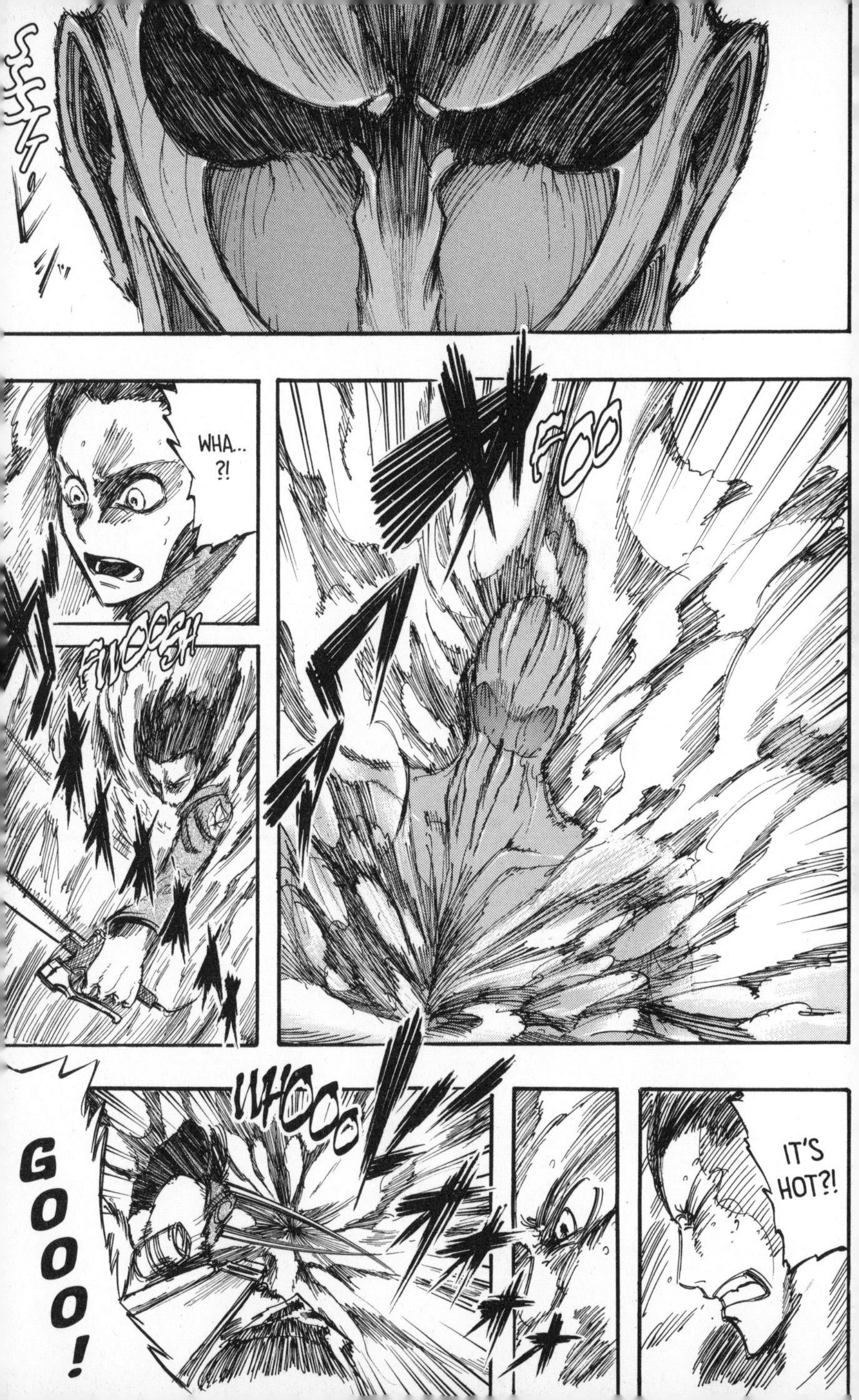
FOO
WHA... ?!
FWOOSH
IT'S HOT?!
WHOOO
GOOOO!

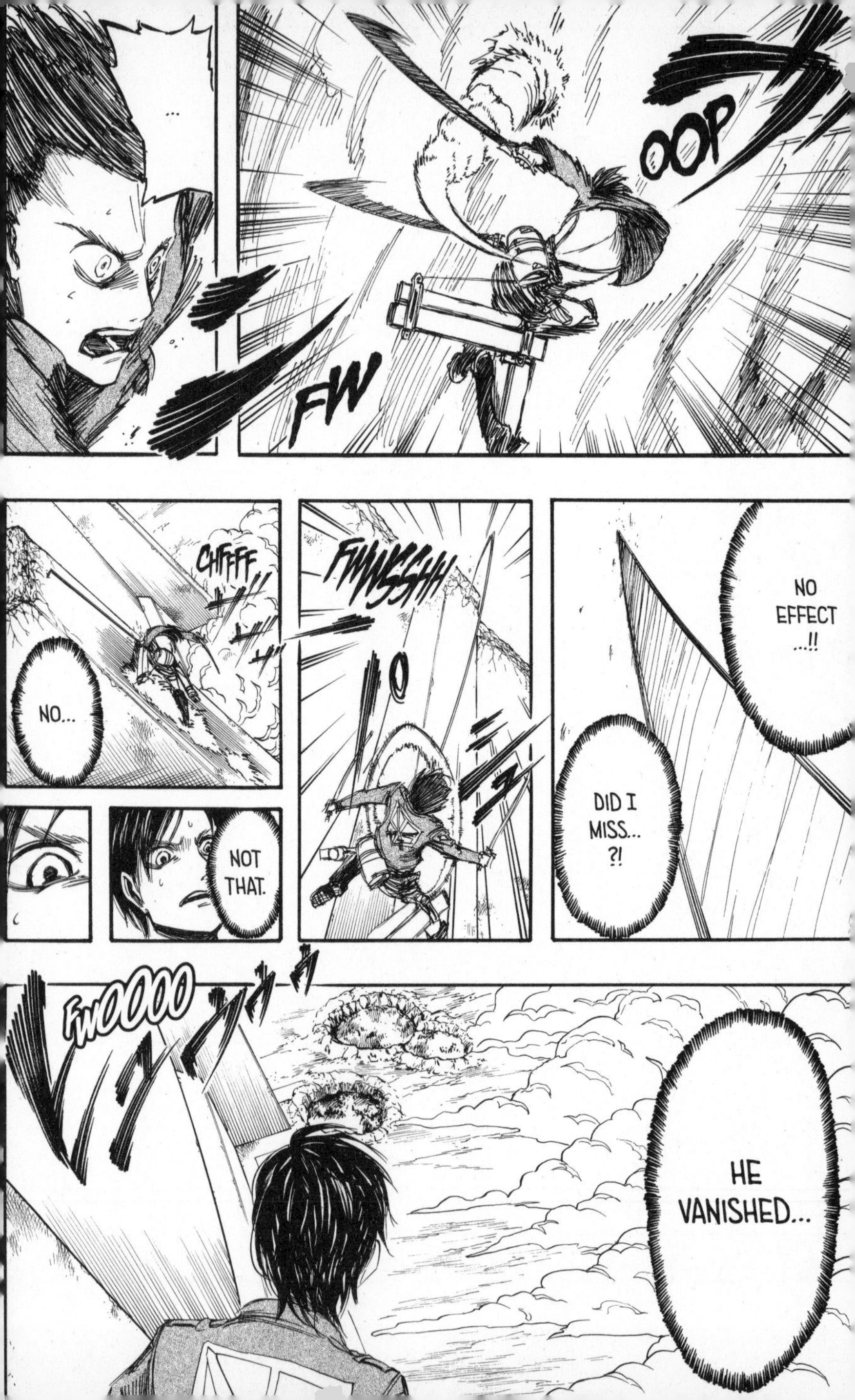

FW
OOP
...
NO EFFECT ...!!
DID I MISS... ?!
FWASSHH
CHFFFF
NO...
NOT THAT.
FWOOOO
HE VANISHED...

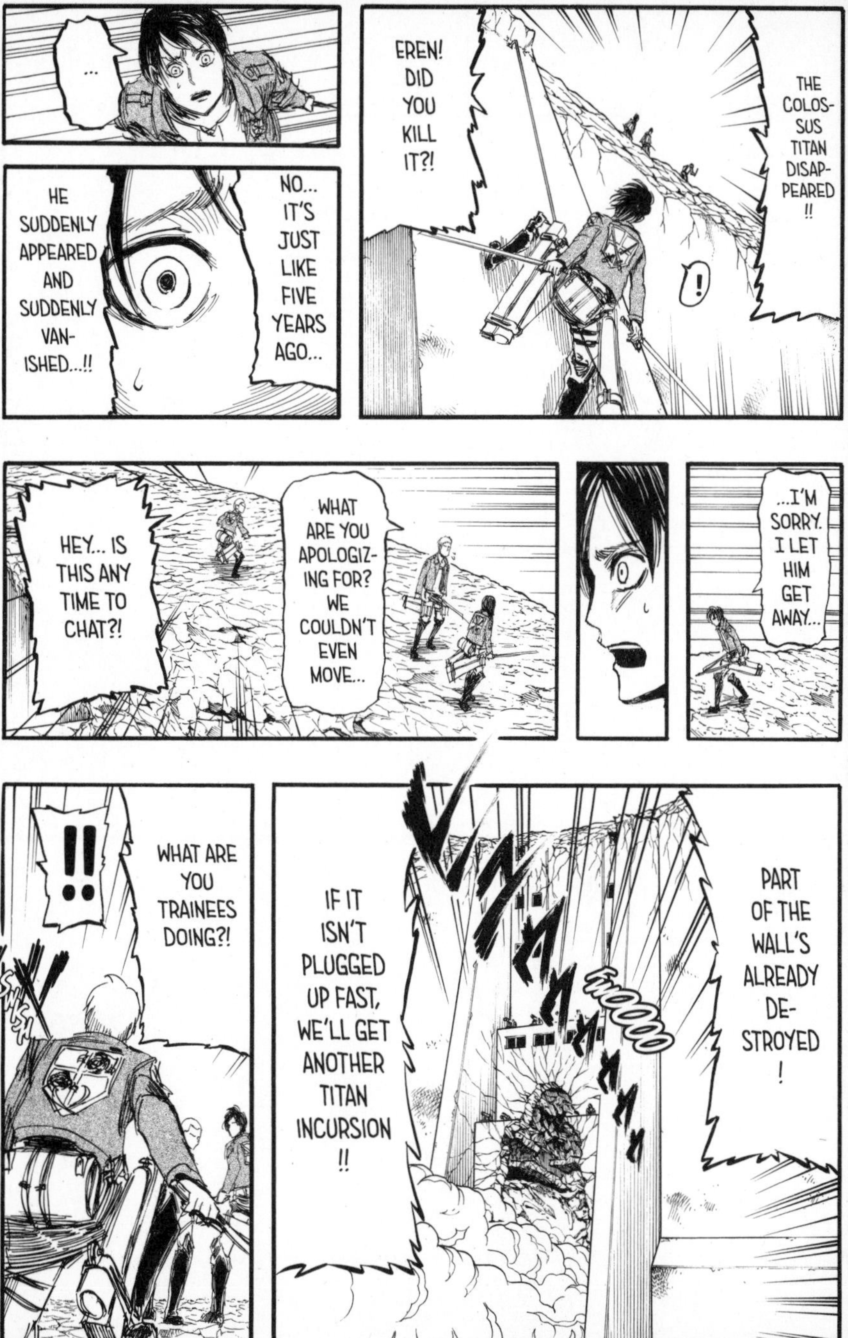

THE COLOSSUS TITAN DISAPPEARED!!
EREN! DID YOU KILL IT?!
!
...
NO... IT'S JUST LIKE FIVE YEARS AGO...
HE SUDDENLY APPEARED AND SUDDENLY VANISHED...!!
...I'M SORRY. I LET HIM GET AWAY...
WHAT ARE YOU APOLOGIZING FOR? WE COULDN'T EVEN MOVE...
HEY... IS THIS ANY TIME TO CHAT?!
PART OF THE WALL'S ALREADY DESTROYED!
FWOOOO
IF IT ISN'T PLUGGED UP FAST, WE'LL GET ANOTHER TITAN INCURSION!!
WHAT ARE YOU TRAINEES DOING?!
!!
SHSH

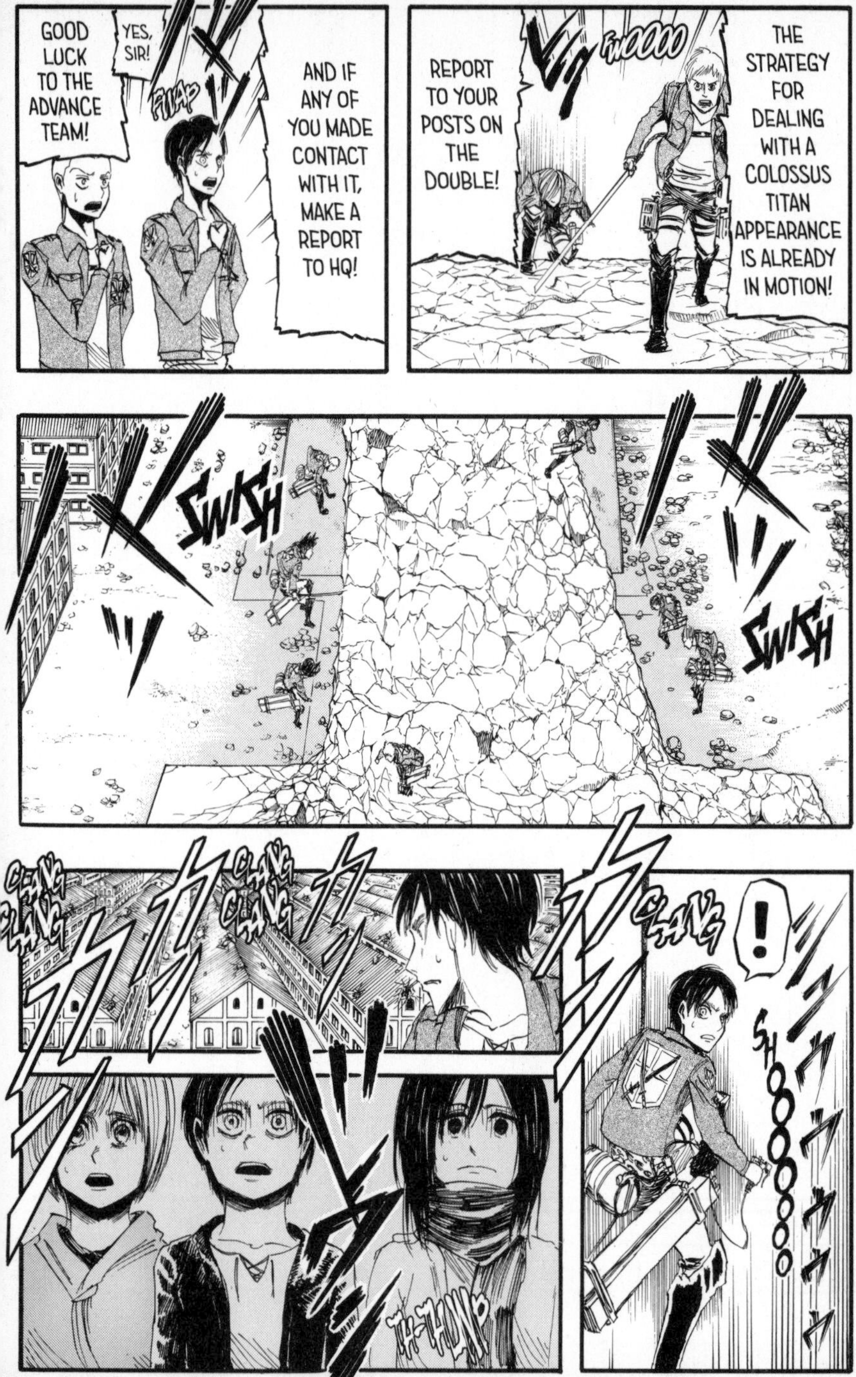
THE STRATEGY FOR DEALING WITH A COLOSSUS TITAN APPEARANCE IS ALREADY IN MOTION!
FWOOOO
REPORT TO YOUR POSTS ON THE DOUBLE!
AND IF ANY OF YOU MADE CONTACT WITH IT, MAKE A REPORT TO HQ!
FWAP
YES, SIR!
GOOD LUCK TO THE ADVANCE TEAM!
SWISH
SWISH
!
CLANG
SHOOOOOOOO
CLANG CLANG
CLANG CLANG
TH-THUMP

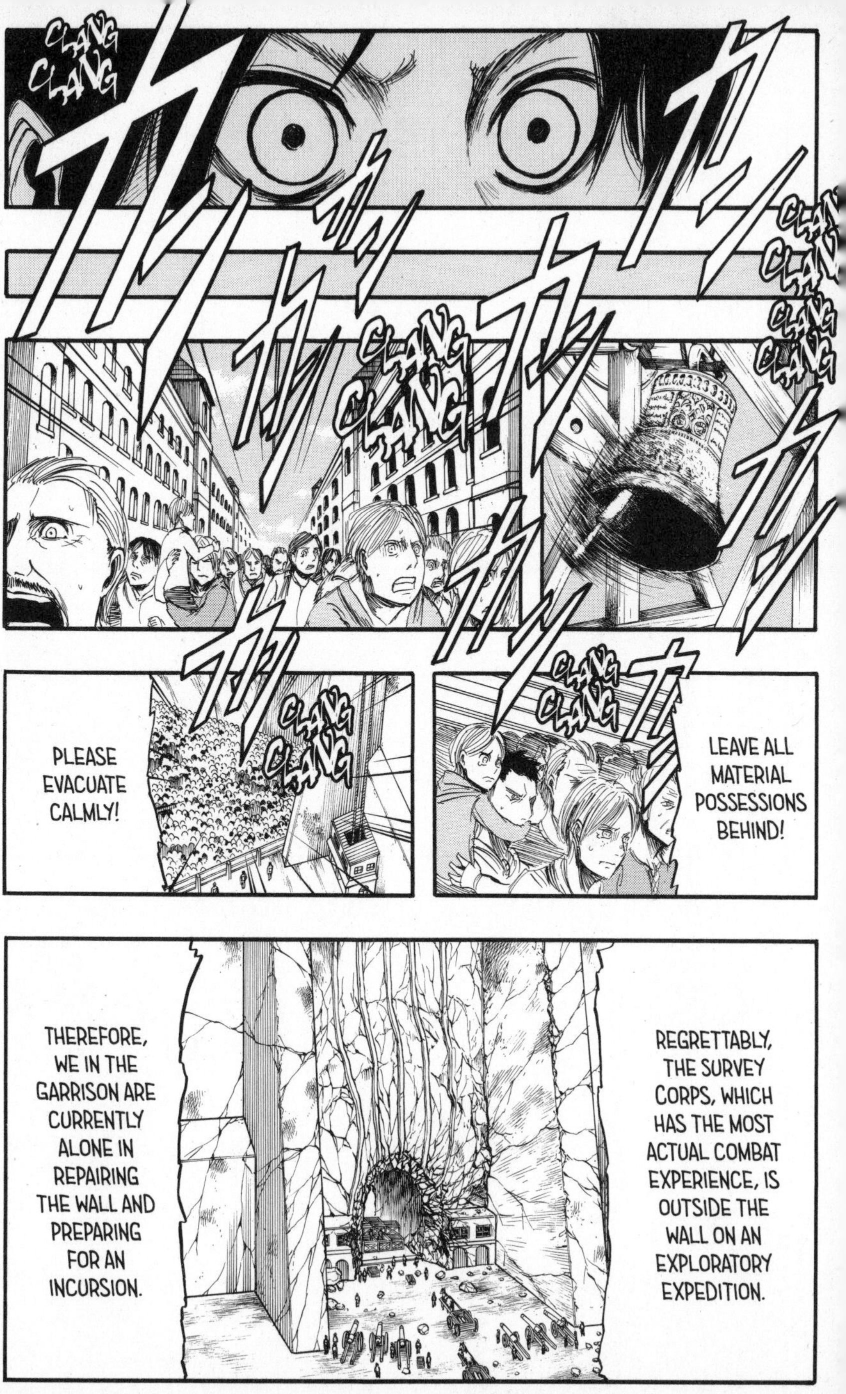

CLANG CLANG
CLANG CLANG CLANG CLANG
CLANG CLANG
CLANG CLANG
LEAVE ALL MATERIAL POSSESSIONS BEHIND!
CLANG CLANG
PLEASE EVACUATE CALMLY!
REGRETTABLY, THE SURVEY CORPS, WHICH HAS THE MOST ACTUAL COMBAT EXPERIENCE, IS OUTSIDE THE WALL ON AN EXPLORATORY EXPEDITION.
THEREFORE, WE IN THE GARRISON ARE CURRENTLY ALONE IN REPAIRING THE WALL AND PREPARING FOR AN INCURSION.

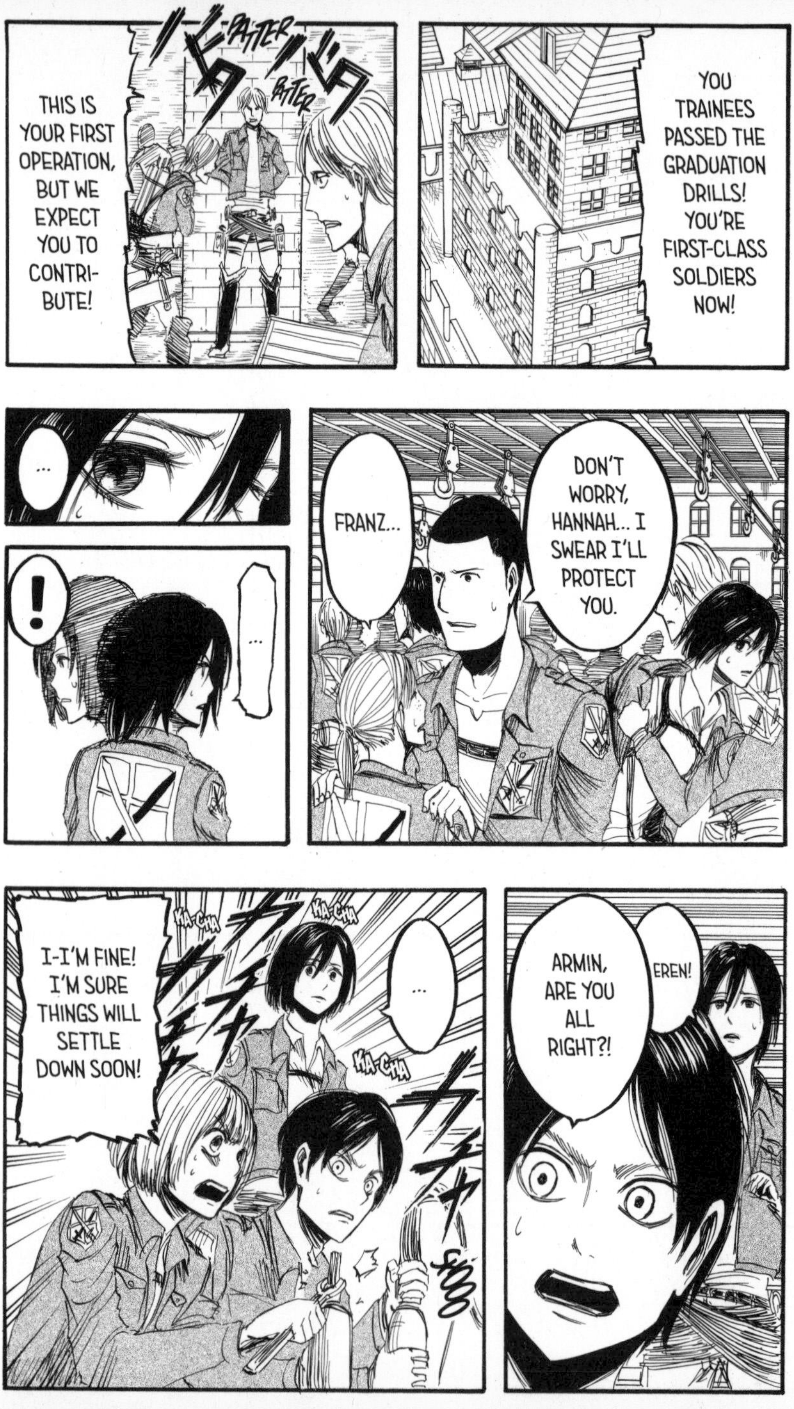
YOU TRAINEES PASSED THE GRADUATION DRILLS! YOU'RE FIRST-CLASS SOLDIERS NOW!
PATTER
PATTER
THIS IS YOUR FIRST OPERATION, BUT WE EXPECT YOU TO CONTRI-BUTE!
DON'T WORRY, HANNAH... I SWEAR I'LL PROTECT YOU.
FRANZ...
...
!
...
EREN!
ARMIN, ARE YOU ALL RIGHT?!
KA-CHA
...
KA-CHA
KA-CHA
I-I'M FINE! I'M SURE THINGS WILL SETTLE DOWN SOON!

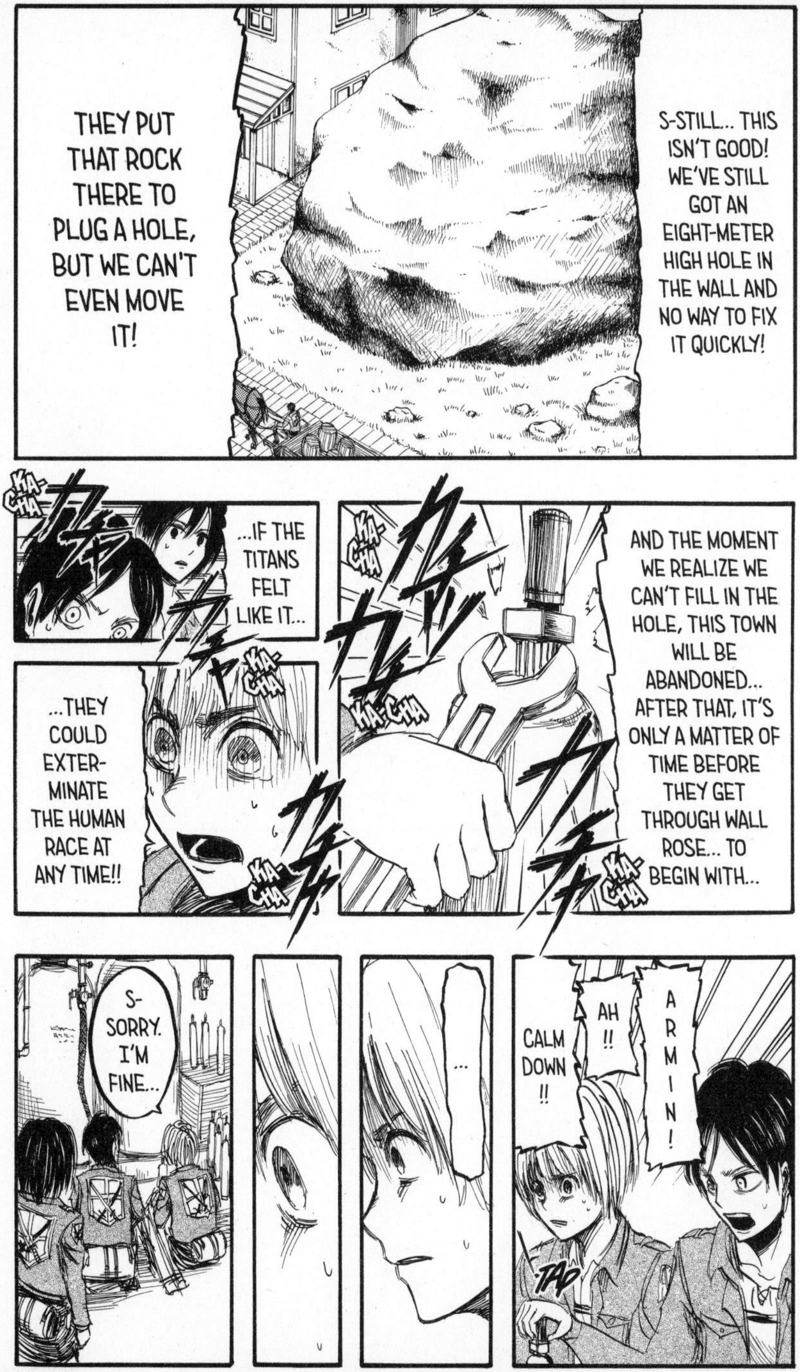
S-STILL... THIS ISN'T GOOD! WE'VE STILL GOT AN EIGHT-METER HIGH HOLE IN THE WALL AND NO WAY TO FIX IT QUICKLY!
THEY PUT THAT ROCK THERE TO PLUG A HOLE, BUT WE CAN'T EVEN MOVE IT!
KA-CHA
AND THE MOMENT WE REALIZE WE CAN'T FILL IN THE HOLE, THIS TOWN WILL BE ABANDONED... AFTER THAT, IT'S ONLY A MATTER OF TIME BEFORE THEY GET THROUGH WALL ROSE... TO BEGIN WITH...
KA-CHA
KA-CHA
KA-CHA
KA-CHA
...IF THE TITANS FELT LIKE IT...
KA-CHA
...THEY COULD EXTERMINATE THE HUMAN RACE AT ANY TIME!!
KA-CHA
ARMIN!
AH!!
CALM DOWN!!
TAP
...
S-SORRY. I'M FINE...

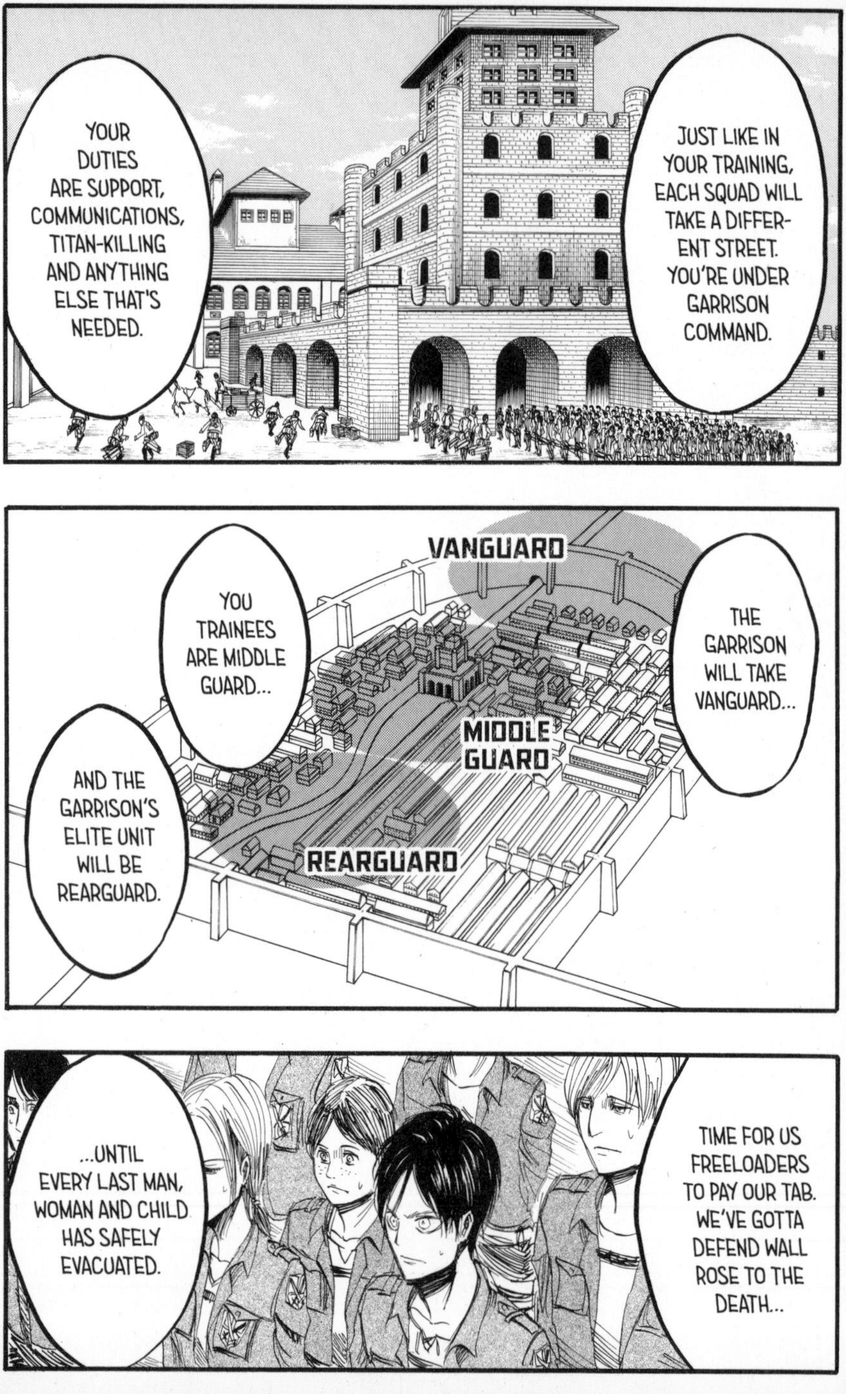
JUST LIKE IN YOUR TRAINING, EACH SQUAD WILL TAKE A DIFFERENT STREET. YOU'RE UNDER GARRISON COMMAND.
YOUR DUTIES ARE SUPPORT, COMMUNICATIONS, TITAN-KILLING AND ANYTHING ELSE THAT'S NEEDED.
THE GARRISON WILL TAKE VANGUARD...
VANGUARD
YOU TRAINEES ARE MIDDLE GUARD...
MIDDLE GUARD
AND THE GARRISON'S ELITE UNIT WILL BE REARGUARD.
REARGUARD
TIME FOR US FREELOADERS TO PAY OUR TAB. WE'VE GOTTA DEFEND WALL ROSE TO THE DEATH...
...UNTIL EVERY LAST MAN, WOMAN AND CHILD HAS SAFELY EVACUATED.

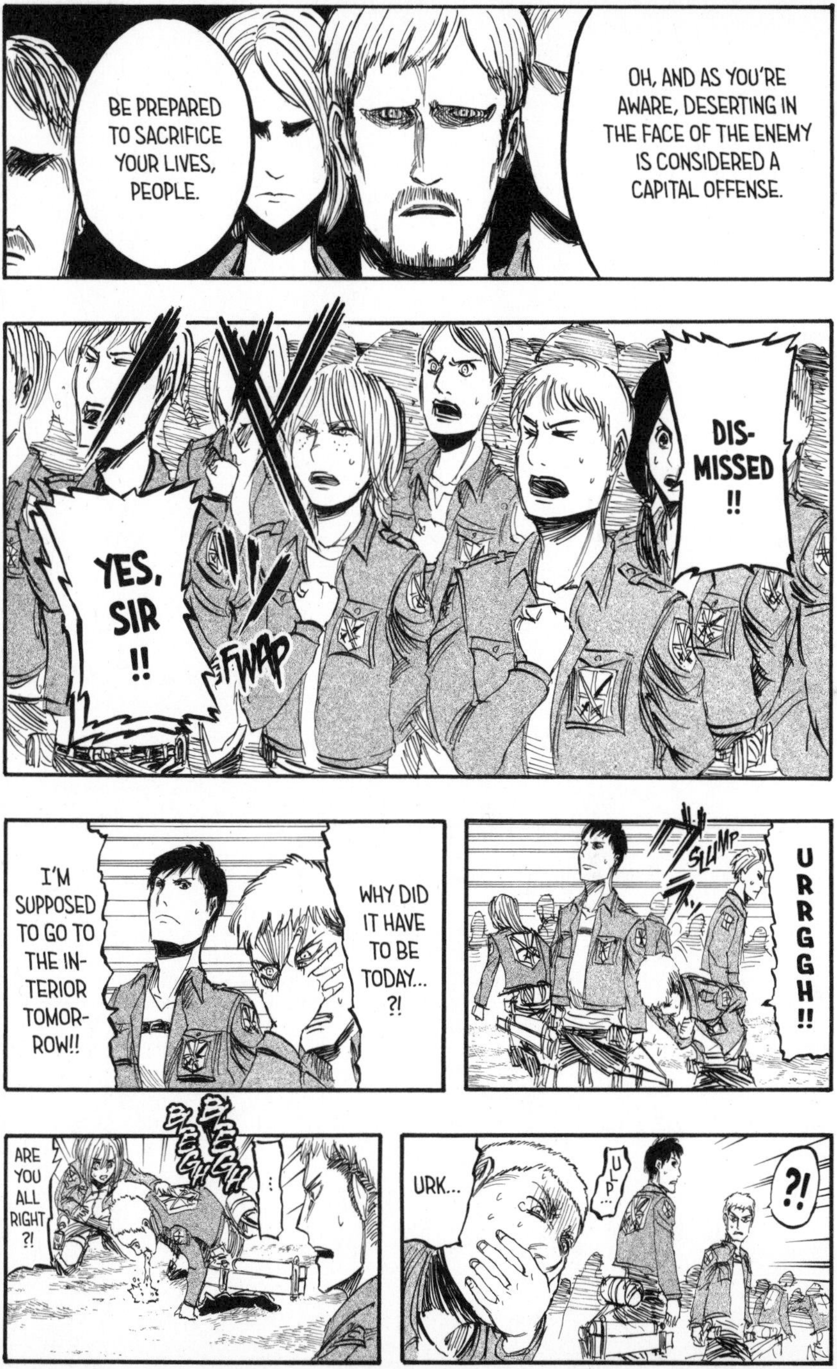
OH, AND AS YOU'RE AWARE, DESERTING IN THE FACE OF THE ENEMY IS CONSIDERED A CAPITAL OFFENSE.
BE PREPARED TO SACRIFICE YOUR LIVES, PEOPLE.
DIS-MISSED !!
YES, SIR !!
FWAP
URRGGH!!
SLUMP
WHY DID IT HAVE TO BE TODAY...?!
I'M SUPPOSED TO GO TO THE IN-TERIOR TOMOR-ROW!!
?!
ULP...
URK...
...
BLEGH
BLEGH
ARE YOU ALL RIGHT ?!

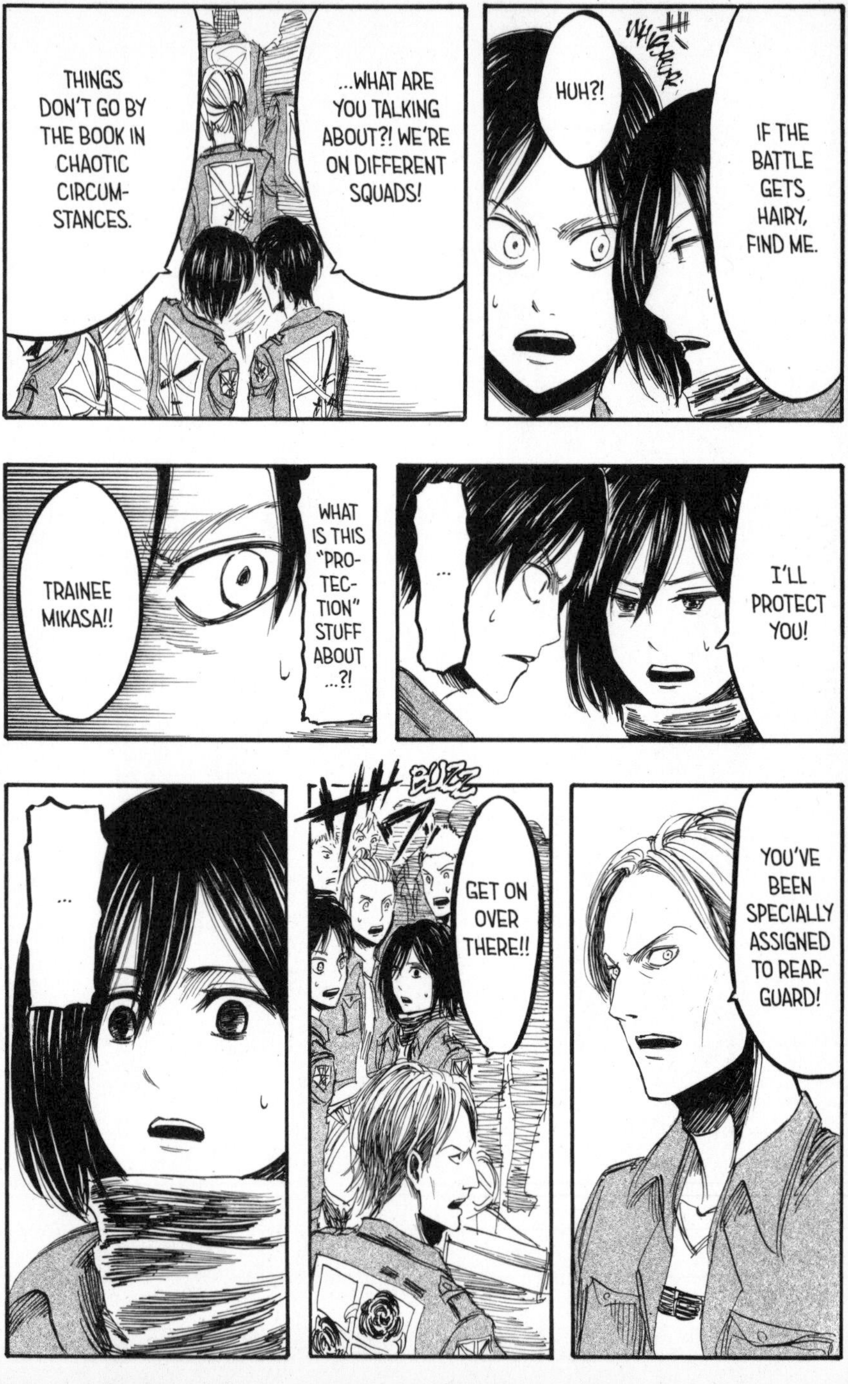
IF THE BATTLE GETS HAIRY, FIND ME.
HUH?!
...WHAT ARE YOU TALKING ABOUT?! WE'RE ON DIFFERENT SQUADS!
THINGS DON'T GO BY THE BOOK IN CHAOTIC CIRCUM-STANCES.
I'LL PROTECT YOU!
...
WHAT IS THIS "PRO-TEC-TION" STUFF ABOUT ...?!
TRAINEE MIKASA!!
YOU'VE BEEN SPECIALLY ASSIGNED TO REAR-GUARD!
BUZZ
GET ON OVER THERE!!
...

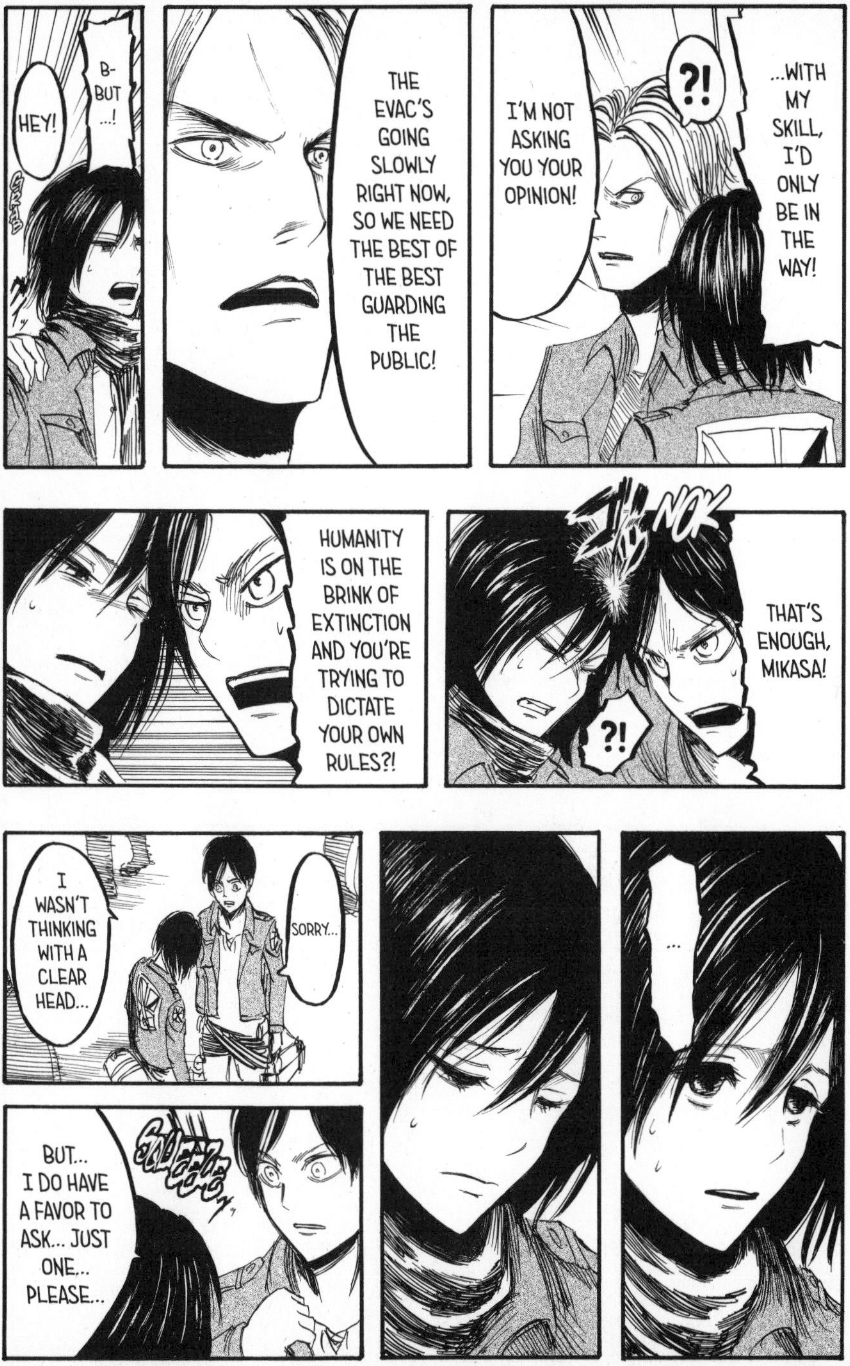
...WITH MY SKILL, I'D ONLY BE IN THE WAY!
?!
I'M NOT ASKING YOU YOUR OPINION!
THE EVAC'S GOING SLOWLY RIGHT NOW, SO WE NEED THE BEST OF THE BEST GUARDING THE PUBLIC!
B-BUT ...!
HEY!
THAT'S ENOUGH, MIKASA!
?!
HUMANITY IS ON THE BRINK OF EXTINCTION AND YOU'RE TRYING TO DICTATE YOUR OWN RULES?!
...
SORRY...
I WASN'T THINKING WITH A CLEAR HEAD...
BUT... I DO HAVE A FAVOR TO ASK... JUST ONE... PLEASE...

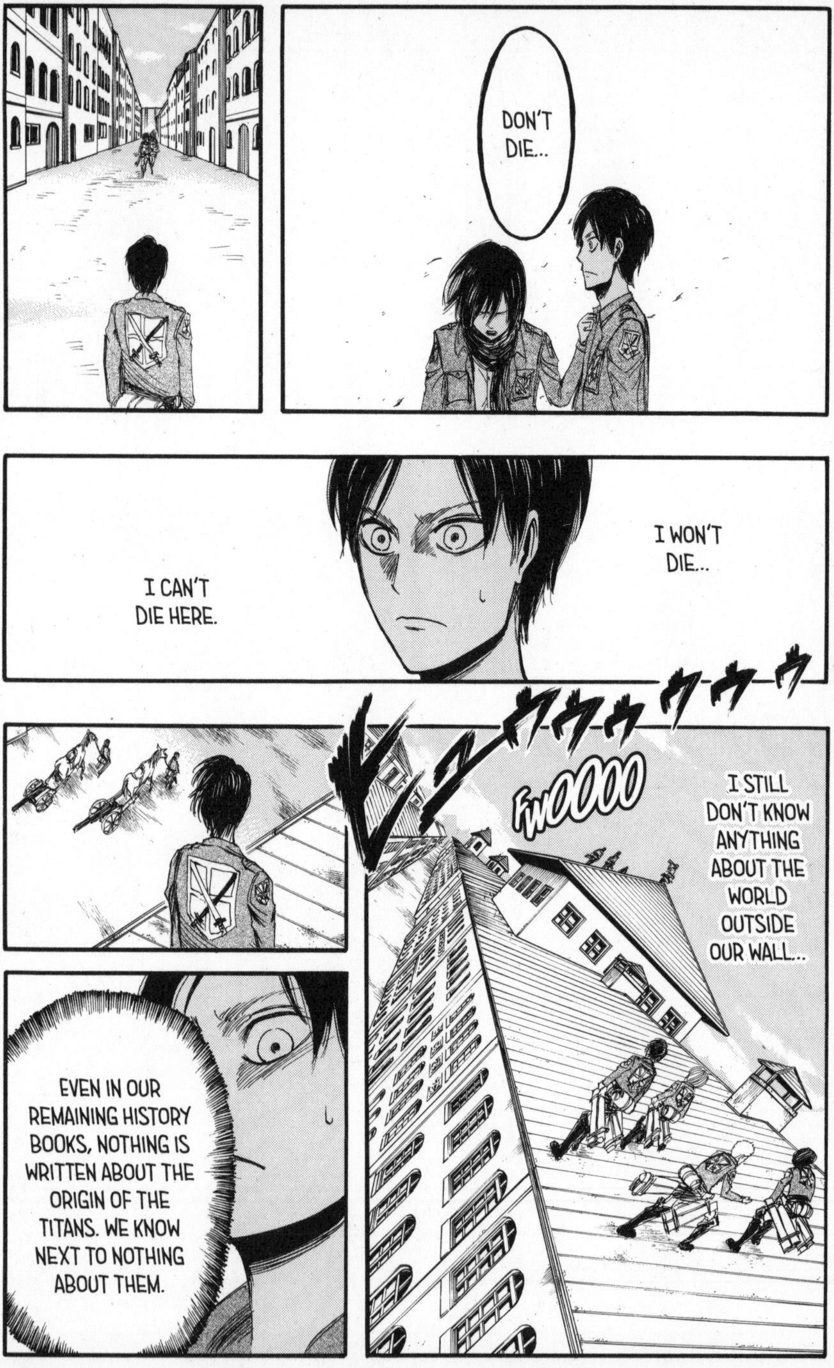
DON'T DIE...
I WON'T DIE...
I CAN'T DIE HERE.
FWOOOO
I STILL DON'T KNOW ANYTHING ABOUT THE WORLD OUTSIDE OUR WALL...
EVEN IN OUR REMAINING HISTORY BOOKS, NOTHING IS WRITTEN ABOUT THE ORIGIN OF THE TITANS. WE KNOW NEXT TO NOTHING ABOUT THEM.

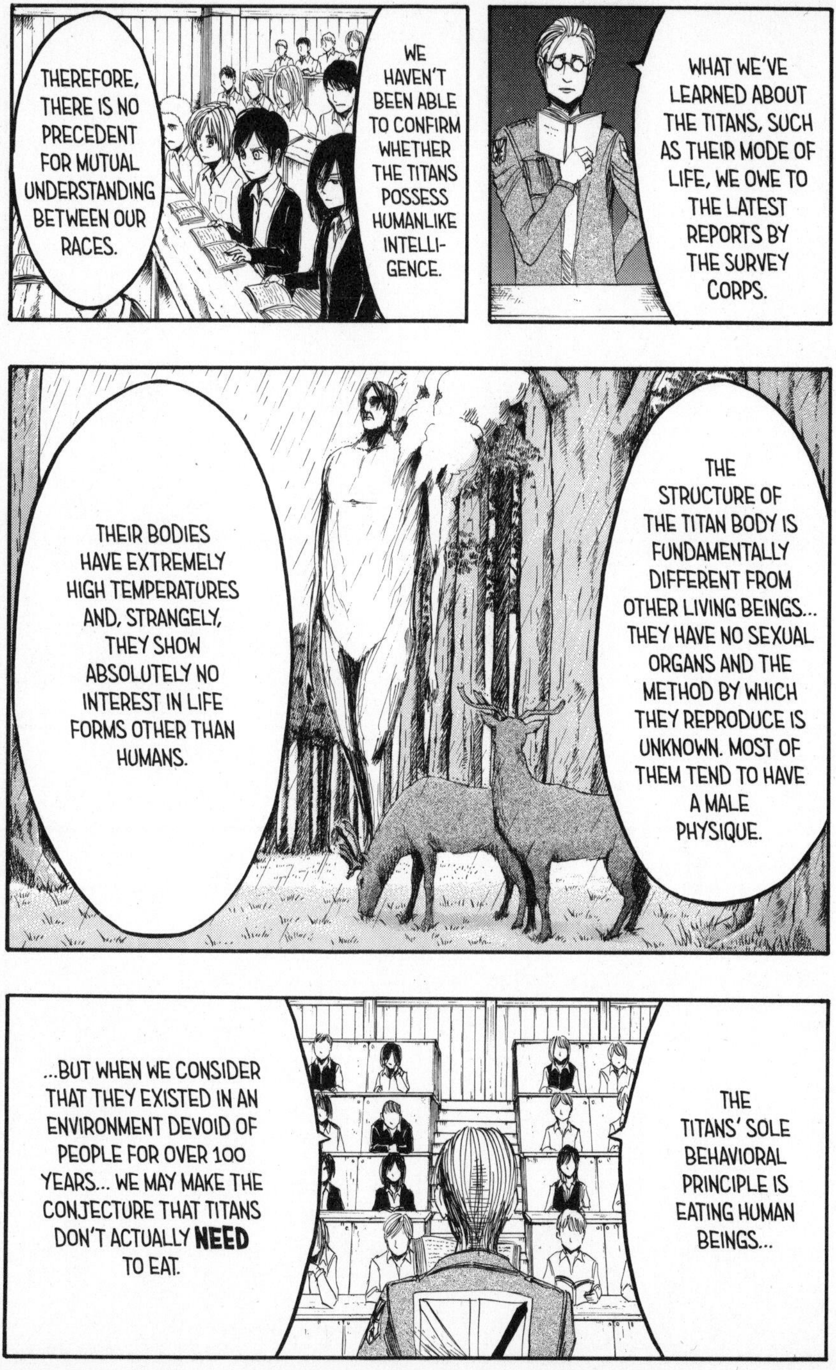
WHAT WE'VE LEARNED ABOUT THE TITANS, SUCH AS THEIR MODE OF LIFE, WE OWE TO THE LATEST REPORTS BY THE SURVEY CORPS.
WE HAVEN'T BEEN ABLE TO CONFIRM WHETHER THE TITANS POSSESS HUMANLIKE INTELLI-GENCE.
THEREFORE, THERE IS NO PRECEDENT FOR MUTUAL UNDERSTANDING BETWEEN OUR RACES.
THE STRUCTURE OF THE TITAN BODY IS FUNDAMENTALLY DIFFERENT FROM OTHER LIVING BEINGS... THEY HAVE NO SEXUAL ORGANS AND THE METHOD BY WHICH THEY REPRODUCE IS UNKNOWN. MOST OF THEM TEND TO HAVE A MALE PHYSIQUE.
THEIR BODIES HAVE EXTREMELY HIGH TEMPERATURES AND, STRANGELY, THEY SHOW ABSOLUTELY NO INTEREST IN LIFE FORMS OTHER THAN HUMANS.
THE TITANS' SOLE BEHAVIORAL PRINCIPLE IS EATING HUMAN BEINGS...
...BUT WHEN WE CONSIDER THAT THEY EXISTED IN AN ENVIRONMENT DEVOID OF PEOPLE FOR OVER 100 YEARS... WE MAY MAKE THE CONJECTURE THAT TITANS DON'T ACTUALLY **NEED** TO EAT.

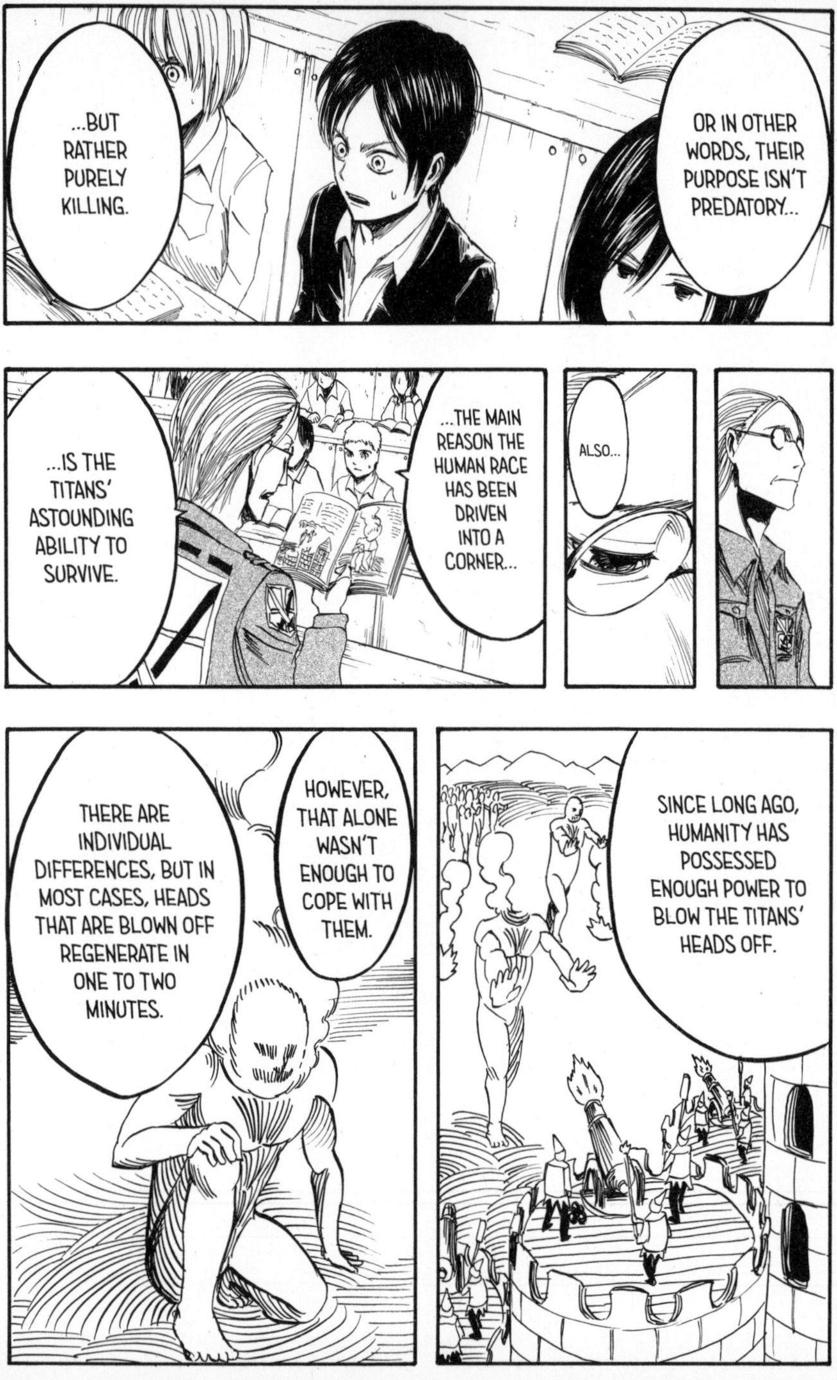
OR IN OTHER WORDS, THEIR PURPOSE ISN'T PREDATORY...
...BUT RATHER PURELY KILLING.
ALSO...
...THE MAIN REASON THE HUMAN RACE HAS BEEN DRIVEN INTO A CORNER...
...IS THE TITANS' ASTOUNDING ABILITY TO SURVIVE.
SINCE LONG AGO, HUMANITY HAS POSSESSED ENOUGH POWER TO BLOW THE TITANS' HEADS OFF.
HOWEVER, THAT ALONE WASN'T ENOUGH TO COPE WITH THEM.
THERE ARE INDIVIDUAL DIFFERENCES, BUT IN MOST CASES, HEADS THAT ARE BLOWN OFF REGENERATE IN ONE TO TWO MINUTES.

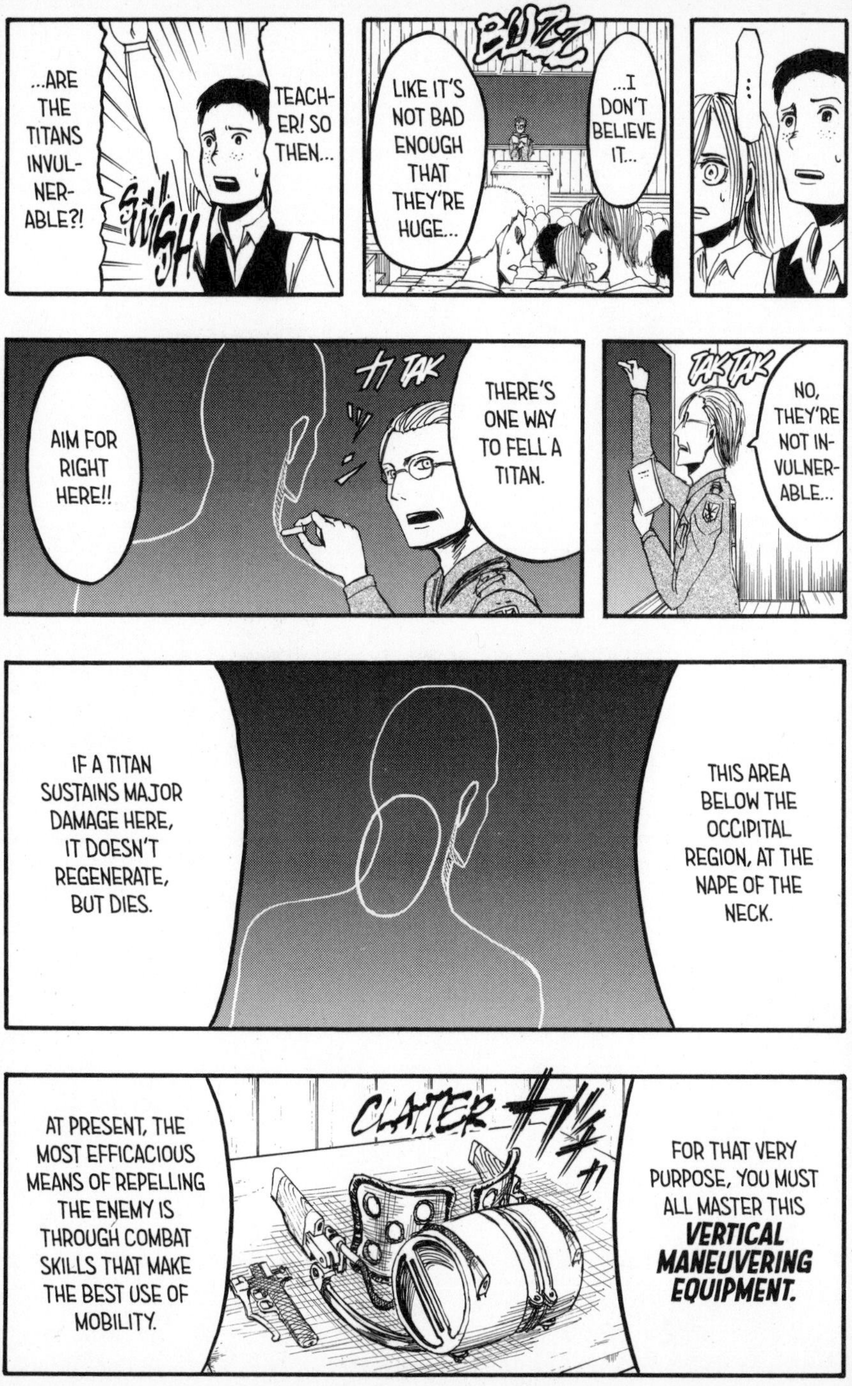
...
BUZZ
...I DON'T BELIEVE IT...
LIKE IT'S NOT BAD ENOUGH THAT THEY'RE HUGE...
TEACHER! SO THEN...
...ARE THE TITANS INVULNERABLE?!
SWISH
TAK TAK
NO, THEY'RE NOT INVULNERABLE...
THERE'S ONE WAY TO FELL A TITAN.
TAK
AIM FOR RIGHT HERE!!
THIS AREA BELOW THE OCCIPITAL REGION, AT THE NAPE OF THE NECK.
IF A TITAN SUSTAINS MAJOR DAMAGE HERE, IT DOESN'T REGENERATE, BUT DIES.
AT PRESENT, THE MOST EFFICACIOUS MEANS OF REPELLING THE ENEMY IS THROUGH COMBAT SKILLS THAT MAKE THE BEST USE OF MOBILITY.
CLATTER
FOR THAT VERY PURPOSE, YOU MUST ALL MASTER THIS **VERTICAL MANEUVERING EQUIPMENT.**

EACH HAND USES THE GRIP OF THIS DEVICE TO OPERATE THE SYSTEM.
THE FIRING MECHANISM AT BOTH SIDES OF THE WAIST LAUNCHES AN ANCHOR.
STEEL WIRE DISCHARGED FROM INSIDE A CYLINDER IS REELED IN THROUGH PRESSURIZED GAS.
THIS RE-PLACEABLE BLADE IS YOUR WEAPON.
IN ORDER TO CUT THROUGH A CHUNK OF TOUGH MEAT, THE BLADE IS MADE TO BE FLEXIBLE.
YOU USE THESE TWO BLADES TO SLICE THROUGH THE AREA.
IF THE ATTACK HITS THE TITAN'S VITAL SPOT, IT DIES INSTANTLY, BEFORE ITS REGENERATIVE SYSTEM CAN KICK IN.
FINALLY...
FINALLY...
...WE CAN BE USEFUL.

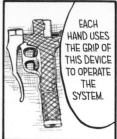

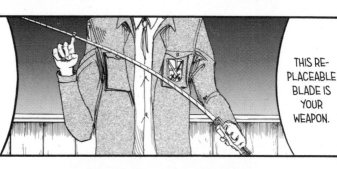

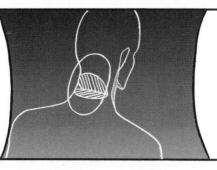

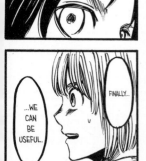

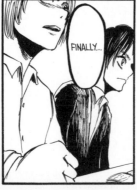

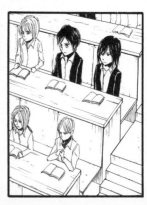

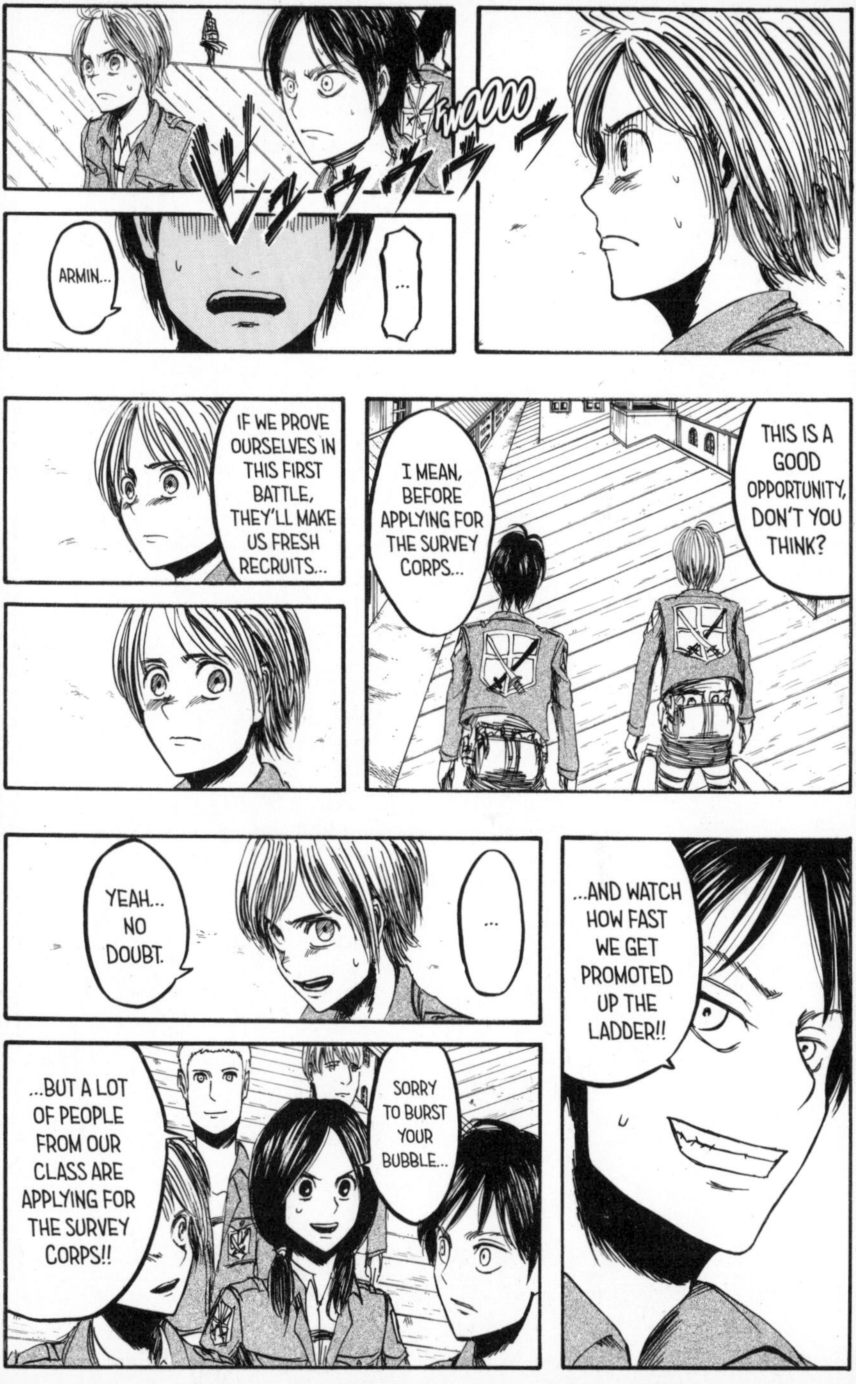
FWOOOO
...
ARMIN...
THIS IS A GOOD OPPORTUNITY, DON'T YOU THINK?
I MEAN, BEFORE APPLYING FOR THE SURVEY CORPS...
IF WE PROVE OURSELVES IN THIS FIRST BATTLE, THEY'LL MAKE US FRESH RECRUITS...
...AND WATCH HOW FAST WE GET PROMOTED UP THE LADDER!!
...
YEAH... NO DOUBT.
SORRY TO BURST YOUR BUBBLE...
...BUT A LOT OF PEOPLE FROM OUR CLASS ARE APPLYING FOR THE SURVEY CORPS!!

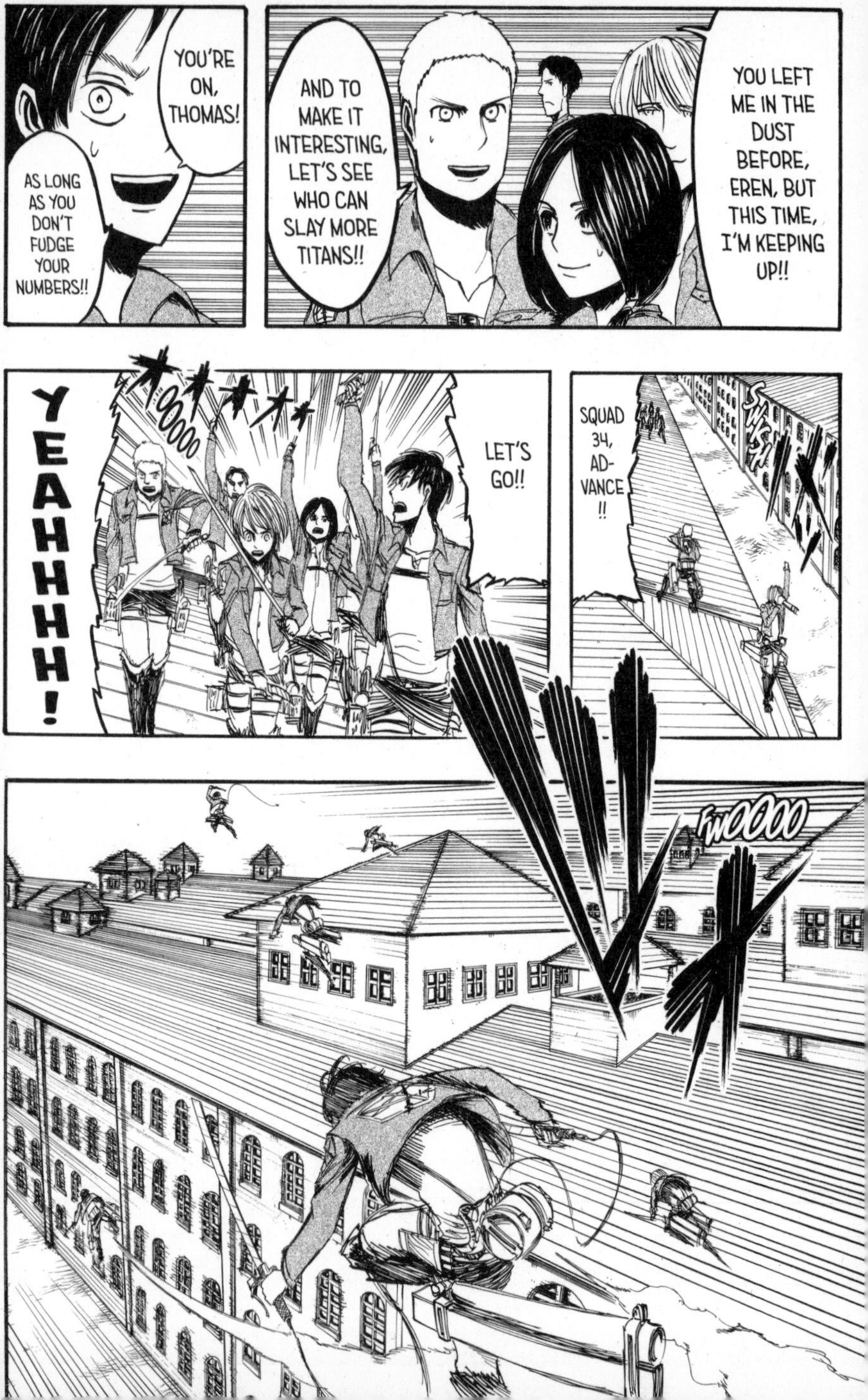
YOU LEFT ME IN THE DUST BEFORE, EREN, BUT THIS TIME, I'M KEEPING UP!!
AND TO MAKE IT INTERESTING, LET'S SEE WHO CAN SLAY MORE TITANS!!
YOU'RE ON, THOMAS!
AS LONG AS YOU DON'T FUDGE YOUR NUMBERS!!
SWISH
SQUAD 34, ADVANCE!!
LET'S GO!!
YEAHHHHH!
FWOOOO

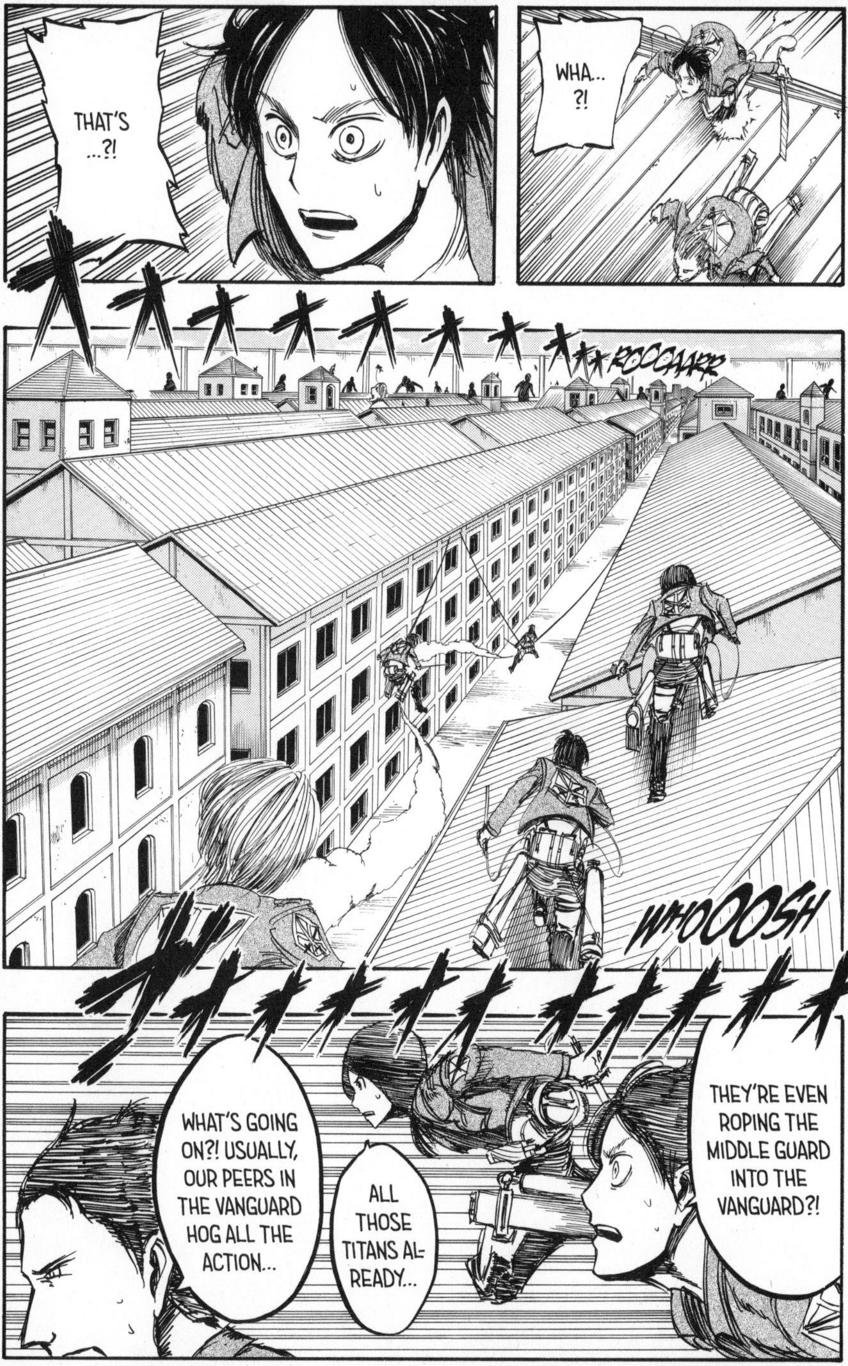
WHA... ?!
THAT'S ...?!
ROOOAARR
WHOOOSH
THEY'RE EVEN ROPING THE MIDDLE GUARD INTO THE VANGUARD?!
ALL THOSE TITANS AL-READY...
WHAT'S GOING ON?! USUALLY, OUR PEERS IN THE VANGUARD HOG ALL THE ACTION...

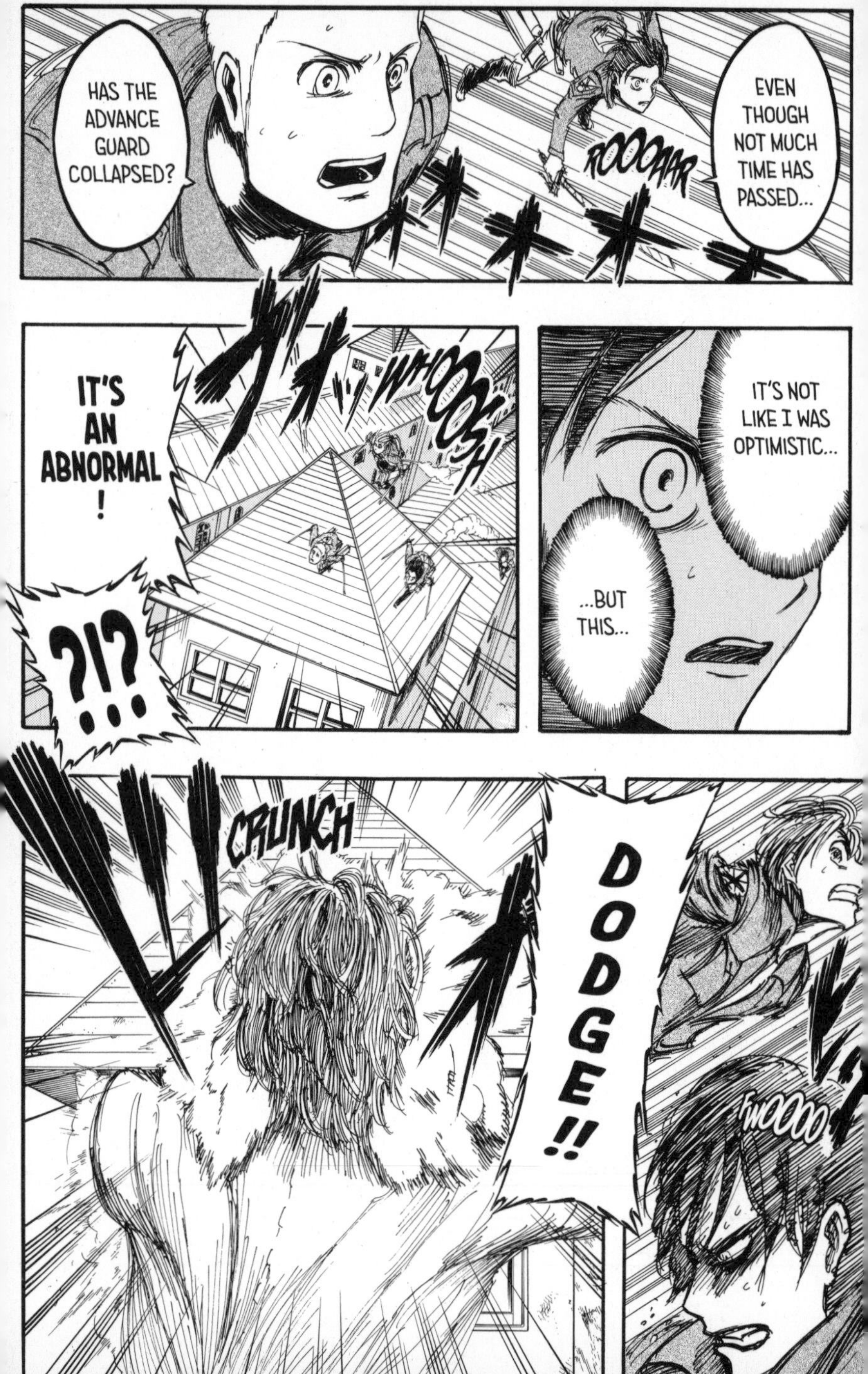
EVEN THOUGH NOT MUCH TIME HAS PASSED...
ROOOAAR
HAS THE ADVANCE GUARD COLLAPSED?
IT'S NOT LIKE I WAS OPTIMISTIC...
...BUT THIS...
WHOOOOSH
IT'S AN ABNORMAL!
?!?
FWOOOO
DODGE!!
CRUNCH

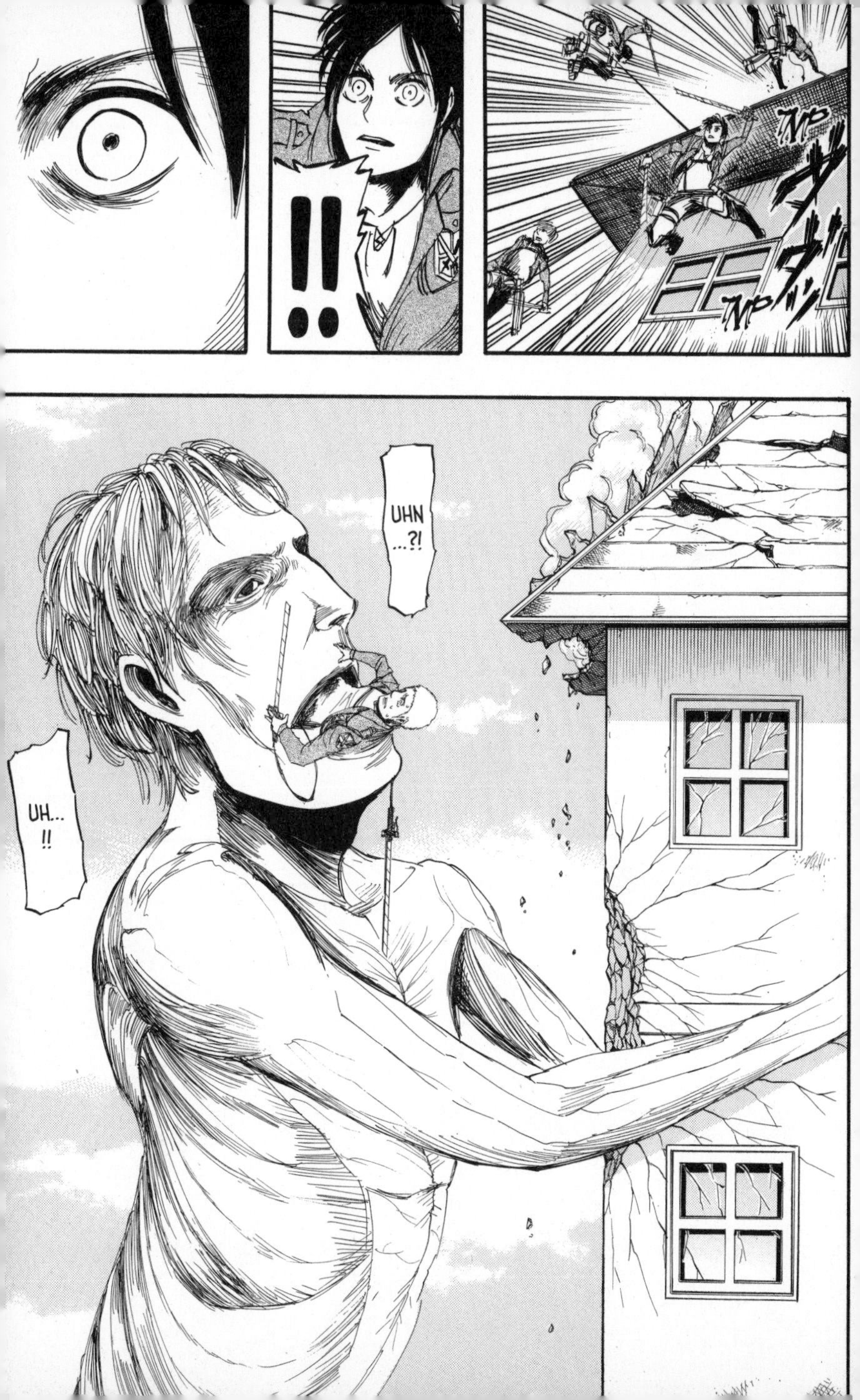
TMP
TMP
!!
UHN ...?!
UH... !!

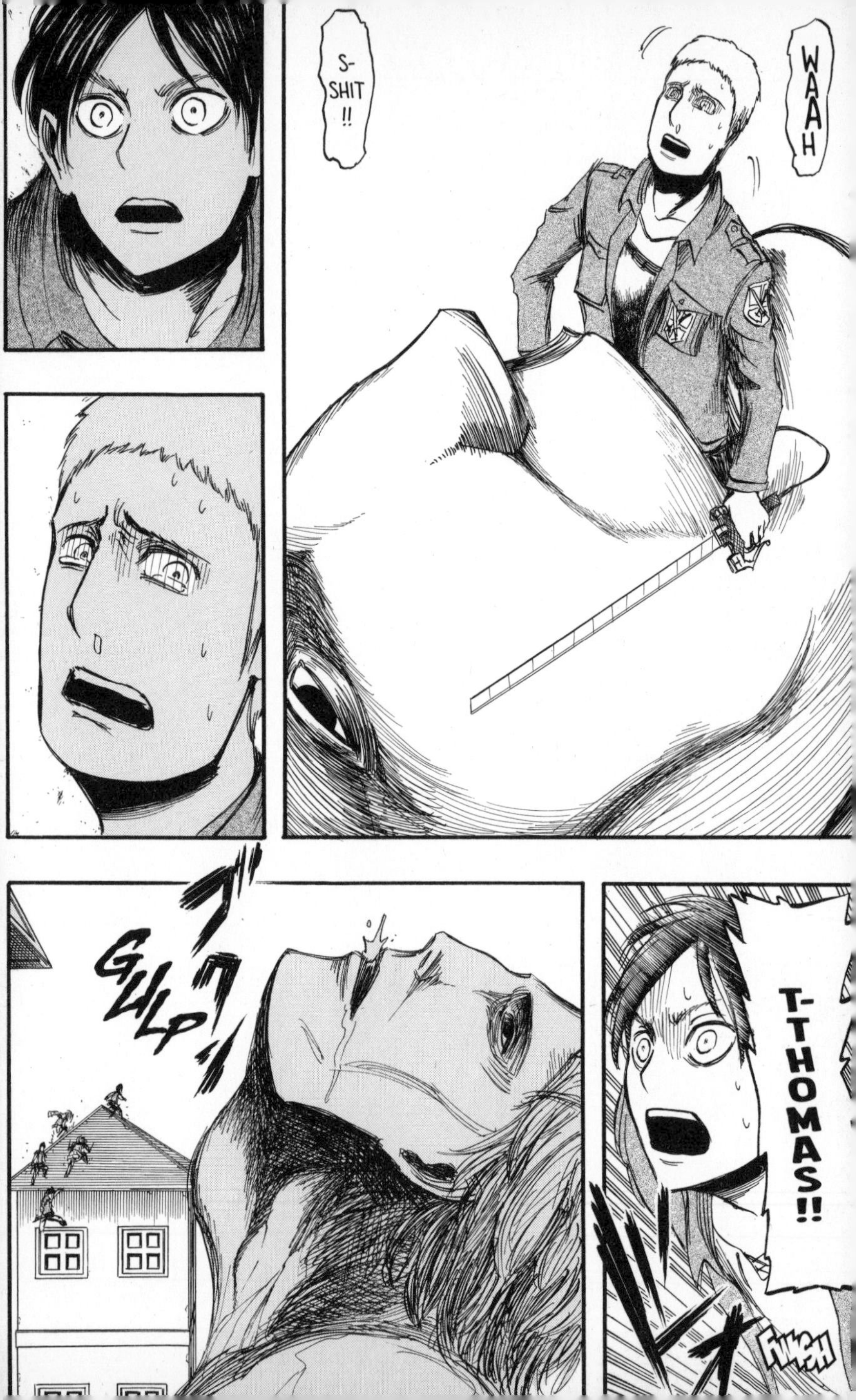
WAAH
S-SHIT!!
T-THOMAS!!
FWISH
GULP

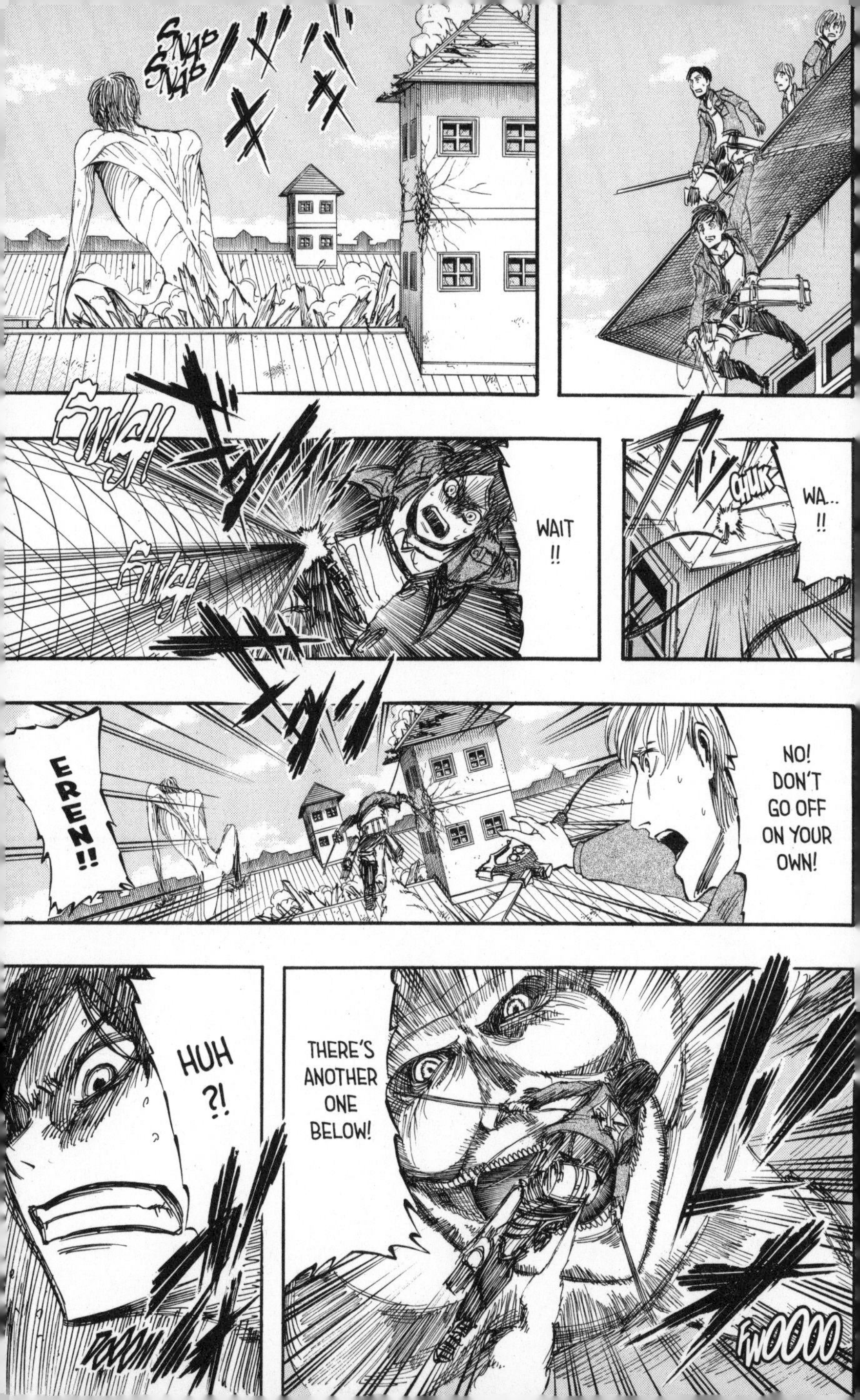
SNAP SNAP
CHUK
WA... !!
WAIT !!
NO! DON'T GO OFF ON YOUR OWN!
EREN!!
THERE'S ANOTHER ONE BELOW!
FWOOOO
HUH ?!

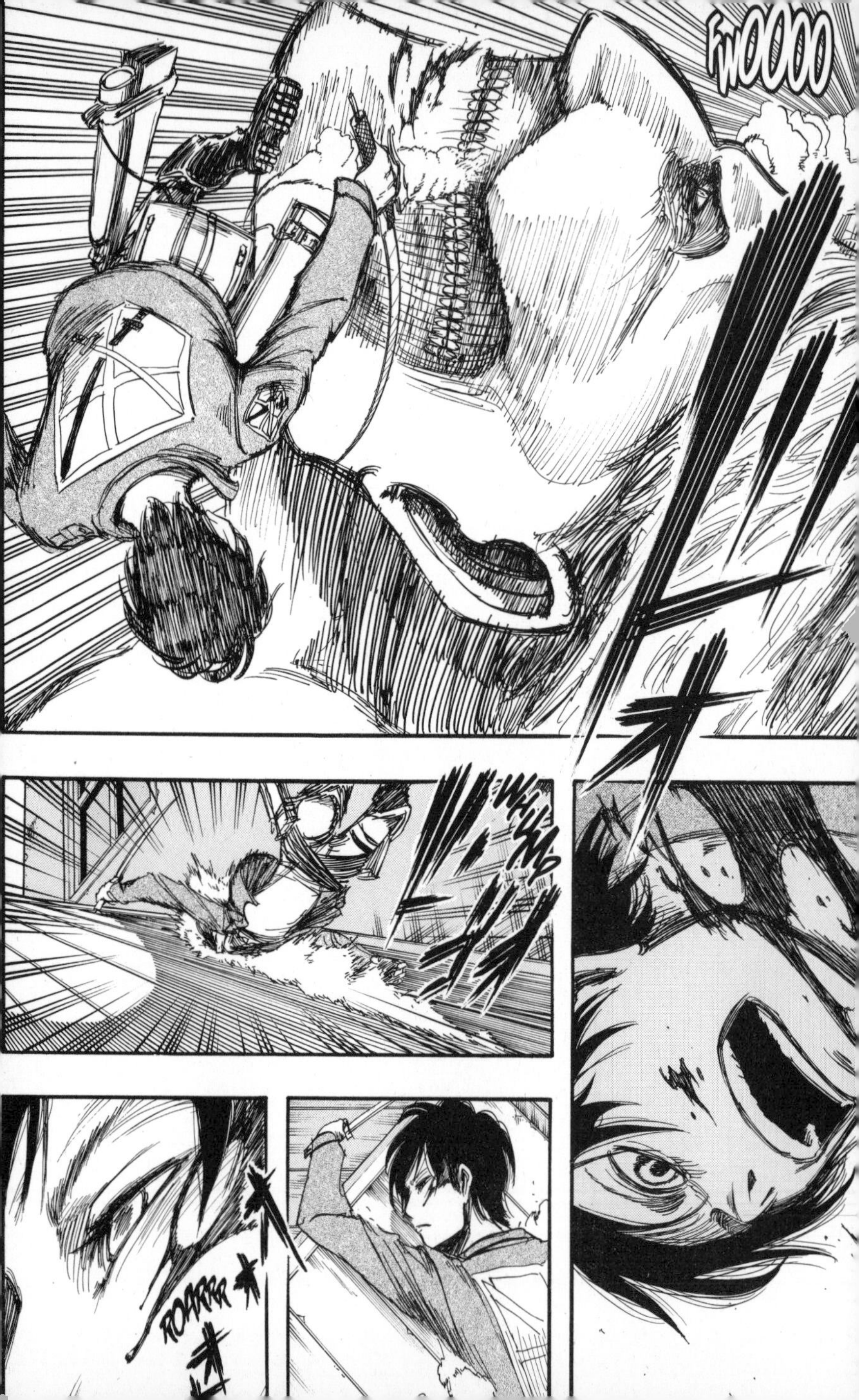
FWOOOO
WHUNG
ROARRR

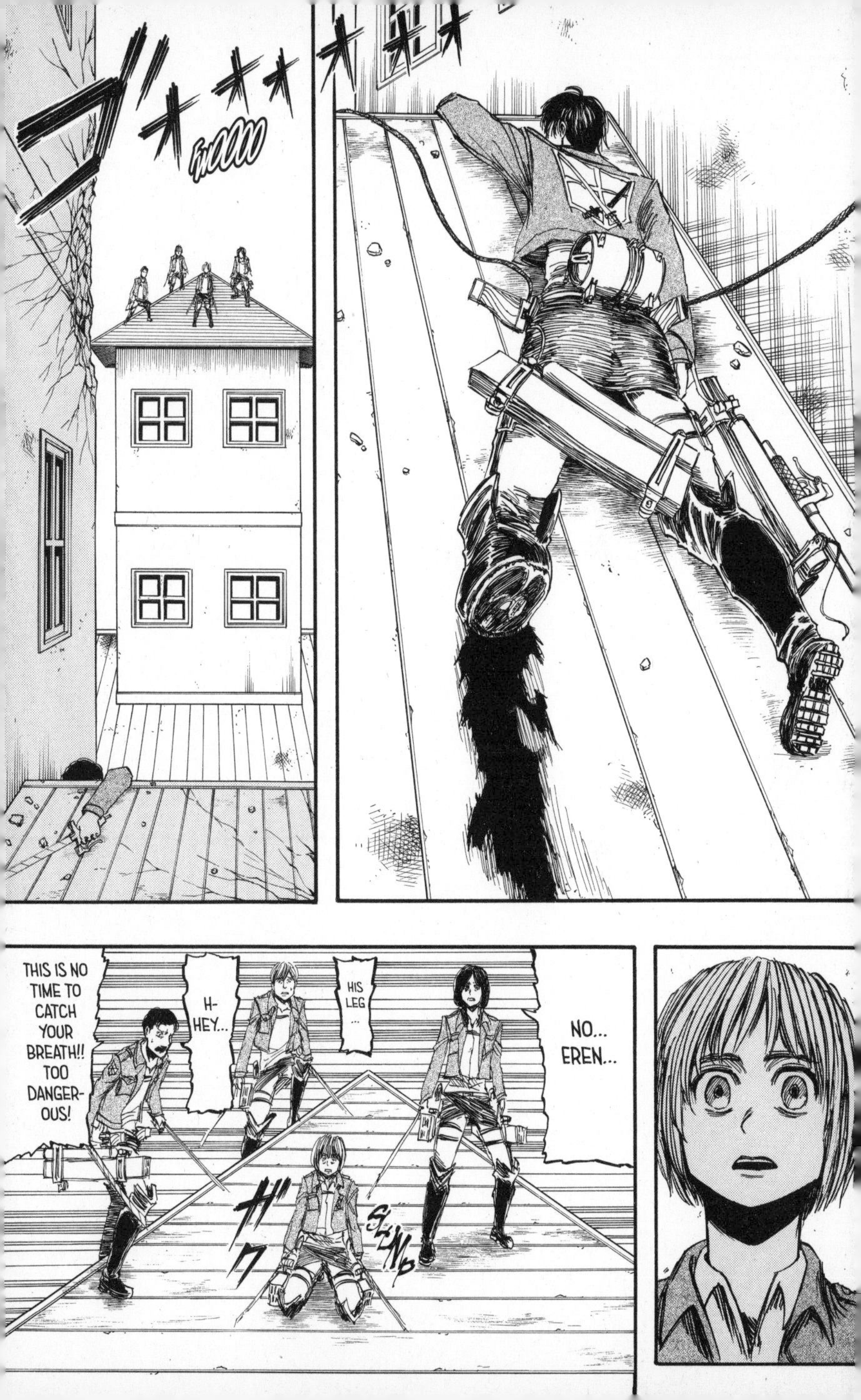
FWOOOO
NO... EREN...
HIS LEG ...
H- HEY...
THIS IS NO TIME TO CATCH YOUR BREATH!! TOO DANGER- OUS!
SLUMP

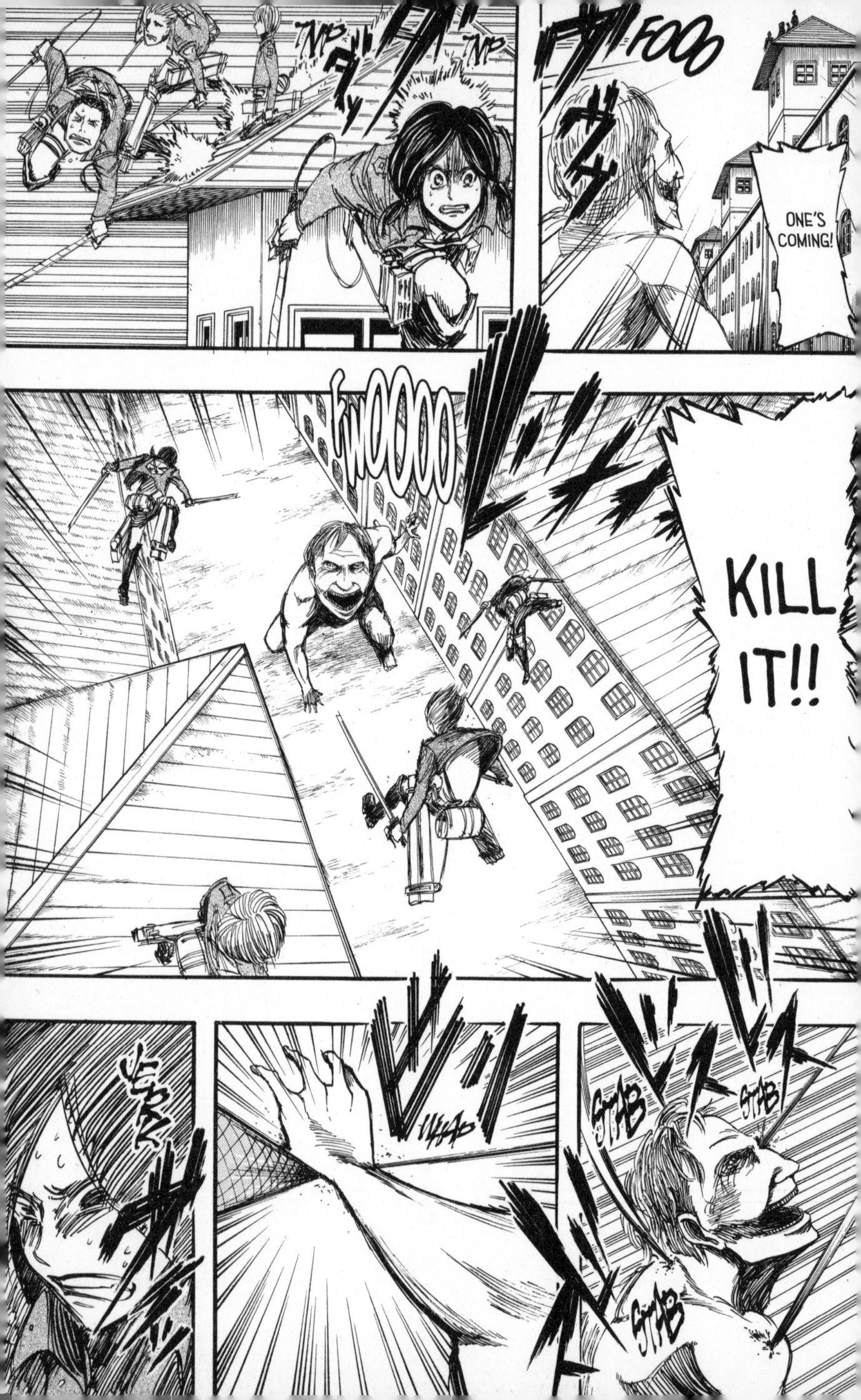
FOOO
ONE'S COMING!
TMP
TMP
FWOOOO
KILL IT!!
STAB
STAB
STAB

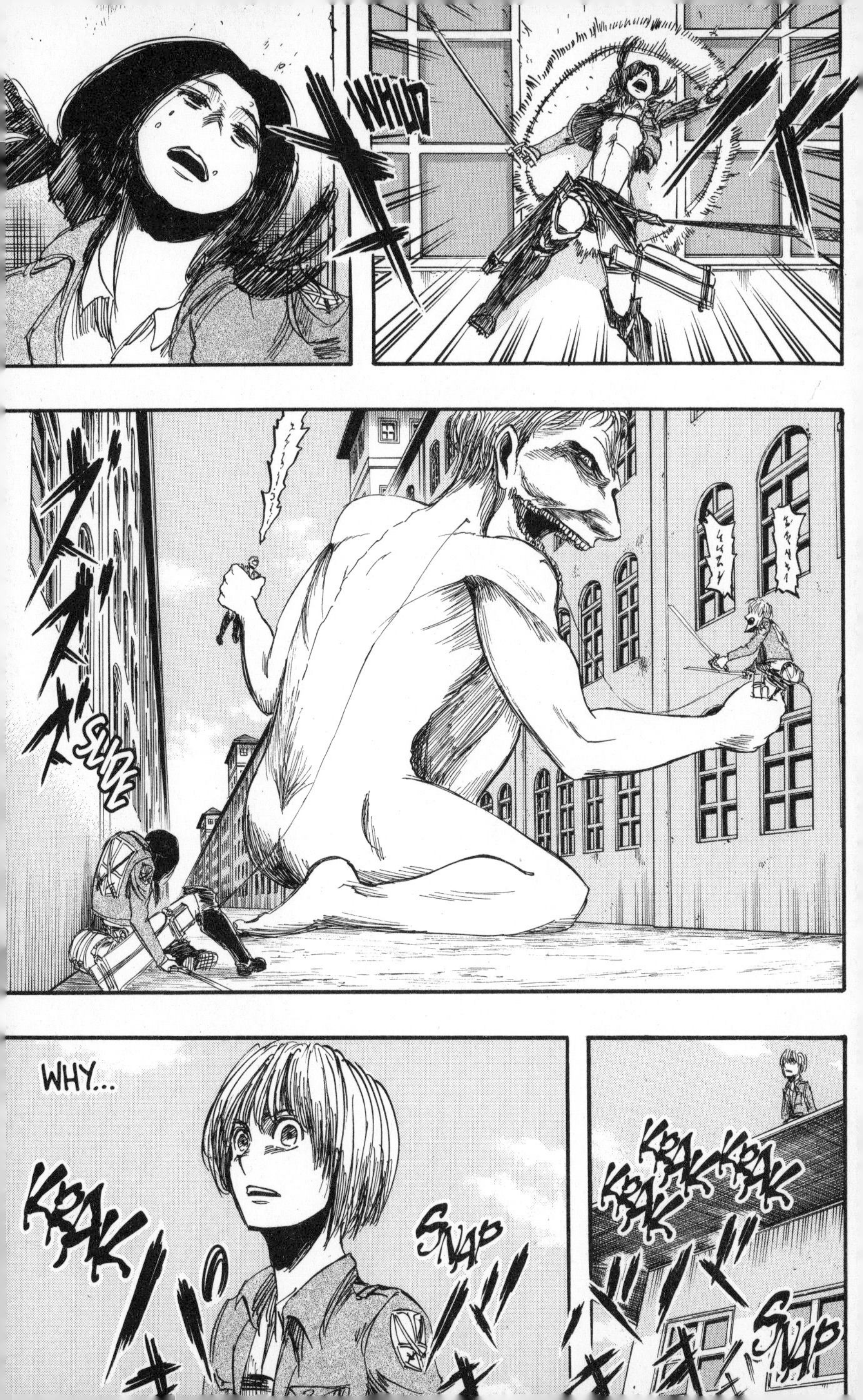
WHUD
KRAK KRAK KRAK KRAK
SNAP
WHY...
KRAK
SNAP

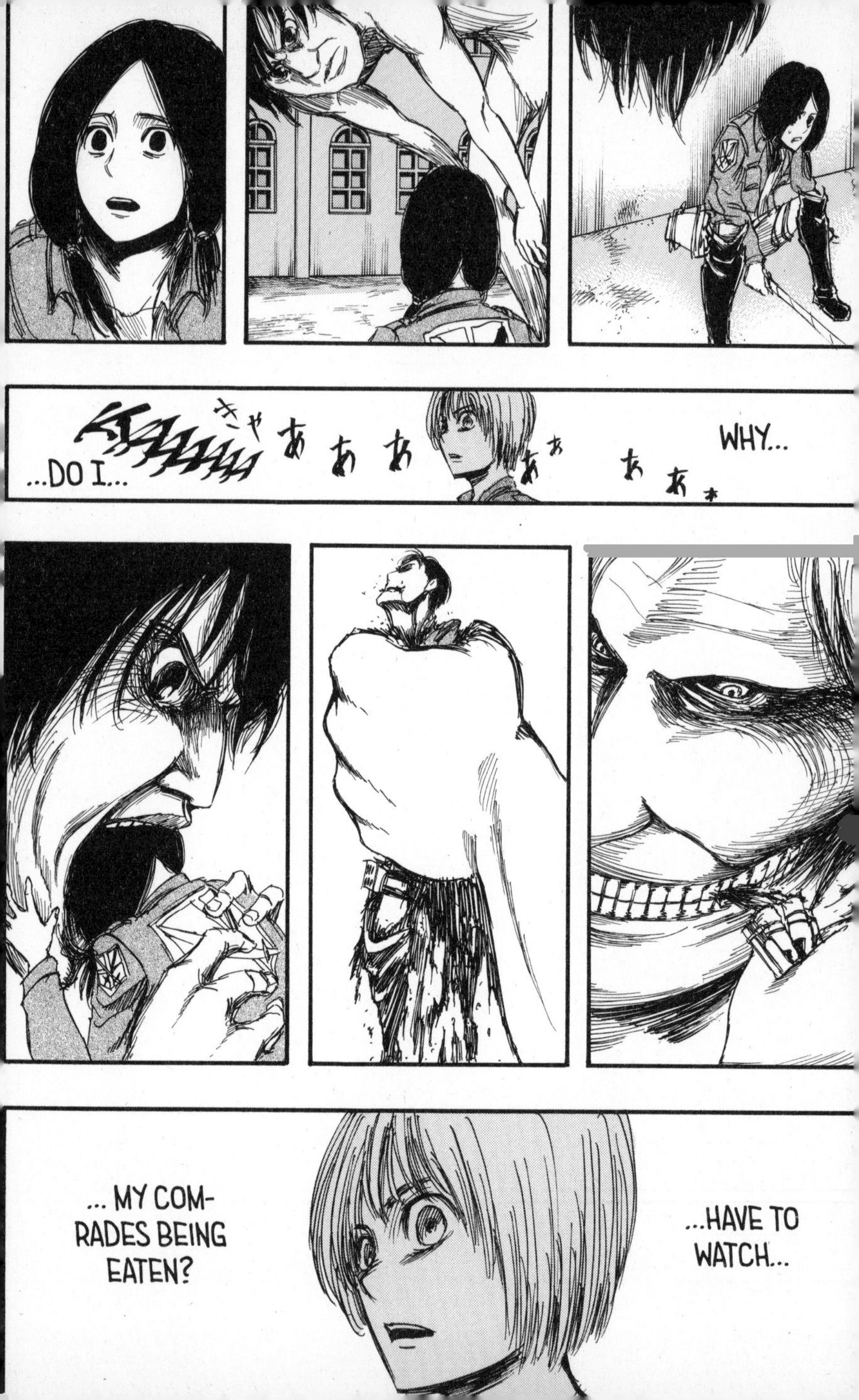
WHY...
...DO I...
...HAVE TO WATCH...
... MY COM-RADES BEING EATEN?

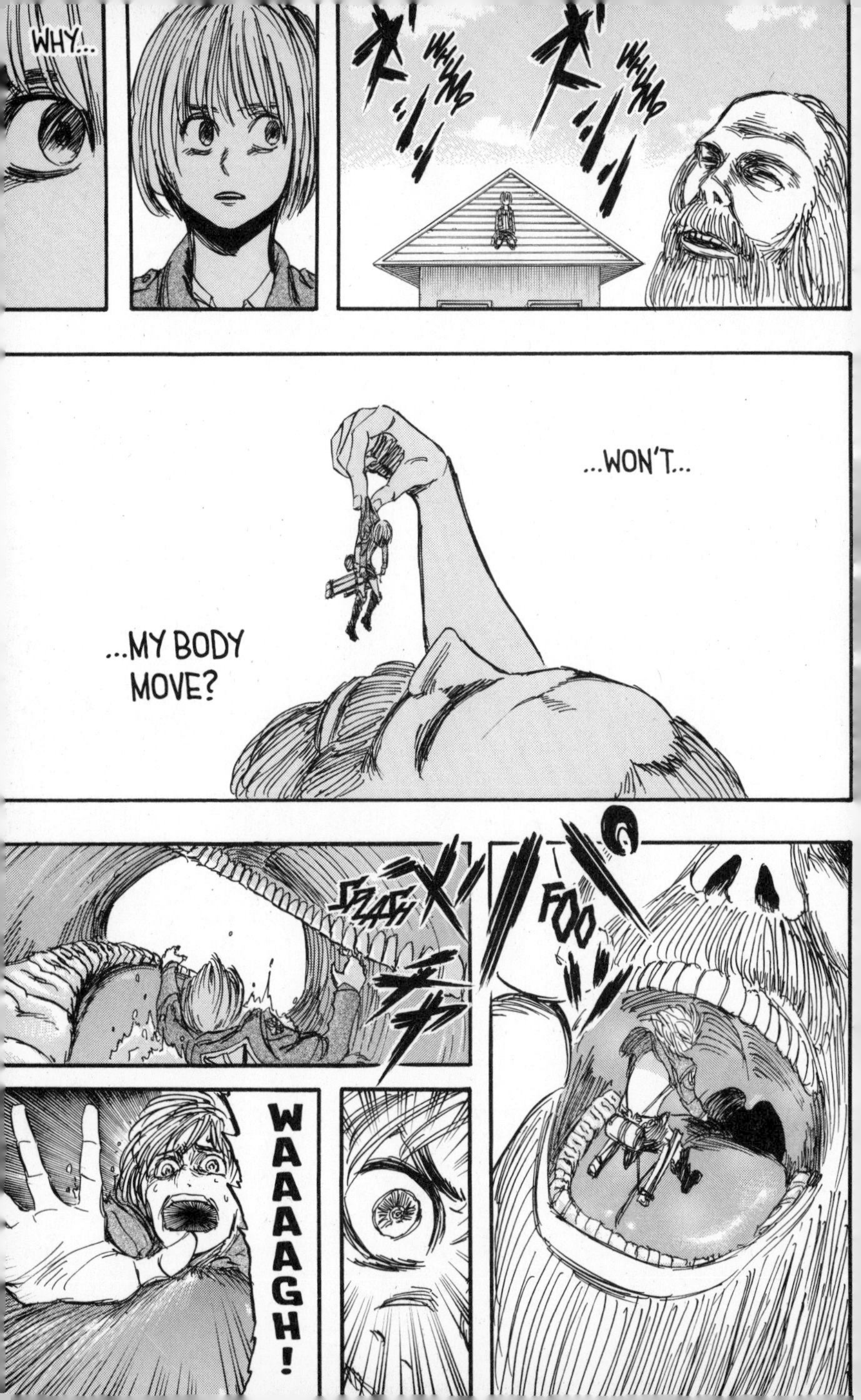
WHY...
...WON'T...
...MY BODY MOVE?
FOO
SPLASH
WAAAAGH!

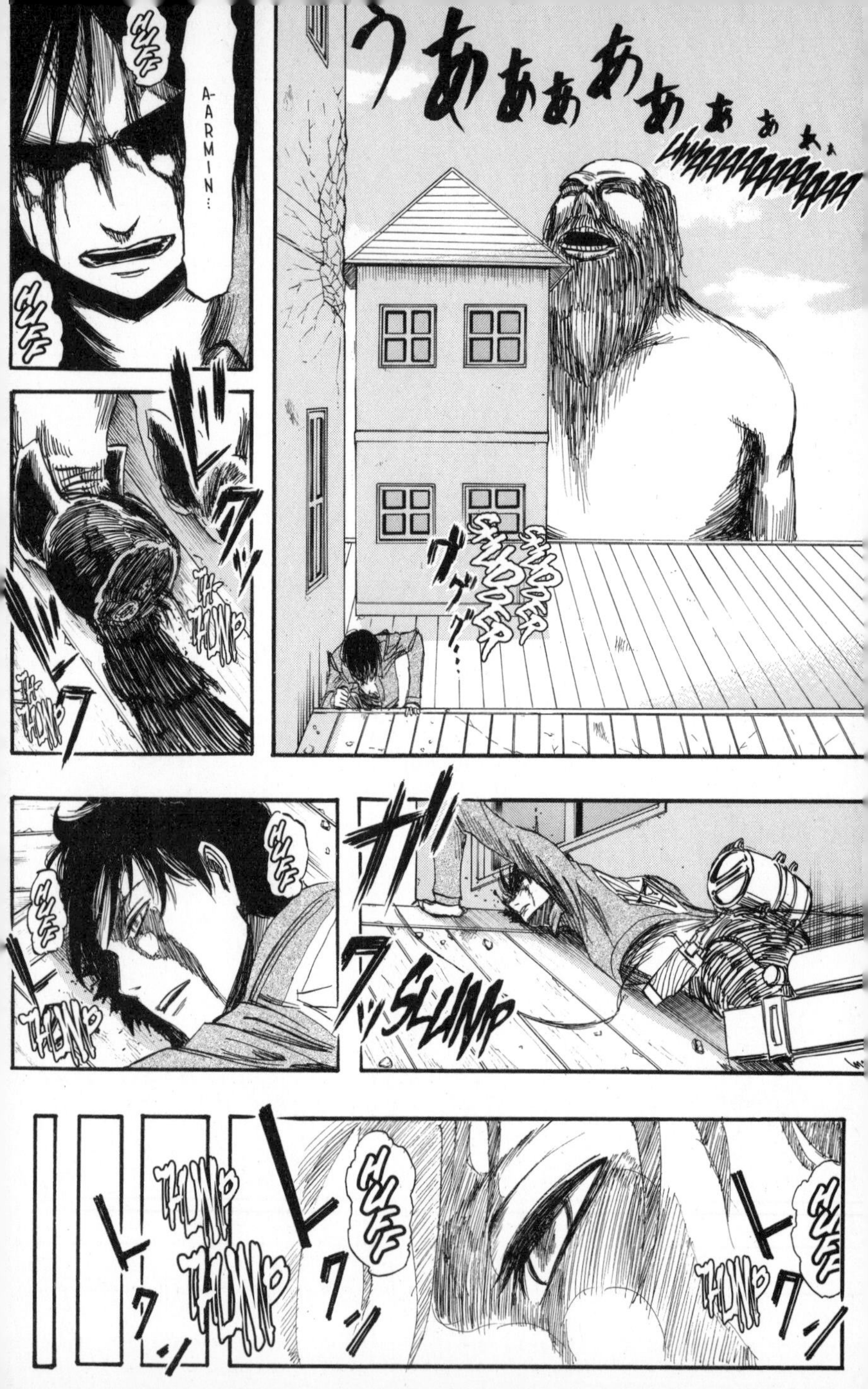

うあぁぁあぁぁぁぁぁ
UWAAAAAAAAAAAA
SHUDDER SHUDDER
ググ…
HUFF
A-ARMIN…
HUFF
THUMP
THUMP
SLUMP
HUFF
HUFF
THUMP
HUFF
THUMP
HUFF
THUMP
THUMP

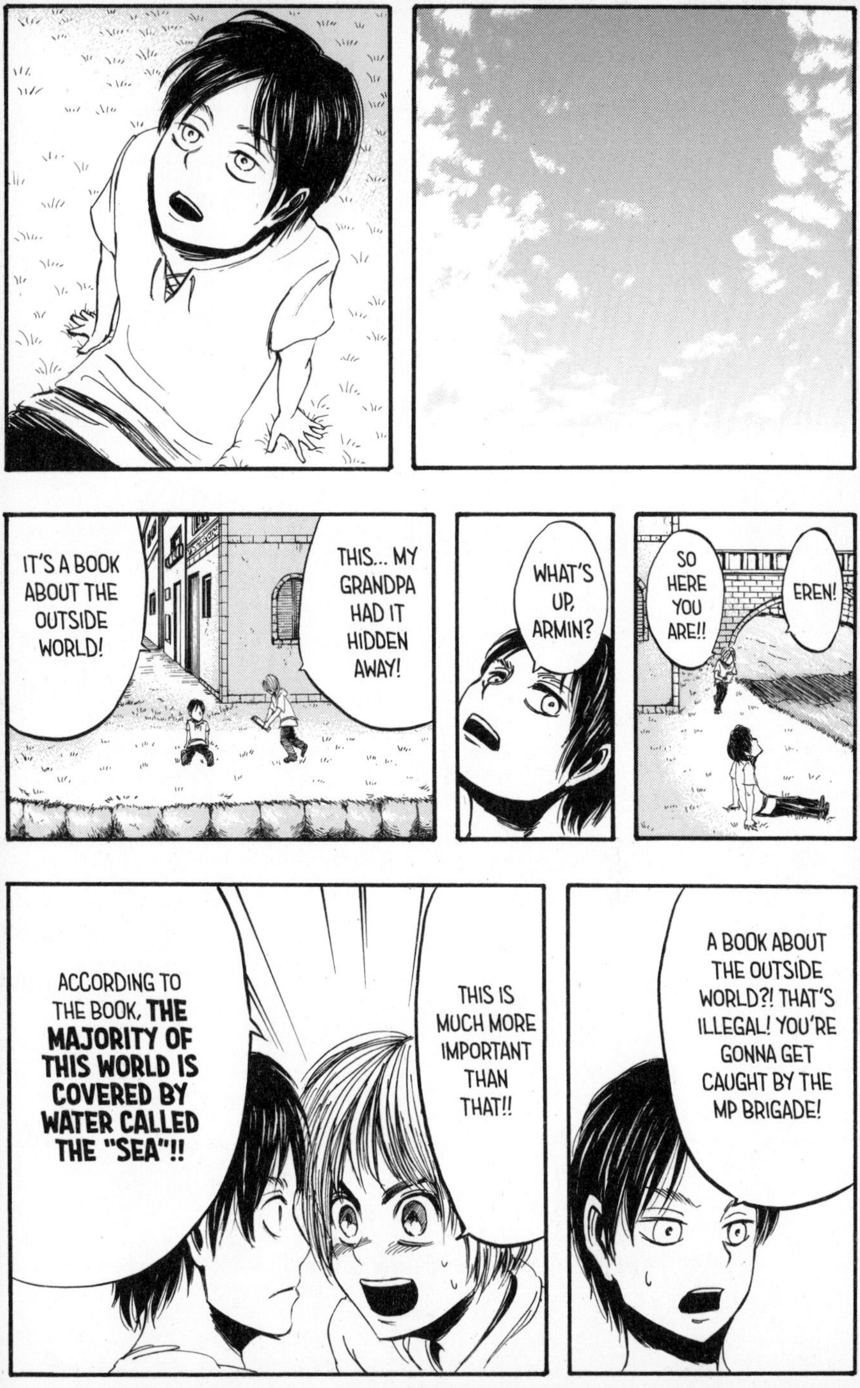
EREN!
SO HERE YOU ARE!!
WHAT'S UP, ARMIN?
THIS... MY GRANDPA HAD IT HIDDEN AWAY!
IT'S A BOOK ABOUT THE OUTSIDE WORLD!
A BOOK ABOUT THE OUTSIDE WORLD?! THAT'S ILLEGAL! YOU'RE GONNA GET CAUGHT BY THE MP BRIGADE!
THIS IS MUCH MORE IMPORTANT THAN THAT!!
ACCORDING TO THE BOOK, **THE MAJORITY OF THIS WORLD IS COVERED BY WATER CALLED THE "SEA"!!**

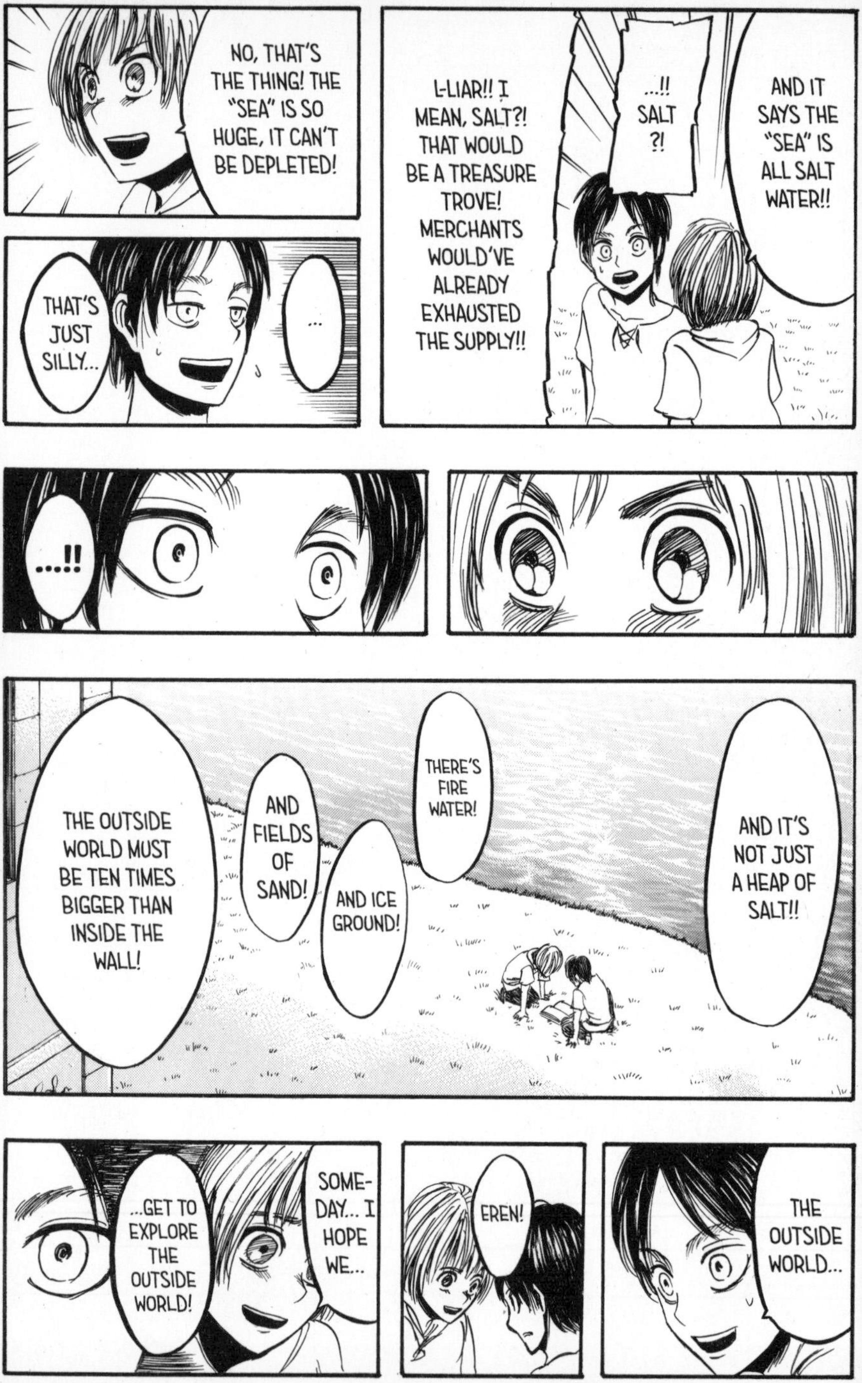
AND IT SAYS THE "SEA" IS ALL SALT WATER!!
...!! SALT ?!
L-LIAR!! I MEAN, SALT?! THAT WOULD BE A TREASURE TROVE! MERCHANTS WOULD'VE ALREADY EXHAUSTED THE SUPPLY!!
NO, THAT'S THE THING! THE "SEA" IS SO HUGE, IT CAN'T BE DEPLETED!
...
THAT'S JUST SILLY...
...!!
AND IT'S NOT JUST A HEAP OF SALT!!
THERE'S FIRE WATER!
AND ICE GROUND!
AND FIELDS OF SAND!
THE OUTSIDE WORLD MUST BE TEN TIMES BIGGER THAN INSIDE THE WALL!
THE OUTSIDE WORLD...
EREN!
SOME-DAY... I HOPE WE...
...GET TO EXPLORE THE OUTSIDE WORLD!

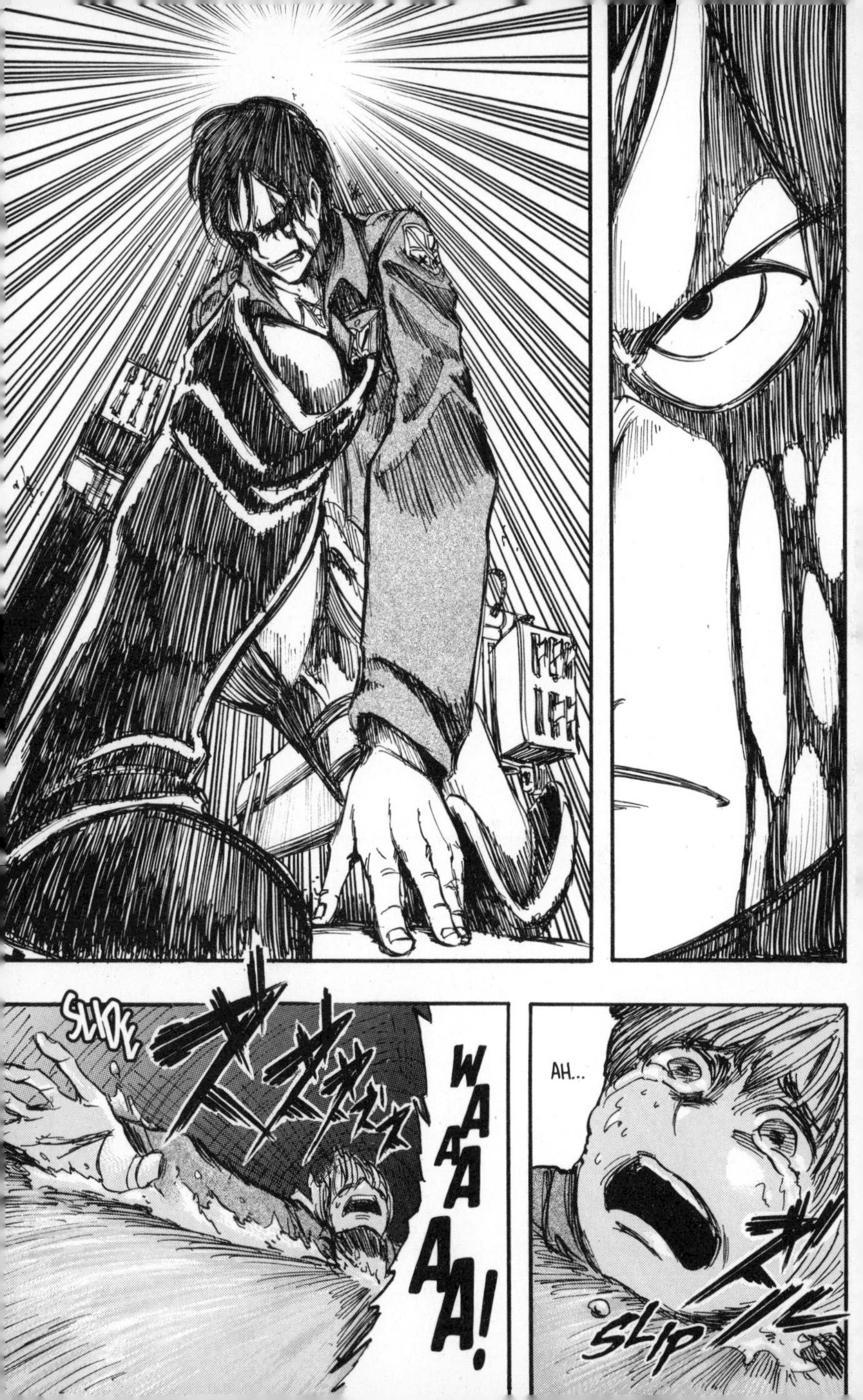
AH...
SLIP
SLICK
WAAAAA!

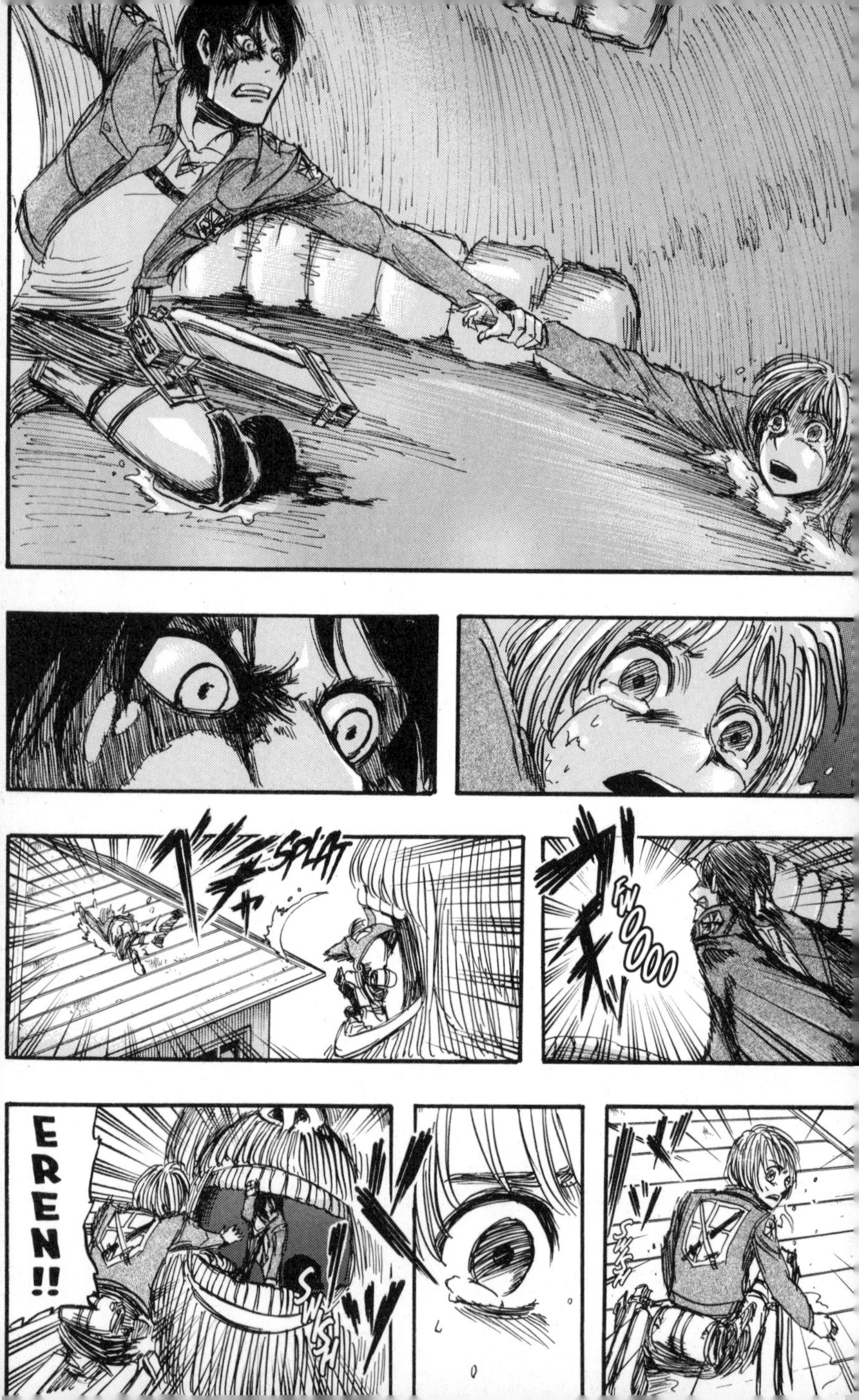

FWOOOO
ベチャ
SPLAT
SWISH
EREN!!
SWISH

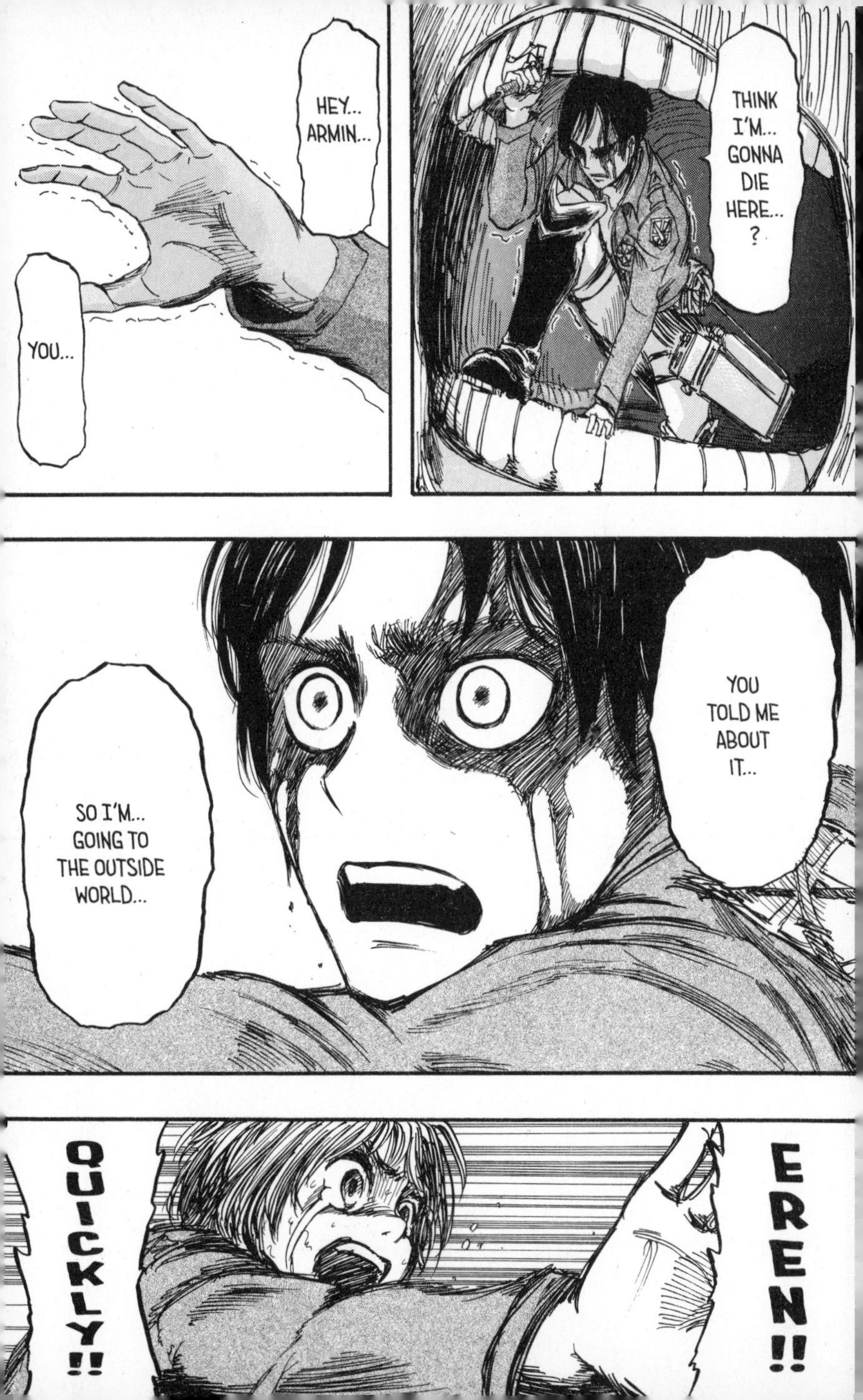
THINK I'M... GONNA DIE HERE...?
HEY... ARMIN...
YOU...
YOU TOLD ME ABOUT IT...
SO I'M... GOING TO THE OUTSIDE WORLD...
EREN!!
QUICKLY!!

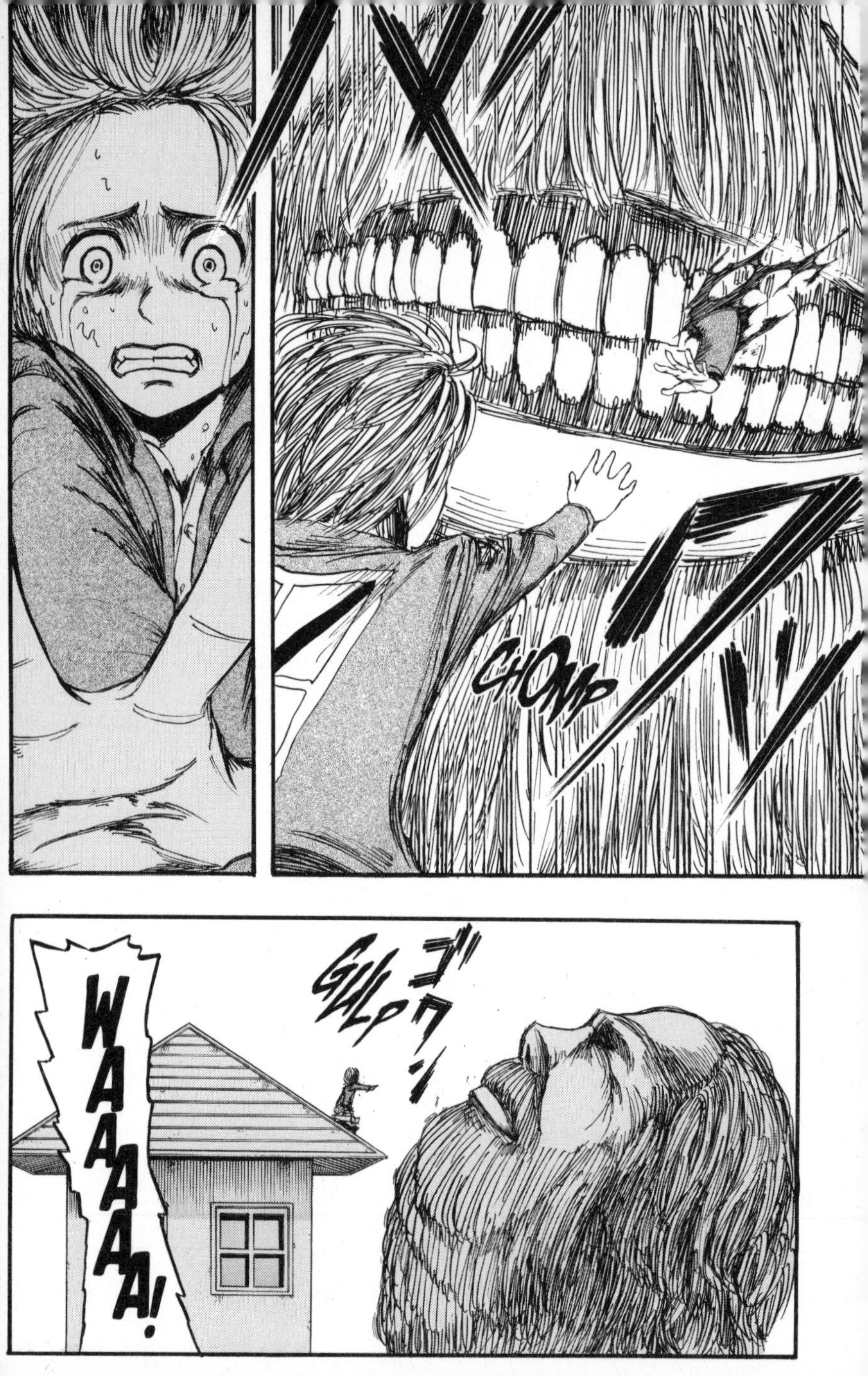
CHOMP
GULP
ゴクン
WAAAAA!

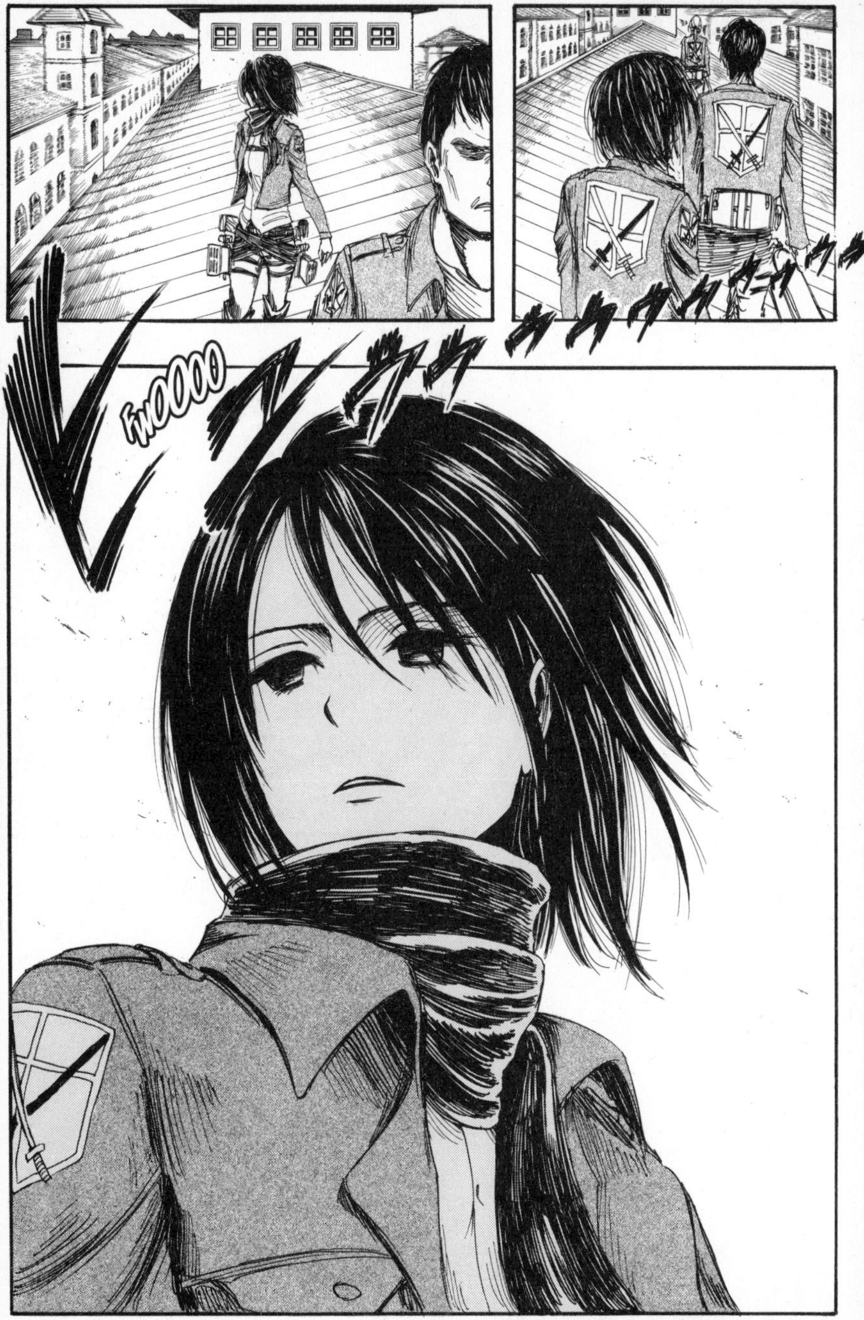
FWOOOO

Continued in Volume 2

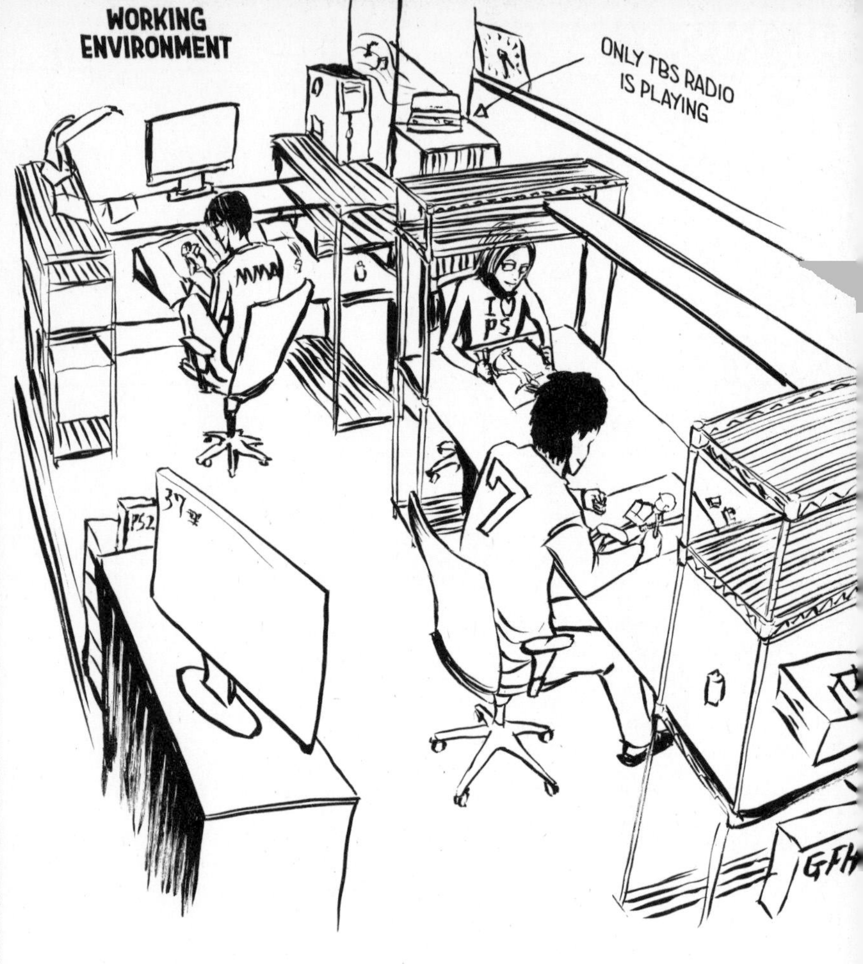
WORKING ENVIRONMENT
ONLY TBS RADIO IS PLAYING
MMA
I♡PS
7
PS2
GFH

SHINX-SAN
OUMI-SAN
SOMETIMES TAKANIWA-SAN

EVERYONE WHO READ
"ATTACK ON TITAN"

THANK YOU VERY MUCH

ULTRA-SPECIAL BONUS!!*

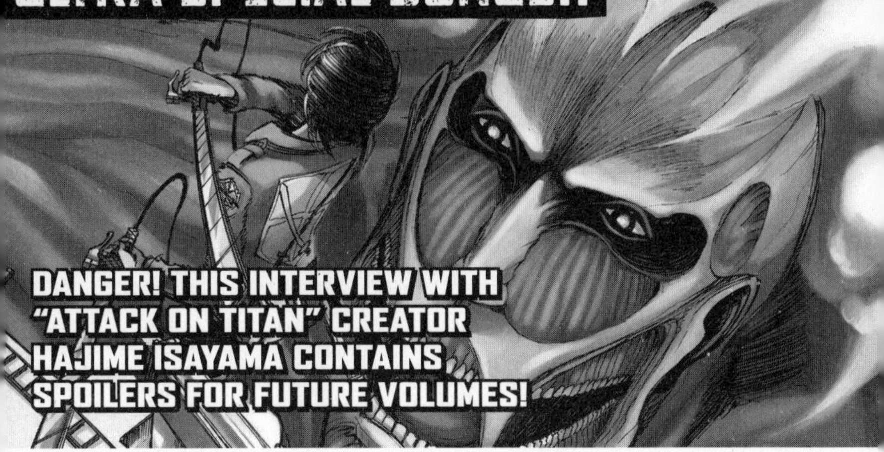

DANGER! THIS INTERVIEW WITH "ATTACK ON TITAN" CREATOR HAJIME ISAYAMA CONTAINS SPOILERS FOR FUTURE VOLUMES!

Japanese readers sent in questions to ask Mr. Isayama, and his editor asked him a few. Here we present his answers. Just be careful: Some of them contain major spoilers for later volumes! We recommend you read Vol. 2, then come back and read this interview.

EDITOR: Thank you for being here today. We've received a lot of questions from the readers. Please answer to the best of your ability.
MR. ISAYAMA: I have a feeling most of my answers will be boring, but... fire away. Nothing is taboo.

Then let's begin. "Why did you decide on giants as the theme of this work?"
ISA: Well, giants are kind of gross, aren't they? That's why.

"Has anything in your life changed since the series has become so popular?"
ISA: I got a weird phone call from my bank. They were wondering about the sudden increase of funds in my savings, so they probably thought I was running some bank transfer scam. (Laughs.)

"Do you have a way to clear out the cobwebs when you're tired or when you need to decide some important story point?"
ISA: Shadowboxing with the hanging lamp cord in my house is very soothing.

"What made you decide to become a manga artist?"
ISA: I just decided one day, is all. I had a habit of doodling and daydreaming anyway, so I was fortunate that my interests were compatible with something that's profitable.

"Mr. Isayama, what is your fetish?"
ISA: I have a body hair fetish.

"How do you get over those times when making manga gets tough?"
ISA: I don't. (Laughs.) I think it's always equal parts tough and fun.

"Where do you get your ideas for stories?"
ISA: This doesn't have to do with creating stories, but when I'm half-awake, like just before I drift off to sleep, my mind gets flooded with information I've seen or heard subconsciously. I call it "Super Enlightenment Time." And this is true, I'm not kidding.

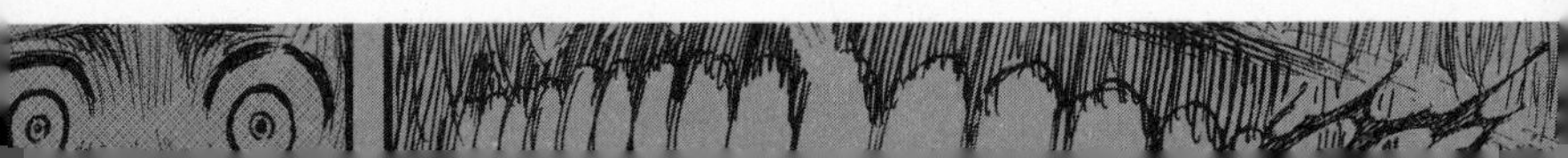

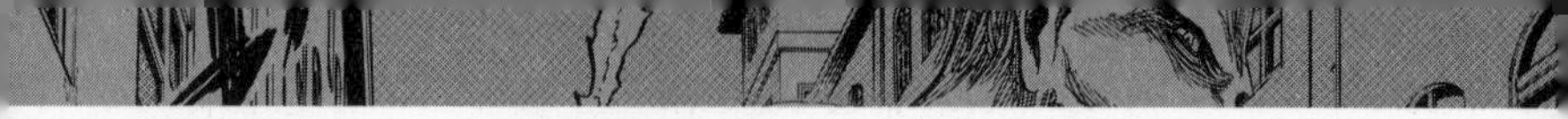

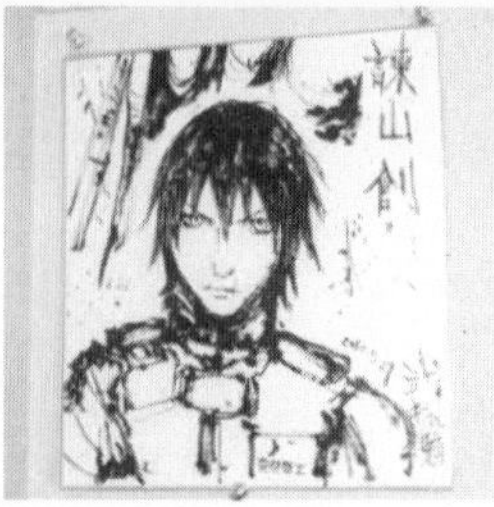

A signed sketch by an artist Mr. Isayama respects, Mr. Nihei. It's a treasured possession that hangs on his wall.

On to the next question... "Is there a manga artist whom you respect?"
ISA: There are plenty of them. Of course, there are my fellow manga artists in Betsu Maga, but also Tsutomu Nihei, Ryoji Minagawa, Kentaro Miura, Hideki Arai, Tooru Mitsumine, and I could go on and on. I'm still a fledgling.

"Who is your favorite character in Attack on Titan?"
ISA: That would be Jean. Jean comes right out and says what he's thinking, even if it's something you normally couldn't say. That's what I like about him.

"Out of all the manga you've read, what influenced you most?"
ISA: ARMS.

"How far ahead do you have Attack on Titan plotted out?"
ISA: In broad strokes, I've got it pretty well thought out to way, way down the line. And I've got outlines that say like, such-and-such a truth will be revealed in volume 5 and around volume 10, this situation is going to happen. See, if I didn't decide these things before it sees publication, I wouldn't even be able to come up with ideas. Although I don't flesh it out until I'm actually working on it...

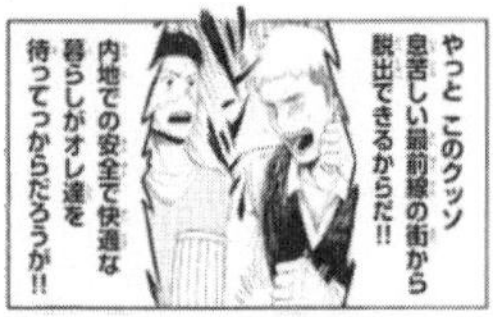
やっとこのクソッ息苦しい最前線の街から脱出できるからだ!!
内地での安全で快適な暮らしがオレ達を待ってっからだろうが!!

Jean Kirstein. I like the name, too.

"What do you think of Miyajima (Masanori Miyajima)?"
ISA: He's got a permanent crease on his nose from his glasses.

"Aren't you going to have female Titans?"
ISA: I wonder if I should say this... They're rare.

"I always forget how the kanji for 'Isa' in your last name goes. Is there a good way to remember how to write it?"
ISA: You can write it however. I'll answer either way.

"Mr. Isayama, I want to see where you work!"
ISA: That's the one thing I hope you'll cut me some slack on! I really don't want to show you, since it's a mess...

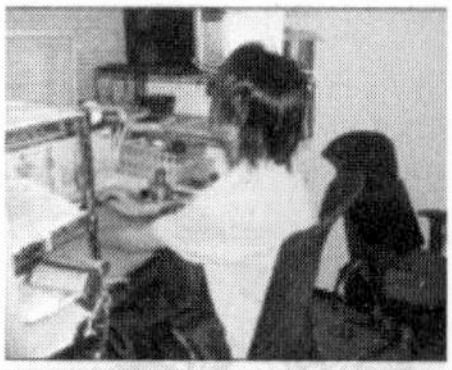

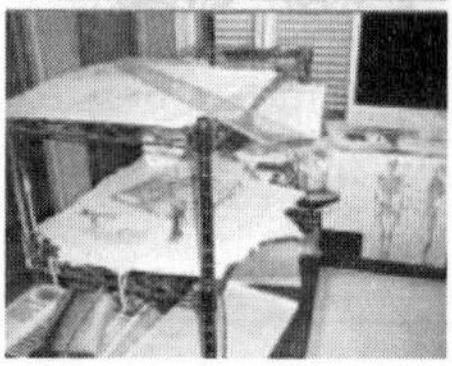

We went ahead and took photos of Mr. Isayama's studio.

"If you were on a desert island and could only have three things, what would you choose besides me and a guitar?"
ISA: Other than you and a guitar, I guess I would bring a U.S. military fleet.

"Mr. Isayama, what were you like as a child?"
ISA: I don't really want to recall my childhood...

"Do you use a model for the Titans?"
ISA: For the Titan version of Eren, I use martial artist Yuushin Okami's body as a model. My ideal is the physique of a middleweight mixed martial artist. I only use the shape of the body as a model.

"I'm guessing that drawing Titans after a long time would do things to your mind. Do you have nightmares about them?"
ISA: I don't think giants are really scary in the first place, so no, never.

"What's the scariest thing in the world?"
ISA: A bunch of middle school girls looking at me and going, "Eww" while laughing.

"Please tell me your basic one-month schedule."
ISA: I take a week to storyboard and three weeks to draw.

"Mikasa is always wearing the scarf she got from Eren. Doesn't she get hot?"
ISA: She doesn't wear it when it's hot outside.

"Mr. Isayama, at what age did you start drawing?"
ISA: I have a memory of being praised for a drawing I did of a dragon when I was in kindergarten.

GONG
11
UFC
Go for the Top!
イザ、頂キへ
岡見勇信
Yūshin Okami, whom Mr. Isayama uses as a model.

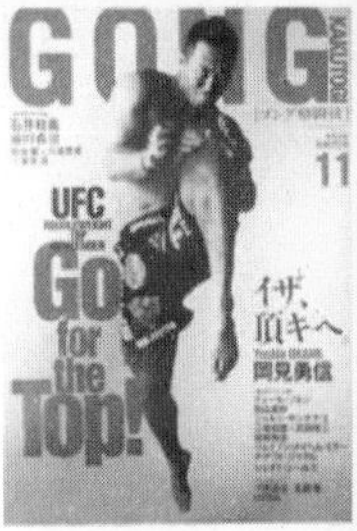

"Are you ever mistaken for the artist who does (soccer series) Giant Killing?"
ISA: Just recently, my own editor made that mistake.

"What manga do you recommend right now?"
ISA: All-Rounder Meguru and Iron Wind!!

"Mr. Isayama, which Attack on Titan character most resembles you?"
ISA: Hmm... Mr. Hannes and the Garrison soldiers in volume 1 who sit around drinking booze.

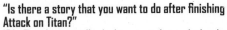

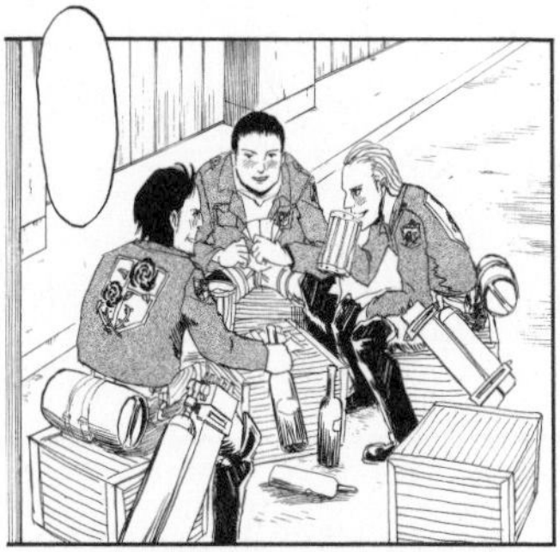

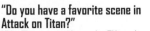

These Garrison soldiers drink alcohol in the middle of the afternoon. Surely Mr. Isayama doesn't do *that* at work?!

"Is there a story that you want to do after finishing Attack on Titan?"
ISA: There's a story I've had in my mind since high school. If I get lucky enough for it to be published someday, I hope everyone reads it!

"Do you have a favorite scene in Attack on Titan?"
ISA: The scene where the TV studio gets taken over and rock music plays. Sorry...

"What's your favorite food?"
ISA: I'm not really into food.**

"How do you spend your free time?"
ISA: Drooling as I surf the net.

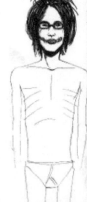

"What would you look like if you were a Titan, Mr. Isayama?"
ISA: I'm sure I'd look something like this. (Laughs.)

Thank you very much! One last question. "From what page does the story really get going?"
ISA: Just wait for the 420th page and up! Please keep reading!

Scary in a way...

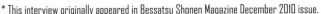

* This interview originally appeared in Bessatsu Shonen Magazine December 2010 issue.
**Apparently, if he's not careful, he'll drop to 40 kilos [88 lbs] without realizing it...

Preview of

Attack on Titan,

volume 2

We're pleased to present a preview from **Attack on Titan,** volume 2, now available from Kodansha Comics. See our Web site (www.kodanshacomics.com) for details!

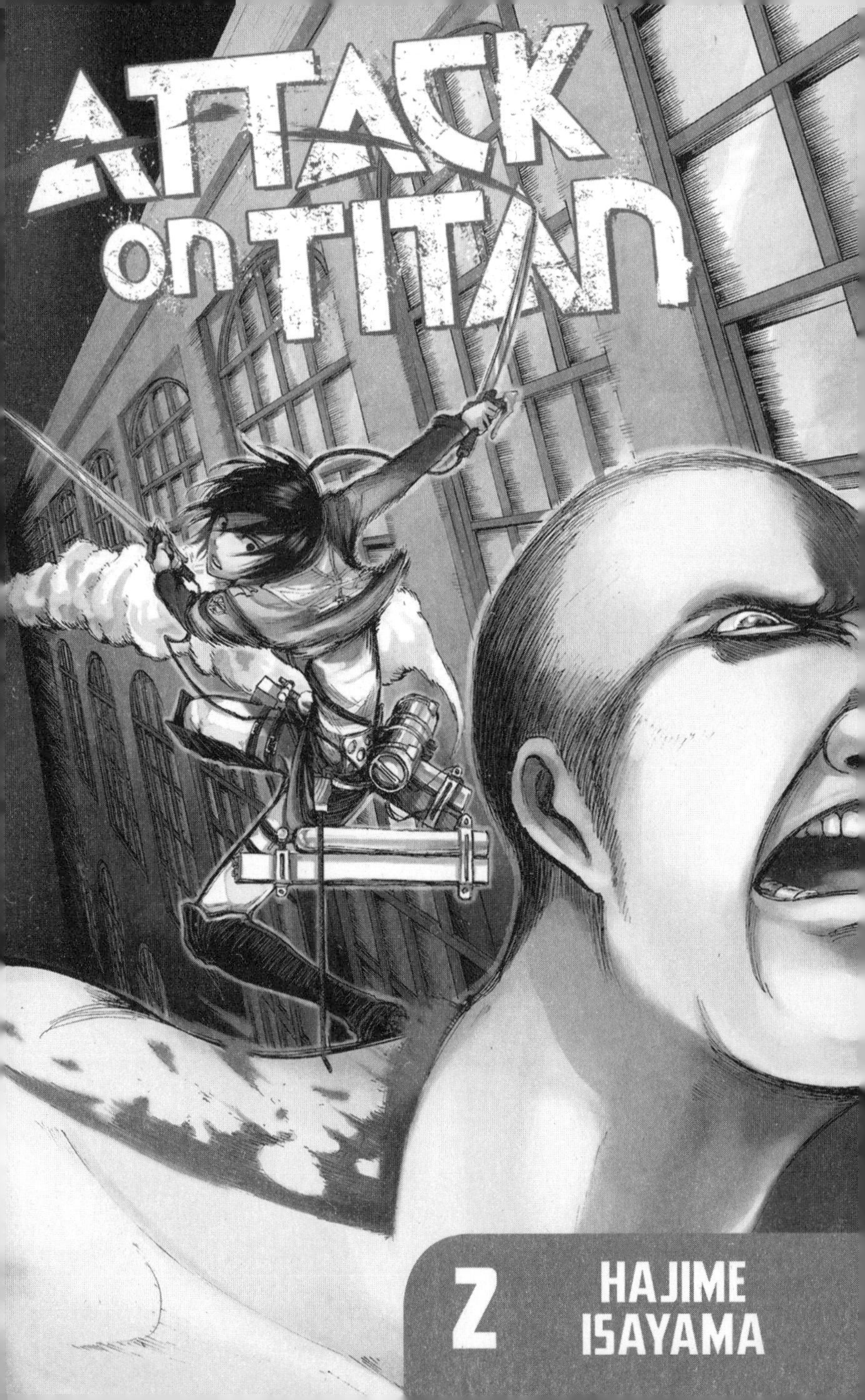

ATTACK ON TITAN
2
HAJIME
ISAYAMA

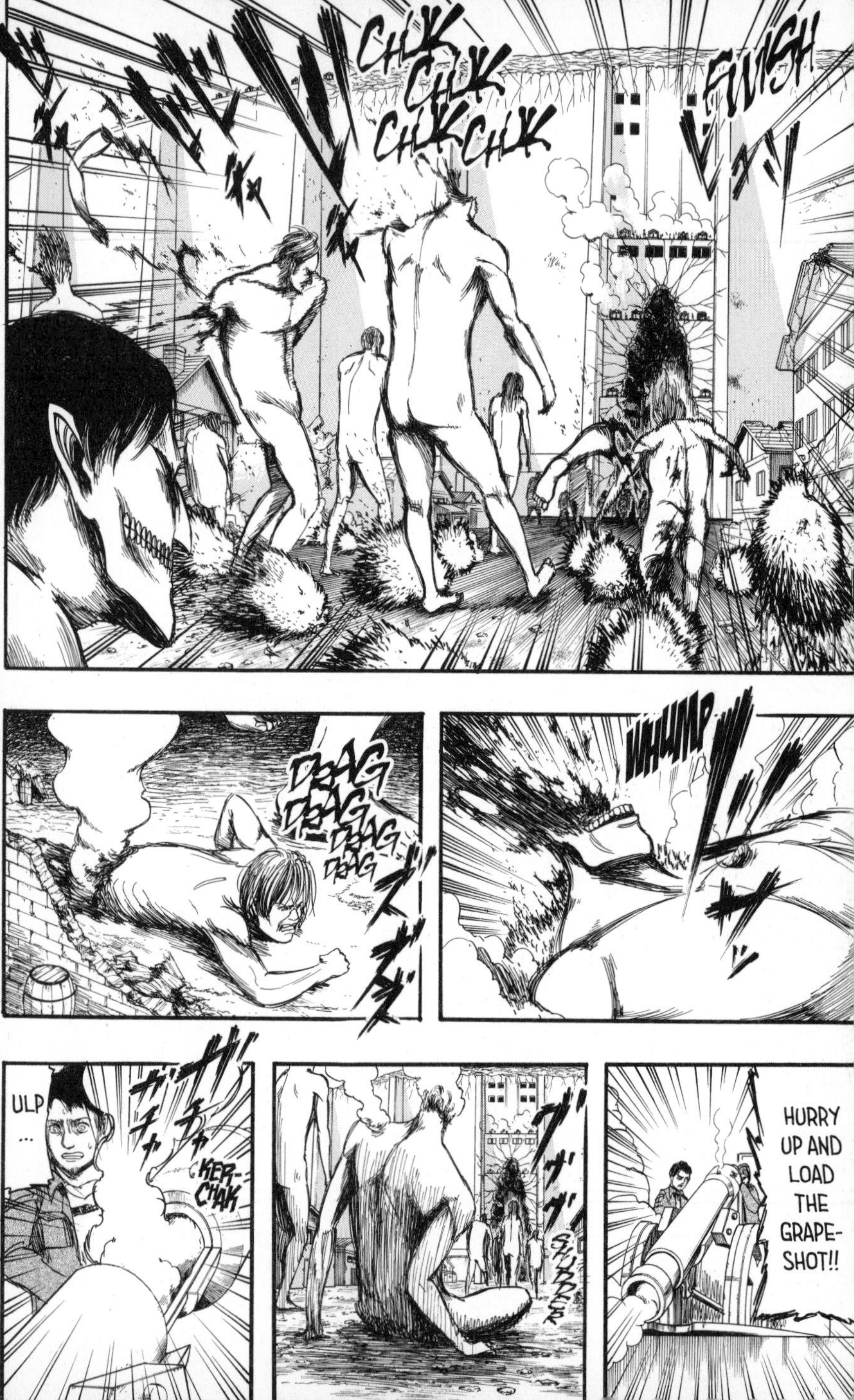
FWISH
CHUK CHUK CHUK CHUK
WHUMP
DRAG DRAG DRAG DRAG DRAG
HURRY UP AND LOAD THE GRAPE-SHOT!!
SHUDDER
ULP ...
KER-CHAK

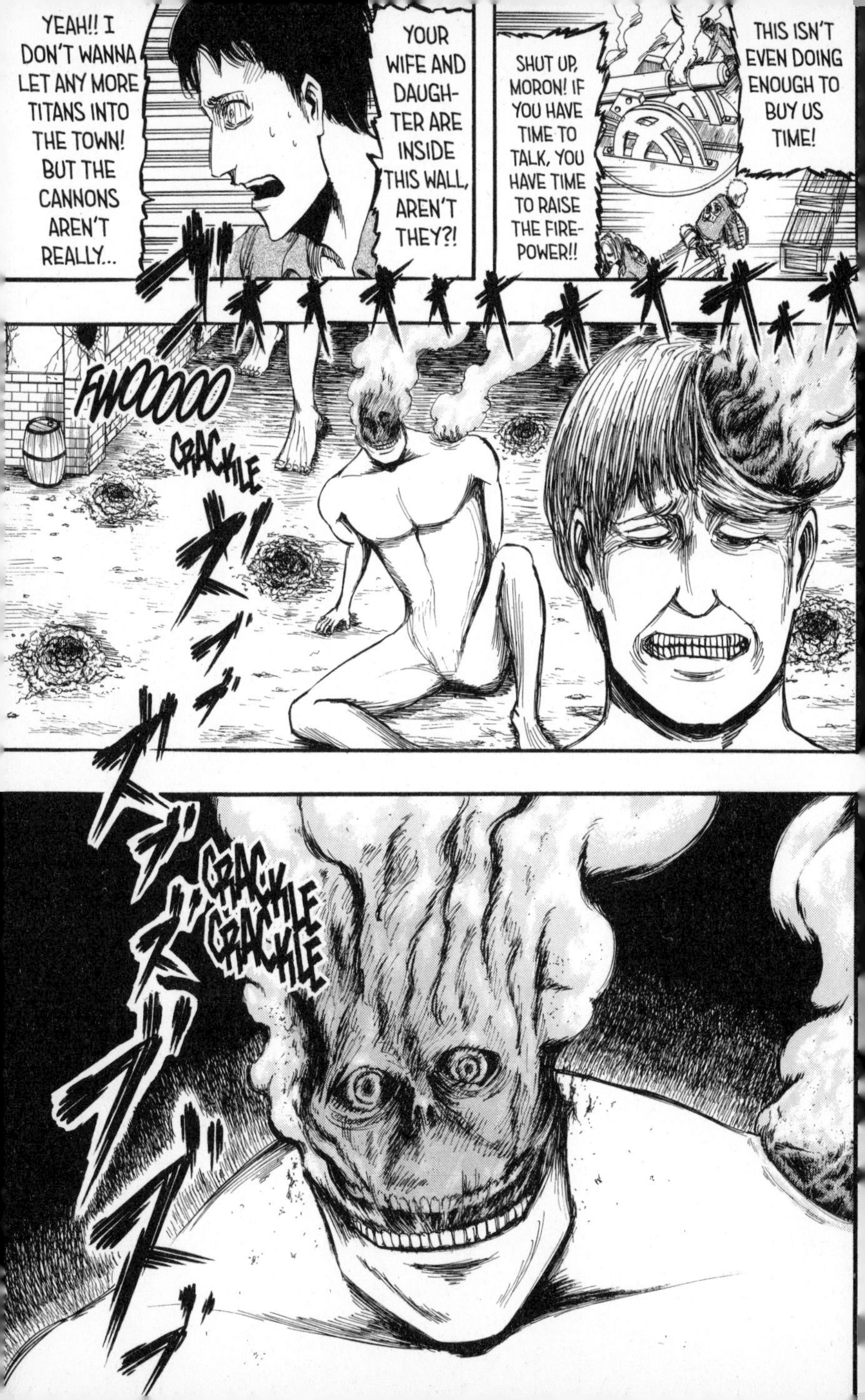
THIS ISN'T EVEN DOING ENOUGH TO BUY US TIME!
SHUT UP, MORON! IF YOU HAVE TIME TO TALK, YOU HAVE TIME TO RAISE THE FIRE-POWER!!
YOUR WIFE AND DAUGHTER ARE INSIDE THIS WALL, AREN'T THEY?!
YEAH!! I DON'T WANNA LET ANY MORE TITANS INTO THE TOWN! BUT THE CANNONS AREN'T REALLY...
FWOOOOOO
CRACKLE
CRACKLE CRACKLE

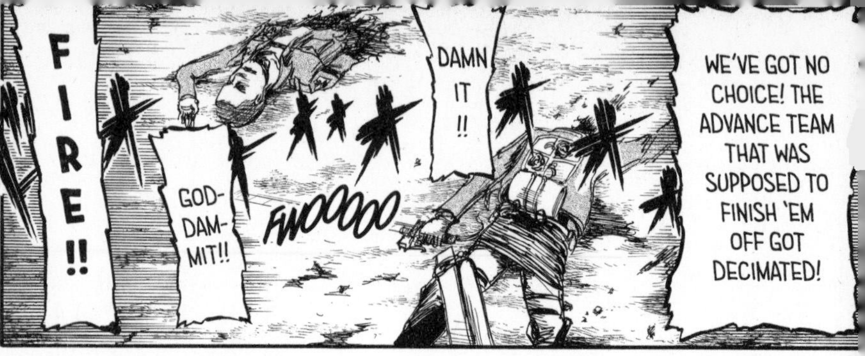
WE'VE GOT NO CHOICE! THE ADVANCE TEAM THAT WAS SUPPOSED TO FINISH 'EM OFF GOT DECIMATED!
DAMN IT!!
FWOOOOO
GOD-DAM-MIT!!
FIRE!!

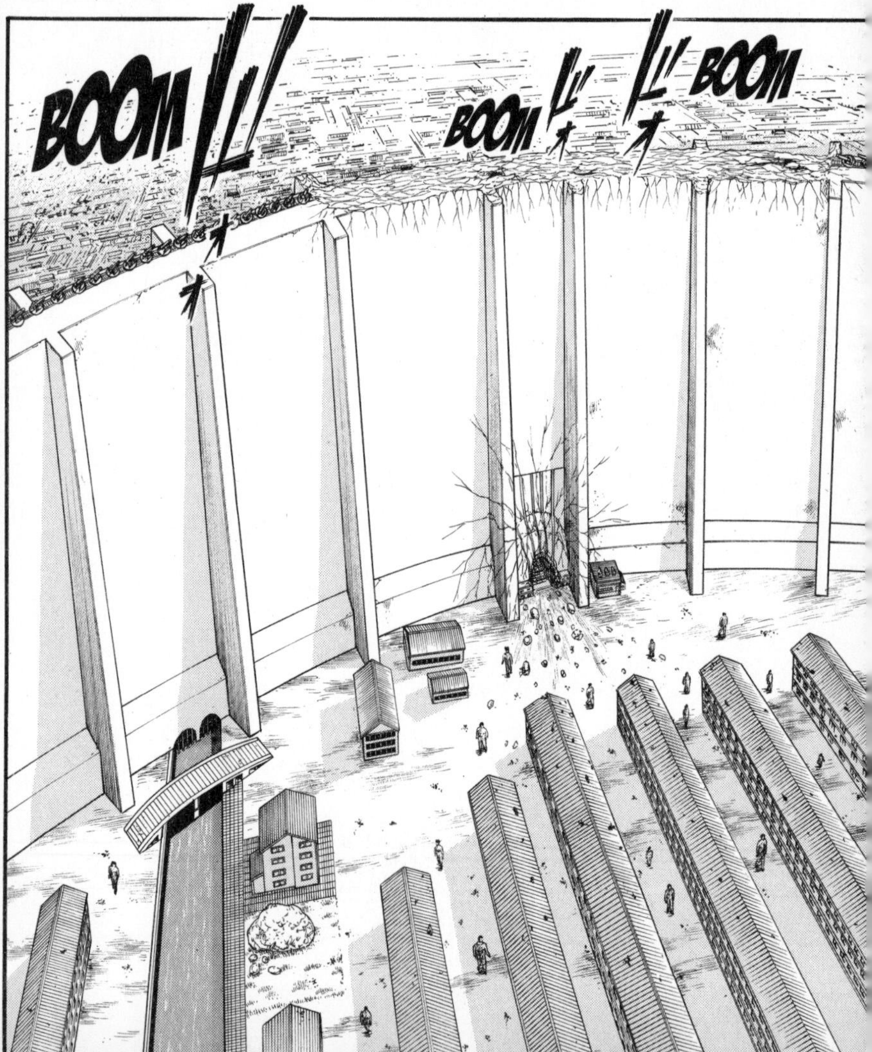
BOOM
BOOM
BOOM!!

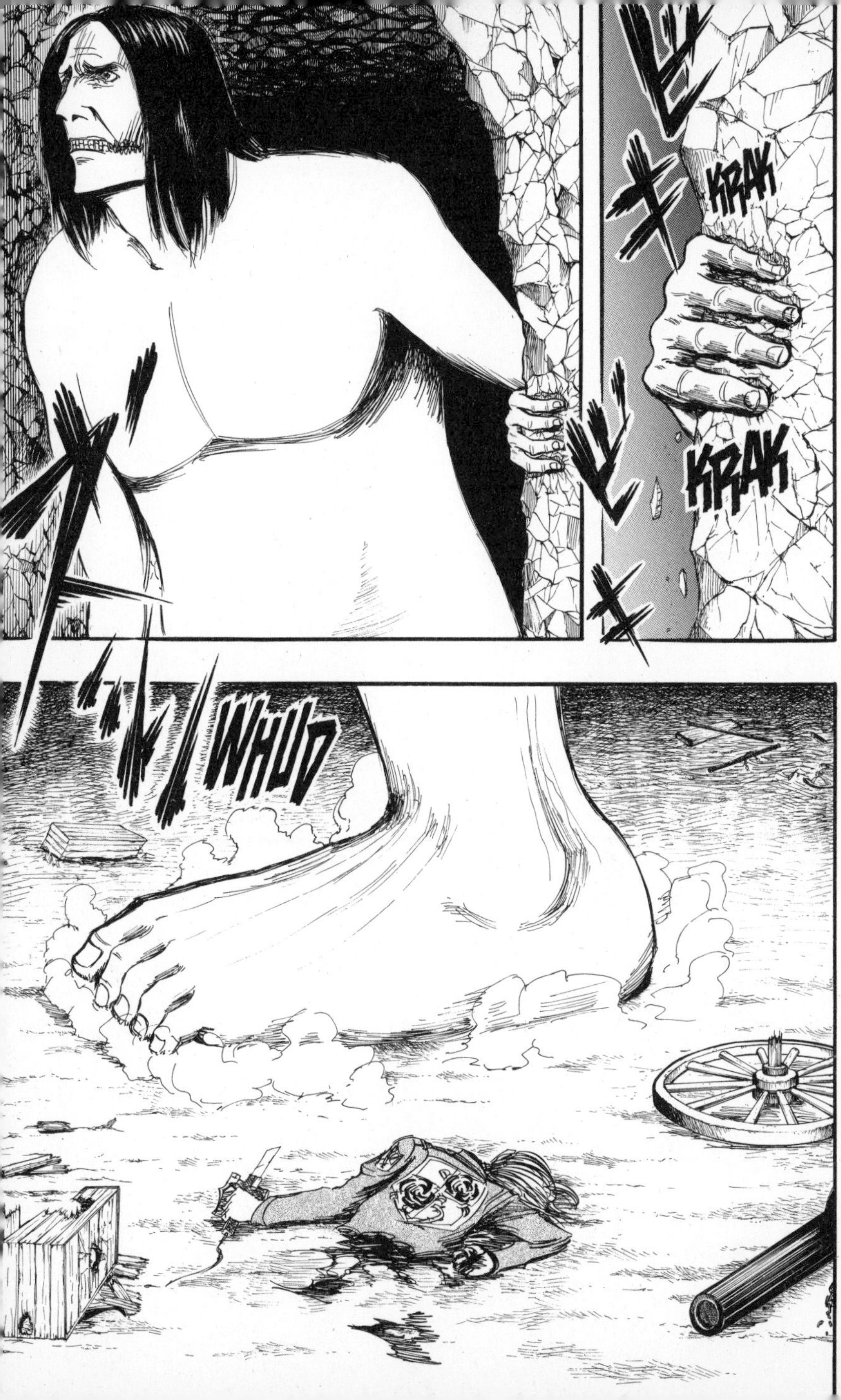
KRAK
KRAK
WHUD

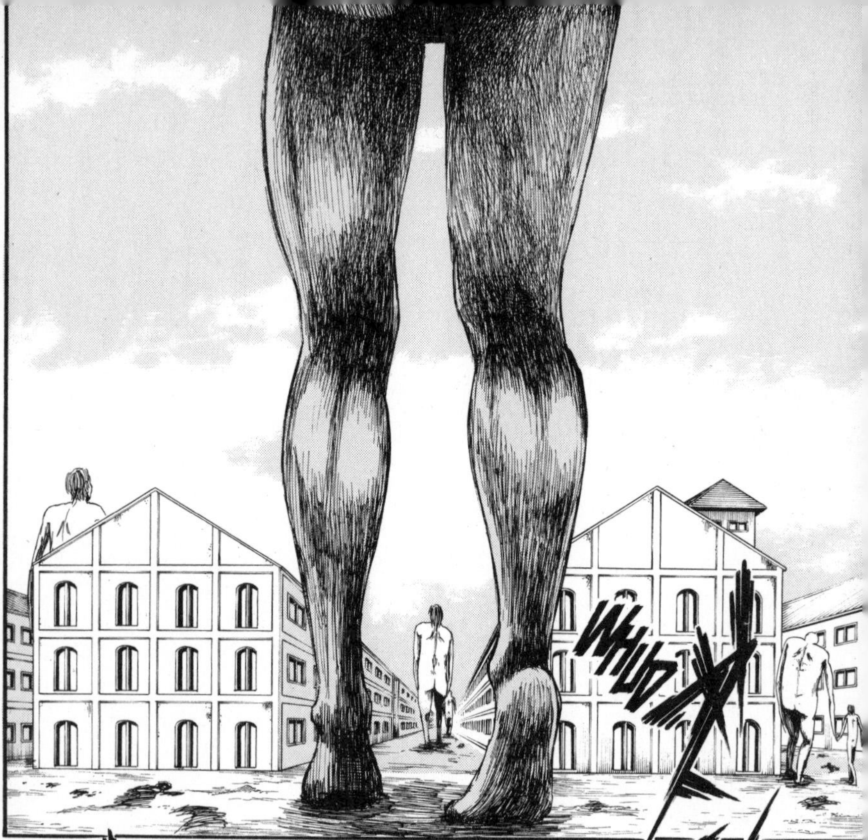
WHUD

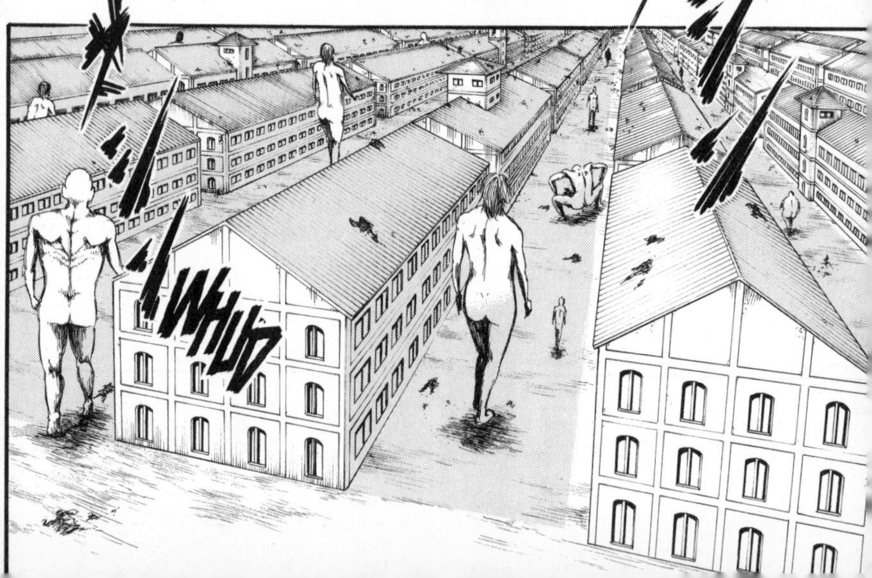
WHUD

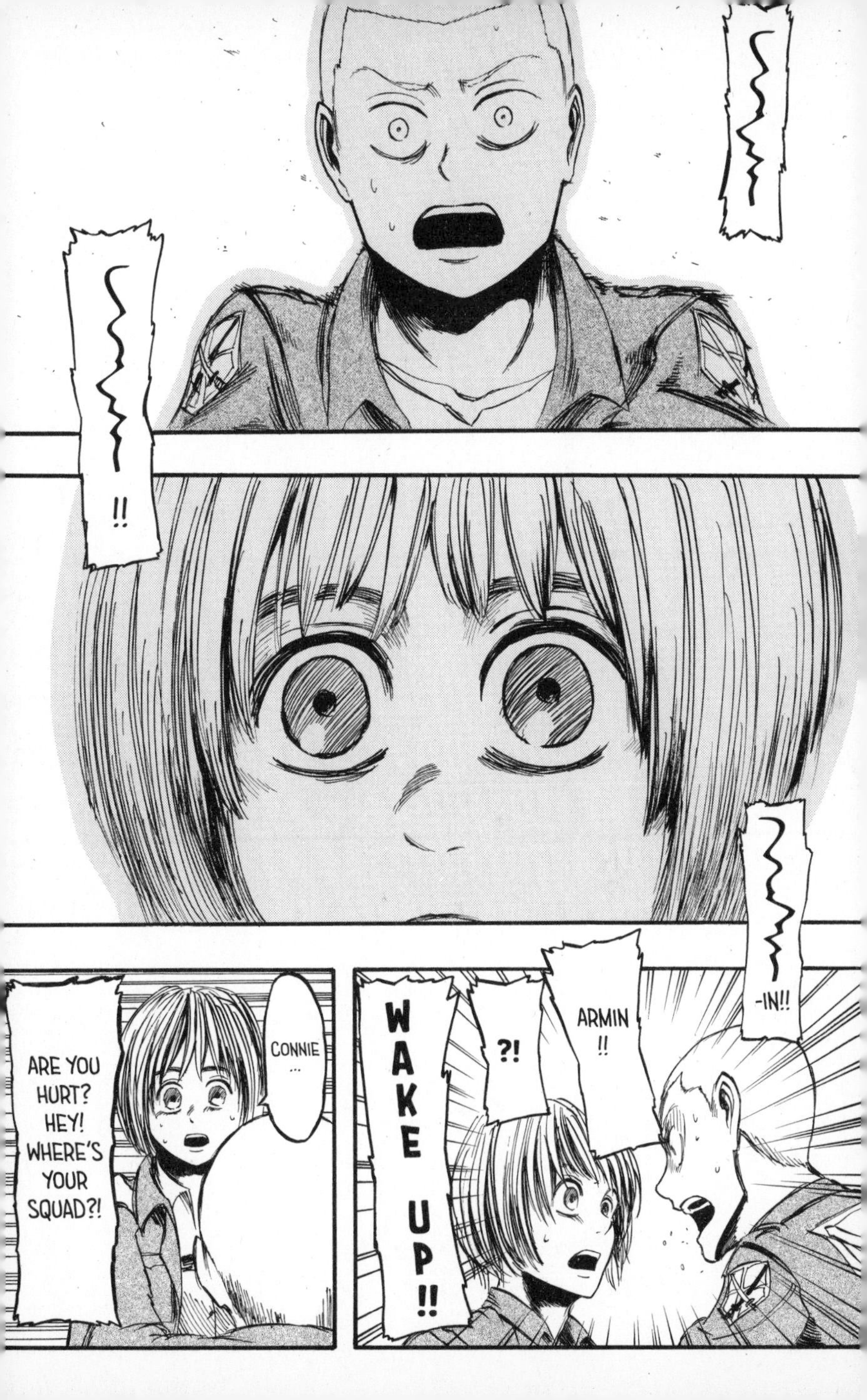
!!
-IN!!
ARMIN !!
?!
WAKE UP!!
CONNIE ...
ARE YOU HURT? HEY! WHERE'S YOUR SQUAD?!

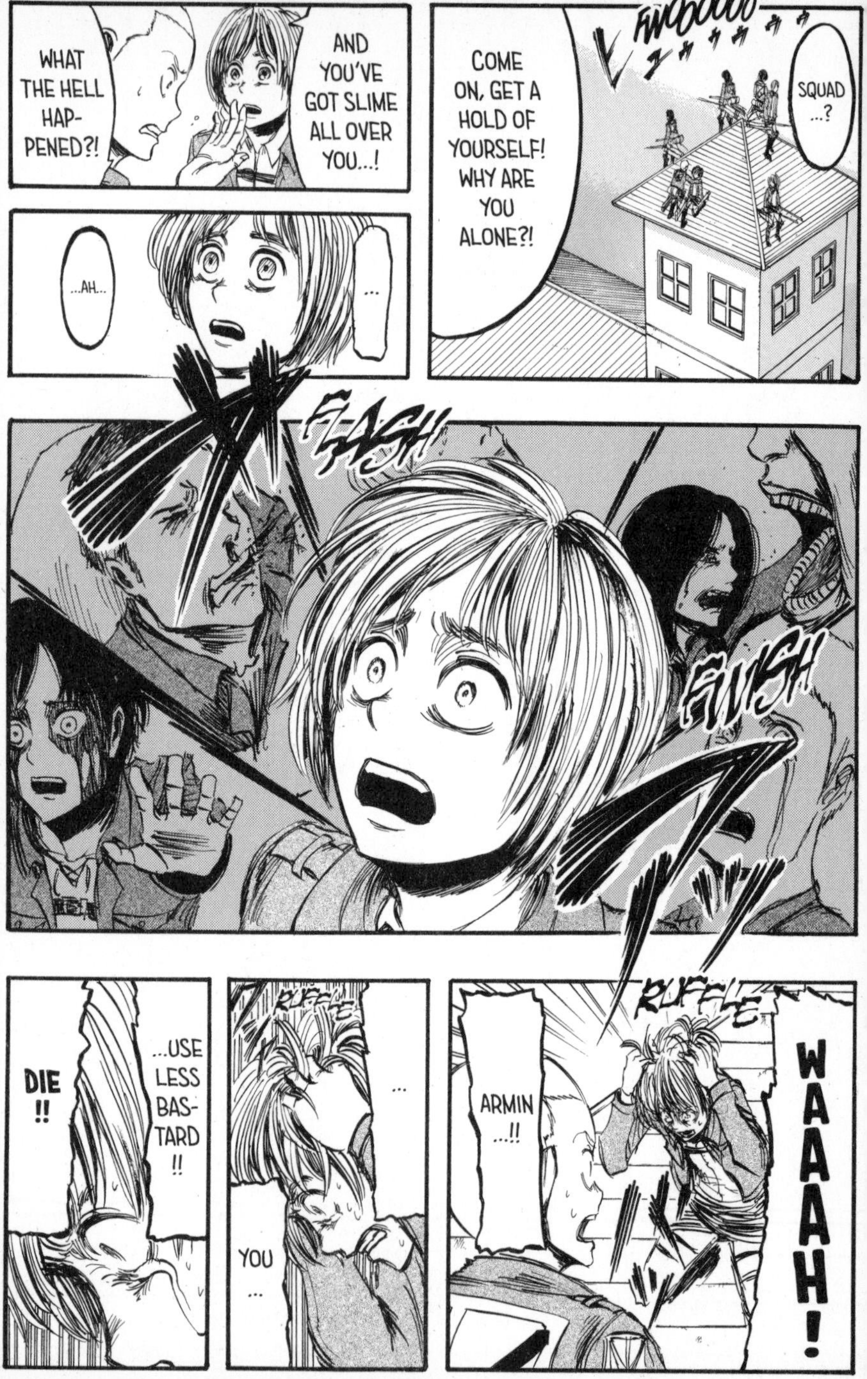
FWOOOOOO
SQUAD ...?
COME ON, GET A HOLD OF YOURSELF! WHY ARE YOU ALONE?!
AND YOU'VE GOT SLIME ALL OVER YOU...!
WHAT THE HELL HAP-PENED?!
...
...AH...
FLASH
FWISH
WAAAH!
RUFFLE
ARMIN ...!!
RUFFLE
...
YOU ...
...USE LESS BAS-TARD !!
DIE !!

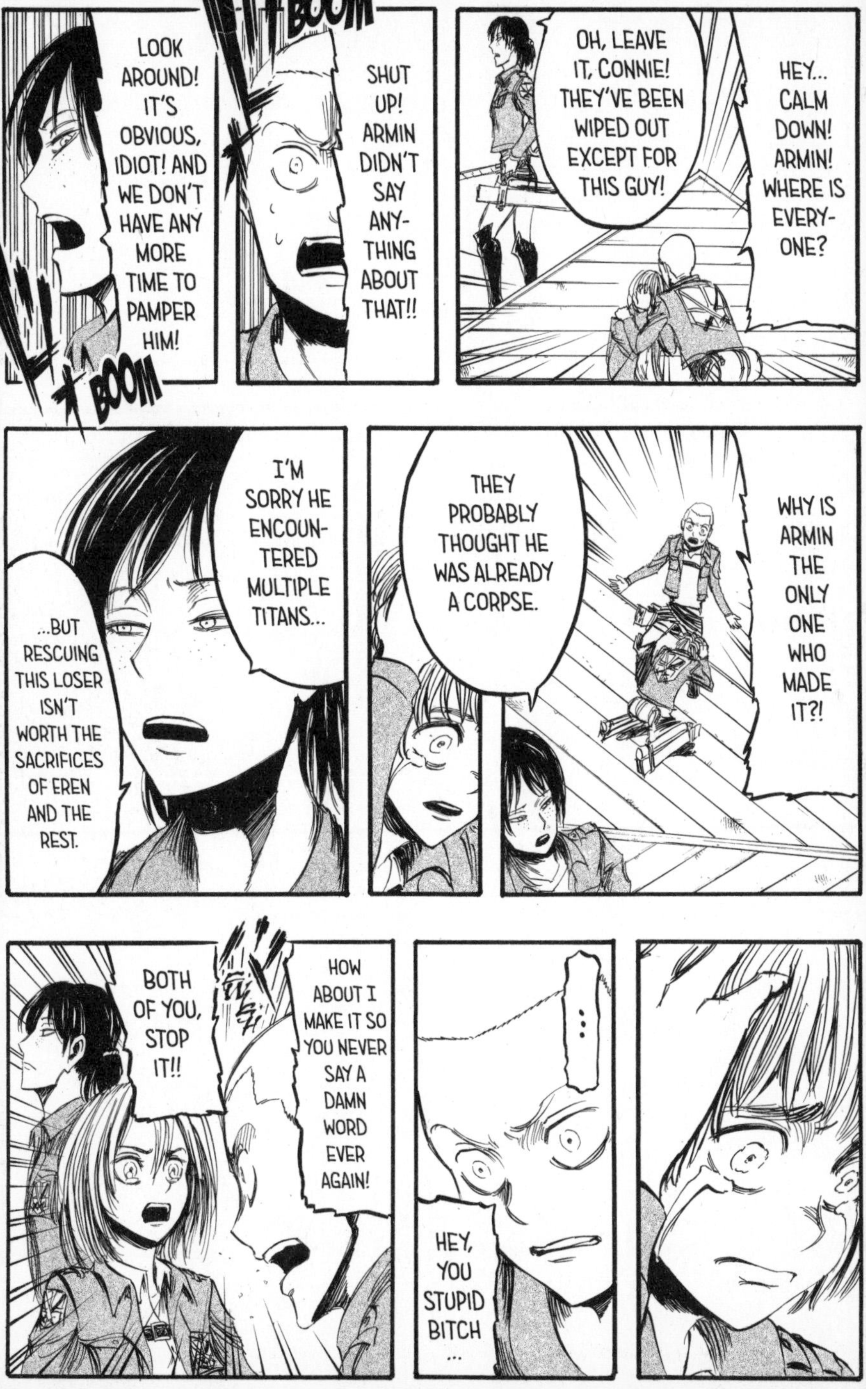
HEY... CALM DOWN! ARMIN! WHERE IS EVERY-ONE?
OH, LEAVE IT, CONNIE! THEY'VE BEEN WIPED OUT EXCEPT FOR THIS GUY!
BOOM
SHUT UP! ARMIN DIDN'T SAY ANY-THING ABOUT THAT!!
LOOK AROUND! IT'S OBVIOUS, IDIOT! AND WE DON'T HAVE ANY MORE TIME TO PAMPER HIM!
BOOM
WHY IS ARMIN THE ONLY ONE WHO MADE IT?!
THEY PROBABLY THOUGHT HE WAS ALREADY A CORPSE.
I'M SORRY HE ENCOUN-TERED MULTIPLE TITANS...
...BUT RESCUING THIS LOSER ISN'T WORTH THE SACRIFICES OF EREN AND THE REST.
...
HEY, YOU STUPID BITCH ...
HOW ABOUT I MAKE IT SO YOU NEVER SAY A DAMN WORD EVER AGAIN!
BOTH OF YOU, STOP IT!!

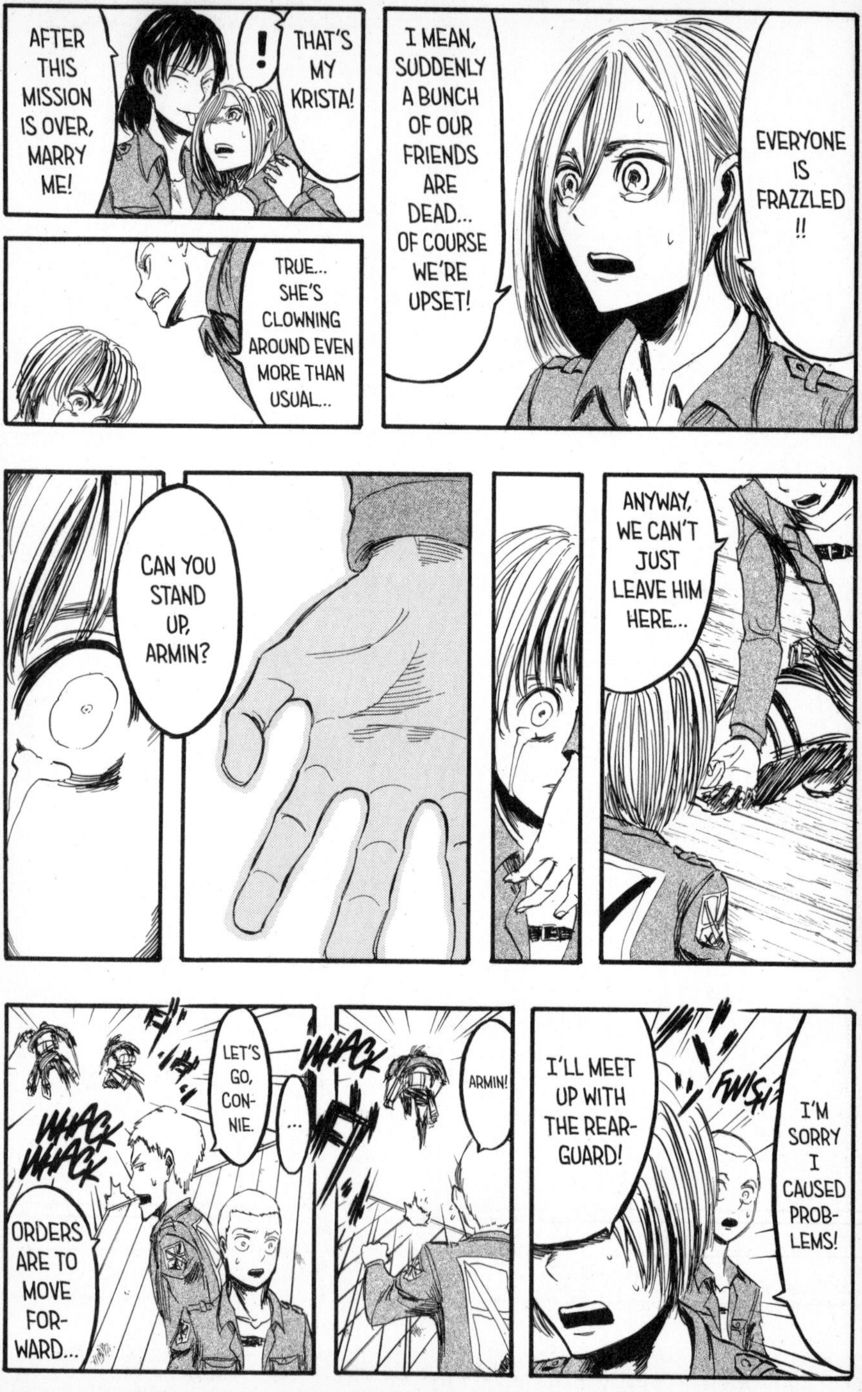
EVERYONE IS FRAZZLED!!
I MEAN, SUDDENLY A BUNCH OF OUR FRIENDS ARE DEAD... OF COURSE WE'RE UPSET!
THAT'S MY KRISTA!
!
AFTER THIS MISSION IS OVER, MARRY ME!
TRUE... SHE'S CLOWNING AROUND EVEN MORE THAN USUAL...
ANYWAY, WE CAN'T JUST LEAVE HIM HERE...
CAN YOU STAND UP, ARMIN?
I'M SORRY I CAUSED PROBLEMS!
FWISH
I'LL MEET UP WITH THE REAR-GUARD!
ARMIN!
WHACK
...
LET'S GO, CONNIE.
WHACK WHACK
ORDERS ARE TO MOVE FORWARD...

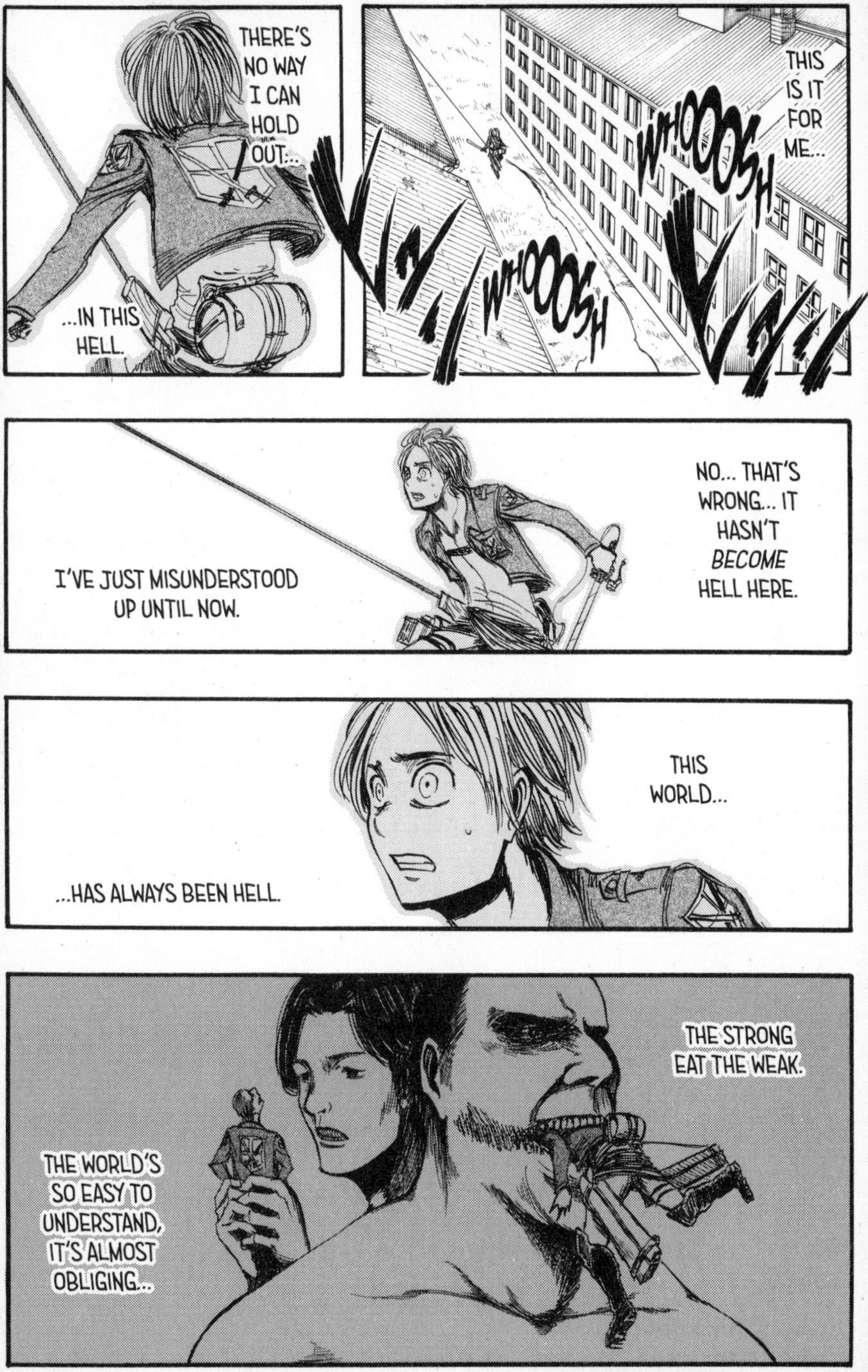
THIS IS IT FOR ME...
WHOOOSH
WHOOOSH
THERE'S NO WAY I CAN HOLD OUT...
...IN THIS HELL.
NO... THAT'S WRONG... IT HASN'T *BECOME* HELL HERE.
I'VE JUST MISUNDERSTOOD UP UNTIL NOW.
THIS WORLD...
...HAS ALWAYS BEEN HELL.
THE STRONG EAT THE WEAK.
THE WORLD'S SO EASY TO UNDERSTAND, IT'S ALMOST OBLIGING...

Attack on Titan volume 1 is a work of fiction. Names, characters, places, and incidents are the products of the author's imagination or are used fictitiously. Any resemblance to actual events, locales, or persons, living or dead, is entirely coincidental.

A Kodansha Comics Trade Paperback Original

Published in the United States by Kodansha Comics, an imprint of Kodansha USA Publishing, LLC, New York.

Publication rights for this English edition arranged through Kodansha Ltd, Tokyo.

First published in Japan in 2010 by Kodansha Ltd., Tokyo.

ISBN 978-1-61262-024-4

Original cover design by Takashi Shimoyama (Red Rooster)

Printed and bound in Germany by GGP Media GmbH, Poessneck

www.kodansha.us

29 28 27 26 25 24 23
Translator: Sheldon Drzka
Lettering: Steve Wands

You are going the *wrong way!*

Manga is a *completely* different type of reading experience.

To start at the *BEGINNING*, go to the *END!*

That's right! Authentic manga is read the traditional Japanese way--from right to left, exactly the opposite of how American books are read. It's easy to follow: just go to the other end of the book, and read each page--and each panel--from the right side to the left side, starting at the top right. Now you're experiencing manga as it was meant to be.